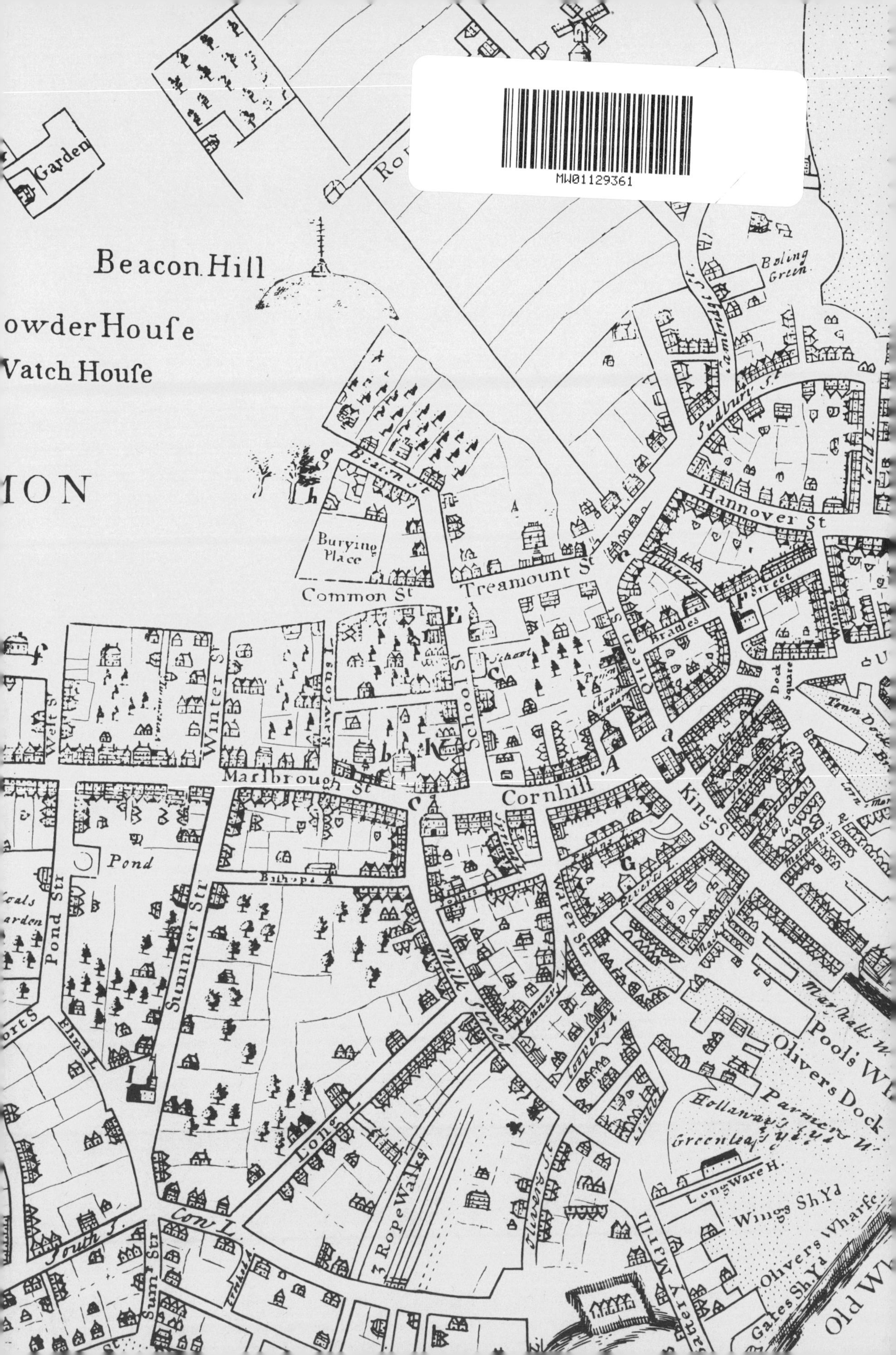

MW01129361
Garden
Beacon Hill
owder Houſe
Vatch Houſe
ION
Boling Green
Sudbury St
Hannover St
Beacon St
Burying Place
Treamount St
Common St
Queen St
School St
Winter St
West St
Marlbrough St
Cornhill
King St
Dock Square
Pond
Pond Str
Summer Str
Milk Street
Water Str
Long
3 Rope Walks
Cow L.
South L.
Battery March
Long Ware H.
Wings Sh.Yd
Olivers Wharfe
Olivers Sh.Yd
Gates Sh.Yd
Olivers Dock
Pools Wh
Greenleafs Yd
Hollaways Yd
Old Wh

Suffolk University

A HISTORY OF SUFFOLK UNIVERSITY

1906 – 1996

Suffolk University

A HISTORY OF SUFFOLK UNIVERSITY

1906 – 1996

David L. Robbins

Boston, Massachusetts

Suffolk University, Boston, Massachusetts

ISBN 0-9652812-0-5

Produced by Creative Services/University Media Services

Cover photo: Richard Pasley
Photography: Suffolk University Archives, Fabian Bachrach, Kindra Clineff,
David Comb, Greig Cranna, Jeffrey Dunn, John Gillooly Pictures Co., Susan Lapides,
Cindy Lucio, Javier Lucio, Richard Pasley, Bill Walcott.

Contents

Dedication

Old age hath yet his honour and his toil;
Death closes all; but something ere the end,
Some work of noble note, may yet be done,
Not unbecoming men that strove with Gods.
The lights begin to twinkle from the rocks;
The long day wanes; the slow moon climbs, the deep
Moans round with many voices. Come, my friends,
'Tis not too late to seek a newer world.
Push off, and sitting well in order smite
The sounding furrows; for my purpose holds
To sail beyond the sunset, and the baths
Of all the western stars, until I die.

–Alfred, Lord Tennyson, *Ulysses*

This essay was, and is, for Thomas Anthony Fulham, sixth president of Suffolk University, 1970-80, who died on March 30, 1995, at 79, still in possession of every faculty.
Godspeed, President Fulham . . .

Introduction

The first seven chapters of this book were written between 1979 and 1981. In writing them, I was part of a team, a Heritage Committee, charged with producing "Pamphlets #2-#8 of the Suffolk University Historical Pamphlet Series" (eventually, chapters 1-7) and composed of a core of editors and a corona of Suffolk "lifers" representing most, if not all, of the University's various constituencies. The Heritage Committee's ultimate product appeared in 1982: a bound volume entitled *Opportunity's Open Door,* comprising newly redacted forms of all seven previously published Heritage Project essays.

Heritage Committee Publications

Working thirteen years later as an individual, it has been my editorial decision to leave those first seven chapters largely unchanged from their original versions. Historical revision is always a complicated, controversial process, and the revision of any specific historical text also raises the spectre—both in the reviser and in the observing audience—of intellectual dishonesty. So, in most cases, I have left the original text (which has itself become, in a sense, not only a history but an historical document) alone, adding only the new eighth and ninth chapters in an effort to bring the work's narrative—and its analysis—up to date and down to the present.

Although 1979 was not so very long ago, chronologically or historically speaking, I cannot help feeling, in rereading the version of events produced at that time, that its author was, as Vladimir Nabokov would have it, "gaspingly young." Over the subsequent decade-and-a-half, as is the human lot, my responsibilities, my life, and my mental universe have altered, as has my perspective on certain matters included in, or excluded from, *Opportunity's Open Door.* If we have no parallax, we have nothing.

The Heritage Committee

David L. Robbins, Professor of History, Chairman
William C. Amidon, Director of Alumni Programs–Law School
Louis B. Connelly, Director of Public Relations
John Griffin, Life Trustee, Suffolk University
P. Richard Jones, Director of University Archives
Alfred I. Maleson, Professor of Law
Joseph H. Strain, Professor of Educational Administration and Speech, Associate Dean of the College of Liberal Arts and Sciences
Arthur J. West II, Chairman and Professor of Biology
Edward G. Hartmann, Emeritus Professor of History, Senior Editor
Patricia I. Brown, Assistant Law Librarian, Assistant Editor
John C. Cavanagh, Chairman and Professor of History, Assistant Editor
Ann D. Hughes, Assistant Professor of English, Assistant Editor
Stanley M. Vogel, Professor of English, Assistant Editor

Chapter 1 Setting the Scene

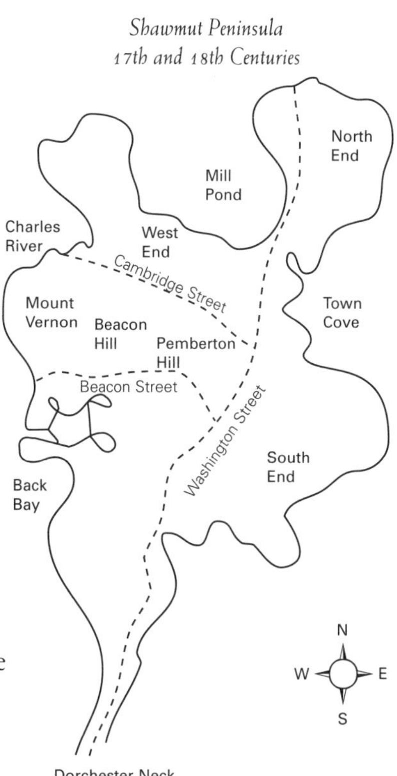

The aim of this chapter is to set the stage for those which will follow: to enlighten our readers about the early history and development of the neighborhood to which Gleason Archer first brought his Suffolk School of Law in 1907. The Temple Street, or Northeast Slope, area has long been the neglected stepchild of Beacon Hill; it has failed, until recently, to capture either attention or affection. The district's past has suffered from a similar neglect. In the Boston 200 *Official Bicentennial Guidebook,* Temple Street is one of the few Beacon Hill thoroughfares on which the compilers have not managed to place at least one historical landmark; and the area around it is ignored in their projected Beacon Hill walking trail.[1]

What follows, then, is an attempt to add a recovered past to a rediscovered present; to illuminate the origins and evolution of the Temple Street area and its successive populations.

From its foundation in 1630 until early in the eighteenth century, Boston grew rapidly. Its growth, however, was confined mainly to the east coast of the Shawmut Peninsula, east of the present line of Washington Street. As the waterfront areas became characteristic of an expanding seaport, the western half of the peninsula—including the Common and the "Trimountain," as it was called—remained rural and sparsely settled.

William Blaxton home on southwest slope of Beacon Hill

This "Trimountain," from which Tremont Street takes its name, was a long ridge with three peaks, which ran east to west across the western half of the Shawmut Peninsula. All three peaks were much higher and more prominent than they are today. They were called, from east to west, Cotton (or Pemberton) Hill, Beacon Hill, and Mount Vernon. Cotton Hill was divided from Beacon Hill where Bowdoin Street now lies; Beacon Hill was separated from Mount Vernon along the present line of Joy Street. The central prominence was named for the beacon which had stood upon it since 1635 to warn the colonists of impending invasion.

The Trimountain formed a "hilly background" behind the town.[2] It served as upland pasture for the town's cattle, and as a location for the long, narrow wooden sheds known as ropewalks. In them, hemp was twisted into the rope cordage so necessary to a seaport town. Smelling strongly of hot pitch, these ropewalks were relegated in Boston, as in any maritime community, to the outlying districts. Thus, in the seventeenth century, the Trimountain had only a tiny daytime population, almost none of which remained there after nightfall.

Following the Glorious Revolution of 1688 in England, the commitment of the English government to colonial commerce grew steadily. Boston's maritime trade burgeoned, and the town's population rose from 7,000 in 1690 to 16,000 in 1740. By 1720, Boston was the largest town in British North America.[3]

Throughout the early eighteenth century, the populated area of the city expanded westward, across the present line of Washington Street and toward the Trimountain. By the 1720s, the eastern blocks of Cambridge Street on the northern side of the Trimountain, and of Beacon Street on the south, were built up. Both thoroughfares, however, stopped abruptly at the town's rural outskirts. Beacon Street ended at the foot of Beacon Hill, and

Cambridge Street terminated in a bowling green near what is today Bowdoin Square. Year by year, though, the increasing population resulted in extension of both streets. By 1733, Cambridge Street had reached the Charles River, while Beacon Street had been pushed west beyond the current site of the State House. The Hancock family constructed an impressive new residence on the Trimountain side of Beacon Street in 1737, just west of the present State House.[4]

Motivated by this extension, and by the possibility of turning their upland pastures to higher profit, many Trimountain landowners began to divide their fields into streets and housing lots, and to put the lots up for sale on the bull market of the 1730s. In 1737, the Tay family laid out in their pasture lands Tay Street and a smaller street farther up Beacon Hill, and divided the street frontage into lots. Tay Street was renamed Temple Street in 1769; the smaller street became Hill Street in 1788, then Derne Street in 1806.[5]

The Hancock house (1737-1863), first of the elegant residences constructed on the Trimountain.

The Minot family, whose pasture lay to the west of the Tay land, cleared George Street along the western boundary of their holdings in 1732. Other families laid out Middlecott Street and Belknap's Lane, in 1727 and 1734, respectively. George Street was later given the name Hancock Street; Middlecott Street became Bowdoin Street in 1824; and Belknap's Lane is today part of Joy Street.[6]

The subdividers along Cambridge Street, however, were caught in an economic squeeze. From 1740 on, Boston's share of the colonial trade began to slip rapidly; by the 1750s, it was only the third largest port—and city—in the colonies, behind Philadelphia and New York. The developers of the 1730s had expected that Boston's population would continue to increase, but between 1740 and 1760 it actually fell by a thousand souls. The real estate market collapsed, and Trimountain land remained low in value.

Because of the deflated real estate values, the building of ropewalks proliferated between 1740 and 1790. One of these occupied the present site of the Donahue Building. Next to this ropewalk, the owner, Matthew Ridgeway, laid out Ridgeway Lane in 1769. Three other ropewalks lay west of Hancock Street, just north of present-day Pinckney Street, and Myrtle Street was constructed in the 1750s to allow access to them. Still another stretched down the east side of Hancock Street, south of what is today Derne Street.

While most of the remaining land continued to be used for pasture, one enterprising fellow, Thomas Hodson, in 1764 began to chop up his worthless subdivision on the south side of Derne Street for gravel and fill. Hodson's early assault on Beacon Hill initiated what was to become a common practice in the nineteenth century.[7]

Of the few lots that were sold, several parcels went to solid families with a spirit of adventure; two of their wooden farmhouses, built in 1787 on Temple Street, were long the oldest surviving structures on Beacon Hill.[8] Toward the Charles River, however, Trimountain lots were purchased by "a mixed and more or less questionable sort of people": freed blacks, barbers, coachmen, waiters, musicians, laundresses, seamen, gamblers, tavernkeepers, pimps, and harlots.[9] The last-named plied their trade on the slopes of what is now decorously known as Mount Vernon—a bowdlerized version of the original name, Mount Whoredom.

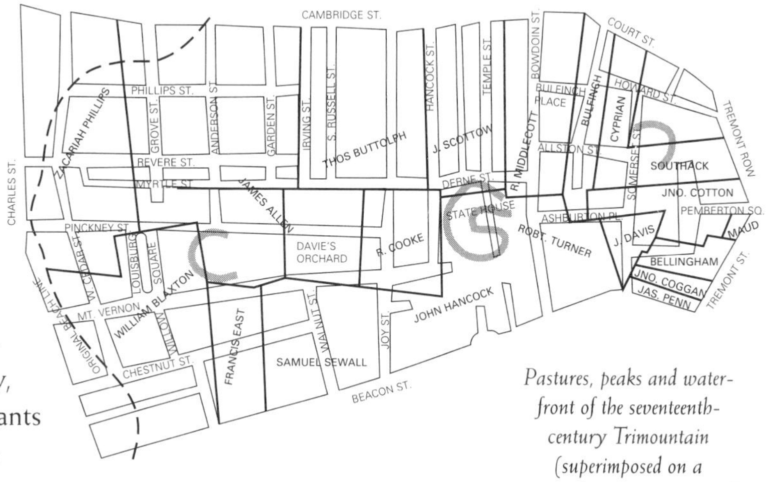

The slump of the mid-eighteenth century left Boston with a stable population and a stagnant economy, in which artisans and merchants were concerned mainly with meeting local demand. The impact of this recession kept the city from expanding its geographical limits of 1740. In the mid-eighteenth century, compared to New York, Boston was a "small town"; it was a city built, in contrast to other leading cities in the colonies, mainly of wood, not brick.[10] Despite the great expectations of the landowners, the Trimountain remained undeveloped. Most of it, especially the Beacon Hill area, retained its rural aspect until the end of the century. Throughout this period, the rocky ridge was popularly considered to be either a "torrent of vice" or a backwater, depending on the viewpoint.[11]

Pastures, peaks and waterfront of the seventeenth-century Trimountain (superimposed on a twentieth-century street grid by Allen Chamberlain).

Brahmins After the end of the Revolution, however, there was an increase in commercial activity with the commencement of the China trade (1790). Encouraged by new opportunities and enterprises, and by the fortunes to be made from them, more people came to Boston. In the forty years following the Revolution, the city's population more than tripled, from 18,000 in 1790 to 60,000 in 1825. The geographical expansion that had marked the early years of the eighteenth century resumed in the early years of the nineteenth. Property on the Trimountain, off both Cambridge Street to the north and Beacon Street to the south reverted to pre-slump values, which continued to rise. For those who were tired of the crowded old city east of Washington Street, and could afford the move, the slopes of the Trimountain offered rural living that was convenient to town.

In 1793 the completion of the West Boston Bridge, from the end of Cambridge Street across the Charles River to Cambridge, made Cambridge Street the most direct route to Harvard College and the west.[12] Well-to-do merchant families began to regard the open land along the Cambridge Street extension with favor. The young architect Charles Bulfinch (whose family had lived since 1724 in the outlying area of Cambridge Street, later known as Bowdoin Square) provided prosperous Bostonians with brick houses worthy of New York, Philadelphia, or even London. Beginning in the early 1790s, Bulfinch, followed by a number of other architects, built a series of fine homes along Cambridge Street. The most notable Bulfinch creations were the first Harrison Gray Otis house (1796) across from the Temple-Hancock block, and the Joseph Coolidge mansion (1792) between Temple and Bowdoin Streets, with gardens running up the east side of Temple Street. The old West Church, erected on Cambridge Street in 1737, was elegantly rebuilt in 1806 by Asher Benjamin; and construction of Massachusetts General Hospital was begun in 1817, from a design by Bulfinch.[13]

The Massachusetts State House on Beacon Hill

While Bulfinch and his patrons were building up Cambridge Street, the Massachusetts General Court made a decision which added greater incentive, and value, to that development. In the early 1790s, the legislators of the Commonwealth approved a plan to move the State House out of downtown Boston and to the still relatively inexpensive rural land on the Trimountain. They purchased a site for the new State House from the Hancock estate on Beacon Hill, not far from the former location of the beacon. Work on the building was begun in 1795 and completed by 1798.

Even before work had begun, however, a well-informed group of real estate speculators, calling themselves the Mount Vernon Proprietors, was buying up the land which abutted the State House site on the Beacon Street side of the Trimountain. They acquired for development purposes the entire south slope of Mount Vernon, and what remained of the south slope of Beacon Hill. Streets and lots were laid out along the previously untouched slope; these included the present Mount Vernon and Pinckney Streets. In the process, the crest of Mount Vernon was shorn of about sixty feet of earth.

By 1800, the attraction of the new State House resulted in Bulfinch's receiving a number of commissions to build along the south slope; the most influential of these was a move by the Harrison Gray Otis family to the new development in 1800. The area opened by the Mount Vernon Proprietors proved attractive to well-to-do Boston families for the next forty years, and new building along both the Cambridge Street and Beacon Street slopes proceeded apace.

A Bulfinch-designed home on Mt. Vernon Street

The building boom on the Trimountain offered opportunities to the middle and artisan classes as well as to the affluent. Some successful builders—artisans as well as architects—used their profits to buy land in the West End (the area north of Cambridge Street) and on the north slope of the Trimountain, adjacent to the Mount Vernon Proprietors' tract.[14] There they constructed sturdy houses, most in wood, a few in brick or stone. On Temple, Hancock, and other north slope streets, successful craftsmen lived side by side with the professional and commercial classes. All of them were drawn by the lure of new housing, more open land, and a quieter residential neighborhood than that which they had left.

The once rural slopes of Beacon Hill were steadily built up: first the less fashionable north, then the south. They were "tolerably, but not densely" inhabited in 1814; but within thirty years, settlement was thick, with vacant land in short supply.[15] By the 1820s, the growing pressure of a "respectable" population had forced the city to clean up the prostitution on the isolated northwest slope of "Mount Whoredom." Grace Episcopal Church (later the First Methodist Church), built in the fashionable Gothic Revival style, was opened on Temple Street in 1835 to serve a genteel Beacon Hill and West End congregation. The Church of the Advent, also Episcopal, was established in the West End in 1844; it moved to near Bowdoin Square in 1847 in order to bring the religious principles of the Oxford Movement to the same socially exclusive constituency addressed by Grace Church. The Trinitarian Congregationalist Church was also drawn to the Northeast Slope by the increasing number of "proper" inhabitants. Since 1809, the Park Street Church had been the nearest Trinitarian rival to the Unitarian Congregationalists in the West Church. However, in 1831, under the charge of Lyman Beecher, the Trinitarians opened the building on Bowdoin Street which now houses the Church of St. John the Evangelist.[16] During his brief pastorate there, Beecher lived on Temple Street, in one of the eighteenth-century farmhouses referred to earlier. In this house—located on what is now the Suffolk University Alumni Park—the Reverend Mr. Beecher received regular letters and visits from his illustrious children, Harriet (author of *Uncle Tom's Cabin*) and Henry Ward Beecher. Nearby, at 20 Hancock Street, lived Senator Charles Sumner; like the Beechers, he was noted for his anti-slavery activities.

Several other anti-slavery luminaries also lived in the neighborhood: Julia Ward Howe, at 32 Mount Vernon Street; and Bronson Alcott, with his daughter Louisa May (author of *Little Women*), at 20 Pinckney Street. More perplexing in his attitudes, but still a key player in the anti-slavery drama, was Daniel Webster, whose home was at 57 Mount Vernon Street. The Northeast Slope was a hotbed of abolitionist activity, containing a strong black community which dated from the eighteenth century. The city's first black school was built in the 1830s on Joy Street, and several Underground Railroad "stations" were to be found in the immediate area. In Smith Court, off Joy Street, stands the African Meeting House, built in 1806 and now the Museum of Afro-American History. Here William Lloyd Garrison held the first meeting of the New England Anti-Slavery Society in 1832.[17]

Cutting down Beacon Hill (1811)

The last beacon had been blown down in 1789; it was replaced the following year by a Bulfinch monument to the heroes of the Revolution. But in response to the growing demand for space on the Trimountain, Bulfinch's monument at the top of Beacon Hill was torn down in 1811. The land on which it stood was sold, and the wooden stairs leading up to the former monument site from the top of Temple Street were dismantled. The crest of Beacon Hill was lowered some sixty feet to make it more suitable for building; the removed earth was used to fill the Mill Pond for land development, just as the top of Mount Vernon had previously been used to fill the Charles riverfront.

In 1820, Temple Street was extended across Derne Street. After crossing Derne, Temple Street continued straight up and over the lowered top of Beacon Hill, to an intersection with Mount Vernon Street. The first Boston English High School was built on the west side of the Temple Street extension in 1820, facing Derne Street.

Pemberton Hill, the only remaining peak of the Trimountain, was leveled in 1835, partly to fill the land where North Station now stands and partly to make way for a block-development of the area where the peak had stood. It was, at the time, the sole surviving "unimproved" district of the Trimountain. However, within a decade, Pemberton Square had been built on the site, and Ashburton Place had been cut through to connect it with Bowdoin Street.

The spacious grounds of the early homes gave way, as time went by, to solid blocks of brick row houses. Such buildings came to characterize a growing number of areas on Beacon Hill, Mount Vernon, and Pemberton Hill. The increased demand for Beacon Hill land contributed, in 1843, to breaking up the grounds of the old Coolidge mansion at the northern end of Temple Street. In that location, there was erected on the east side of Temple Street a block of brick row houses which still stands.[18]

Boston street railway (ca. 1900)

Change Temple Street was, like most of Beacon Hill, still part of the most fashionable neighborhood in Boston in the 1840s. Nonetheless, residents were becoming discontented with the increasingly cramped surroundings. Many old families were also dismayed when, late in the decade, the city began work on a cavernous granite reservoir atop Beacon Hill, west of the Temple Street extension. And from the 1850s on, increasing commercial use of Cambridge Street brought more noise and bustle—along with an unwanted social element, the tradesman—to an already crowded district. Faced with all this, many unhappy inhabitants of Beacon Hill chose to move into more spacious homes in newly opened areas: the Back Bay for the very well-off, the South End for those of more moderate means.[19]

Increased crowding on Beacon Hill was no figment of nostalgic imaginations. Boston's population had grown from the 60,000 of 1825 to 135,000 in 1850; by 1875, the number of inhabitants was 340,000, six times what it had been a half-century earlier. Much of this increase was caused by large, then tidal, waves of immigration: from Ireland in the 1840s and 1850s; from Eastern Europe (primarily Polish and Russian Jews) during the '70s and '80s; and from Italy at the century's end.

These immigrants were first confined to the Fort Hill and North End areas. Street railways, however, began operating in Boston in 1855; and as the railway network expanded, so did the possibilities which it opened to Boston's immigrants. Access to this network would allow many members of immigrant families to travel quickly and inexpensively to places of employment far beyond their previous range. Several lines ran through the West End, including one along Cambridge Street; Bowdoin Square was the terminus for the Cambridge Street line, and a number of others terminated at Scollay Square.

From 1860 on, one ethnic group after another surged out of its original enclaves and into the West End. Some members of each group even settled on the north slope of Beacon Hill. A few of the new residents sought an outlet for their hard-earned capital; many wanted better housing; but most came in search of convenient and economical public transportation. Whatever the reasons for it, however, the influx of these "new" people helped to encourage the flight of Trimountain families to the developing neighborhoods on the outskirts of the city.[20]

For the same reasons that were causing the old residents to leave, newly affluent and socially ambitious families chose not to move to Beacon Hill. Consequently, rents and property values on the Trimountain began to fall. Speculators, or less socially acceptable families, took advantage of the situation; and their presence in increasing numbers drove other old families to depart. As this exodus increased, many who provided services for the well-to-do also decided to move; thus the neighborhood was opened to a new population and a changing economy.

Pinckney Street

Throughout the third quarter of the nineteenth century, the Temple Street area retained a mixed, if changing, population. A number of conservative families, perhaps heartened by the close proximity of the State House and by the separation from the North End, remained in the area to stem the encroachment of the boardinghouse, the speculator, and the small merchant. Such resistance continued far longer, and was more effective, in this district than in any neighborhood of the West End.

During the late nineteenth and early twentieth centuries, a changing population, demanding low-priced apartments, brought with it a new building boom. Unlike the construction spurt of the early nineteenth century, however, this boom produced mainly apartment houses; indeed, it produced the majority of the tenements which are today so widespread on the Cambridge Street side of the Trimountain. The continuing resistance of the Temple Street area to this trend is evidenced by the fact that, of all the north slope streets, Temple, Hancock, and Bowdoin have the fewest of these tenement houses.[21] Nevertheless, during the last quarter of the nineteenth century and the first quarter of the twentieth, the neighborhood was clearly in transition from one-family residences to lodging houses, tenements, and small retail businesses.

The change from an upper middle to a lower middle class neighborhood became more evident with each passing year. A number of houses on Temple Street had store fronts added to them. Many homes fell into decay, either through their owners' neglect or despite their efforts. Grace Episcopal Church on Temple Street was abandoned to the Methodists in 1864. In 1863, the Bowdoin Street Church shut its doors. Into that deserted Trinitarian Congregationalist structure, the Episcopal Church of the Advent moved, for temporary refuge from the growing congestion and hurly-burly of the Bowdoin Square area. By 1868, however, construction had begun on a new building for the Advent congregation on Brimmer Street, well away from the West End. With the completion of the new structure in 1883, the Bowdoin Street Church renounced its pretensions to social and religious fashionability. It remained in Anglo-Catholic hands, but was transformed into a mission church for the English-based Cowley Fathers, who still occupy the premises. Finally, in 1892, the old West Church (Unitarian Congregationalist) closed, for lack of a congregation.[22]

Boston's Old City Hall on School Street

In 1888, the entire upper part of Temple Street, above Derne, was cleared; it was then incorporated into the State House grounds for the building of an Annex, the foundation stone of which was supplied by the Beacon Hill Reservoir. A stone staircase, still traversed daily by Suffolk students, was built to give access to the new State House grounds from what was left of Temple Street. A replica of Bulfinch's 1790 monument was erected on the new grounds in 1898. The walkway at the top of the newly-built stone staircase from Temple Street cut through the exact location of Bulfinch's original monument, which had been set up where the old beacon had once stood. Rather than move the sidewalk or the stairs, it was decided to place the new monument slightly to the east of the original, where it now stands.[23]

Law School The Northeast Slope in the early twentieth century was in every sense a mixed neighborhood. It had close ties to the West End, that legendary settling basin of nationalities left by the successive crests of immigrant floods out of the North End. Martin Lomasney, the greatest of the ward bosses, ran the West End, and at his side James Michael Curley learned the political trade.[24]

On the edge of this ethnic tidal basin, and touched only by the highest tides of immigration, lay the Temple Street (Northeast Slope) area. Near to the West End, it was also an easy walk from the legal and political centers of Boston and Massachusetts. The expanded State House, the newly constructed Suffolk County Court House in Pemberton Square, and the City Hall on School Street were all close by. Although many daytime occupants of this governmental and judicial center had withdrawn to the Back Bay by 1900, a few still inhabited Beacon Hill. Most of these, it is true, lived in the Mount Vernon Proprietors' development on the south slope, but a few hardy outcroppings of the political stratum had escaped erosion by the tides of immigration on the Northeast Slope. All around them, however, property values were falling, and the neighborhood was filling with people who had fled European shores in search of the American dream.

Concern about how that dream could be realized was on the minds of many Americans. The turn of the twentieth century saw the inauguration of the "Progressive Era." The "Progressives" were a varied collection of reformers with numerous foci for their reformist activities; they seemed, however, to hold one belief in common. They saw themselves as "true" Americans, ardent disciples of the gospel of hard work and self-help, who were caught between two very dangerous forces. One was the flood of immigrants coming to these shores, with unrealistic expectations of success in the New World, but with very little of the training or skills needed to function in American society. The other was what the Progressives saw as the sinister rich: economic, political, and social monopolists who were organizing to exclude new entrants from their ranks, and conspiring against freedom of competition and equality of opportunity in American life.

Young Gleason Archer

Ignorant and frustrated immigrants, the Progressives warned, could easily be made dupes, either by socialist demagogues or by monopolistic interests. In both cases, the "true" Americans would be the real victims. As a preventative, the Progressives aimed to educate the immigrants. This would enable many of the new arrivals to understand the basic values of American life, and would provide them with skills that might allow some of them to get ahead. Immigrant families would thus have it demonstrated to them that the self-help ethic they were being asked to accept was based on fact. The Progressives believed that once acculturated in this manner, the immigrants would naturally turn against both socialists and monopolists; they could then be readily enlisted under the Progressive banner and the leadership of the "true" Americans.

Gleason Archer, a law student at Boston University in 1905, was much influenced by this Progressive strain in American thought. He came from a Maine Yankee family, and while still in law school he began to offer tutoring in law to men from immigrant families. Upon his graduation and admission to the Bar in 1906, Archer opened an evening law school at his home in Roxbury to "serve ambitious young men who are obliged to work for a living while studying law."[25] But if

Archer's school was to succeed, a new location was necessary which would suit both his purpose and his constituency.

In 1907, the Suffolk School of Law, as Archer called it, was moved to a neighborhood perfectly adapted to its aims and prospective students, a setting which has played a key role in its continuing growth.[26] Close on one side were the legal and political centers for the state and city; close on another was the West End, a key concentration point of Archer's immigrant constituency; between the two lay an area easily accessible from the trolley terminal at Scollay Square and Park Street, or from North Station. Here, in border territory—an area of strategic location, but of low rents and property values—Archer chose to locate his school.

. . . Archer chose Suffolk as the "most appropriate [name]." "To be sure," he said, "it was the name of a county in Massachusetts, but it was also an old English name derived from the more ancient 'Southfolk.' "

A coalition of educational vested interests ridiculed the Law School, and steadily opposed its growth. Progressive that he was, Archer had expected such "sinister" opposition, and he denounced it as "the Educational Octopus," adapting his term from Frank Norris' anti-monopolistic Progressive novel of 1901.[27] In spite of the "Octopus," the Suffolk School of Law expanded rapidly, outgrowing first one home and then another.

Archer was careful, however, to keep each successive location for his school within the border zone. The first in-town location for the School had been in Archer's law offices at 53 Tremont Street, the present site of the Three Center Plaza. Classes were held there from 1907 until 1909, when Archer moved them to the Tremont Temple. In 1914, rising registrations necessitated a third relocation. Although he would have preferred Pemberton Square, in the shadow of the Suffolk County Court House, Archer had to content himself with a building at 45 Mount Vernon Street, near the Julia Ward Howe and Daniel Webster homes. Archer's law classes remained at 45 Mount Vernon Street—later the home of Suffolk University's School of Management—until 1921; but, once again, despite his having built an Annex in 1915, the demand for the educational services which he offered outgrew the space available.

Under the pressure of increasing enrollments after World War I, the Suffolk Law School (so named in 1914, when it was chartered to grant degrees) was forced to remove to larger quarters; it was transferred to the current site of the Archer Building, on the corner of Derne and Temple Streets. Archer particularly liked the situation immediately behind the State House, just on the fringe of the West End, and within walking distance of the inexpensive public transportation which carried the members of many immigrant families to and from the nearer suburbs. Here, in a location perfectly suited to its mission, he built a permanent home for his school.

The neighborhood in which Archer chose to build was, as we have seen, a mixture of many elements. By 1920, the immigrant population had come to outnumber the "native" group even on the Northeast Slope. Predominant among the ethnic groups in the Temple Street area were Eastern European Jews, with an admixture of Italians, Poles, and Irish. The black population had virtually deserted the Northeast Slope for the South End by this time; the African Meeting House in Smith Court had been converted into a synagogue.

Suffolk Law School, 45 Mt. Vernon Street (1914)

In addition to the immigrant communities with their tenement housing and small storefronts, however, there existed another element: a substantial population of law students and law clerks inhabited the Northeast Slope during the early part of the twentieth century. Students from the nearby law offices, and from several of the new law schools, rented rooms on Beacon Hill. Clerks and officials from the Suffolk County Court House, as well as young lawyers with practices recently opened in the area, did likewise.

The new Court House had been opened in 1893 in Pemberton Square. Around it clustered law offices; Tremont and State Streets were particularly favored locations. Boston's commercial expansion during the nineteenth century had created opportunities in business and government for men with general legal knowledge, as well as for practicing attorneys. The traditional preparation for a law career was for the aspirant to apprentice himself in the office of an established firm.

By 1870, increased demand, as well as the growing extent and specialization of legal knowledge, was rendering the old system inadequate. It still functioned in Gleason Archer's time, but with each year it required a larger supplement from newly-founded law schools. These new schools offered formal classes to much larger groups than could ever be accommodated to read law at firms, and by 1920 they were rapidly superseding the old system.

Harvard Law School was the only such institution in the Boston area from its foundation in 1817 until 1872, when the Boston University Law School was opened on Beacon Hill. After that time, growing demand made the schools multiply with comparative rapidity. The YMCA (later Northeastern) Law School was founded in 1898; the Suffolk School of Law followed in 1906; and the Portia Law School—for women—was established in 1908.[28]

Gleason Archer's law school operated only on a part-time basis. There were no day classes until 1924, and even then the day classes met only several hours a day, three days a week. This schedule made Suffolk an ideal place to study law for working men from the immigrant communities of Boston and the near suburbs: they could usually manage the time necessary for class attendance and for study while retaining full-time jobs.

Since Suffolk had no full-time students until 1943, it required in the earlier period no full-time faculty. Lawyers could be invited to come over from their nearby offices to teach for several hours once or twice a week. Because of the minimal time and energy required of the faculty, their remuneration could be kept correspondingly small. Thus, tuition could be held down to a cost which the school's immigrant constituency could afford.

President Coolidge (seated at right on the dais) at the laying of the cornerstone of the Archer Building (1920)

Governor Calvin Coolidge laid the cornerstone of what is today the Archer Building, at 20 Derne Street, in 1920, and work on the structure was completed a year later. An Annex was added at 51 Temple Street in 1924; and in the same year Archer had a giant electric sign—which proclaimed "Suffolk Law School"—placed on top of his new building as a gesture of defiance against the "Educational Octopus."[29]

University In 1927, an Alumni Clubhouse was installed at 73 Hancock Street, where it remained until 1939. A College of Liberal Arts was opened in 1934, and in the following year classes were transferred to 59 Hancock Street, on the southwest corner of Hancock and Myrtle Streets. In 1937 the College of Liberal Arts returned to the University (Archer) Building, which had been remodeled and expanded from three to five stories. Meanwhile, a Graduate School of Law, a College of Journalism, and a College of Business Administration had been founded, in 1935, 1936, and 1937, respectively.

The various branches of Archer's school were incorporated as Suffolk University in 1937. The divisions of the new University were established on the model of the Law School; each offered an evening school education to working men (and women, after 1934), especially to first- and second-generation immigrants. Students from the West End, and from immigrant families in the near suburbs who could now afford to commute to central Boston, formed an ideal constituency for the University. And, with the exception of the war years between 1942 and 1945, growth in all divisions of the

University continued steadily, due in large measure to the healthy symbiosis between the University and the community it was designed to serve.

Beginning in the late 1950s that symbiosis was seriously disrupted, as the Boston Redevelopment Authority undertook the West End Renewal Project. This much criticized effort at "urban renewal" destroyed the West End north of Cambridge Street and exiled its population. Soon, all that was left of the West End was a small fringe area on the north slope of Beacon Hill. Almost simultaneously, the B.R.A. began to destroy old Scollay Square, to make room for the new Government Center. The character of the surrounding area was changing rapidly and drastically, and both Suffolk University and the Northeast Slope community were forced to develop plans that would allow them to escape the fate of the neighborhood to which they had been so closely allied.

59 Hancock Street, Home of the College of Liberal Arts from 1935 - 1937

Between 1970 and 1980, a cooperative community effort rehabilitated the Northeast Slope area. A number of houses on Temple Street and on adjoining streets were completely remodeled; the old store fronts were removed from many buildings; and the old West Church was restored to religious use. During the same period, Suffolk University began to recruit and to attract a more suburban constituency. Much of this constituency was made up of the second and third generations of immigrant families who, through the exertions and good fortune of the first generations, had been able to leave the inner city and the contiguous suburbs for the more middle-class suburbs. For the most part, they were no longer people on the outside of the American dream looking in, but people living that dream. As Boston's immigrant families were assimilated into American life—often with Suffolk's help—both the mission of the University and the kind of people it served underwent changes.

Drawing on this new, middle-class pool of students, the University grew extensively between 1965 and 1981. In 1966, the Frank J. Donahue (Law School) Building was opened at 41 Temple Street, on the site of the old First Methodist Church just north of the original University Building; the Methodists had removed to the West Church in 1962. The new building was named for Judge Donahue, a long-serving Trustee and former Treasurer of the University.

With the transfer of the Law School, the College of Liberal Arts took over most of the old University Building; it was promptly renamed the Archer Building, in honor of the founder and his brother Hiram, a faculty member and Law School Trustee from the early history of the institution. The original Ridgeway (Student Activities)

Building, at 148 Cambridge Street, was added in 1969; after twenty years of negotiations with the University's Beacon Hill neighbors, it was demolished and completely rebuilt between 1989 and 1991. In 1972, the Business School—known today as the Frank Sawyer School of Management—reoccupied the original Beacon Hill location of the Law School at 45-47 Mount Vernon Street, displacing the New England School of Law (formerly the Portia Law School). During the 1970s, the University's administrative offices were housed at 56 Temple Street and 100 Charles River Plaza—occupied in 1971 and 1973, respectively. In 1981, these offices, along with the entire School of Management, moved to 8 Ashburton Place.

The Frank Sawyer Building at 8 Ashburton Place

The John E. Fenton Building, which provided space for much of the College of Liberal Arts and Sciences, was opened in 1975 at 32 Derne Street, on the site of the old Wright and Potter printing plant. The new building was named to commemorate Judge Fenton, late Chairman of the Board and fifth President of the University. The Frank Sawyer Building at 8 Ashburton Place (erected for the City Club in 1913, and acquired by the University from the United Way of Massachusetts Bay in 1978) was a twelve-story structure in the shadow of the Suffolk County Court House, very near the Pemberton Square site Archer had wanted for his law school in 1914. This addition clearly reflected the University's continuing efforts to adapt itself to its changing environment and mission. During these fifteen years of growth, Suffolk brought a new student element into a neighborhood already characterized by its heterogeneity, with the usual problems and rewards of adjustment on both sides.

So extensive was the expansion of the University over this period, that it was at times viewed as a rival, and not as a partner in development, by the surrounding Northeast Slope community. Imaginative and constructive steps were taken, however, to restore the traditional cooperation between the University and other residents of the neighborhood. University facilities and classes, for example, were made accessible to many local inhabitants, and a close working relationship was established with the Museum of Afro-American History. But the most successful and promising example of cooperation between the University and the community was the creation of Temple Walk, which was opened in 1977. This pedestrian street and mall ran the length of Temple Street, providing residents of the area with an urban park, and the University with its first semblance of an outdoor campus. The opening of Temple Walk was greatly facilitated by inclusion in the Beacon Hill Historic District;

this recognition as a historical landmark was doubly important, in that it also protected the Temple Street area from the kind of "renewal" that destroyed the West End north of Cambridge Street—a fate long feared by Northeast Slope community organizers.[30]

These achievements stood as models both of neighborhood self-help in urban regeneration, and of enlightened cooperation between town and gown. They boded well for a maintenance of the good relationship between Suffolk University and the surrounding neighborhood, long made possible through the University's pursuit of the mission assigned to it by Gleason Archer: community service.

Chapter 2 Gleason L. Archer

History has demonstrated that the great leaders of every age were, almost without exception, born in poverty, denied educational advantages in boyhood, and obliged to educate themselves at odd moments while doing a man's work in the world. The same immutable principle is in operation today—the earnest souls who now toil in the evening schools to fit themselves for life will be found in the front ranks of our civilization of tomorrow.

–*Gleason L. Archer* (1923)[1]

Gleason L. Archer, founder of Suffolk University

Gleason L. Archer was the founder of Suffolk Law School. He was the first and longest-serving President of Suffolk University. He was the prime mover of the institution for over forty years.

Until recently, however, Archer's memory had become strangely obscured at the school he established. Most members of the Suffolk community recognized his name, but they knew it primarily through a folklore of garbled and fantastic tales. About the man himself, his career, and his heritage, a curious ignorance persisted.

The eclipse of Archer's reputation owed something to design. Strife between Archer and the Trustees precipitated the President's resignation in 1948. Angry and hoping to end Archer's forty-year personification of the school, the Trustees took drastic action. A veil was drawn over Archer's portrait. His name was expunged from the University's catalogues and, as much as possible, from its consciousness. As the founder's name faded from awareness, however, so did a sense of his achievements; Suffolk University forgot its roots.[2]

Only in recent years has any movement from this position taken place. Gleason Archer's death in 1966 ended a quarter-century of mutual recrimination. Since then, the Dean's name has reappeared in the College and Law School catalogues. His portrait has been restored to public display. A law scholarship and a University building have been named for him. Many materials—including the founder's prototype Suffolk Law School ring—have been donated to Suffolk by the Archer family, and an Archer Archives has been established to house them.[3]

Suffolk University is now in the process of reintegrating its heritage, and the work of Gleason Archer forms a central part of that inheritance. The man and his work remain partly in shadow. This essay is intended to introduce Gleason L. Archer to his beneficiaries in the clear light of day.

He was, says one witness,

"A big man, well proportioned with gray and thinning hair over a high forehead, and wearing glasses. Dean Archer, while friendly and humorous, fairly radiates the scholastic air. He is a man of enthusiasms."[4]

Archer remained throughout his life a "man of enthusiasms," of strong opinions and vigorous actions. The occasional quixotic episodes do not vitiate the worth of his causes.

The man who founded Suffolk University to benefit aspiring young men of the working class, did so because he himself had come from poverty and had labored for success. His youth, in fact, was remarkably like those of the Horatio Alger heroes so popular with his generation.[5]

Gleason Leonard Archer was born into the rural poverty of the Maine frontier, on October 29, 1880. His home was a wilderness hamlet, Hancock County Plantation #33, known "by courtesy of the Post Office Department" as Great Pond.[6] It lay thirty-five miles northeast of Bangor, in the midst of an unbroken forest. For several months a year the Yankee settlement was cut off from the outside world.

Isolation had produced generations of inbreeding; the eighty souls who occupied Great Pond's nineteen homes were all "cousins or close relatives." Gleason's father, John Sewall Archer, and his mother, Frances Martha Williams were first cousins. Although neither knew it, their common ancestors had come to America on the *Mayflower.*[7]

Gleason Archer as a high school student

John Archer was a blacksmith, but the limited population and remoteness of the area forced him to supplement his earnings by seasonal work as a woodcutter. As the size of his family grew, he became more dependent on lumbering to make ends meet. One by one, the boys were removed from school and required to join their father at the cabin several miles from Great Pond which served as the family logging "camp."

Gleason was the third son in a family that eventually included seven boys and one girl.[8] At thirteen, like his brothers, he began work at the "camp." Since he weighed only seventy-six pounds, however, and cut rather a comic figure as a lumberjack, the new recruit was assigned cooking duties. He became quite proficient at his job, and the cook's post remained his for nearly six years, even after he began to equal his brothers in size.

Removal from school did nothing to dull Archer's appetite for knowledge. He became, and remained for the rest of his life, a voracious reader and a compulsive writer. Every spare moment found him poring over a borrowed book or a precious sheet of stationery. The young autodidact's intense desire for education did not go unrecognized even by his family. Nor did his talent. He became a local celebrity when several of his articles appeared in the *Ellsworth American,* a Bangor-area newspaper.

The following autumn, Archer's family provided him the opportunity which they knew he deserved. His uncle, Leonard S. Williams, had attended the Cobb Divinity School of Bates College, in Lewiston. Williams became a Free Baptist minister and settled in Sabattus, a suburb of Lewiston. There, some hundred miles from Great Pond, the Reverend Mr. Williams found a place for his nephew: in October 1899, Gleason became chore boy for physician Frank E. Sleeper. As payment for his services, young Archer was to receive bed and board during his studies at Sabattus High School.[9]

He spent most of the next three years in Sabattus. While still in high school, Archer was appointed Sabattus reporter for both the

Lewiston Journal and the *Webster Herald*. He also edited the all-state *Maine High School* magazine. Having entered Sabattus High School as a sophomore, he graduated in June 1902—valedictorian in a class of six.

There was a scholarship waiting at Bates College, but Archer's first visit to Boston convinced him that his future lay on Beacon Hill: Boston University had a law school, which Bates did not. Gleason borrowed money for tuition, and went to join his older brother Hiram in the metropolis. The younger Archer planned to attend the College of Liberal Arts for two years, and then to transfer to the Legal Division.

Gleason Archer arrived in Boston in September 1902, with no money for rent or living expenses. He was determined, however, to extend his education. If that meant living frugally and supporting himself by odd jobs, then he was willing; sacrifice and privation were nothing new to the Archer family. During his first year at college, Gleason shared a room with Hiram at 83 Myrtle Street.[10] He worked six days a week as a waiter to pay his share of the rent. This left him with a meager sixty cents a week for meals and other necessities.

Gleason Archer arrived in Boston in September 1902, with no money for rent or living expenses. He was determined, however, to extend his education. If that meant living frugally and supporting himself by odd jobs, then he was willing; sacrifice and privation were nothing new to the Archer family.

At the end of his first college year, young Archer secured a job at the Cotocheeset, a resort hotel near Wianno on Cape Cod. His strength and vigor were just returning after the deprivations of the school year, when he shattered his left knee in a fall. Only in Boston was medical expertise available that could prevent permanent disability. On borrowed crutches and in the teeth of a howling gale, he began the painful journey.

The jolting coach carried only one other passenger: George A. Frost, a summer resident of Wianno and president of the renowned Boston Garter Company. Much Archer's senior, Frost evinced a paternal concern for his injured companion. A conversation began, and—typical and improbable Alger touch—the wealthy man who met the youthful hero by accident admired his pluck, and brought him under his patronage. By the time the stage reached Barnstable railroad depot, Gleason Archer was George Frost's protégé.

The young invalid was taken immediately by parlor car to Boston. There he was met by Frost's coachman, and conveyed to the Newton Hospital, of which George Frost was president and principal benefactor. No charges for medical care, or for his month-long convalescence at the hospital, were ever sent to Archer.

Loans from Mr. Frost allowed Gleason Archer to complete his studies at Boston University free from deprivation or distraction. By the spring of his second year, he was already attending law courses. After formally entering the Law School, he completed the three-year curriculum in two. Graduation came in June 1906, and was quickly followed by admission to the bar. In August, Gleason Archer was invited to join the State Street law firm of Carver and Blodgett—on George Frost's recommendation.[11]

Archer's benefactor refused all monetary reimbursement for his loans. They were, he told the young lawyer, "an investment in human life." The only repayment he wanted, Frost insisted, was that "if you ever have a chance to pass this favor along to other boys, do it for me." The response was quick and sure. What he really wanted to do, young Archer told his patron, was to open an evening law school. Thus, he could pass his good fortune on to others like himself, by making it possible "for such young men to qualify as lawyers while working for a living."[12] Archer was not without teaching experience. There had been a brief term at the Great Pond school while he was still a student at Sabattus High. More important, he had begun in October 1905 to tutor a group of working men in the principles of contract law. The class had been short-lived, but several of its members urged Archer to renew his endeavor. Mr. Frost shared their enthusiasm, and he pledged his support for the new school.[13]

George A. Frost met the youthful Gleason Archer on a coach ride and became the school's foremost backer until his death in 1938.

A first-floor apartment in Roxbury was quickly located, and there, at 6 Alpine Street, the first classes of "Archer's Evening Law School" took place on September 19, 1906. That warm night as the lecture closed, all nine auditors were glued to their seats—by the new varnish on Archer's second-hand chairs. Once they tore themselves away, however, word spread that there was something more than varnish holding men to their places in the young educator's front room. Gleason Archer had found his life's work. George Frost remained the school's foremost backer until his death in 1936. And, somewhere, Horatio Alger was smiling.[14]

Archer's experience confirmed the world-view with which he grew up, the gospel of self-help. According to that gospel those individuals who worked hard and sacrificed to improve themselves would be rewarded with success; the sluggards who did not would be punished by failure. This was the message carried by Horatio Alger and his fellow evangelists of the late nineteenth century. But only free competition, they asserted, would allow economic justice to prevail. Thus, in Gleason Archer's eyes, the precondition that made possible his success, and the salutary success of hard workers like him, was equality of opportunity. The struggle to maintain it in American society provides the organizing principle of his life.

The young schoolmaster was not alone in his concerns. Social tensions were emerging in the early twentieth century that worried many Americans. Industrial development and urban growth were changing the nation. Unparalleled immigration and concentration of wealth struck many people as threats to the unlimited individual opportunity that made America unique.

Many unskilled American workers were fearful that lower-paid immigrant labor might replace them; their incentive for "self-improvement" through education was thus greatly strengthened. These "true" Americans were natural champions of the Horatio Alger ethic. But others in American society, Archer and his allies felt, were being tempted by the new conditions to respond in more sinister ways. Self-made men were forgetting their roots; banding together against new talent, they strove to close the very doors through which they themselves had escaped poverty.

Archer felt he was speaking as a "true" American when he denounced such monopolists for the threat they posed to the nation and its traditions. His concern was that, denied advancement, some "true" Americans might attempt to subvert equality of opportunity for the new immigrants. This, in turn, could lead the new arrivals to fall back on the political traditions of their homelands. The overwhelming number of immigrants could thus open the shores of America to socialism and/or the paternalistic welfare state. With the advent of either one, free competition and the incentive to achievement would disappear. The "true" American, it was feared, would go the way of the passenger pigeon.[15]

Gleason Archer and other "Progressives" saw only one way to save him, and the ethos which he embodied. The octopus of monopoly had to be fought wherever it was found; equality of opportunity had to be protected from its tentacles. Archer's personal crusade aimed to keep every level of education open to all—rich and poor, "true" American and immigrant alike. He fought any attempt by special interests and government to favor one individual or group over another. And, above all, he opposed any attempt to interfere in the free competition of the academic marketplace.[16]

Archer's Evening Law School grew rapidly. A law classmate, Arthur W. McLean, joined Archer on the "faculty" in the spring of 1907. By June, the school had outgrown the Roxbury flat. To handle its growing demands on their time, Archer and McLean consolidated their legal commitments by becoming law partners. When the new firm opened downtown offices at 53 Tremont Street in September, the suite doubled as law classrooms three nights a week.

The new location, combined with Archer's genius for obtaining free publicity, provided a fillip to attendance. The Dean, as he soon styled himself, was indefatigable. He taught, and handled all administrative duties. He courted political speakers, baited suffragettes, raced trains in his car, and gave away scholarships by popular vote—anything to call attention to the school. But when one of his first students passed the bar exam in 1908, the publicity eclipsed the Dean's efforts. Roland E. Brown was a machinist by trade, and news of his achievement swelled registration. In December 1908, Archer gave up law practice to devote full time to his Suffolk School of Law.[17]

He immediately assumed the task of writing textbooks for the school. His first effort, *Law Office and Court Procedure,* was begun in January 1909. Little, Brown, and Company, a prestigious law publisher, brought it out the next winter. When *Ethical Obligations of the Lawyer* followed within the year, it was an unprecedented event; the obscure Archer had provided two of Little, Brown's three new texts for 1910. When T. H. Flood and Company of Chicago snapped up his next two books, Archer's reputation was established.

As the Dean's reputation and his school grew, so did his assured readership. From 1916 on, Archer dispensed with independent publishers. Each new text, and each new edition of an old text, was printed at the Wright and Potter plant on Derne Street; all appeared under the imprint of the Suffolk Law School Press. Archer wrote quickly, almost obsessively. He worked long after midnight, between packed days. By adhering to his murderous writing schedule, he produced between 1916 and 1930 ten new texts and five new editions for use at the school. During that time, he averaged one law book per year, in addition to his other writing and his backbreaking administrative duties. By 1931, a majority of the courses at Suffolk Law School were equipped with textbooks written by the Dean.[18]

After 1909, school business competed with writing for Archer's attention—and usually won. When he closed his law office, Archer moved the school to the Tremont Temple Spacious quarters and electric lighting offered a striking contrast to the old location, and numbers steadily increased.[19] Economical evening classes were proving popular with working men bent on "improvement." But as Archer's school grew, so did his responsibilities.

He made few efforts to share them. A three-man Advisory Council was set up by Archer in 1908. When the school incorporated as a charitable educational institution three years later, a seven-man Board of Trustees was established. Neither body seriously diluted Archer's authority nor reduced his duties. The Board regularly elected him its Treasurer; in this capacity, he wielded financial control over the institution of which he was also Dean. The combination of duties exhausted Archer, but it also left him with a free hand in school affairs. He served as Dean until 1942 and Treasurer until 1946; his close friend Thomas J. Boynton chaired the Board of Trustees from 1911 until his death in 1945. As long as the pairing lasted, Suffolk was Gleason Archer's school.

The Dean's duties had grown so demanding by 1914 that Archer became literally a full-time resident of the school. Enrollment jumped when Suffolk Law School was granted power to confer degrees; new energies and new facilities were required. Archer mortgaged his home to purchase a new school location at 45 Mount Vernon Street, and moved with his family to the top floor of the building.[20]

By 1930, Archer and his "family" had made Suffolk one of the world's largest law schools.

During the seven years they lived there, Dean Archer worked at the school from 9am until 9:30pm, six days a week. He taught, administered, lobbied, kept accounts, and acted as press agent. He personally directed the building of an annex in 1915, and when that proved inadequate, plunged into an expansion campaign. For it, Archer solicited funds, negotiated loans, engaged builders, fought strikers, and again supervised construction. His house was remortgaged, and his capital was invested in the undertaking. Personal borrowing was backed with added insurance on his life. The Dean was even forced by the scope of his exertions to give up teaching. When Archer moved with his family in 1921 to the top floor of the new structure on Derne Street, he had pledged himself for every aspect of the building.[21]

The incautious pledge, however, was soon redeemed; by 1930, Archer and his "family" had made Suffolk one of the world's largest law schools. The Dean, his wife Elizabeth, and their three children retained the top floor apartment until 1937. From the "imperial suite," as he called it, Archer supervised school affairs twenty-four hours a day. Mrs. Archer's father, the Reverend Henry S. Snyder, had been appointed Assistant Treasurer and Superintendent at the school in 1914, he and his wife lived with the Archers from that time on. Their son, H. Rossiter Snyder, also helped in the treasurer's office when the need arose. Gleason's brother Hiram had taught at the school as early as September, 1907. He was appointed Director of the Review Department in 1915, and thus became the first full-time faculty member. Elected a Trustee in

1930, Hiram Archer actively served Suffolk until his death in 1966. The Dean's younger son, Gleason, Jr., also became a Trustee in 1939; like Hiram, he continued to teach at the institution after his election to the board. His sister Marian managed the Bookstore and served as Advisor to Women after 1934. Her husband, Paul MacDonald, headed the Placement Bureau, and went on to become Bursar. Julia Archer, daughter of the Dean's eldest brother, served on the office staff, while the Dean's younger brother Harold was brought from Maine to work at the school in 1926; he preceded Marian as Bookstore Manager.[22]

Hiram J. Archer

Maine provided the Suffolk "family" with a number of recruits. Dean Archer never forgot his origins. He brought to Suffolk all three sons of the uncle who in 1899 had found him a place in Sabattus. Upon graduation from the law school in 1927, Kenneth Williams joined Hiram Archer on the full-time faculty. Both his brothers also graduated from Suffolk; to pay living expenses as students, Leonard was appointed Recorder at the school, while Gerard became Assistant Engineer, then Librarian. Roger Stinchfield, who preceded Leonard as Recorder, followed in his cousin Kenneth's footsteps. Shortly after graduation in 1930, Stinchfield was appointed a faculty member by Gleason Archer. The Dean also became patron to a number of Maine boys who were unrelated to him. Monitors at Suffolk were always theology students at Boston University, but most other administrative positions were put in the hands of Archer's "Maine mafia." In these destitute students he saw himself, and he loved playing George Frost to them.[23]

Archer's office staff rounded out his "family." Chief among them was the indefatigable, indispensable Catharine C. "Kay" Caraher. Hired as the Dean's secretary at seventeen in 1919, she became Archer's most trusted assistant. With Hiram Archer and, later, Kenneth Williams, Caraher handled the day-to-day running of Suffolk Law School until her resignation in 1939. The ingenious, and unique, system of selling class admission "tickets" was her creation: tuition payment and class attendance could thus be computed simultaneously. She headed up a close-knit band of Irish Catholics in a predominantly Yankee administration. Caraher's sister Margaret "Peg" Gillespie, Dorothy McNamara, and her sister Evelyn Reilly together compiled over a century of service to the school. Gillespie succeeded her sister as Law School Secretary in 1939, and the beloved "Dotty Mac" remained a Suffolk fixture for forty-six years as Bursar and Alumni Director. All were part of the Dean's "family." They received frequent invitations to join Archer and his relatives at

Archer's Norwell estate, on fishing trips, or for drives in the Dean's old Stearns Knight.

At the head of his clan, Archer was tireless. He wrote the school catalogues, founded an Alumni Association, edited the *Alumni News*, and provided the association with a home. He recruited "family" member Alden Cleveland as Alumni Secretary and resident caretaker. When activities shifted to Norwell for the summer, Dean Archer held open house. There he marshaled a formidable array of Maine frontier skills. He cooked, fished, farmed, pruned, cut wood; he even constructed a trout pool and built a log cabin by hand. His relentless activity provided an example to his household which none could match—but which none could disregard.[24]

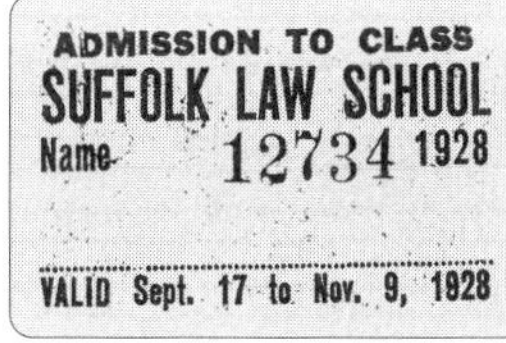

Law School class admission ticket

The remarkable success of Suffolk Law School by 1930 was a "family" achievement; a sense of mission passed from the Dean through his staff to the students themselves. Prosperity, however, resulted from more than morale. Gleason Archer was offering a very marketable product, as the 2,600 men who filled his school in 1927 testified. Evening classes allowed students to retain jobs. A part-time faculty kept costs down and tuition low. The case method was discarded as unsuitable to part-time students. And there were no entrance requirements; Archer offered every man an opportunity to study law.

His approach provoked hostility. Suffolk's Trustees petitioned in 1912 for the right to grant degrees; their request sparked the fiercest educational struggle in the Massachusetts legislature's history. The resistance, Archer argued, came from arrogant monopolistic interests. This "Educational Octopus," Archer asserted, despised the common man, the "true" American; it was dedicated to the preservation of privilege. Had not President Lowell of Harvard taken a personal hand in the legislative proceedings, and a Harvard overseer sneeringly denounced Archer's attempt to "turn cart horses into trotters"?[25]

Suffolk's Dean sought help from an unfamiliar quarter. Archer had been a Republican from the cradle, born into a community where there were "not more than four Democrats of voting age."[26] Republican complicity in the effort to "control" education shocked him, however; the attack on free competition contradicted his fundamental beliefs. As a result, Archer was soon in contact with top Democratic leaders. Irish almost to a man, they were no strangers to the fight against exclusiveness and privilege. Thomas Boynton was a local Democratic chairman. Through him, General Charles Bartlett, James Vahey, and Joseph O'Connell were brought onto the Board of Trustees. Their mediation brought Martin Lomasney and Mayor

James Michael Curley into the fray. After a three-year legislative battle, Archer and his allies finally won. They even managed to unseat Governor Eugene Foss in the process. Newly-elected Democrat David Walsh signed the Suffolk Law School charter on March 10, 1914.

Archer's Democratic ties did not end with the charter fight. Lomasney, "the splendid old War Horse of the West End," remained Suffolk's champion until his death in 1933.[27] His loyalty confirmed the importance attached to Archer's school by the West End constituency. Curley, too, was a constant supporter. The Mayor made Archer a member of his "brain trust." He appointed the Dean to a number of executive commissions, and in 1930 designated him Vice-Chairman of the Boston Tercentenary. Although Archer never could accept Democratic machine politics, he respected Curley, Lomasney, and their colleagues as fellow campaigners for equality of opportunity.[28]

The Dean repeatedly appealed to the legislature and its Democratic majority for aid against his "monopolistic" antagonists: the Board of Education, the Bar Association, the Bar Examiners, the Board of Collegiate Authority, and, ultimately, even his own Trustees. The General Court, Archer asserted, was "close to the people"; it therefore had both the power and the responsibility to override selfish dictates by committees, boards, and professional associations. The Democratic Party defended legislative primacy against bureaucratic usurpation and private interest. At least until the advent of the New Deal, Gleason Archer and the Democrats were natural allies.[29]

His first encounter with the "Educational Octopus" left Dean Archer profoundly suspicious of any movement to "control" education in the name of "standards." When the American Bar Association proposed in 1921 to require two years of college for admission to the bar, Archer was outraged. He viewed the action as an attempt to exclude workingmen from law study, to make law a "millionaires' racket." After all, less than two percent of Americans in 1921 could afford the privilege of attending college. Behind the proposal, he saw the hand of the "educational trust." The same sinister interests that had opposed Suffolk's charter in 1912 were now moving, he believed, against all schools of Suffolk's type. Tuition costs already excluded newcomers from the universities which formed the "Educational Octopus." The monopolists, Archer argued, were now out to close the legal profession to all except graduates of their chosen universities, just as, early in the century, they had closed the medical profession. Harvard Law School and Boston University Law

School were singled out as centers of militant monopolism. The Association of American Law Schools was denounced as a pressure group for the exclusive "University" law schools. It had been AALS activity which pushed the new "standard" through the ABA Section of Legal Education.[30]

Suffolk's Dean led opposition to the "college monopoly." For the next ten years, Archer criss-crossed the country. He attended ABA conventions and addressed associations; he spoke to groups of lawyers, to law educators, and to the general public. He lobbied in legislatures and cooperated with sympathetic legislators, like Martin Lomasney in Massachusetts. His enemies labeled him a "reactionary" for his opinions and his rejection of the case method; they sought to discredit him by denouncing Suffolk as a "proprietary school" dedicated only to maximal profits. He took the abuse, exposed the distortions and fought on. To counterbalance the AALS, Archer organized in 1922 the National Association of Day and Evening Law Schools. The campaign earned him honorary degrees from two charter members of the new association. More important, it left him with a permanent hostility toward all accrediting bodies and toward any form of educational "control." Finally, it made him a public figure. By 1929, Gleason Archer was a nationally recognized spokesman for "equality of opportunity."[31]

Gleason Archer, radio personality

It was a speech on that very topic which led Dean Archer into radio broadcasting. He took the microphone as a substitute speaker at WBZ-WBZA on September 29, 1929. Within a fortnight, he had his own show; his hard-line broadcasts on crime and criminal law immediately won attention for him and his school. A natural showman, Archer grasped the possibilities of radio; he developed a passion for the new medium.

Mayor Curley in 1930 appointed him Chairman of the Boston Tercentenary Radio Broadcasting Committee. In that capacity, Archer delivered the inaugural Tercentenary radio address; he also assembled, through the National Broadcasting Company in New York, a nationwide network for his Tercentenary historical broadcasts. When these ended, public response had been so impressive that NBC asked Dean Archer to begin a series on legal issues. "Laws That Safeguard Society" remained an NBC staple for three years. Dean Archer traveled weekly to WEAF in New York, where his network transmission originated. His facility for popularization also led to an historical series on WBZ-WBZA which lasted from 1930 until 1934.[32]

Subsequent publication of material from both series attested Archer's popularity, and that wide appeal opened the doors of many broadcasting luminaries. David Sarnoff, Rudy Vallee, and John Shepard of the Yankee Network were all brought by Archer into Suffolk affairs. John Clark, Program Director at WBZ, became a close friend. The inside knowledge gained from them eventually enabled Archer to produce his two-volume *History of Radio*; a pioneering effort when published in 1938-39, it remained for years the authoritative statement.[33]

His school, however, remained Archer's first love. He never hesitated to exploit for its sake the exposure and the connections which he derived from broadcasting. During a time of economic depression, Suffolk needed all the help it could get.

That aid was all the more necessary because, as the twenty-fifth anniversary Jubilee approached, Gleason Archer had ambitious plans for his law school. He had long fought the "educational trust" over the college requirement for bar admission. Now, he proposed to banish the specter of a "college monopoly" in the professions by opening a college that working people could afford. The new college, he asserted, would become a "haven of opportunity," and Suffolk "a great evening University."[34]

The original Suffolk University seal

Expansion followed the founder's blueprint. During the prosperity of the late twenties, Archer had purchased Beacon Hill property against just such an eventuality. He had already given 73 Hancock Street to the Alumni Association; his building at 59 Hancock Street, however, was quickly readied to receive the new "collegiate department."[35] The Suffolk College of Liberal Arts was founded in 1934. To its charter was affixed the signature of James Michael Curley, by then Governor of the Commonwealth; he also received the College's first honorary degree. Three years later, the Main Building at 20 Derne Street was expanded from three stories to five. The structure had been designed in 1920, on the Dean's insistence, to accommodate the added weight. When the state legislature approved a charter creating Suffolk University in 1937, Archer became the first President of the new institution. The founder's vision had been realized. Of that realization, however, there was an ironic consequence. For the first time since 1914, no residential space was available at Suffolk; reconstruction of the school drove Gleason Archer and his family from it.[36]

In a larger sense, too, the events of 1937 prepared the founder's departure. Expansion during the Depression was a bold step; when war followed, the University was left with no income to service its mortgage. Archer, as Treasurer, had built no endowment to cover such crises. By 1945, University finances were in a desperate condition.

So were relations between President Archer and the Trustees. The 1937 charter had raised the number of Board members from seven to eighteen. New membership undermined the Board's docility; Archer's management encountered unprecedented scrutiny, which became more insistent as conditions deteriorated. The President, for his part, had been sensitive to criticism throughout his life; he tended to view those who disagreed with him as "enemies." Years of success, culminating in the triumphs of 1937, had pushed him from self-assurance to complacency. A self-made man and a rugged individualist, he found it hard to view the Board's "control" as anything but conspiracy against him, his values, and the school that embodied them.

Archer's abhorrence of "control" contributed, as well, to other frictions with the Trustees. The President was reluctant to seek ABA accreditation because it would mean submitting Suffolk Law School to "regulation." Accreditation, however, seemed a matter of growing urgency to Trustees like Hiram Archer and Frank Donahue, as well as to Frank Simpson, who replaced Gleason Archer as Dean in 1942. The maverick status of Suffolk and its founder worried them; they wanted to standardize Suffolk education with that given at "quality" law schools, and they saw ABA requirements as a useful guide in that process.[37]

A second conflict arose over President Archer's views on New Deal efforts at "control." By 1936, he was convinced that New Deal "liberalism" was not furthering, as it professed to do, equality of opportunity. Archer viewed it, instead, as a confused mixture of socialism and monopolistic paternalism. As a Progressive, he had spent much of his life fighting these twin threats to "true American" free competition; and like many other former Progressives, he turned on the New Deal. Archer denounced Roosevelt's "alien-minded" advisors who, he insisted, were working to transform the United States into "a Bureaucratic Totalitarian State—with themselves as perpetual overlords." He broke with Governor Curley in 1936 and associated himself with the National Jeffersonian Democratic Party, an anti-Roosevelt splinter group. Eight years later, the American Democratic National Committee revived the crusade. Suffolk's President became national chairman of the organization; he also produced *On the Cuff*, a scathing attack on the New Deal.[38]

Archer's efforts cost Suffolk indispensable federal programs during the wartime financial crisis. They also earned him the enmity of several more Trustees. Bernard Killion, Roosevelt campaign treasurer in Massachusetts, was furious; he was supported in his indignation by Bretton Woods proprietor David Stoneman and by Judge Donahue, who had for years been a major figure in Massachusetts Democratic politics.[39]

At war's end, a majority of the Board viewed as imperative the retirement of their sixty-five year old President. His abilities were still redoubtable; but his rogue-elephant style contrasted sharply, in their view, with the needs of the University in an increasingly corporate and bureaucratic educational world.

The sequel was unedifying. Three years of acrimony and litigation finally ended in August 1948, with President Archer's tearful departure. Most of his remaining "family" went with him.[40] Archer had transferred formal ownership to the Board in 1914, but Suffolk had been "his" school—as Dean, Treasurer, and President—for over forty years. Enforced withdrawal was profoundly difficult. He never did fully understand the reasons for his ouster; a belief that he was the victim of injustice dogged him for the rest of his life, as did a terrible sense of loss.[41]

"It is my most sincere desire," the founder pleaded, "that the compact I made with George Frost fifty years ago may continue to animate the University."

Archer remained indomitable, however. At 67, he was still an entrepreneur. Immediately after his dismissal, he purchased a Pembroke farm; there he initiated the growing of cultivated blueberries in Massachusetts. He founded, and for years presided over, the Massachusetts Cultivated Blueberry Association. The Pembroke Historical Society appointed him Director. In 1963, Archer married his old friend Pauline (Wilfong) Clark; he was 83, she 57. They sold the blueberry nursery, but Archer remained vigorous and active until stricken with cancer in 1965. He died, just three months after his brother Hiram, on June 28, 1966.[42]

Gleason Archer's valediction to Suffolk came during the Jubilee Year of 1956. "It is my most sincere desire," the founder pleaded, "that the compact I made with George Frost fifty years ago may continue to animate the University." Only in that way could the institution's efforts be, as Archer asserted his "life interest" had always been, "vitally focused upon the preservation to present and future generations of that democracy in education and in the opportunities of life which our ancestors transmitted to us."[43]

The words evoke Horatio Alger; but no more fitting epitaph could be found for Gleason L. Archer. Nor could any pronouncement more accurately delineate the heritage bequeathed by him to the University he founded.[44]

Chapter 3 *The Law School, 1906–1981*

Gleason L. Archer founded Suffolk Law School to be an "open door of opportunity"[1] for immigrant and American-born workingmen. For years, he fought efforts by the American Bar Association (ABA) and the Association of American Law Schools (AALS) to establish "quality control" standards for legal education through legislation or voluntary accreditation guidelines. Such "regulation," Archer feared, would drive the cost of forensic training or its prerequisites beyond the means of most Americans. His school was vilified by the professional associations as the seat of mediocrity, but Archer's opposition to exclusive standards was never opposition to educational excellence as such. He worked steadily to improve the quality of education offered at Suffolk Law School, and as high school and college instruction became widely affordable, many at

Gleason Archer (left) with Rudy Vallee at the building that bears Archer's name

Suffolk who shared his goal of educational excellence came to accept as constructive the net influence of accreditation criteria. Although considered code words for elitism and exclusivity at the height of Archer's battles with the ABA and AALS, "quality" and "excellence" were eventually accepted as watchwords at the school he had founded.

This chapter aims to trace the steps, occasionally hesitant or painful, by which Suffolk Law School, Dean Archer's "haven of opportunity,"[2] became the Suffolk University Law School which by 1981 was proudly engaged in a "Campaign for Excellence."[3]

When Gleason L. Archer resigned as Dean of Suffolk University Law School in 1942, he had occupied that position since founding the school thirty-six years earlier. Archer's institution, like urban evening schools across the country, served native and immigrant workingmen who could not afford the time or money for a traditional legal education, or who would be excluded from older law schools by barriers of socio-economic prejudice. Since nearly all of Archer's students worked full-time during the day, evening classes allowed them to retain their jobs. The school was open only three nights a week; and each course met only once weekly, giving students time to assimilate course material. A part-time faculty and a minimal administrative staff kept salary costs down and tuition low; after 1915, a free employment bureau helped students to find the jobs necessary for continued attendance. Gleason Archer was determined to keep his law school financially accessible to any ambitious working man, of any age or background.[4]

He was also determined that potential students should not be barred for their educational deficiencies, as they were from many conventional legal programs. Throughout the period of explosive growth at Suffolk Law School (1909-30), Dean Archer maintained a policy of open admissions. There were no entrance requirements; every man was offered an opportunity to study law. A person who lacked the high school education required before he could take the Massachusetts bar examination could obtain it by attending Suffolk's Summer Preparatory Department (established in 1910) during each summer of his law school career.[5] He could thus earn a law degree and the equivalent of a high school diploma concurrently. Clearly, problems could arise from this attempt to combine high school training with a legal education; and there was, understandably, a high attrition rate among Archer's students. Only about thirty percent of those entering the law school went on to graduate; but these included many impecunious young men who might otherwise have been denied access to the legal profession.[6]

Archer's approach proved so attractive that by 1924 he could claim Suffolk Law School was the world's largest. Between 1909 and 1930, enrollments increased from 114 to 2207; the faculty expanded from nine to 34, but the number of students grew seven times faster. Such growth was overwhelming; it forced Archer to improvise a series of ingenious operational adjustments. In many ways, he was simply evolving a methodology to accommodate the effects of his *laissez-faire* educational philosophy, according to which no one should be excluded and, consequently, no enrollment limits set. The procedures he adopted, however, accelerated Suffolk Law School's divergence from the ABA and the AALS, while also providing prime targets for external, and later internal, criticism of Archer's administration.

By 1924 Archer could claim Suffolk Law School was the world's largest. Between 1909 and 1930, enrollments increased from 114 to 2207; the faculty expanded from nine to 34, but the number of students grew seven times faster.

Classroom monitors became necessary to preserve decorum, and accurate record-keeping could only be maintained through the introduction of class admission tickets. The flood of registrants forced Archer to abandon moot court exercises and to replace them with a lecture course on "Practice and Pleading."[7] It also ended any thoughts entertained by Archer of a dalliance with the "case" method of teaching law, and definitively wedded him to the "black letter" approach.

The Socratic "case" technique was rapidly displacing "black-letter" methodology in leading law schools; nevertheless, Dean Archer concluded that the "case" method, unless substantially modified, was unsuitable for the instruction of part-time students. Developed by Dean Langdell of Harvard in 1870, it stressed reading of "landmark" cases and independent evolution by each student of the legal principles embodied in them. Such an approach required expensive casebooks and extensive time outside class for reading and reflection. The case method, Archer asserted, forced students to "disregard the accumulated wisdom of the past" and thus was "a pitiful waste of human effort."[8] He was convinced that students with full time jobs had neither the time nor the energy to "reinvent the wheel" in each aspect of law. Dean Archer considered more efficient, and therefore retained, the older "black letter" method, which relied on lectures and textbooks where the law was reduced to a set of rules, and which stressed memorization rather than inductive reasoning. In his judgment, however, the final nail in the case method's coffin was a practical one; the Socratic classroom dialogue required by the case method was impracticable at Suffolk given the Law

School's very high student-teacher ratio (and reduction of that ratio would have meant an unacceptable increase in educational costs). Thus, though the case method was becoming standard in university law schools during the 1920s, black-letter law was entrenched at Suffolk Law School.

For his rejection of entrance requirements and the case method, Gleason Archer's ABA and AALS enemies labeled him a "reactionary"; but the Dean's embattled relations with outside accrediting agencies certainly did not mean that he was unconcerned with quality education in his own school. As early as 1913, prizes were being awarded at Suffolk for student academic achievement; during the prosperous 1920s, the awards increased steadily in number, and scholarship funds were attached to them.

Suffolk Law School freshmen (1911)

As burgeoning enrollments made it difficult to give individual attention to students, the Dean modified accepted black-letter procedure to provide it. The result was what Archer dubbed the "Suffolk method." To the customary combination of explanatory lectures, regular in-class review, and the Dean's black-letter texts, it added a new element—the work of the Research and Review Department. This body, originally called the Department of Problems and Quizzes, was created in 1915 by Gleason Archer, who appointed his brother Hiram to be its head.[9] The Department prepared monthly quizzes, final examinations, and homework problems upon which students were required to formulate written legal opinions. Hiram Archer and his staff then graded the responses not only for content, but for grammar and spelling as well, since difficulties with written and spoken English were not uncommon among Suffolk students. Corrected exercises were returned, accompanied by a model for comparison; thus, every student received regular criticism on both his writing and his legal analysis. The Dean's predilection for black-letter law gave his students an advantage on bar examinations that stressed memorization over inductive reasoning; but it was the unique personal review component in the "Suffolk method" that permitted the sharpening of individual skills at an institution bursting with students. The result was that a larger number (if not a higher percentage) of candidates from Suffolk passed the Massachusetts bar exam in the 1920s than from any of the four other Boston-area law schools.[10]

When immigration curbs and economic stagnation stemmed the enrollment flood after 1929, Archer seized the opportunity to undertake organizational and methodological innovations. The

Dean's original teaching staff of Boston University graduates[11] had given way by that time to one on which Suffolk Law School graduates[12] predominated; these alumni professors formed the nucleus of Archer's faculty until the Second World War, and they joined in his efforts to improve educational conditions at Suffolk with a zeal which only those who had passed through the system themselves could muster.

The alumni insisted, and Archer acknowledged, that while the individual criticism available from the Research and Review Department was welcome, it was not enough. There was general agreement that, as enrollments fell, the Law School's previously overextended resources could at last be concentrated to provide more personal attention for Suffolk Law students. To this end, a Resident Counselor for first-year students (Kenneth B. Williams) was appointed in 1929. That same year, Dean Archer took a second step to adapt the "Suffolk method" to a smaller student body; although he by no means abandoned his insistence on the primacy of black-letter law for his students, he began a series of simplified, economical casebooks to supplement his texts. To accommodate more discussion, class length was increased in 1932 from 1 1/2 to 2 hours. Eight years later, a period was formally set aside in each class for discussion work, including cases; and in 1941 classes were extended from three days a week to four.

In 1931, Archer ended open admissions at Suffolk, as he had ended black-letter law's monopoly two years before; again, he acted on the advice of his alumni professors. The Dean abolished the Summer Preparatory Department, and required that all applicants be high school graduates. He justified this requirement by citing the dramatically increased access to free high schools. Not only was a high school diploma required, a college degree was urged—and the inducement was a 20% tuition discount for any law student who was a college graduate. To provide a high school background for those who aspired to become Suffolk students, Archer contracted with the Wheeler Preparatory School; by the fall of 1931, it was officially the "preparation department of Suffolk Law School," located in one of Archer's properties at 59 Hancock Street. Beginning in 1932, the space vacated by elimination of the Summer Preparatory Department was employed to house a law summer session composed solely of makeup work for those who had performed unsatisfactorily during the school year.

Archer's acceptance of a high school requirement for Law school admission was quickly followed by state imposition of a college requirement. Since 1921, both the ABA and the AALS had urged passage of a law requiring two years of college training for bar admission. Archer fought this requirement; when it was enacted, he believed that it posed a severe threat to Suffolk's traditional constituency and to the school itself. To counter this threat, the Dean founded the Suffolk College of Liberal Arts.[13] It opened in September 1934, just three months after passage of the objectionable regulation. The part-time, low-tuition college kept access to legal training open to Suffolk's historic clientele; it also provided Suffolk Law students with better pre-legal preparation then ever before. Under these circumstances, Archer's hostility to the college requirement evaporated. In the early 1920s, no argument could have reconciled the Dean to ABA desiderata for "quality" legal education; a decade later, time and altered conditions had, in several instances, accomplished that feat.

In February 1935, Suffolk College received degree-granting powers from the Massachusetts General Court; the same legislation also authorized Suffolk Law School to award the Master of Laws (LLM) degree. The Law Alumni Association had offered post-graduate lecture courses at its 73 Hancock Street Clubhouse since November 1927; in the fall of 1935, the lectures became part of the LLM program offered by the newly-founded Suffolk Graduate School of Law. The graduate department never attracted more than a hundred students at a time into its two-year program, but, in the Dean's eyes, it represented another step toward "respectability."

Almost necessarily, the next step was development of the Law Library. There had never been a full-time Librarian at Suffolk before 1936, when Archer recruited M. Esther Newsome. At first, she was in charge only of the College Library at 59 Hancock Street; but in 1937, when the two collections were combined after reconstruction of the 20 Derne Street building, she became University Librarian. Under her supervision, the law collection grew from seven thousand volumes to over ten thousand in 1941. The new Library, located on the third floor of what is today the Archer Building, could hold forty-five thousand books and had a seating capacity of almost three hundred.

Many members of the Suffolk Law School community supported Dean Archer's rapprochement with "respectability"; indeed, some proved rather more enthusiastic about it than the Dean. As enrollments fell during the 1930s to half the 1927 level, there was increased pressure on Archer to conform to the recommended policies and practices of the professional associations. His colleagues and his alumni alike expressed growing concern about the character—and even the fate—of a law school repeatedly denounced by the ABA.

Hiram Archer became his brother's severest critic. He found an ally in one of the school's most influential alumni, Frank J. Donahue, recently appointed to the Superior Court bench. When the University charter of 1937 raised the number of Trustees from seven to eighteen, the pair saw their opportunity.[14] Many of the Board's added members lacked the docility of Gleason Archer's hand-picked incumbents; under Hiram's leadership, the new Trustees subjected President Archer's management to unprecedented scrutiny, which became more insistent as conditions deteriorated.

Judge Frank J. Donahue

The dissidents demanded the standardization of Suffolk legal education with that given at "quality" law schools, normalization of relations with the ABA, and early ABA accreditation. Under the circumstances, the President was forced to compromise with them. His statements on the case method became steadily more measured, and his rejection of ABA accreditation standards less and less strident. In the 1940 Law School catalogue, he even went so far as to claim that, except for its insufficiency of full-time faculty members, Suffolk Law School satisfied all ABA accreditation requirements.

To a growing number of Trustees, however, Gleason Archer's progress toward accreditation seemed too slow. Archer, on his side, could not convince himself of the ABA's good faith, and, because of their long-standing mutual antagonism, ABA officials were equally distrustful of Archer. Many Board members viewed the Law School as the nucleus of the University, and, as financial conditions worsened, they became increasingly impatient with President Archer's belief that the future of the University lay with the Colleges. Each election after 1941 brought a new Law School advocate to the Board; in 1945, Judge Donahue himself became a Trustee.

To save his authority as President and Treasurer, Gleason Archer capitulated to demands by Law School adherents on and off the Board: he resigned as Dean of the Law School. In September 1942, he was replaced by Frank L. Simpson. The President and the Board both approved of Simpson's appointment, and both also agreed on his mandate to obtain ABA accreditation for Suffolk University Law School.

Frank Simpson was Archer's old friend and contemporary; he was a graduate of Boston University Law School, and he had begun a thirty-seven year teaching career there during Gleason Archer's last year as a student. The new Dean came to Suffolk as a critic of the case method, but he very quickly fell under the influence of Hiram Archer and Frank Donahue. With their advice and cooperation, Simpson had carried out a revolution by 1948.

In September 1943, Suffolk became a full-time day law school.[15] Hiram Archer remained a faculty stalwart, and he was joined in devoting his time exclusively to teaching by three other professors. Among these were two whose long-term contributions left indelible marks on Suffolk Law School: future Dean Donald R. Simpson, a B.U. graduate like his father Frank Simpson; and the venerable Raymond T. Parke, a Harvard alumnus who for two decades served as Suffolk's self-appointed arbiter of quality. One of several part-time instructors recruited by Frank Simpson was Mary Frances Pray, a Portia Law School graduate with an LLM from Suffolk, who thus became the first woman to serve on the Law School's teaching staff.[16] After a lapse of thirty years, a moot court was reestablished[17]; an office apprenticeship course was begun under Pray's direction; and an office laboratory was set up. Seminars were introduced, while fundamental courses were lengthened by a semester to provide time for collateral reading and reflection. Monitors and class admission tickets were phased out. The summer make-up classes of the pre-war period were replaced by a full-fledged law summer session. This new summer program offered Suffolk Law School's first elective courses since 1915; they constituted less than 20% of any student's program, but even this provided a marked contrast to Dean Archer's compulsory curriculum. The Research and Review Department was abolished; orthodox casebooks replaced the Archer texts; and by the spring of 1946 the old Suffolk Law School "system" had been completely demolished.

So had the ethnic stratification of the pre-war era. Apart from his office staff, Dean Archer had maintained a predominantly Yankee administration; the student body, by contrast, was mainly Irish Catholic. During the 1940s, Archer's alumni captured his school.

Their leader was Judge Frank J. Donahue. To undermine the thirty-year hegemony of Gleason Archer's small band of Yankee Trustees, Donahue used his influence to help bring a number of Irish Catholic Suffolk Law graduates onto the Board after 1937. Their support, and Donahue's aggressive advocacy of Law School accreditation, resulted in his election as Chairman of the Board in 1946. He was the first Chairman not hand-picked by Gleason Archer, and in many ways his election marks the end of the Archer era at Suffolk. Donahue chaired the Board of Trustees until 1948. Then, from 1949 until 1969, he occupied the pivotal position of University Treasurer. He chaired the Law School Committee of the Board during four decades, ending in 1975. From his position of Olympian authority, Judge Donahue managed to restore solvency after the wartime financial debacle. To do so, he scrutinized every area of University expenditure, retaining ultimate control even over the purchase of library books. His work as principal organizer of the Law School alumni for forty years earned him his nickname, but it accurately reflected the scope of his other contributions as well: Frank Donahue was "Mr. Suffolk."[18]

His chief subordinate was Bursar Dorothy M. McNamara. She was not, however, the usual subordinate. McNamara had been part of Gleason Archer's office staff for fourteen years before becoming Bursar in 1941; besides Hiram Archer, she was the only member of President Archer's official "family" to remain at Suffolk after his resignation in 1948. She served as Bursar until 1964, then as Alumni Secretary for another ten years; during nearly a half-century, she served, and shaped, the University. Her position as a link to the school's past, her central day-to-day role on campus, and the concern she unfailingly manifested for Suffolk students conferred on "Dotty Mac" a prestige and popularity which surpassed that of any other Suffolk University official, including Donahue himself. The Treasurer and the Bursar differed in their priorities. The Judge's preoccupation was with helping the school, its prestige, and its fiscal stringency; Miss Mac's was with the students. Many graduates of Suffolk Law School will admit gratefully that they would not be practicing law today had not Dorothy McNamara's lenience permitted them to overcome tuition difficulties. She retained in practice after 1948 Gleason Archer's indulgence of student financial delinquencies, and kept Suffolk Law School "the school with a heart." If Judge Donahue was "Mr. Suffolk" to the world, Dorothy McNamara was "Miss Suffolk" to the students.

It was from Donahue, however, that the support came which the "baleful, autocratic"[19] Frank Simpson needed to "standardize" the Law School with ABA accreditation requirements. An Endowment Fund was incorporated in 1950. The Library's law collection doubled by 1953, as did law scholarships between 1948 and 1951. The addition of Thomas Reed Powell, the aged but nationally-acclaimed constitutional scholar, and John L. Hurley, who had recently been appointed an advisor to the ABA Section of Legal Education, strengthened Simpson's full-time faculty, while another recruit, John F. X. O'Brien, remained a Suffolk institution for thirty years.[20]

By 1949, Law School enrollments had increased nine-fold over the wartime nadir of sixty students. Although attendance was only a fifth what it had been in Archer's heyday, the pre-war pattern of masculine predominance persisted. Women constituted barely one percent of Suffolk Law students. Most of their male counterparts were veterans whose legal education was financed by G.I. Bill funds. Three times more Law School entrants came from the Suffolk Colleges than from any other undergraduate institution; and, despite the two-year college requirement for admission, only 25% of all entering students possessed bachelor's degrees.

When Dean Simpson retired in June 1952, Suffolk Law School still lacked ABA accreditation; his "standardizing" reforms, however, had brought the school to the very threshold of approval. President Walter M. Burse, aided by Acting Law Dean John O'Brien, completed Simpson's work. Since replacing Gleason Archer as President in 1948, Burse, a Harvard-trained lawyer, had worked tirelessly to get the Colleges accredited—both for their own sake and as a prerequisite to ABA sanction for the Law School. In December 1952, the New England Association of Colleges and Secondary Schools approved the Colleges, and the way was opened for ABA accreditation.

In December 1952, the New England Association of Colleges and Secondary Schools approved the Colleges, and the way was opened for ABA accreditation.

John G. Hervey, Dean of the University of Oklahoma Law School, headed the ABA accreditation program during this period. Over several years, his advice to Burse, O'Brien, and Director of Libraries Edward G. Hartmann allowed them to bring Suffolk into conformity with ABA standards. When formal application for ABA approval was made, Hervey's advocacy of Suffolk Law School's cause helped open the way for accreditation despite pockets of residual hostility in the Section of Legal Education. The American Bar Association approved Suffolk University Law School in August 1953; Gleason Archer's old antagonist had been beaten—or, rather, joined.

The achievement, however, was slow to yield tangible rewards. The tumultuous changes of Dean Simpson's tenure, immediately succeeded by the emotional hurricane of the accreditation fight, made accurate evaluation of the school's position in their aftermath difficult. Frank Simpson's sudden departure, followed by President Burse's retirement two years later, left the Law School without a clear sense of direction. Professor O'Brien's appointment as Dean in July 1952 was, upon his own request, purely an interim one; he was to carry out a holding action until a strategy could be evolved for future development and for securing the full benefits of accreditation to Suffolk Law School.[21] That O'Brien was asked to maintain this holding posture for four years was not his fault; but the resultant extended paralysis had consequences that nearly proved fatal to the Law School.

At a time when the blessings of accreditation should have been accruing to Suffolk, Dean O'Brien's caretaker status, and his consequent inaction, allowed the Law School to drift toward crisis. Postwar law school enrollments at Suffolk (and nation-wide) peaked in 1949. As the pool of those eligible for G.I. Bill assistance shrank in subsequent years, attendance plunged. In the last years of Frank Simpson's Deanship, and throughout Dean O'Brien's tenure, applications and admissions fell alarmingly.[22] By 1956, there were fewer than three hundred students at Suffolk Law, half the 1949 figure. Only a third were enrolled full-time, while women constituted a mere four percent of total registration.

Like his predecessor, Dean O'Brien operated with only a skeletal administrative staff; therefore, as revenue dropped, he was forced to cut back in other areas. Library acquisitions fell to a trickle. Electives were cut back to compose only ten percent of the curriculum, and the summer session was discontinued entirely. The LLM program maintained only a tenuous existence. O'Brien's termination of the office apprenticeship laboratory also meant dismissal of its instructor, the school's only female faculty member. In 1956, there were no more full-time faculty members than there had been in 1943. Many instructors were elderly, and 25 out of 29 taught only part-time. Even Hiram Archer had to admit that the Law School was "deep in the red,"[23] supported only by income from the Colleges.

The world was changing around Dean O'Brien's school, and its traditional student reservoirs were evaporating. New programs and new initiatives were necessary to guarantee survival; new sources of applicants had to be tapped. The Simpson regime had laid the foundation of a university law school on the ABA pattern. Now, a new Dean was needed, one who possessed the vision, resolution, and support to build on Simpson's foundation an edifice of the quality which it was capable of supporting. That mandate fell, in July 1956, on Frederick A. McDermott.

Dean McDermott's appointment promised long-term leadership toward educational excellence. He was young (not yet fifty), energetic, and academically well-connected. A graduate of Harvard

Law School, he had taught for twenty years at Boston College Law School. His scholastic credentials, like those of his immediate predecessors (both B.U. Law graduates) reflected the postwar regime's rapprochement with the institutions Gleason Archer had denounced as parts of an "Educational Octopus." Shortly after taking office, the new Dean even opened formal relations with the once-dreaded AALS, and, with Alumni Association backing, attended the annual meeting of that organization in 1957.

During McDermott's eight years as Dean, the full-time faculty grew from four to ten. Those he appointed formed the nucleus of the Law School's teaching staff for decades afterward; they included Malcolm M. Donahue (the Judge's son), David J. Sargent, John J. Nolan, and Alfred I. Maleson.[24] Catherine T. Judge had been appointed as a separate Law School Registrar in 1955; after she completed her LLM at Suffolk in 1960, Dean McDermott expanded her duties to include part-time teaching.

A Legal Internship program with the office of Middlesex County District Attorney James O'Dea (a pioneer program for the region) was instituted in February 1957, and a similar arrangement was concluded two years later with the Attorney-General of the Commonwealth. Law clerkships also became a regular feature of the Law School's program for upperclassmen. An Estate Planning Contest was introduced in 1957, and, three years later, Moot Appellate Court and National Moot Court competition began. In 1959, a Student Bar Association (SBA) was founded.

As programs were diversified and competition increased, Dean McDermott also insisted that additional scholarship support be made available. The first Law Alumni Association scholarships, twelve in number, had been awarded in 1954; a decade later, there were fifty. Law School scholarship funds doubled, from five to ten thousand dollars, during McDermott's tenure. Four special Trustee Scholarships to the Law School were established for outstanding students entering from the Colleges, and four others were made available annually (one for each school) to graduates of Dartmouth, Holy Cross, Brandeis, and Merrimack. In 1961, a Trustee Graduate Law Fellowship was added, to send one graduating Suffolk Law student yearly to the doctoral or master's program of the recipient's choice.

The LSAT examination was first required for students entering in the fall of 1961, and the part-time program was discontinued for day division students two years later. Admissions, however, grew steadily. During McDermott's Deanship, enrollment trebled, reaching 800 by 1964.[25] Nonetheless, full-time students constituted only a third of this figure, and women only three percent; these proportions were identical with those for 1956, when McDermott had assumed office. Now, however, B.C., B.U., and Northeastern each sent more students to Suffolk Law School than did Suffolk's Colleges (a significant change from 1956), and only three percent of Suffolk Law students still lacked a bachelor's degree (compared to thirteen percent in 1956). Even Harvard College sent several students a year to Dean McDermott's school.

When Frederick McDermott died in March 1964, he left behind him an expanding and developing law school. Under his leadership, the Library's law collection had expanded 30%, from 22,000 to 31,000 volumes. The Law School had shown a profit in each year since 1958, as enrollments continued to rise. As the generation of postwar babies came of age, Suffolk Law School appeared on the verge of a new era of explosive growth to match that of Dean Archer's halcyon days. Where to put those new students, and what impact they would have on educational quality at the school, were the questions that had to be faced by McDermott's successor, Donald R. Simpson.

Dean Frederick A. McDermott

Donald Simpson was the son of former Dean Frank Simpson. Like his father, the younger Simpson had received his law degree from Boston University; he taught briefly at Northeastern, then joined the Suffolk faculty after World War II. In May 1964, he was appointed Dean. During his eight years in office, the school undertook a revolutionary expansion in programs, facilities, and administrative services; faculty expansion was coupled with impressive change in both the nature and number of students.

Under Simpson's leadership, Dean McDermott's programs were maintained or enlarged, while many new options were introduced. The Legal Intern program was expanded to include the Norfolk and Plymouth County District Attorneys' offices, the Boston Corporation Counsel, Lynn Neighborhood Legal Services, and the Legal Aid Society of Greater Lawrence. During the same period, the law clerk program grew to encompass district courts in Middlesex, Essex, and Worcester counties, as well as the Municipal Court of the Roxbury District. An Indigent Defendant Clinical Program was established at the Somerville District Court in 1967. After Wilbur C. Hollingsworth was appointed in 1970[26] as the first coordinator of all Suffolk Law School clinical programs, the Somerville operation was extended—under the name "Suffolk

Voluntary Defenders"—to the Boston Juvenile Court and to district courts in Middlesex, Norfolk, and Essex counties. At that time, the same courts also authorized foundation of a Suffolk Student Prosecutor Program.

To provide the Defenders and the Prosecutors with trained participants, a carefully-supervised moot court program was essential. Dean Simpson therefore appointed Charles B. Garabedian as Suffolk's first full-time moot court director. Under Garabedian, the program prospered. Scholarships were awarded to the three National Moot Court team members each year after 1970; and, in 1972, scholarships were made available to the winners of the newly-founded Justice Tom C. Clark Annual Moot Court Competition—a voluntary contest for second- and third-year students, named to honor the retired Supreme Court jurist.

Moot Court (1959)

In the spring of 1967, the first issue of the *Suffolk University Law Review* appeared. Three years later, scholarships were granted to the editorial staff, while the editor-in-chief was accredited—along with the SBA's President and Evening Division Chairman—to the Law School Committee of the Trustees. *The Advocate,* a legal magazine and journal, published its initial number in the fall of 1968; like the *Law Review,* it was edited by Suffolk Law students and funded by the school.[27]

Many of these new programs were housed in the 41 Temple Street building, the University's first new construction in thirty years. Expansion had been made imperative by rising enrollments, and was financed by increased income from them. Opened in 1966, the new building was named for Judge Donahue in 1971.

The new structure housed, for the first time since consolidation with the College facility in 1937, a separate Law School Library. For three decades, the University Librarians—M. Esther Newsome, succeeded by Dr. Edward G. Hartmann and then Richard J. Sullivan—had been charged with the responsibility of keeping both College and Law School holdings comprehensive and up-to-date. Since Dr. Hartmann's time, however, the real supervisor of the law collection had been Patricia I. "Pat" Brown. A Suffolk Law graduate and bar member, Brown carried out the gigantic task of cataloguing the Library's legal resources. When John W. Lynch was appointed the first separate Law Librarian in 1967, she became the principal "working librarian" on his staff, and played a major role in organizing his new bailiwick. Pat Brown received official designation as Assistant Law Librarian in 1972; by that time, the thirty thousand volumes of 1967 had grown to sixty thousand, necessitating the addition of a full-time Reference Librarian.[28]

Additional space provided by the new building also allowed the University to add separate Law Placement and Law Admissions officers—Anthony J. DeVico and John C. Deliso, respectively. At Donald Simpson's retirement in June 1972, his professional administrative staff had eight members, four times more than when he assumed the Deanship.

As enrollments and space expanded, Dean Simpson's instructional staff also increased—from a total of 31 in 1964 to 50 by 1972. The full-time faculty, which numbered ten at the time of Dean McDermott's death, had doubled when McDermott's successor left office.[29] Simpson's appointments included four Suffolk Law alumni, while Catherine Judge, another Suffolk graduate, gave up her position as a part-time Law Registrar in 1967 to be appointed the Law School's first full-time female teacher. Five years later, she became the first woman at Suffolk Law School to attain the rank of full professor. Upon vacating her old post in 1967, Judge was replaced by Doris R. Pote, the school's first full-time Law Registrar.

Dean Donald R. Simpson (left) with John E. Fenton

An enlarged faculty brought an increased choice of courses for students. Under Dean McDermott, less than ten percent of a student's program was composed of elective courses; by the end of Donald Simpson's Deanship, the proportion had been expanded to 25% for day students and 17% for their evening counterparts. To help fill the new scheduling space, and to serve an increasingly diverse student body, elective courses were introduced which focused on conditions of legal practice in specific states outside Massachusetts.[30]

As if to symbolize that important changes were in progress at Suffolk, the Board of Trustees voted in December 1968 to replace the Bachelor of Laws (LLB) degree, which had been awarded by the Law School since 1914, with a new one, the *Juris Doctor* (JD). In the same year, Dean Simpson received the school's first consulting visitor from the Association of American Law Schools, initiating an evaluation process that culminated nine years later in AALS membership.

Law School scholarship funds grew six-fold during Donald Simpson's tenure as Dean, to sixty-three thousand dollars annually. From 1966 on, a federally-funded Work-Study program also allowed the Dean to expand the existing student-assistant arrangements. It was academic quality, however, and not financial opportunity, which Law School officials counted on most to attract students to Suffolk.

They came, in legions. Between 1964 and 1972, the Law School's enrollment increased 150%, from 800 to 2,000. More than half the students attended full-time in 1972 (compared to only one-third eight years earlier), and the percentage of women was twice what it had been in 1964 (though it was still only seven percent). By the early 1970s, the University of Massachusetts joined B.C., B.U., and Northeastern in sending more students each to Suffolk Law than did the Suffolk Colleges.

David J. Sargent

When Donald Simpson retired in June 1972, Suffolk Law School was again, as in Gleason Archer's heyday, among the world's largest law schools. Where once use of that phrase had conveyed praise, however, now it implied blame. With Suffolk Law's two thousand students in 1972, there went a student-faculty ratio of 100-1. Whether quality legal education could be given under these circumstances was problematical. To reaffirm educational standards required more faculty members, fewer students, or a combination of both; this, in turn, would mean increased costs and higher tuition. Difficult choices had to be made, weighing quality against economy, and a strategy had to be developed by which the two might be reconciled. That was the challenge faced by Donald Simpson's eventual successor as Law School Dean: David J. Sargent.[31]

Sargent was the first Suffolk Law graduate to assume the Deanship on a permanent basis; the Trustees' willingness to appoint an alumnus clearly indicated the school's enhanced prestige and growing sense of its own worth. Dean Sargent's educational views were representative of those shared by an expanding group of younger faculty members. As students in the turbulent late 1960s called for greater freedom of choice, more opportunities for practical involvement, and broadening of the student body itself, their demands found sympathy within the faculty. Dean Simpson had, after all, considerably augmented the proportion of full-timers who had themselves been Suffolk Law students.

By tempering traditionalism with piecemeal concessions, Donald Simpson had managed to prevent major restructuring during his tenure. Changes began, however, from the time he stepped down. Under Dean Sargent, old restrictions were swept away, and new options opened. Conservatism gave way to experimentation as the new regime strove to improve the quality of student life at Suffolk Law School.

Towards this end, a 25% reduction in enrollments, from 2,140 to 1,680, took place between 1972 and 1980.[32] By the latter date, sixty percent of the Law School's students attended the day (full-time) division, compared to just over half eight years before. Competition for a diminishing number of places intensified, eliciting increasingly impressive credentials from successful applicants. Suffolk Law students were still drawn in large numbers from Boston College, the University of Massachusetts, Boston University, Northeastern, Holy Cross, Providence, and the Suffolk Colleges. By the late 1970s, however, contingents also came from Brown, Tufts, Smith, Mount Holyoke, and, of course, Harvard. In 1980, the Law School attracted nearly 40% of its students from outside Massachusetts, up from a 1972 figure of twenty-five percent.

As the student body contracted, the faculty expanded dramatically. Between 1972 and 1980, Dean Sargent doubled, to 45, the number of full-time faculty members, while decreasing to one-quarter the proportion of Suffolk Law graduates in that group.[33] During the same period, the total teaching staff grew from 50 to 95. By 1980, faculty expansion had reduced the astronomic student-faculty ratio of 1972 to a respectable 30-1. In addition, it brought to the school specialists eager to teach courses in their diverse fields. Faculty and student requests produced a reduction in the proportion of required courses—to 60% of a day student's program, and 70% of an evening student's.

The number of elective offerings multiplied to fill the space available. Students were thereby given a significantly greater freedom of choice in shaping their law school experience.

To prepare them for responsible use of this freedom, and to help provide orientation for entering law students, a unified (or "integrated") first-year program was also introduced. At its core were small Legal Practice Skills (LPS) sections, which were added to complement the first-year moot court work. Special Teaching Fellows (often recent graduates) were hired as LPS instructors, and a student-run Moot Court was established.

The Moot Court Board was only one of many opportunities for student participation opened by Dean Sargent. The clinical programs were nurtured and expanded. The Suffolk University Legal Assistance Bureau (SULAB) was founded in 1973, and eight years later still maintained offices in Beverly, its original location, and Charlestown.[34] For those unable or disinclined to participate in the Voluntary Defenders, Voluntary Prosecutors, or SULAB, an Outside Clinical Studies program was established in 1976 to provide governmental or judicial internships. Professor Garabedian, previously director of SULAB, took charge of Outside Clinical Studies, while Special Faculty positions were created for the directors of the three clinical programs.

A Client Counseling Competition and the Philip C. Jessup International Moot Court Competition both began in 1973; a Best Oral Advocate Run-Off Competition was added three years later, for those individuals selected as best oral advocate from each LPS section. In 1977, the Run-Off Competition was named to honor the man who had become Law School Committee chairman in 1976: the Honorable Walter H. McLaughlin, retired Chief Justice of the Massachusetts Superior Court.

David Sargent had been the Student Bar Association's first advisor, and as Dean he manifested tolerance and sympathy toward efforts at law student self-expression and self-government through the SBA. Shortly after he became Dean in 1973, a full scholarship—like the one Donald Simpson had obtained for the *Law Review* editor—was granted to the SBA President; and, in 1977, an attempt was made, although unsuccessfully, to win a similar grant for the Chairman of the SBA Evening Division's Board of Governors. In the meantime, *Dicta*, the SBA-sponsored student newspaper founded in 1972, had already survived longer than any previous SBA publication.[35]

As the faculty multiplied and activities expanded, Dean Sargent strove to improve the services offered to students. A law summer session was reintroduced in 1974, after a lapse of twenty years. The Law Library grew from sixty thousand volumes in 1972 to 140,000 by 1980, necessitating the addition of three new Reference Librarians. During the same period, the Library's seating capacity was increased from 650 to 830, while in June 1979, Law Librarian Edward J. Bander was able to announce the prestigious designation of his facility as a Government Printing Office Depository. A Law School Financial Aid Officer, Marjorie A. Cellar, was hired in 1973; then, two years later, an Assistant Placement Director. In 1975, the University appointed its first separate Law School Development officer. Counting his two Associate Deans, Dean Sargent's professional administrative staff in 1980 numbered fifteen—double the 1972 figure.

To accommodate this growth, the Law School required more space. Library needs combined with classroom and office shortages to create critical pressures. After the Fenton Building was opened in 1975, all College classes were shifted out of the Donahue Building, which was rededicated the next year exclusively for Law School use.

Acquisition of its own building paved the way for Suffolk Law's admission to the AALS; it also provided, along with institution of a separate Law Commencement in 1974, a major stimulus to the Law School's sense of identity.

Dean Sargent's improvements in the quality of student life were dearly bought; in 1975, Law School tuition first significantly exceeded the Colleges', and within five years the difference had grown to $1,000. To help mitigate the socio-economic impact of this dramatic increase, the Law School quintupled scholarship funds, to $300,000, between 1972 and 1979. Special admission and scholarship programs for disadvantaged students were established during the Sargent regime's first year. At the same time, submission of the GAPSFAS (Graduate and Professional School Financial Aid Service) form became mandatory for those applying to the Law School for scholarship assistance, and by 1977 financial aid was being awarded solely on the basis of need. In 1980, fifteen percent of those enrolled received scholarships, while a Guaranteed Loan program—begun in 1977—provided aid to half the student body. Direct tuition subsidies on such a scale were unprecedented at Suffolk Law School. The message, however, was clear, and it represented an interesting inversion: where Dean Archer's maxim once had been that excellence for some could be afforded only if it did not undermine opportunity for many, now Dean Sargent's was that excellence for many could be afforded only if it did not undermine opportunity for some.

By 1981, Suffolk University Law School alumni served on the federal and state bench, in the United States Congress and in the Massachusetts General Court, in national, state, and local government posts. The previous year's graduating class counted members from twenty-one states. What had once been a local law school had established itself as a regional one, and was on its way to becoming national.

On December 27, 1977, Suffolk University Law School was granted full membership in the AALS; the wounds of the Archer era, on both sides, had finally healed. By 1981, Suffolk University Law School alumni served on the federal and state bench, in the United States Congress and in the Massachusetts General Court, in national, state, and local government posts. The previous year's graduating class counted members from twenty-one states. What had once been a local law school had established itself as a regional one, and was on its way to becoming national. There remained the challenge of continued development.

Chapter 4 *The College of Liberal Arts and Sciences, 1934–1981*

The University (later the Archer) Building at 20 Derne Street (1938)

Gleason L. Archer founded the Suffolk College of Liberal Arts in 1934 to serve "the wage-earning multitude of young men and women to whom education in day colleges is impossible."[1] Its parent institution, spiritually and practically, was Suffolk Law School. For thirty years, Archer's Law School kept access to legal education open to workingmen and immigrants; his new foundation was designed to maintain similar "equality of opportunity"[2] for those who sought college training.

As unrestricted immigration peaked in the first decade of the century, traditional elites attempted to protect the "purity" of their professions by organizing professional associations. These associations urged that admission to their respective professions be limited to holders of high school diplomas; in subsequent years, the recommended standard became possession of a college degree. The expense of such prerequisite training would have excluded all but the well-to-do from the professions; in consequence, Archer denounced efforts to establish a "college monopoly" (i.e., a monopoly by college graduates) in the professions—a threat which he considered the most fearful spectre stalking American society.[3] Throughout the 1920s, he fought attempts by the American Bar Association (ABA) to encourage legislative or judicial action which would establish "college monopoly" rules for admission to the bar.

As it became clear that he could not indefinitely postpone implementation of a college requirement, Archer took another tack. In September 1927, he introduced a resolution at the ABA convention calling for establishment in every state of "collegiate training, free or at moderate cost, so that all deserving young men and women seeking admission to the bar may obtain an adequate preliminary education."[4] As gratis or low-priced high school education became widely available during the 1920s, the professional associations concluded that to maintain the "standards" of their professions, a college degree should now be required for admission. The establishment of inexpensive colleges, Archer asserted, would overcome this final barrier against equal opportunity.

As gratis or low-priced high school education became widely available during the 1920s, the professional associations concluded that to maintain the "standards" of their professions, a college degree should now be required for admission. The establishment of inexpensive colleges, Archer asserted, would overcome this final barrier against equal opportunity.

By January 1931, Archer had moved from abstract advocacy to concrete planning. In conversations with Massachusetts Commissioner of Education Payson Smith, he outlined his plan to transform Suffolk Law School into a "great evening University" by adding a college "in which a limited number of required subjects would be offered instead of the vast array of electives."[5] Only through this limitation, Archer felt, could tuition be kept low, and access open. He traced the high cost of college education directly to what he called the "elective system"[6]—the proliferation of elective courses which, during the previous several decades, had replaced simple, required curricula at most traditional colleges. This proliferation necessitated an increase in faculty and classrooms. Both of these factors sent costs skyrocketing. Thus, in undergraduate as in legal education, Gleason Archer was a "reactionary"; he advocated retention of an older, more cost-efficient approach because it seemed to him the only way to keep his school affordable to all.

"College monopoly" rules for admission to the bar were finally adopted in Massachusetts in June 1934; that development impelled Archer toward implementation of his college blueprint. He worked feverishly during the summer to set up the Suffolk College of Liberal Arts as an economical alternative to traditional college training. The "college monopoly" was thus prevented from becoming a monopoly of the rich, while at the same time members of Suffolk Law School's historic constituency were offered at low cost the requisite background for bar admission before entering Archer's law school.[7]

Whatever his concern about the general impact of "college monopoly" rules on the legal profession, Dean Archer clearly realized that without the opening of a college which could prepare his potential law students at a price they could afford, Suffolk Law School might easily wither and die. Thus, the risks of proceeding to develop the College in the midst of a Depression were outweighed by the risks of not proceeding. Costs, however, were to be kept to a bare minimum by restricting the curriculum "as far as possible to cultural subjects that have bearing upon lawyers."[8]

The new department opened in September 1934 as a junior college, and the first year was, by Archer's own admission, "largely experimental."[9] Classes met in the Law School building at 20 Derne Street; this posed few problems for Law School scheduling, however, since the College counted a total of four faculty members, none of whom was employed full-time, and only nine students. At the end of the academic year, the entire first-year class "evaporated"[10]; several entered Suffolk Law School, and the others dropped out.

Archer served as the College's chief executive until 1937. Since his experience in managing undergraduate education was nonexistent, he copied as many features of Suffolk Law School's instruction as he could. As in the Law School, evening classes allowed students to retain full-time jobs. To permit working students to keep up with course material, the College (like the Law School) was open only three nights a week, and each individual class met twice weekly. Classroom monitors and class admission tickets, like those employed at Suffolk Law School, were introduced into the College, while administrative chores in the new academic unit were, with few exceptions, carried out by Archer's Law School staff.

Where emulation would not suffice, Archer was forced to rely on outside advisors, whose recommendations occasionally became sources of later embarrassment. Archer, for example, asked Boston Superintendent of Schools Patrick T. Campbell to help him in choosing suitable instructors. The College consequently began with a faculty consisting entirely of teachers from the Boston Teachers' College and from the city's high schools. Since his new faculty members knew little more of college standards than he did, Archer also requested help from Campbell, and from Dr. Frank W. Wright of the State Board of Education, in laying out a "compact" curriculum to be offered by his small teaching staff.[11] On Wright's suggestion, graduation requirements for the new College were set at 105 semester hours (compared to the 120 frequently demanded in undergraduate institutions). This suggestion was implemented by John Griffin, the College's first Registrar. Griffin, who was to play a critical role in Suffolk University's development for the next half-century, was among the first high school instructors recruited by Archer to teach at the College of Liberal Arts. Beginning in the summer of 1934, he also served as Archer's evening aide for undergraduate curriculum planning. He was appointed Registrar shortly afterward, and, based on the procedure of Boston University (where he was attending classes), began offering credit to in-service teachers for previous teaching experience. Griffin's well-intentioned practice was responsible for the fact that trade school teachers made up a high percentage of the College's early students; however, it also further undermined the institution's academic credibility.[12]

It was only with the arrival of Carrolla A. Bryant as Registrar in 1936, and of Donald W. Miller as Dean a year later, that the fledgling institution began to take on the characteristics of a college. Gleason Archer brought Bryant from New York, where she had been a radio executive at WEAF, to replace John Griffin. She served as Registrar from 1936 until 1946, and during that time was a leading architect of College policies as well as their principal administrator. To her Registrar's duties were added those of College Treasurer, Admissions Director, Executive Secretary, and, not infrequently, Assistant or Acting Dean. She brought an order and discipline to undergraduate affairs which allowed the collegiate departments to develop before World War II, and to survive repeated crises during wartime and immediately after. She had a sharp tongue and an aggressive style of office management; she never inspired in students or colleagues the kind of affection which Bursar Dorothy McNamara elicited. In fact, she quarreled, fiercely and frequently, with both McNamara and her own counterpart in the Law School, Catharine Caraher. But without Bryant's day-to-day contributions, the survival and early growth of undergraduate education at Suffolk would have been inconceivable.

By the time Bryant arrived in January 1936, Gleason Archer had clearly oriented his college to serve the kind of non-traditional constituencies that Suffolk Law School had served since its foundation in 1906. Like its parent institution, the College was to be, in the founder's phrase, an "educational pioneer."[13] Archer had won from the

General Court in February 1935 a charter for the new college to grant degrees; it thus became the first institution in New England at which a student could obtain a bachelor's degree entirely by evening study. It had also, unlike the Law School, been co-educational since its foundation (although there were no female faculty members until after World War II). To help the school's students find full- or part-time jobs that would allow them to earn tuition money, a Placement Bureau was established in September 1935; it was housed—along with the rest of the College—at 59 Hancock Street, one of Gleason Archer's Beacon Hill properties.

Degree-granting powers and the new building helped attract to the College fifty-four students, eight of whom were women, to replace the previous year's "evaporated" class. To retain them, and to attract others, Bryant began to tighten standards. She quickly raised semester-hour requirements from 105 to a much more respectable figure of 120, while eliminating academic credit for teaching experience.[14] She also inaugurated, in July 1936, a six-week Liberal Arts College summer session. Unlike the pre-war Law School summer session, it was not a make-up session but rather offered supplementary courses for students who wanted to accelerate their progress toward a degree.

Suffolk Journal *staff (1958)*

Bryant's arrival freed John Griffin from his duties as College Registrar. During the following two years, he was given primary responsibility by Archer for the establishment of two other "pioneer" evening colleges. Conversations in the spring of 1936 between Gleason Archer and Paul A. Newsome, Executive Secretary of the Massachusetts Press Association, led to the foundation of a Suffolk College of Journalism the following autumn. Griffin and Newsome worked through the summer to set up the new school, which opened on September 22 with Newsome as Dean, two part-time faculty members, and forty students (seven of them women). The *Suffolk Journal,* founded by the Trustees to provide a laboratory experience for Journalism students, began publication in September 1936. One year later, a College of Business Administration opened its doors. This time, Griffin was the one who talked Archer into undertaking the project; the organizational work, carried out during the summer of 1937, was done almost entirely by Griffin, and when the College of Business Administration began operation on September 27, the credit was Griffin's alone.[15] The University charter of 1937, which incorporated Suffolk Law School and the three Colleges as Suffolk University, also gave degree-granting powers to

Griffin's two new professionally oriented colleges; and for his achievements John Griffin was elected to the expanded Board of Trustees created by the new charter.

Paul Newsome lasted less than a year as Journalism Dean; but through him, his sister M. Esther Newsome was recruited in 1936 as the College's first full-time Librarian. The following year, when the 20 Derne Street building was reconstructed, the College and Law School collections were consolidated there, and responsibility for both was given to Esther Newsome. She assumed the title of University Librarian, and served in that capacity until 1948. Her new library was equipped to hold a maximum of 45,000 volumes, and it had a seating capacity of two hundred and thirty. At Newsome's insistence, College collection books, unlike their Law counterparts, were allowed to circulate to students.

Newsome's brother Paul was replaced as Dean of the College of Journalism by Donald W. Miller, who had previously been named Dean of the Liberal Arts College by Gleason Archer after Archer was elected first President of Suffolk University in April 1937.[16] By the fall, Miller had also been named Dean of the College of Business Administration. He thus inaugurated the practice of having all three Colleges administered by a single Dean with a Liberal Arts background. In effect, the two professional colleges were run as departments of the College of Liberal Arts—a procedure which persisted for thirty years.[17]

Dean Miller came to Suffolk with a Harvard Ed.D. and good academic connections. As Archer had done before him, he relied entirely on part-time faculty members. There were no full-time teachers in the Suffolk Colleges until 1946. However, Miller radically changed the nature and quality of his part-time instructional staff. He replaced Archer's high school teachers with college professors, many of whom were previous acquaintances convinced by Miller to teach several nights a week at Suffolk in addition to their full-time duties at Harvard, MIT, or Tufts. During his tenure, a part-time faculty of impressive quality was assembled, and the first steps toward departmental organization and a faculty committee structure were taken. He also initiated the process of differentiating a College administrative staff from its Law School equivalent.

Miller worked closely with Carrolla Bryant to improve internal organization and to impose more rigorous standards. Classes were expanded from three days a week to four in 1937, then to five (to allow for science laboratories) in 1939; class length was also increased, from an hour and a quarter to 1½ hours. A day division and a four-year (full-time) degree program were begun in the College of Liberal Arts in 1938. A year later, day divisions were also introduced in the two professional colleges, although only the five-year (part-time) degree was available to their students until after the war. Major and minor field requirements, universally employed in college curricula, were introduced to Suffolk by Dean Miller. He and his science faculty also began a process which by 1941 had resulted in construction of spacious, up-to-date biology, chemistry, physics, and geology laboratories in the University Building. To attract highly qualified students for the academic program built by Miller, Bryant, and their colleagues, the Trustees in 1939 established thirty competitive scholarships (six full- and twenty-four half-tuition) for entering freshmen.[18]

Dean Archer with winners of a special journalism scholarship, awarded by the Fourth Estate Club (1939)

By the time Dean Miller resigned in April 1939, his professional leadership had established guidelines which set the pattern for future development of the Liberal Arts College, and trained a staff which could be relied upon to follow those guidelines. Although he occasionally chafed at the restrictions it imposed, Miller accepted President Archer's model for a collegiate department with a limited number of courses, few electives, a small faculty, and a consequently low tuition. Within these limitations, he sought to bring the education offered and the personnel offering it to the highest quality Archer's system was capable of sustaining. That commitment, and its transmission to those who worked with and succeeded him, was Dean Miller's lasting legacy to Suffolk University.

By 1940, a separate undergraduate administration of twelve officials had been set up. The Liberal Arts faculty had grown to 27, while the Journalism faculty numbered nine and that of Business Administration three. Student enrollment in the College of Liberal Arts reached a pre-war peak of 160; Journalism and Business Administration also peaked in 1940, at 49 and 22 respectively.[19] The University's first Bachelor of Arts (BA) degree was awarded in 1938, and the initial Bachelor of Science (BS) in 1939. The first Bachelor of Science in Business Administration (BSBA) degree was not awarded until 1943; the first Bachelor of Science in Journalism (BSJ), not until 1948.

After Dean Miller's resignation, his close collaborator Carrolla Bryant defended his standards, and helped to pass them on to the postwar institution. Dean Miller and President Archer had a less than cordial personal relationship. Bryant's endorsement of Miller's vision, however, and the case argued for undergraduate education's growth potential by Archer's close friend Robert E. Rogers of MIT, convinced Archer by 1939 that the future of Suffolk University lay with the Colleges. The College of Liberal Arts, prophesied the President, would soon replace the Law School as the chief income-earning unit of the University, to be succeeded in its turn by the College of Business Administration.[20] He was careful, of course, to add his familiar caveat that "Suffolk's chief mission is and probably always will be to minister to the evening student—the employed student."[21]

Carolla Bryant, Executive Secretary of the University and Registrar of the Colleges

President Archer's commitment to develop the Colleges caused great consternation among Trustees (such as Hiram Archer) and alumni (including Frank J. Donahue) who felt that the Law School always had been and should remain the heart of the institution. In their view, Gleason Archer was diverting to College development monies which would be better spent in preparing the Law School for the accreditation which they felt it so sorely needed. Expansion during the Depression had been a controversial step; when the wartime drop in enrollments left the University without income to service the debts thus contracted, Law School advocates cried that the President's single-minded development of undergraduate facilities had now placed the entire University in jeopardy. As the institution's financial plight approached desperation toward the war's end, their representatives on the Board proposed that the hard-pressed University retrench by abolishing the Colleges. In Archer's opinion, this move would permit the Law School to survive by devouring its children, and he launched an all-out campaign to prevent it.

Archer was seconded in his resistance, and steeled to it, by Carrolla Bryant. As Executive Secretary of the University and Registrar of the Colleges, Bryant managed to keep the Colleges open during the war by discontinuing the day division and retaining only a part-time evening program. She was ordered, however, by the Board of Trustees not to reopen the Colleges in the fall of 1945. Bryant refused to comply, and, using money supplied from Gleason Archer's own pocket, she reopened both the day and evening divisions. Lester Ott, who had taught at Suffolk before the war, was appointed Dean of the Colleges by President Archer.[22] Over opposition by the Trustees and the State Board of Collegiate Authority, Archer appealed to the General Court for help in gaining approval for the Suffolk Colleges as institutions where academic standards justified G.I. Bill funding for their students. Approval was granted in March 1946, and within a month there was a flood of applications from veterans for immediate entry. The Colleges were saved. A special summer session was arranged, with morning, afternoon, and evening divisions, beginning in early June 1946. Shortly after the session began, however, the Trustees punished the defiant saviors of the Colleges for their temerity. Bryant was summarily dismissed, while Archer was deposed as Treasurer and had most of his authority as President stripped from him. The only survivor was Dean Ott, who was spared to maintain at least a tenuous continuity at a time of immense financial opportunity for the Suffolk Colleges.

Ott was charged by the Trustees to rebuild the collegiate departments; in that undertaking, he received an unexpected amount of support from the Board. With Bryant gone and President Archer steadily declining in power until his resignation in 1948, partisan strife over the Colleges diminished. The Law School advocates who had ousted Archer quickly came to realize that, in the changed postwar circumstances, development of the Colleges could contribute to rather than detract from their efforts to accredit the Law School. For one thing, Judge Donahue and his allies had to admit—and it was much easier to do since the former President was not around to remind them—that Gleason Archer had been right about the potential profitability of the Colleges; in the postwar educational boom, income from the collegiate departments far surpassed that from even a prosperous Law School. This income could provide important assistance in preparing Suffolk Law School for accreditation. Once the Colleges had been spared for their economic worth, however, development of them virtually imposed itself on the Trustees; the ABA, it seemed, would not accredit the Law School unless the Colleges were first accredited by the New England Association of Colleges and Secondary Schools (NEACSS).

Thus, the same Trustees who had proposed abolition of the Colleges in 1945, rallied to the cause of College accreditation two years later. One leading figure in the accreditation process which followed was Harvard Business School Professor Arthur W. Hanson, a Suffolk Trustee since 1938, who chaired the Board's College Committee from 1948 until his death in 1965[23]; another was Walter M. Burse, a Harvard-trained lawyer, who succeeded Gleason Archer as University President in 1948. The key figure, however, was Dean Lester Ott. As a Harvard doctoral candidate, he had been appointed to the Suffolk Liberal Arts faculty by Dean Miller in 1939. After the war, Ott was appointed Dean by Gleason Archer because of his familiarity with the pre-war workings of the Colleges. Now, the Trustees turned to Ott, with his Harvard background, to rebuild those Colleges; in place of Archer's economical part-time model, he was instructed to employ—as Dean Frank Simpson was doing in the Law School—a more "respectable" (and accreditable) full-time paradigm.

For help in this demanding process, Ott called on his friend Donald W. Goodrich, an educator and educational administrator of twenty years' experience, whom he appointed as Registrar as soon as Goodrich was released from military service.[24] Together, they set about the task of creating a new order in the Suffolk Colleges. Classes now met five days a week; monitors and class admission tickets were discontinued. A full-time faculty was assembled—with special attention devoted, for accreditation purposes, to the recruitment of Ph.D.'s. The recruits with doctorates included Neilson Hannay, Ella Murphy, Stanley Vogel, Catherine Fehrer, Norman Floyd, George McKee, and Leo Lieberman. Upon their arrival, they joined a full-time teaching staff that counted among its members Harvard Ph.D. Robert Friedman (whose service at Suffolk began in 1941) and a number of instructors who lacked doctorates—such as Joseph Strain, Donald Fiorillo, William Sahakian, John Colburn, and Harold Stone. Many members of this faculty nucleus remained leaders in the institution's development for decades. The Colleges' first female teacher, Ruth C. Widmayer, came to the College of Liberal Arts in 1947, and the first full-time female faculty members—Catherine Fehrer, Ella Murphy, and Edith Marken—all arrived at Suffolk a year after Widmayer. By 1949, there were thirty full-time faculty members in the Colleges; of these, 40% possessed Ph.D.'s.[25] Directors of Student Activities, Guidance, Remedial Reading, Athletics, and Health were appointed, along with an Advisor to Women. From a wartime minimum of five, Dean Ott's undergraduate administrative staff had more than doubled by 1948. The Trustees also pressed the Dean to hire an "accreditable Librarian"[26] to succeed Esther Newsome; in 1948, that position went to Dr. Edward Hartmann, who retained charge of both the College and Law School collections for ten years.[27]

The Colleges' first full-time chairmen were appointed by Dean Ott in 1947, as the faculty was organized first into academic divisions, then a year later into departments.[28] Dean Ott also reorganized and revitalized the system of appointive faculty committees established by Dean Miller before the war.

All this activity was aimed toward eventual accreditation, but it was focused more immediately on addressing the needs of the new majority of Suffolk undergraduates: full-time day students, most of whom were male veterans attending the Colleges with G.I. Bill funding. By 1949, College attendance was thirty times the wartime low of 35, and five times what it had been in 1940.[29]

A program of scholarships, prizes, assistantships, and service scholarships was established in 1948. Fifty Trustee and University half-tuition scholarships were made available, along with a number of full-tuition athletic awards. The newly-founded College Alumni Association also offered several grants.[30] By 1950, a Loan Fund and a University Endowment Fund had also been set up.

Although the attention given to day undergraduates increased steadily during his tenure, Dean Ott never forgot the injunction given him and his colleagues in 1939 by Gleason Archer that Suffolk should always serve the evening student. As the Day (full-time) Division was infused with its own character and an independent identity after 1948, an Evening (part-time) Division was also formally delineated and differentiated for the first time. A separate evening degree, the Bachelor of Science in General Studies (BSGS) was established. To complement the regular evening program, simplified one-night-a-week Adult Education courses were begun.[31] The growing emphasis on full-time day students, and the creation of a separate (somewhat less prestigious) identity for part-time evening division students, represented a deviation from Gleason Archer's plan for the Colleges; but Dean Ott did at least manage to continue offering at Suffolk the evening collegiate instruction unavailable at most traditional undergraduate institutions. The importance Ott attached to the new Evening Division was indicated by his establishment of special evening scholarships in 1948 and by his appointment as Evening Division Director of Robert J. Munce, the man who eventually succeeded him as Dean.

To serve another educational constituency, and to satisfy the Trustees' clamor for greater College "respectability," Ott also founded graduate programs. Although Master of Arts (MA) degrees were briefly available in several traditional Liberal Arts disciplines,[32] the focus of the new venture was primarily on professional training in education and business. Students were admitted in the fall of 1948, and both the Master of Arts in Education and the Master of Science in Business Administration (MSBA) programs were approved by the Board of Collegiate Authority in October 1949. Three months later, the Colleges awarded their first two graduate degrees, and by 1952 post-graduate enrollment had risen to ninety-two.

When Lester Ott resigned in May 1949, the campaign for accreditation was at its height. His successor, Robert J. Munce, inherited responsibility for this critical undertaking.[33] With the help of President Burse, Ott's Registrar Donald Goodrich, Ott's Librarian Edward Hartmann, and many members of Ott's faculty, Dean Munce carried forward the preparations. In December 1952, NEACSS accreditation was granted.[34]

Despite this achievement, student enrollment plummeted in the early 1950s. As the flood of Second World War veterans abated, and as the Korean War made its demands, attendance was cut in half—to less than six hundred. Scholarship money declined, and by 1954 academic programs had been cut so severely that Dean Munce was forced to reply to Trustee requests for further retrenchments that costs in the collegiate departments had been slashed to an "irreducible minimum."[35] Even under these conditions, however, things were far better in the Colleges than in the Law School. Except for a six-month period in 1952, the Colleges remained in the black financially, and it was only this surplus from undergraduate revenues that kept Suffolk's debt-ridden Law School in operation.

Robert J. Munce

Munce served primarily as a pilot who steered the College successfully through stormy seas; he had few opportunities to make innovations or improvements. For his services to the University, however, he was chosen to succeed Walter M. Burse as President in June 1954. For two years after his accession, Munce also remained Dean of the Colleges. In June 1956, with financial conditions alleviated somewhat by slowly rising enrollments and by the University's receipt of a Ford Foundation grant to help pay faculty salaries, the Trustees finally consented to the transfer of the Deanship from President Munce to his long-time Registrar, Donald W. Goodrich.

Goodrich inherited a school in which enrollment had fallen from a high of 1500 in 1947 to 900 in 1956, and whose "income continued to depend mainly on the tuition of male students of military age."[36] The number of full-time faculty members remained virtually unchanged from Ott's time, and much of the personnel remained the same. The proportion of Ph.D.'s (40%) was also unchanged, as was the size of the professional administrative staff.[37] Undergraduate scholarship funds in 1956 totaled exactly what they had seven years earlier ($11,500), and virtually the same number of scholarships (50) were offered. Library accessions, as well, were roughly equivalent.

Although these figures might imply stagnation, in fact the realities of the situation inherited by the new Dean were quite different. The hardships endured by Dean Munce seemed to be over. Admissions had been rising since 1954, and new financial resources were becoming—and continued to become—available to the collegiate departments during Dean Goodrich's tenure; he was thus provided with opportunities his predecessor had never had. Goodrich had been one of the architects of the Colleges' postwar educational structure; his continued presence as Registrar under Dean Munce had provided an experienced, steadying hand at the tiller which discouraged any significant changes in academic policies by Ott's successor. Now that Goodrich was Dean in his own right (while also retaining his post as Registrar until 1966), there was little reason to expect deviation from the academic course he had steered since 1947. Indeed, he did adhere closely to the plan formulated by himself and Dean Ott years before; his expanding resources simply permitted him to implement program and faculty development aspects of it that had hung fire since the late 1940s. In a very real sense, Donald Goodrich picked up where Lester Ott had left off.[38]

The Robert S. Friedman Field Research Station on Cobscook Bay, Edmunds, Maine

Goodrich presided over the development of the Natural Sciences division in the science boom that followed the launching of Sputnik in 1957. The hosting of the Thirteenth Annual Eastern Colleges Science Conference by the Suffolk Science departments in 1959 was the real turning point: the spectacular success of the venture won the enthusiasm and sympathy of the Trustees, Treasurer Donahue, President Munce, and the Dean. Laboratory facilities were renovated and expanded in the fall of 1960, and a Medical Technology program was also inaugurated at that time.[39] A marine biology field research station was established in 1968 on Cobscook Bay near Edmunds, Maine.[40] That same year, the Dean gave his approval to creation of a separate Physics department, and he even authorized experimentation with short-lived Master of Science (MS) programs in Chemistry and Physics.[41]

The Education Department's graduate programs were expanded dramatically during Dean Goodrich's tenure. Training in special-needs education and counseling were stressed, as areas of specialization for the Master of Arts in Education multiplied. A Master of Arts in Teaching (MAT) was offered briefly, and a Master of Education (Ed.M.) degree in counselor education was introduced in 1968.[42]

The increasing social concerns of the 1960s were mirrored in a number of steps instituted under Goodrich's imprimatur. The

Sociology department implemented a group of new social service programs, including Social Work, Crime and Delinquency, Child Care, and an Urban Track. The Psychology department and the Guidance office were separated, freeing both to pursue their increasingly divergent goals and interests. Courses were begun on black, ethnic, and third world history and literature.

Nor were language skills neglected. Upon the insistence of Catherine Fehrer, a Language Laboratory was completed in 1965, and a student exchange program was established with French-, German-, and Spanish-speaking countries. A Remedial Reading office was reestablished, while the English department was expanded under Chairman Stanley Vogel's direction from four to sixteen members.[43]

The Frank J. Donahue Building at 41 Temple Street

Such an ambitious expansion in programs, and in the faculty necessary to teach them, was made possible by steady growth in enrollments from the time Goodrich assumed the Deanship in 1956 until his resignation thirteen years later. By 1969, attendance at the Colleges had reached 3,206, over three times what it had been when Goodrich assumed office. Even excluding the newly autonomous College of Business Administration, enrollments in the two Colleges left under his jurisdiction (Liberal Arts and Journalism) totaled 1,820, twice the comparable figure for 1956.[44] The graduate Education enrollment had expanded from 30 in 1956 to 230, and the new MS programs numbered eight students.

The tuition that came from this rising tide of students permitted a faculty expansion that kept pace with attendance growth. During Goodrich's term as Dean, the full-time faculty of the Colleges more than trebled, from 29 to 96. The proportion of Ph.D.'s among them, however, remained steady at forty percent.[45]

The Colleges remained, as they had been since their foundation, primarily teaching institutions; faculty research was assigned a low priority.[46] As the number of faculty members increased, however, so did the diversity of their expertise. They asked, understandably, to be allowed to teach at least some courses in their areas of specialization; and when the requests were repeatedly granted, the number of elective courses multiplied rapidly to fill the space made available after 1966 by the opening of the Donahue Building.[47] Whatever the beneficial effects, and they were many, the result clearly represented a challenge to Gleason Archer's insistence on a compact faculty and to his rejection of the "elective system."[48]

To provide students with better services, Goodrich increased the size of the professional administrative staff by fifty percent during his term. He formally surrendered his position as College Registrar in 1966 to Mary Hefron; in turn, he was rewarded with the title of University Vice-President by a Board of Trustees grateful for his achievements as Dean. The first Dean of Students (D. Bradley Sullivan) also took office under the Goodrich administration, and the original Ridgeway Building was acquired in 1969 to serve as a student union.[49] When Edward Hartmann resigned as Director of Libraries in 1958 to assume full-time teaching duties, he was succeeded by Richard Sullivan. Under Sullivan's direction, the College Library was completely reorganized and its collections developed. After 1967, formal appointment of a Law Librarian permitted Sullivan for the first time to devote his full energies to the College Library, which was entirely renovated during 1968 and 1969. Seating capacity was increased from 300 (which it had been since 1948) to over 400, and book storage capacity was significantly expanded.

Although circumstances led him to compromise several tenets of Gleason Archer's College plan, there was one aspect of Archer's vision to which Donald Goodrich adhered faithfully: abiding concern for the evening student. It was Goodrich's conviction that the evening student should not only be given the opportunity to attend the Suffolk Colleges, but, if Suffolk's tradition meant anything, should also be given parity of treatment with full-time day undergraduates. Goodrich was ably seconded in this position—and quickly harried back to it if he strayed—by Joseph Strain. Three months after Goodrich assumed office in 1956, Strain, an Archer-era graduate of the Liberal Arts College, was appointed Assistant Dean in charge of the Evening Division. He proceeded to completely reorganize the Evening Division and to restore the position of the evening student. Adult Education courses were discontinued; all courses offered at night were now to be equivalent to their daytime counterparts. The BSGS degree was retained, but Evening Division students were given the option of undertaking BA or BS programs if they chose to do so. Evening students had constituted 14% of the colleges' enrollment in 1948; under the Goodrich regime, that proportion rose from 26% in 1956 to 40% in 1969. The quantitative increase was significant, but the qualitative change was crucial; parity was being restored to the evening student.

In 1967, the College of Business Administration was made a separate administrative unit with its own Dean; at that time, the College of Liberal Arts was renamed the College of Liberal Arts and Sciences.

In 1967, the College of Business Administration was made a separate administrative unit with its own Dean; at that time, the College of Liberal Arts was renamed the College of Liberal Arts and Sciences. Donald Grunewald was appointed the Business School's first

Dean, and his performance was so impressive that, when Goodrich retired as Liberal Arts Dean and University Vice-President in June 1969, Grunewald was named to succeed him in both capacities.

Grunewald held a Doctor of Business Administration degree from the Harvard Business School. He was an imaginative, pragmatic, and flexible administrator who was determined to minimize Suffolk's internal conflicts in an era of turbulence and political self-assertion by accommodating faculty and student demands whenever possible. Under him, the trends that had begun in the last years of Goodrich's tenure continued and accelerated. The faculty and the student body continued to expand, electives to proliferate, awareness of social problems to increase, and control of students' lives by administrative regulations to diminish. Between 1969 and Grunewald's resignation in 1972, the full-time Liberal Arts teaching staff increased by 22%, from 80 to 98; the proportion of Ph.D.'s, meanwhile, remained at forty percent.[50] During Dean Grunewald's brief tenure, Liberal Arts attendance increased 10%; by 1972, there were 1,746 undergraduates and 396 graduate students.[51]

Dean Michael R. Ronayne, Jr.

Grunewald also sought to discourage unrest—at least that which might arise over internal University issues—by improving educational conditions and options. An Environmental Technology program was established in 1971, and within a year Biochemistry and Clinical Chemistry majors had been introduced. An affiliation with Beth Israel Hospital was set up for Clinical Chemistry students, and another was concluded with the Museum of Science. The SAFARI (Study at Foreign Academically Recognized Institutions) Committee was organized in 1970 to facilitate overseas study. Two years later, the CROSS (Career-Related Opportunities in Spanish and Sociology) program was introduced to begin the preparation of social workers with bilingual competence.

In addition, the Dean's training had sensitized him to the value of efficient administration in preventing dissatisfaction. To this end, he expanded his professional administrative staff from 13 in 1969 to 25 three years later.[52] An International Student Advisor was appointed in 1971 to provide assistance to an expanding number of foreign students. A year later, the school's first transfer student counselor, Ellen Peterson, was added to the Admissions office. Her addition was rendered imperative by a steady increase in the number of tax-supported two-year community colleges, which from the late 1960s on began to preempt a portion of the "college of opportunity" role that had been embraced by Suffolk's collegiate departments since their foundation. Before the end of the 1970s, half of the Liberal Arts student body consisted of men and women who had transferred to Suffolk from other institutions.[53]

When Donald Grunewald resigned in June 1972 to accept the presidency of Mercy College, he was succeeded by Michael R Ronayne, Jr. Ronayne was selected, at least in part, for the skill he had demonstrated at working within the committee system of faculty governance established under his two predecessors. He was also the first Ph.D. named to the Deanship.

Ronayne was a chemist by training, and he presided over a continuing development in undergraduate science programs. Suffolk's Chemistry department, for example, received American Chemical Society accreditation in 1973.[54] Three years later, the Biology department organized a Marine Science program which utilized the facilities of the school's Robert S. Friedman Cobscook Bay Laboratory; by 1980, a link had also been established with the interdisciplinary MIT Sea Grant program. In addition, the late 1970s saw a major expansion in computer capacities and computer training. Establishment of a Data Processing office in 1978, along with introduction of a Computer Science Applications Certificate program and a Computer Science major, impelled the University to install two in-house 1.5 megabyte PRIME 750 computers—the first in 1980, and the second a year later.

Significant development under Ronayne's regime also took place in a number of other disciplines. Suffolk's undergraduate programs in Education were approved in 1975 for participation in the Interstate Certification Compact, which qualified graduates of those programs to teach in thirty-one states. Meanwhile, the Education department's graduate programs continued to expand in diversity; a Certificate of Advanced Graduate Study (CAGS) program in counseling, for example, was begun in 1980, as was an In-Service Institute to offer short courses for Boston-area teachers. During the period after 1972, the University Counseling Center also undertook an impressive expansion in its services.[55] The Sociology department continued its growth during the 1970s, as well; BS programs were introduced in Health Services and Human Services, while Sociology became by 1975 the largest Liberal Arts undergraduate major. The Government department set up internships with a number of state officials, and began an association with the Washington Center for Learning Alternatives (WCLA) in order to provide students with experience in national government. Dean Ronayne also presided over the rebuilding—begun by Allan Kennedy and carried on by Edward Harris—of a Communications and Speech department and a highly competitive forensics program, centered around the Walter M. Burse Debating Society.[56]

The College of Journalism had continued to function and to attract students since its foundation in 1936. For almost its entire history, however, it had been administered as a department of the Liberal Arts College; and for almost two decades after 1952, the Journalism "College" was composed entirely of part-time instructors, one of whom, William Homer, served as its head. Under Ronayne, the College of Journalism was officially demoted to the much more appropriate status of a department. Meanwhile, new chairman Malcolm Barach, the first full-time member of the Journalism faculty in twenty years, began work on a revitalization of the program.[57]

During Dean Ronayne's tenure, the College Library's collection reached 90,000 volumes. When Richard Sullivan retired in 1975, Edmund Hamann succeeded him as College Librarian. Hamann greatly expanded the Library's resources through memberships in NELINET, a computerized bibliographical network, and in the 660,000-volume Fenway Library Consortium. By 1980, his staff of full-time technical and reference librarians had more than doubled since separation of the College and Law School Libraries in 1967.

Growth occurred in a number of other administrative areas, as well. Between 1972 and 1981, Dean Ronayne's professional staff increased from 25 to 37. In 1975, the first College Development officer was appointed. Establishment of a Financial Aid office helped scholarship funds climb by 1980 to $802,000 (plus $2.3 million in federal assistance)—four times the 1972 figures.[58] By 1981, over 40% of Liberal Arts undergraduates received financial assistance.

Undergraduate enrollment in the College of Liberal Arts and Sciences remained steady at around 1,700 in the eight years after Ronayne's accession; attendance in the graduate Education programs, meanwhile, even declined slightly (from 396 to 287).[59] After three decades as the economic mainstay of the University, the Liberal Arts College was said by some to be surrendering its numerical and financial predominance—as Gleason Archer had predicted that one day it would—to the Business School; in fact, this was a misleading assertion, since Liberal Arts faculty members continued to teach 40% of the courses taken by students registered in the School of Management.

As community and state colleges multiplied and increasingly challenged Suffolk's uniqueness as a "college of opportunity," the Liberal Arts College had to rely more and more on the excellence of its offerings to compete for students even from its traditional constituencies. The improvement and expansion of programs and services during the Ronayne era also helped to encourage diversification of the Liberal Arts student body.[60]

That student population, in any case, displayed a zeal for involvement and extra-curricular activities unmatched in either the Law School or the School of Management. Organization, and an effective student government, allowed College students to gain attention for their grievances; both factors helped win establishment in 1974 of a Commencement separate from the Law School ceremony. In addition, student agitation helped, as it had done in the case of the Donahue Building, to bring about acquisition of new physical facilities. The Fenton Building, opened in 1975, was devoted entirely to College programs; and the Sawyer Building, opened in 1981, permitted the convenient consolidation of many College and University services (including those of a new College Library) under one roof.

The John E. Fenton Building at 32 Derne Street (1970s)

Like the Liberal Arts student body, the College faculty remained virtually unchanged in numbers under the Ronayne regime; the full-time faculty remained at approximately 100 from 1972 until 1981.[61] Its quality, however, improved steadily; the proportion of Ph.D.'s doubled, from 40% in 1972 to 80% eight years later. Research gradually came to be recognized by the Board and the administration as a desirable supplement to teaching responsibilities in at least some cases[62]; the Ronayne era thus offered a wider latitude of acceptable applications for the faculty's creative energies than any previous period in the College's history.

By 1981, the College of Liberal Arts and Sciences provided a balanced program of excellence, opportunity, and community service.[63] The school's undertakings and its mission had grown well beyond what Gleason Archer had initially envisioned for it. The purposes and results of this development, however, could only have left the founder well pleased.

Chapter 5 *The Frank Sawyer School of Management, 1937–1981*

The foundation in 1937 of Suffolk University's "newest professional department,"[1] the School of Management, resulted from collaboration between John Griffin and Gleason L. Archer. Both men combined academic interests with entrepreneurial skills and a well-developed business sense. The school they established reflected that mixture of concerns. As a practical matter, it would help provide additional income for Suffolk University; but the new school also excited its founders by the possibilities it offered for the extension of intellectual analysis in the field of management. In the approach that it took to business education, the School of Management again accurately reflected the dual interests of Griffin and Archer. From the first year of the school's existence, that approach stressed "the impressive value of combining educational theory and daily

The College of Business Administration, 45-47 Mt. Vernon Street (1972)

wage-earning experience.[2] Forty years later, the School of Management catalogue still emphasized the crucial significance of "blending academic knowledge with practical skills."[3]

The year 1981 marked not only the seventy-fifth anniversary of Suffolk University's founding, but also the centenary of America's first collegiate school of business—the Wharton School of the University of Pennsylvania. In the decades since the foundation of the School of Management, both Suffolk's Business School and the self-proclaimed "mainstream" business schools like Wharton had undergone significant changes in their roles and in their conceptions of themselves. What follows is an attempt to trace those changes in Suffolk University's School of Management, and to relate those internal changes to broader trends in professional management education.

Suffolk University's School of Management was founded in 1937. The College of Business Administration, as it was then known, was designed to provide another "open door of opportunity" for the "wage-earning multitude of young men and women"[4] served by the Journalism College, the College of Liberal Arts, and Suffolk Law School. The new school's principal architect, under the watchful eye of University President Gleason L. Archer, was John Griffin. Griffin shared Archer's vision of a new college to provide easily accessible education in business skills to the working men and women who formed the University's primary constituency. As a practical man of business, however, John Griffin's aspirations for the new school went beyond provision of a service. Since there were many more business professionals in the world than lawyers or journalists, the programs offered by the College of Business Administration promised eventually to attract a larger student body than the other academic units.[5]

Since 1906, many students had attended Suffolk Law School not to obtain degrees or to enter the legal profession, but to take courses which would provide them with legal information and skills that would be applicable in business. If this same pattern—some degree students, others attending individual courses to obtain specific kinds of expertise—could be cultivated in the new Business School, Griffin was confident of its success. His arguments convinced even Archer that the College of Business Administration would one day surpass both the Law School and the Liberal Arts College as a source of revenue for the University.[6]

While attending classes at Boston University, Griffin had been impressed by the prosperity of the business school there. In the spring of 1937, he convinced Archer that a similar unit should be established at Suffolk. Griffin, a Harvard MBA, worked through the summer to organize and start the College of Business Administration, which was authorized to grant degrees by the University charter of 1937. When it opened in September, Griffin had succeeded in attracting only two faculty members, both of whom taught part-time, and a student body of six men and two women. Of the courses slated to be taken by the students as part of their five-year (part-time) degree program, over half were offered by Liberal Arts instructors. Only two business courses were available that first year: Accounting and Introductory Business Administration. Accounting, Griffin asserted, would be the "cornerstone" of the new curriculum.[7]

All Business courses met in the University Building at 20 Derne Street. To accommodate students with full-time jobs, and also the part-time faculty necessary to minimize tuition, each course met only two nights a week. Daytime classes were begun in 1939, but until after World War II only a part-time (five-year) Bachelor of Science in Business Administration (BSBA) degree program was available. As a result, not until 1943 was the Business College's first degree awarded.

Since 1906, many students had attended Suffolk Law School not to obtain degrees or to enter the legal profession, but to take courses which would provide them with legal information and skills that would be applicable in business.

Despite Gleason Archer's confidence in its future, the College of Business Administration became—and remained for thirty years—something of a stepchild in the University. Donald W. Miller was appointed Liberal Arts Dean in 1937, with a clear mandate to develop the Liberal Arts departments. Miller's successes within his own college led President Archer to confer on him authority over the College of Journalism (founded in 1936) and the Business College. The new Dean's background and priorities were ill-suited to his added responsibilities. Business School development was subordinated to that of the Liberal Arts College, and the resulting neglect contributed to the College of Business Administration's initial failure to fulfill John Griffin's rosy expectations. By 1940, attendance was only twenty-two, compared to 160 in the College of Liberal Arts[8]; a faculty of three part-time instructors was dwarfed by the Liberal Arts instructional staff of nineteen.

The pattern of authority established by Dean Miller persisted long after his departure. Until 1967, the College of Business Administration operated as a department under the supervision of a "Dean of the Colleges"—whose primary charge was the Liberal Arts

College, and whose background, consequently, was without exception non-business. Although there was a separate "chairman" of the Business "department" after 1946, his suggestions and curricular initiatives were subject to approval by the Dean of the Colleges and by faculty committees on which Liberal Arts representatives predominated. This was a slow, frustrating process, and it reduced the Business School's attractiveness to students by severely hampering its ability to adjust to the shifting needs of the business community.

Walter M. Burse

There were sporadic—but always short-lived—efforts made to provide the Business College with greater autonomy. In 1944, John F. X. O'Brien, who had taught in both the Business School and the Liberal Arts College before the war, was appointed Dean of the College of Business Administration.[9] O'Brien had proposed to the Trustees that, in preparation for the flood of ambitious veterans at war's end, the Business School be transformed into a College of Business and Governmental Administration which would offer a number of its programs in cooperation with the Law School and the Liberal Arts College. It was an imaginative and far-sighted design, which would be largely achieved by the late 1970s; but under the University's severe wartime financial constraints, it was an idea whose time had not yet come. O'Brien's tenure as Dean, and his experiment, ended abruptly in 1945 when Liberal Arts hegemony was restored by the appointment of historian Lester Ott as Dean of the Colleges.

During the late 1940s, there was discussion among the Trustees of again appointing a separate Business School Dean.[10] After Walter M. Burse replaced Gleason Archer as President in 1948, he spoke of appointing an Advisory Council for the Business School like the one he established in 1949 for Journalism. The Business School Committee of the Trustees, on which John Griffin and Harvard Business School Professor Arthur W. Hanson had served since 1938, was reconstituted after the war, and Hanson was appointed to chair it. The Business School Committee, however, had ceased to meet by 1950, and the other two initiatives came to naught as the University's energies were focused in another direction by the quest for Law School and College accreditation.

The first full-time faculty members were appointed in the College of Business Administration, as in the other collegiate departments, in 1946. Day classes now met five days a week, and a full-time (four-year) BSBA program was inaugurated, complementing the part-time (five-year) program that had been offered since 1937.

The pre-war emphasis on Accounting continued under Maurice Sklar, the Business department's first postwar chairman.[11] After John Mahoney assumed the chair in 1949, that emphasis was maintained, notwithstanding the introduction of two other major-field programs—Management and Marketing—during Mahoney's tenure. That tenure lasted for eighteen years, until 1967, when Mahoney finally surrendered his chairmanship of the Business department to a full-fledged Dean.

Mahoney's principal colleague throughout those two decades was Harold Stone, who remained a faculty leader for over thirty years. After his arrival at Suffolk in 1947, Stone became the chief architect of the Business School's postwar Accounting program. He also designed a Master of Science in Business Administration (MSBA) degree program, which was begun in 1948. The State Board of Collegiate Authority approved the program in October 1949; three months later, the first graduate received his degree.

Beginning in 1946, the postwar surge in enrollments predicted by O'Brien took place. Veterans with G.I. Bill funds flocked into Suffolk's Business School. When the high-water mark was reached in 1948, over 500 students, twenty-five times the 1940 figure, were attending the College of Business Administration—compared to 600 in the College of Liberal Arts.[12] The Business faculty expanded to meet the increased demand; by 1948, there were four full-time members, and eight others taught part-time.[13]

Despite the prosperity of the late 1940s, the Business School's postwar dependence almost exclusively on male students soon caused serious problems. During the Korean War, enrollments fell even more than in the Liberal Arts College—to a third of 1948 levels by 1953. As in the Law School and the Liberal Arts College, however, the years after 1956 began a new era of growth for the College of Business Administration. By 1958, Business attendance had reached 650, 30% greater than a decade earlier.[14] The number of graduate Business students stood at twenty-eight in 1958,[15] compared to forty-nine in graduate Education. Liberal Arts and Business undergraduate enrollments were virtually equal, however, which represented a clear gain for the Business School. Between 1948 and 1956, the full-time Business faculty had remained at four; it reached seven in 1958.[16] By that time, Mahoney and Stone had been joined as full-time faculty members by Dion Archon, along with alumni Benson Diamond and Martin Donahue.[17]

The Business School's obvious growth in the late 1950s, and the possibilities for much greater development offered by the projected expansion in the college-age population during the 1960s, reawakened the Trustees to the hitherto-neglected potential of the College of Business Administration. In 1957, the Deanship was offered to Trustee Arthur W. Hanson upon his retirement from the faculty of the Harvard Business School. Hanson declined, but the Board's confidence enabled him to begin a process which, within twenty years, allowed the Business School to realize its potential. He won election to the Board in 1960 for Daniel C. Bloomfield, former Executive Vice-President of the Retail Trade Board of Boston and a Visiting Consultant on Distribution at Harvard. Together, Hanson and Bloomfield worked to gain approval from the Trustees for a Business Advisory Council to provide suggestions and connections for strengthening the College of Business Administration. Once approval was obtained, both men devoted tireless effort to convincing local businessmen to serve. By January 1961, a membership had been assembled that included future Trustees George Seybolt, Stephen Mugar, Joseph Sullivan, Thomas Fulham and John Chase; Seybolt was elected Chairman of the Advisory Council in October 1961. That same year, Fulham and Sullivan were elected to the Board of Trustees, followed a year later by Seybolt and Mugar—and in 1965 by Chase. All five steadily gained influence and support among the Trustees, and Seybolt in 1966 was elected Chairman of the Board. Meanwhile, Chase, who succeeded Seybolt as Chairman of the Business Advisory Council, was also appointed in 1965 to convene and chair a special Business School Committee of the Trustees. The committee included John Griffin, along with Fulham, Seybolt, Sullivan, and Mugar, and its task was to consult with the Advisory Council and the Business faculty on methods of improving and strengthening the College of Business Administration. After Seybolt became Board Chairman, Chase's special committee was recognized as a standing committee of the Board, to replace the standing Business School Committee whose work had been discontinued in 1948.[18]

In the early 1960's, Trustee attitudes began to change in favor of Business School development and campus facilities expansion. . . . it was the second most important watershed in the University's history.

The additions of the early 1960s provided a healthy injection of prominent businessmen among the Board's judges and lawyers, and that injection clearly marks the point at which Trustee attitudes began to change in favor of Business School development and campus facilities expansion. Second only to the transfer of power from Gleason Archer to his Trustees, it was the most important watershed in the University's history.

John Chase's new Business School Committee in early 1966 secured the consulting services of Professor Gordon Marshall of the Harvard Business School to survey the College of Business Administration and to submit a comprehensive evaluation of it and its place in the field of business education. Marshall's recommendations for change included strengthening of the faculty, expansion of library facilities, transformation of the College of Business Administration into a "distinct entity" within the University, and enlistment of a competent Dean with the appropriate authority. He also concurred with the recommendation given the University by the New England Association of Colleges and Secondary Schools (NEACSS) reaccreditation team in 1962 that the graduate Business program be either further developed or abandoned. Upon receipt of his findings, the Business School Committee and Board Chairman Seybolt authorized Marshall to select a candidate for the Deanship to be presented to the Trustees. The candidate he recommended was Harvard DBA Donald Grunewald, who was confirmed by the Board in December 1966 as Business School Dean. At Grunewald's request, the Trustees established the Graduate School of Administration (GSA)—an academic unit separate from the College of Business Administration although headed by the same Dean—and assigned to it responsibility for graduate Business programs at Suffolk University.[19] They also changed the name of the School's graduate Business degree from Master of Science in Business Administration (MSBA) to the more conventional Master of Business Administration (MBA).

Donald Grunewald

The College which Donald Grunewald inherited had developed considerably during the previous decade. John Mahoney and Harold Stone had acquired accreditation from the New York State Regents for the school's Accounting program.To encourage and reward academic excellence, the Trustees in 1963 had introduced a Daniel Bloomfield Scholarship, awarded annually to the outstanding undergraduate in the College of Business Administration.[20] Three years later, four Graduate Business Fellowships were established, to be awarded purely on a merit basis. In 1966, as well, the Business School first required the Educational Testing Service Graduate Business Examination of all applicants for the MSBA program.[21] Between 1958 and 1967, undergraduate enrollment in the College of Business Administration remained virtually unchanged, at 650, while Liberal Arts undergraduate attendance doubled, to 1,200. The number of graduate Business students, however, increased six-fold, to 170.[22] Meanwhile, the full-time Business faculty expanded by 60%, from seven in 1958 to eleven nine years later.[23]

Dean Grunewald assumed office in January 1967. He served only two years as Business School Dean,[24] but his brief tenure was important because it set the tone for all that was to follow. Grunewald and his faculty introduced a broader range of undergraduate programs to complement the Business School's historic emphasis on Accounting.[25] A Finance and Banking evening major was initiated as part of an affiliation with the American Institute of Banking, and an affiliation was also established with the School of Insurance. Joel Corman, one of Grunewald's earliest faculty appointments, began revitalization of the MBA program. As part of the development effort, the school's first MBA Extension Center was set up in 1967 at Raytheon in Lowell.[26] Grunewald began the establishment of a separate appointive faculty committee structure for the Business School, thereby alleviating somewhat the problems long posed by a system in which Liberal Arts-dominated committees had to approve all changes in the Business College's programs or curricula.[27] He also divided the Business School into two departments for the first time, appointing Harold Stone chairman of an Accounting department and retaining control himself of the Business Administration department.[28] At Grunewald's insistence, computerization and instruction in computer techniques were begun at Suffolk. He even arranged for several early conversations between Suffolk University and representatives of the American Assembly of Collegiate Schools of Business (AACSB).[29]

During only two years in office, Grunewald increased the size of the full-time faculty by 45%, from eleven to sixteen. Those he recruited raised the proportion of full-time faculty members with MBA degrees to over eighty percent.[30] Student enrollments during Grunewald's tenure kept pace with faculty expansion. Undergraduate attendance rose from 650 to over a thousand (54%), while the number of graduate Business students more than doubled, from 170 to 368. In the same period, Liberal Arts undergraduate attendance grew only half as fast (25%), although the graduate Education programs kept pace with their Business counterpart.[31]

When Donald Grunewald became Dean of the College of Liberal Arts and Sciences in 1969, Robert C. Waehler succeeded him as Business School Dean. Waehler came to Suffolk after twelve years of teaching Accounting and Taxation at Boston University. His background, however, also included experience as director of student activities at Burdett College. Consequently, he was sensitive not only to academic priorities, but also to the need to defend and improve the quality of student life at a fast-growing institution like the Business School.[32]

During Waehler's five-year term as Dean, undergraduate Business enrollment rose sixteen percent, while graduate Business attendance grew thirty percent.[33] To accommodate this growth, Waehler increased the size of the full-time Business Faculty from sixteen to twenty-one (including the Business School's first full-time female faculty member).[34] For better organization of his expanding faculty, Waehler doubled the number of academic departments from two to four. He split the Business Administration department into three new departments—Finance, Management, and Marketing—and assigned a faculty member to chair each one. Although Dean Grunewald had managed the Business School with no separate professional administrative staff, the demands imposed by continued development led Dean Waehler to add an Assistant Dean and an Administrative Assistant. To promote better conditions for the Business School's expanding faculty and student body, the University also reacquired during Waehler's tenure the building a 45-47 Mount Vernon Street.[35] That structure housed the College of Business Administration and the Graduate School of Administration until 1981; it also provided the Business School with its own building for the first time.

Dean Waehler continued development of the Extension program begun by Donald Grunewald; graduate and undergraduate Business courses were offered at Western Electric in North Andover from 1970 until 1975. He also experimented with a number of non-degree programs, including seminars, conferences, and institutes. An evening Retailing Seminar was established in 1970, an Institute of Real Estate Appraisers in 1971, and a seminar series on consumer affairs (in cooperation with the Consumer Affairs Foundation and the Better Business Bureau) two years later.[36]

Despite the significance of these initiatives, Waehler's most impressive innovation was his introduction of a Public Management program to serve government employees at the state, federal, and municipal levels. The instrument for establishment of the new program was the Center for State Government Management, which was set up at the Business School in 1973 with funds from the New England Regional Commission. The Center's director was Richard McDowell, and its aims included implementation of graduate and undergraduate Public Administration programs, provision of short-term educational and training programs in Public Management, and the promotion of research on public management and policy problems. Within four years, most of these aims had been accomplished. A Master of Public Administration (MPA) degree program and an undergraduate major in Public Management were established in 1973, along with a Public Management and Administration Advisory Council to oversee them. By 1977, a new Public Management department had been created in the Business School, and a Bachelor of Science in Public Administration (BSPA) undergraduate degree program begun.[37]

Dean Richard L. McDowell

The success of the Center for State Government Management (later renamed the Center for Public Management) so impressed the Trustees that when Robert Waehler stepped down as Business School Dean in August 1974, they named the Center's director, Richard L. McDowell, to the Deanship.[38] The new Dean immediately joined with his faculty in a vigorous campaign for greater autonomy and a stronger Business School identity within the University. Early in McDowell's Deanship, the Business School's faculty governance structure became genuinely independent of Liberal Arts control for the first time in University history.[39] McDowell's faculty was authorized by the Trustees to convene its own Faculty Assembly and to elect for itself academic governance committees to replace the joint bodies on which Business School representatives had previously been badly outnumbered by Liberal Arts members.[40] When the Business School Faculty Assembly voted in 1979 that the College of Business Administration/Graduate School of Administration be renamed the School of Management (SOM), the action underlined the School's commitment to professional education in both the public and private sectors. However, it also reflected the continuing effort to strengthen the School's identity in the University and in the community. In 1995, the School of Management (SOM) was renamed the Frank Sawyer School of Management (SSOM), to honor the late University benefactor Frank Sawyer.

Increased autonomy for the School of Management was also in conformity with professional accreditation requirements of the American Assembly of Collegiate Schools of Business (AACSB) and of the National Association of Schools of Public Affairs and Administration (NASPAA). From 1975 on, Dean McDowell and his faculty, supported by the Trustees' Business School Committee, began to take steps to meet AACSB accreditation standards; beginning in 1976, an AACSB consultant visited the school each year. Graduate and undergraduate curricula and degree programs were reviewed and brought into line with AACSB and NASPAA standards. Full-time faculty members possessing doctorates replaced many part-time instructors. Between 1974 and 1981, the full-time faculty doubled, from twenty-one to forty-two; the proportion with doctoral degrees rose from ten to fifty percent.[41] Administrative support also improved, with the appointment of an Executive MBA Director, a Director of Cooperative Education, a Director of Academic Computing, and an Assistant Dean of Advising and Administration.[42] In 1979, data-based management was introduced; working data were circulated to School of Management faculty members, who could thus cooperate with the professional administrative staff in planning development of the School and provision for faculty needs.[43]

In 1980, Public Management department chairman David Pfeiffer was able to announce that Suffolk's MPA program had successfully met NASPAA's peer review criteria. The program thus became one of only four approved in the New England region, and one of only forty-five programs approved (out of over 180 that applied for approval) nation-wide.

One of McDowell's first undertakings as Dean was to create a private-sector equivalent to the Center for Public Management. In November 1974, an Institute for Business Management was set up, to offer "non-credit educational and training activities"[44] like those presented by the Center for Public Management. The Institute, however, aimed to provide "continuing non-academic professional educational opportunities for the business community"[45]— short courses, workshops, and conferences, on the model of the Retailing Seminar program established in 1970 by Dean Waehler. As early as 1975, the Center for Public Management and the Institute for Business Management were served by a common Conference Coordinator; two years later, they were merged to form the Management Education Center, which thus became the "focus for professional education and training activities for business, government, and non-profit organizations served by Suffolk University."[46] To provide a standard by which these non-academic, non-credit activities could be measured, and the time invested in them rewarded, McDowell in 1975 convinced the Trustees to accept the convention of using Continuing Education Units.

The professional education function, which Dean McDowell believed to be so important to the Business School's continued vitality, was further developed in 1975 by institution of a Saturday Executive MBA degree program. Six years later, an Executive MPA program was established. The Satellite (Extension) Centers, offering undergraduate and graduate courses, multiplied to include a Merrimack Valley Center at Bradford College in Haverhill, MPA courses in Swampscott, and in-town courses at the Massachusetts Public Welfare Department and at Boston City Hall. However, as the School's expanded on-campus library and computer resources were increasingly integrated into academic course work, the Satellite Centers were closed.[47]

Meanwhile, additions and improvements were being made to the Business School's degree programs.[48] A Computer Information Systems major, the sixth major offered by the School of Management faculty, was introduced in 1980; it was supported by the resources of the School's new Academic Computing Center (established in 1979) and of the University's two 1.5 megabyte PRIME 750 computers (acquired in 1980 and 1981). Affiliations were also arranged with a number of agencies, firms, institutions, and organizations. These affiliations, and several other new programs, exemplified the Business School's expanded commitment to "blending academic knowledge with practical skills."[49] For example, through the Small Business Institute, Management students satisfied class assignments by serving as consultants to local businesses.[50] In 1980, a Cooperative Education/Internship program was also instituted, to supplement a student's academic training with intervals of practical work experience.[51]

By 1980, there were 1,560 undergraduates and 1,200 graduate students enrolled in the School of Management; undergraduate attendance had risen 25% since 1974, while graduate registrations had trebled.[52] The Mount Vernon Building had offered temporary relief from the problem of overcrowding. By the late 1970s, however, continued expansion in enrollments had necessitated larger physical facilities. The School of Management's transfer in 1981 to the twelve-story Frank Sawyer Building not only alleviated the space problem; it also provided greatly improved conditions for students, faculty members, and administrators.

Between 1974 and 1980, a notable transposition took place. At the beginning of McDowell's Deanship, the total number of students enrolled in the Business School came to 72% of the number registered in the Liberal Arts College; six years later, the situation was reversed.[53] Gleason Archer's prophesy had been fulfilled: the School of Management had become Suffolk University's largest academic unit.

Numerical expansion, however, was not the only goal of Gleason Archer and John Griffin for the Business School. They saw it as an educational "pioneer,"[54] bringing part-time and evening collegiate business education to employed students for whom university business schools had previously made no provision. For decades after the foundation of Suffolk's College of Business Administration, major U.S. business schools continued to disdain the kind of programs Suffolk offered. After 1960, however, nationally oriented professional management schools gradually discovered the value and validity of part-time, evening, and non-degree programs. They began to experiment in a field where Suffolk had thirty years of experience, and their entry drew part-time business programs into the mainstream of university education for management.

University benefactor Frank Sawyer in front of the building named after him

At the same time that the "mainstream" was being diverted in Suffolk's direction, many elements that characterized major business schools were introduced into the School of Management. The curriculum was strengthened. Administrative and student services were upgraded. Graduate programs were expanded and broadened. Research was encouraged, and a faculty was recruited that represented strong university preparation as well as professional experience.[55] In 1979, a Mission Statement issued by the faculty reaffirmed the school's historic commitment to provide professional education opportunities for the working public. It noted, however, the increasingly high educational expectations of working men and women,[56] and emphasized that a commitment to excellence was fundamental to the continued provision of opportunity. By 1981, the School of Management's efforts to fulfill both commitments had established it in the regional mainstream of professional management education.

Suffolk Law Schoo

Awaiting the 1937 commencement ceremony, graduates look forward to their promising careers. The University, as well, prepares for the future as construction of the additional floors proceeds at the Archer Building.

SUFFOLK JOURNAL

The SUFFOLK JOU

The Suffolk Ram

SENIOR HOP N

"FINEST YEARBOOK POSSIBLE" GOAL OF SENIOR PRESIDENT

Recognition Day Awards Given To 55 Students

"Who's Who"

JOURN

DONAHUE

FIRST IN S

SUFFOLK UNIVERSITY
Invitation

SUFFOLK UNIVERSITY
HONESTAS ET DILIGENTIA
BOSTON
1906
SVFFOLK LAW
CONDITA
MCMVI
BOSTON

Suffolk University

Chapter 6 A Social History, 1906–1981

Gleason L. Archer insisted throughout his life that the University he founded was "dedicated to the cause of the working classes, from whose ranks he himself had sprung."[1] His first students were painters, dyers, printers, cashiers, laborers, and salesmen; by 1908, over twenty-five occupations were represented at Suffolk.[2] Beginning in the 1920s, however, Archer acknowledged that "bankers, brokers, businessmen, federal, state, and municipal officials" were also "numbered in every class."[3] As white collar workers supplemented the artisan base at Archer's school, a mixture was created that characterized the University's student body for decades; in most academic divisions, it remained the formula for success in 1981.

Suffolk Law students (1938)

The "controlling motive" of Archer's school was "to give every student his chance."[4] Those whom Archer expected Suffolk University to serve were a projection of his self-image: honest, diligent working people who sought education in order to enhance their social status and the contribution they could make to society. To their ambition and hard work, Archer aimed to add what George Frost had added to his—the good fortune of having a patron concerned with making affordable the education so earnestly sought. This combination of "pluck and luck" was Horatio Alger's prescription for his heroes' success[5]; it was also the one which had carried Gleason Archer out of the working class. For those who possessed the integrity and determination to follow the founder's path, Suffolk University presented an "open door of opportunity."[6]

Suffolk undergraduates in class (1941)

What follows is an attempt to understand the people who took part, as students, faculty, administrators, or alumni, in seventy-five years of the Suffolk University experience. Who were they? Why did they come? How did they interact with one another? What were the forces at work on them? Most important, how did this combination of personalities and circumstances contribute to making Suffolk University what it had become by 1981?

When Suffolk University was founded in 1906, unquestioned and unrestricted immigration had been the central fact of American life for forty years.[7] By the first decade of the twentieth century, many Americans were being forced to confront the implications. Thousands of new immigrants arrived each day. Even more disturbing, an American-born second generation increased every year in numbers and maturity, demanding full rights of participation in the society to which their mothers and fathers had come in search of opportunity.

Traditional leadership groups in American society took steps to safeguard their predominance. High school diplomas, then college degrees, took on unprecedented importance, as newly-founded professional associations strove to secure state regulations requiring such credentials for access to professions. Poorer immigrant groups were thereby excluded.

This emphasis on degrees, however, also created intense pressure for expanded educational facilities and opportunities. Institutions of higher learning were few, exclusive, and costly. Many new schools, therefore, were founded. Often they catered to poorer "native" Americans who sought degrees that would distinguish them from their immigrant competitors. Some, even more odious in the view of traditional leadership groups, also aimed at the immigrants. Only through education, their founders argued, could the new arrivals be "Americanized," and thus immunized against left- or right-wing political demagoguery. A few educators also saw their institutions as instruments of economic self-help for immigrant groups.

From the foundation of Suffolk University, Gleason L. Archer assigned it the "real pioneer work" of "making lighter and surer the path of aspiring young men born in poverty, denied educational advantages in boyhood, and obliged to educate themselves at odd moments while doing a man's work in the world."[8]

The founder insisted that Suffolk's "chief mission" was and probably always would be "to minister to the evening student—the employed student."[9] These "earnest souls who toil in the evening schools," he asserted, would be found "in the front ranks of our civilization of tomorrow"[10]; the "honesty and diligence" of the new University's students would help make Horatio Alger's rags-to-riches stories come to life.

In Archer's view, his school provided a "haven of opportunity" for "the leaders of the working classes throughout Greater Boston."[11] As a Progressive—and Progressivism was as distinctly a product of early twentieth-century conditions as was Suffolk University—he believed it to be part of his school's vital mission to maintain equality of opportunity in education against conspiratorial efforts on the part of the "sinister rich" to close the channels of social mobility in America.[12] If social and educational opportunity were significantly eroded, Archer insisted, immigrants and native-born workingmen alike would quickly lose faith in the gospel of self-help preached by Horatio Alger and those like him. Suffolk's founder was convinced that, faced with a contradiction between theory and practice, many of these ambitious workmen might turn "dangerous,"[13] attracted by a socialist movement previously foreign to American soil. It was left to "true Americans" like himself, Archer felt, to prevent this catastrophe by fighting the selfish machinations of the rich, by rallying to the defense of the potentially oppressed poor, and by insuring the provision of educational opportunity to those less fortunate. Not only would such action help protect American society against socialism, but it would also allow "true American" Progressives like Archer to proselytize working-class people to their point of view. These Progressives could thus provide themselves with an army of political supporters that could spell the difference in their struggle against vested monopolistic interests in America.

In Archer's view, his school provided a "haven of opportunity" for "the leaders of the working classes throughout Greater Boston." As a Progressive—and Progressivism was as distinctly a product of early twentieth-century conditions as was Suffolk University—he believed it to be part of his school's vital mission to maintain equality of opportunity in education against conspiratorial efforts on the part of the "sinister rich" to close the channels of social mobility in America.

In addition, then, to its role as a springboard to success for individual workingmen, Archer's school was also an instrument to "dispel prejudices, class hatreds, and propaganda calculated to foster class warfare"—thereby assuring the emergence of "sound leadership" from the "ranks of the underprivileged."[14] The liberation function and the control function were finely balanced in this program; the line between championship of the workers' cause and patronizing of the workers themselves was a thin one. Were they being freed by education to be themselves, to evolve their own values; or were they simply being freed to obey their educators more willingly? The struggle—sometimes conscious, sometimes unconscious—to resolve the tensions that grew out of the historical conditions in which Suffolk University was founded, has provided one of the central themes in the social history of the institution.

Registration (1965)

Throughout his forty-two years at the University, Gleason Archer obviously thought of himself as performing an on-going act of philanthropy; through his school, he was passing on to his poor and immigrant students the opportunity given to him by George Frost to obtain a level of education which he could not otherwise have afforded. As he considered the backgrounds from which Suffolk students came, however, Archer was—and remained—convinced that "it was of course necessary for me to exercise a paternal oversight"[15] over the school's students, its extra-curricular activities, and its alumni. Not only did he assert his tutelary authority as Dean, and later President; he demanded continued "loyalty" to the school (i.e., deference to the Dean's judgment) from alumni long after they had graduated. It was probably unintentional, but there was a hint of patronizing and condescension in the way the self-made Yankee "philanthropist" regarded (and addressed) his poor, disadvantaged, and predominantly non-Yankee "beneficiaries."

The Dean's tutelary approach set the tone for relations between his administration and the University's students until his alumni ousted him during the 1940s.[16] Even after the dominant ethnic elements in the administration became identical to those in the student body, the paternalistic habits learned by many of the new Trustees as students at Suffolk proved very difficult to break. Student and alumni self-government grew steadily in the decade after Gleason Archer's departure in 1948; its growth was inhibited, however, by administrative reluctance to share responsibility, and by student and alumni hesitancy to assume it. During the 1960s, student self-confidence developed considerably, as resistance to authority increased throughout American society. Mediation by a new generation of Trustees and administrators—ethnically similar to their senior colleagues, but less intractably paternalistic—ultimately permitted the

University to accommodate emphatic student and alumni demands for a participatory role. It was 1971, however, before the administration finally endorsed alumni association autonomy and officially encouraged every student "to assume responsibility for his own affairs as much as possible."[17]

This slow transformation in administrative, student, and alumni attitudes also reflected long-term changes in the composition of the student body. During the 1920s, Archer prominently advertised the school's "cosmopolitanism,"[18] his code word for ethnic diversity. Over twenty national groups were represented at Suffolk. Protestants, Catholics, and Jews, whites, blacks, Asians, and Amerindians all attended; but, Archer asserted: "race and creed are forgotten in the common tasks of the library and the classroom. A spirit of comradeship develops in all classes that makes for true Americanism."[19] That this "true Americanism" was the Americanism proffered them by "true American" Progressives like Archer did not seem to disturb Archer-era students at Suffolk.[20] They, and their successors for decades, looked to the University's faculty and administration for guidance, leadership, and opinions.

During the 1920s, Archer prominently advertised the school's "cosmopolitanism," his code word for ethnic diversity.

At any given time before World War II, half of Suffolk Law School's students were Irish in background—of immigrant stock, but second or (more commonly) third generation Americans. Another quarter was composed of more recent immigrants, mainly East European Jews and Italians; some of these students were newly arrived in this country, but the second generation predominated. Poor Yankees (from English or Scottish families long resident in New England) constituted the final quarter.[21]

Although the flood of immigrants to the United States had been stemmed after 1920 by immigration quotas,[22] the ambitious second generation produced an enormous impact on American society in the years that followed. Even when members of that second generation did not enter schools themselves, their competition drove many other Americans to seek degrees that would maintain or improve their own competitive position. High school attendance, for example, rose from 10% of the high school age group in 1910 to 50% in 1930.[23]

The Suffolk Colleges, established in the 1930s, were designed in part to serve the same competitive degree-seeking that had created the boom in high school education. Both "native" working people and those of immigrant stock were attracted to the new undergraduate institutions. Interestingly, low-income Yankee students in the

Colleges outnumbered students from Irish backgrounds until after the Second World War—forty percent to thirty percent. The remaining quarter of the student body was composed, as in the Law School, primarily of students from Italian and Jewish backgrounds.

Before World War II, Boston proper was home for more Suffolk students, Law and College, than any other locality; contiguous communities like Roxbury, Dorchester, Somerville, Cambridge, and South Boston provided the next largest delegations. Then came cities on the North Shore or north of Boston—Lynn, Lowell, Lawrence, Medford, Revere—which were linked to the Hub by an effective rail network. South Shore communities were generally underrepresented, at least partially due to inadequacies in public transportation. Archer's school served primarily an urban-based, lower middle or working class constituency—hard-working men and women seeking to realize the American dream.

Law School students (1974)

Despite the dislocations of the Second World War and the immediate postwar period, G.I. Bill funds enabled the University to retain a substantial portion of all its traditional constituencies. Although male veterans became the predominant element in both the law and undergraduate student bodies for almost a decade after 1945, the distribution of ethnic backgrounds remained almost identical to that of the 1930s.[24] At Suffolk Law, Irish students still predominated, followed by Yankees, Jews, and Italians; in the Colleges, Yankee and Irish students each constituted a third of the registration, while Italians and Jews again made up the balance. Nor did the towns from which the University drew its enrollment change substantially after the war. At a time when more and more people were moving to the suburbs, it was Boston and the inner ring of contiguous urban communities that continued to provide the bulk of Suffolk's law and undergraduate students.[25]

Within two decades, however, the geographic and socioeconomic origins of Suffolk students had begun to change. At the Law School, the traditional preponderance of working-class students from Dorchester, Roxbury, Somerville, and Cambridge gave way after 1970 to a numerical ascendancy of students from middle-class suburbs like Newton, Brookline, Quincy, Arlington, and Framingham. By 1980, forty-three states were represented; nearly 40% of Suffolk Law students came from outside Massachusetts, compared to 25% in 1972, 4%, in 1956, and 1% or less before 1950.[26] The Colleges, meanwhile, continued to draw many students from traditional working-class centers like Boston, Dorchester, Cambridge, and Medford;

four-fifths of Suffolk's undergraduates lived with their parents, half financed their own education, and 80% worked at least part-time. In 1980, however, the Liberal Arts College and the School of Management were also attracting students in substantial numbers from such middle-class communities as Quincy, West Roxbury, Arlington, and Newton.[27] Only a few College students came from west of Worcester, 5% from outside Massachusetts, and 2% from abroad.[28]

Ethnically, there continued to be more law students of Irish descent than from any other background. They no longer constituted a majority, however; only about 35% of Suffolk Law School students after 1970 were identifiably Irish. Another quarter was composed of Yankees, who thus approached the Irish proportion more closely than ever before. By 1980, the percentage of students from Italian backgrounds equaled the Jewish figure, while both groups (at 15% each) formed larger proportions of the Law School's student body than ever before. As traditional residence patterns had done, older ethnic patterns persisted longer in the Colleges than in the Law School. After 1966, the proportion of College students from Irish backgrounds did surpass that of Yankee students for the first time (33% to 28%); but those two groups continued to constitute, as they had since the 1930s, two-thirds of the Colleges' enrollment. The remaining third, as well, retained its historic composition of Italian and Jewish students—though by 1980 the proportion of Italian students (16%) had outgrown the Jewish figure (10%).[29]

Although the Law School diverged more sharply in 1981 from the attendance patterns typical of the University's first six decades, significant—if less apparent—changes had also taken place in the College population. In the Liberal Arts and Management student bodies, the proportion of students from recently-immigrated families had declined steadily, along with the foreign-born segment of the American population.[30] During the 1960s and 1970s, the proportion of suburban students grew—while that of working-class and recently-immigrated students shrank—more in the Law School than in Liberal Arts or Management. Both trends, however, characterized all three of the University's academic units. The greater self-confidence of suburban students, and the student body's broadened familiarity with democratic institutions and the American way of life, combined to undermine long-standing habits of deference and to produce steadily escalating demands for student and alumni participation in University governance.

There was African-American representation in Archer's law school early in its history; the first black graduate, Thomas Vreeland Jones, received his degree in 1915.[31] Until after World War II, blacks at Suffolk totaled approximately 2% of the student body, a percentage equal to the African-American proportion of Boston's population. Such black percentage equivalence was very rare at institutions of higher learning during this period. Other non-white racial groups were also represented, though in proportions far below even those for black students. Suffolk's first Asian graduate[32] received his degree in 1922, and three years later Nelson D. Simons, "chief" of the Pequot tribe, became the school's first Native American alumnus. The first African-American to receive a degree from the Colleges was awarded his BSBA in 1948; the recipient, Herbert L. Lyken, also became in 1970 the first black to serve on the Business School faculty.

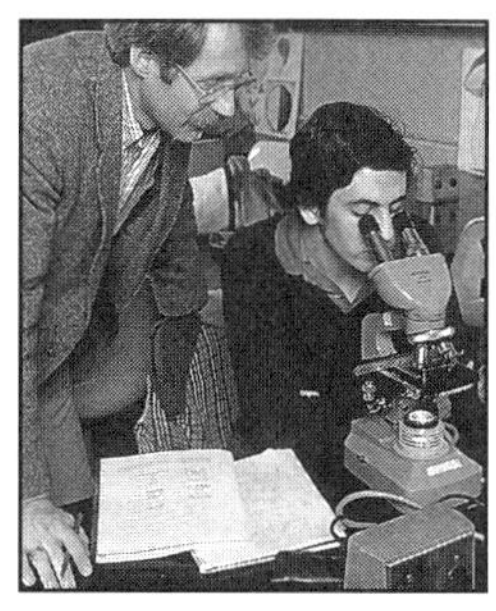

Biology laboratory (1985)

After 1946, however, the proportion of AHANA (African-American, Hispanic, Asian, and Native American) students at Suffolk no longer kept pace with the increasing non-white proportion of Boston's population. As at most institutions of higher learning, it was only during the racial difficulties of the 1960s that this was recognized as a problem. Once it was, a wide-ranging program to increase AHANA representation was undertaken—after 1968 in the Colleges, and after 1972 in the Law School. Special scholarships for disadvantaged students were instituted in 1968 in the Colleges and extended to the Law School five years later.[33] William Hannah became in 1970 Suffolk's first full-time black teacher; and within the next two years the work of Professor Edward Clark brought an affiliation between the University and the Museum of Afro-American History.[34] An Affirmative Action/Equal Opportunity officer joined Suffolk's professional administrative staff in 1972; that same year, Professor Hannah was appointed Suffolk's first Minority Student Advisor (a part-time post), and a Committee on Minority Student Affairs was created to assist and advise him. Despite these efforts, the undergraduate AHANA population at Suffolk remained small; it hovered around five percent (four-fifths black)[35] for the remainder of the decade, while that in the Law School reached only 2% (half black) by 1980. In that year, 3% of the full-time Liberal Arts faculty was composed of African-Americans, but there were no full-time black teachers in either the Law School or the School of Management.

Nearly a third of Suffolk's black student community was drawn from abroad—especially from the West Indies and various

African states. The number of these and other international students in the Colleges began to grow significantly during the late 1960s, after Suffolk's name was added to a United States Information Service list of schools which accepted overseas students. In 1960, twenty-six students came to the University from sixteen countries; by the mid-1970s, that figure had grown to 150 students from thirty-eight countries.[36]

At the school's first closing exercises on May 18, 1908, Dean Archer had announced that although women (none of whom had yet been admitted) might be the intellectual equals of men, he would not have any of them in his classrooms, because of the flirtation that would inevitably arise.[37] Women were formally barred from Suffolk Law School until 1937; and from 1925 until that date, the Dean's catalogue prominently billed Suffolk Law as "A Man's School."

Marian Archer MacDonald and Gleason Archer at commencement (1937)

Gleason Archer's daughter Marian was the first woman to attend Suffolk Law School; she entered in the fall of 1933.[38] Her performance was impressive, and this[39] convinced Archer to make the College of Liberal Arts that he founded in September 1934 co-educational from the start. Even so, Archer's College catalogue clearly stated throughout the pre-war period that the administration reserved the right "to limit the number of young women who may enter in any one year."[40] Both the College of Journalism and the College of Business Administration were founded on a co-educational basis, and, after Marian Archer MacDonald's graduation in 1937, the Law School was opened to women from outside the founder's family.[41]

By 1940, women composed a quarter of the University's undergraduate population, although they constituted less than one percent of Law School enrollment. As veterans filled all divisions of the school after 1946, however, the population of female students in the collegiate departments declined to that of the Law School. Both stood at around 3% in 1946. During the next fifteen years, the proportion of women in the Colleges grew steadily, if slowly, to 11% by 1960[42]; while the Law School figure remained virtually unchanged. Within the collegiate departments, the center of the expansion in women's enrollments was the Liberal Arts College; the College of Business Administration remained at or below Law School levels.[43]

By 1965, the proportion of women in the Liberal Arts College had reached nearly 30%, although both the Law School and the Business School still hovered around the 4% mark. Five years later, the College of Business Administration and the Law School had reached 6%; during the same period, the College of Liberal Arts increased the female proportion of its enrollment to nearly 40%.[44] It was the 1970s, however, that brought University-wide changes in the number of women in attendance, the quality of their lives as students, and the support facilities available to them. By 1980, more than half of Liberal Arts students were women. Meanwhile, the proportion of female students in the Business School had trebled, from 6% in 1970 to 18% a decade later.[45] Most dramatically, the proportion of women in the Law School jumped over the same period from 6% to 35%.[46]

Law School students (1995)

Senior citizens have found a place in the Suffolk University tradition throughout the school's history. As early as the 1920s, students at Suffolk Law School ranged in age from seventeen to sixty; Gleason Archer did not concentrate solely on those of traditional "student age," but encouraged people of all ages to come to his institution.[47] In 1973, the University established a program whereby senior citizens could attend Suffolk classes tuition-free—on a space-available basis—with full academic privileges; upon successful completion of a course, semester-hour credit toward a degree was awarded. The Senior Citizens' Program gained Suffolk nation-wide attention, especially through the media interest manifested in degree recipients like octogenarian Charles L. Niles (BS '77, Ed.M. '79) and Rosalie L. Warren, who was seventy-nine when she received her BS degree in 1980 *magna cum laude.*[48] Partly as a result of the program's appeal, the age range among Suffolk students was even greater in 1980 than it had been during the Archer era; students from sixteen to eighty were to be found on the University's busy campus.

Student activities have played an important role, over the years, in helping to shape Suffolk's diverse student body into a community. As prosperity came to Suffolk Law School after 1914, optimistic attempts were made to add extra-curricular activities typical of more traditional institutions. Some flourished briefly, but they soon died or became dormant; at a workingman's school, few had extra time to donate.[49]

A College of Journalism was founded in 1936, and a College of Business Administration in 1937; like the College of Liberal Arts, they were dwarfed in student population by the Law School. As part of an attempt to create a "collegiate" atmosphere, a program of extra-curricular activities was established. To compensate for the meager number of participants available from the Colleges, law students were actively encouraged to join the program. Their numbers rapidly became preponderant, and, throughout the pre-war period, law students dominated the extra-curricular program.[50] In 1939, a Student Council was established—the first suggestion of student government at Suffolk. It was an elected body; each of the three Colleges chose three representatives, while the much larger Law School designated twelve. The Council's first president was law student Samuel P. Hyland. President Archer had some misgivings about the impact on his institution of extensive student participation; he stipulated that the activities a student might engage in could "at any time [be] limited" by the administration to "safeguard student health and scholarship."[51] Nevertheless, the student organizations founded in the late 1930s proved very durable; each of the five organizations that existed at Suffolk in 1940 was the progenitor of an equivalent association at the University in 1981.[52]

The first Student Council (1939)

After 1946, returning veterans increased enrollment in the college departments to six times the pre-war size—and to three times the Law School's diminished enrollment. The revitalized Colleges were thus enabled to reclaim, and to bar law students from participating in, most student activities programs.[53] A Student Government for the Colleges (later renamed the Student Government Association, or SGA) was set up; its first elections were held in February 1946, and Laurence V. Rand was chosen its first president.[54] By 1949, there were over twenty-five student organizations, five times the number that had existed ten years earlier.[55]

Edgar DeForest presided over the postwar prosperity as Director of Student Activities between 1948 and 1953. When he resigned, however, prosperity had given way to hard times. The Korean War sent enrollments plummeting, and retrenchment across the board in the extra-curricular program was one result.[56] The SGA President noted a "low ebb" of student spirit in 1951, and University President Walter M. Burse observed that students were probably "worn out" by the crowded extracurricular schedule of previous years.[57] By 1954, the twenty-five active student organizations of 1949 had been cut to under a dozen.

The man who became Student Activities Director at this critical juncture was Professor John Colburn. He served in that position for fifteen years, from 1953 until 1968. Like his predecessors, he served as only a part-time director,[58] but the contributions which his energy and enthusiasm made to the recovery and subsequent vigor of the activities program can never be accurately calculated.

As enrollments in the collegiate departments and the Law School began slowly to rise after 1956, the extra-curricular programs in both were resuscitated. By 1961, combined action by Colburn and the SGA had won reinstitution of a student activities fee and introduction of a student activities period for the Colleges. An elected student government for the Law School (the Student Bar Association) was established in 1959.[59] Four years later, the Evening Division Student Association (EDSA) was organized to represent evening and part-time students in the collegiate departments; by 1971, it had transformed itself into an elective, genuinely representative organ of student government.[60] By the time John Colburn resigned as Director of Student Activities in 1968 to assume full-time teaching duties, there were again twenty-five student organizations on campus; this was more than double the number when he took office, and equal to the number of student clubs at the height of the postwar boom. His perseverance had restored health to the student activities program and had extended it—as it had been extended in 1949—to the limits imposed by the Director's part-time status and by the University's restrictive physical facilities.[61]

Social Club (1949)

In 1966, the opening of the Donahue Building, and the appointment of D. Bradley Sullivan as the University's first Dean of Students, opened a new phase in the development of student activities at Suffolk.[62] The new building alleviated the space problem, allowing student organizations to multiply and the complexity of their involvements to increase; the new Dean assumed the expanded (and complicated) administrative responsibilities thus created.

Sullivan inherited a situation in which an apparently optimistic outlook for the development of student activities contrasted sharply with the mood of the student body. Student leaders and the administration had been severely at odds since the early 1960s, as students challenged the traditional "paternal oversight" exercised by administrators over student affairs. In its place, the students demanded increased autonomy and a participatory role in managing those areas of University life that directly affected their lives. Student organization and agitation had played a significant part in propelling the Trustees out of their long-maintained fiscal conservatism and into a building program necessary to supplement the increasingly inadequate facilities of the old University Building.[63] Even as the Donahue Building opened in 1966, the administration and Trustees only with difficulty acknowledged the influence—or even the legitimacy—of student activism in shaping the University's evolution. For their part, student leaders had difficulty believing that the Board's—and the administration's—new direction could be self-motivated, the result of internal changes in membership. Pressure, the student leaders felt, had been necessary to win all past concessions, and continued agitation would be required to defend what had been granted and to obtain a continued hearing for student grievances. The danger was that in the resulting confrontation the opportunities for development offered by the school's new facilities would be overlooked or neglected, to the detriment of all concerned.

The original Ridgeway Building at 148 Cambridge Street (1970s)

Sullivan's job, then, was to mediate between the students and the administration in an attempt to resolve the crisis of conflicting views. At his suggestion, a Joint Council on Student Affairs—composed of student, faculty, and administrative representatives—was set up in 1967. Within two years, that body had produced a Code of Justice to regulate disciplinary proceedings against students; some called it a "student bill of rights."[64] It was then incorporated into a much more comprehensive Joint Statement on the Rights and Responsibilities of Students, which received final approval from the Board of Trustees in 1977. The Joint Statement superseded previous guidelines drawn up by University administrators alone; it thus marked an important commitment by the administration to share at least some responsibilities with student leaders. Although he could make no headway on SGA demands for a student Trustee, Sullivan did help students secure representation on a number of faculty committees. He also helped them to win accreditation for student representatives to relevant Trustee committees—for Liberal Arts students to the College Committee in 1969, and for business students to the Business School Committee two years later.[65] In the fall of 1969, long-standing student demands for a "student union"[66] were also addressed (if not perfectly satisfied) by the opening of the Ridgeway Building for use as a student activities center. By the early 1970s, Sullivan had built the bridges and laid the organizational groundwork necessary for constructive interaction between students and the administration.

Dean Sullivan thus helped make available a great deal of energy for the development of student activities and organizations that might otherwise have been expended in contention. In addition, he won authorization to convert the part-time Director of Student Activities position into a full-time post. When John Colburn resigned in 1968, he was succeeded by the first full-time Director of Student Activities: alumnus William J. Lewis. During the ensuing thirteen years, Lewis and his successors[67] witnessed an unparalleled expansion in extra-curricular programs throughout the University.[68] By 1980, there were eleven student organizations functioning in the Law School (not counting the moot courts or the clinical programs) compared to only one fifteen years before. In the collegiate departments, meanwhile, the twenty-five organizations of 1968 had by 1980 grown to forty-six, including thirty-eight in the Liberal Arts College and eight in the School of Management.[69]

By 1981, the relationship between the University's administration (including the Trustees) and the student body had altered substantially from what it had been in Gleason Archer's day. Unfettered paternalism had been renounced; far from discouraging student participation in extra-curricular activities and University decision-making, the administration actually cultivated it. As early as 1974, the Board of Trustees officially decreed that "student input is welcomed and encouraged at all levels of University governance, including the Board level,"[70] and to facilitate interaction with student leaders a Trustee Student Affairs Committee was set up in 1979. One of the first acts of the new committee was to pass a resolution, which was then endorsed by the full Board of Trustees, that reflected the new spirit infusing the administration's relationship with the students and with the school's other constituencies. That resolution pledged that the Board "will support efforts to improve the communications between the Suffolk University Board of Trustees and the Suffolk University community, and will welcome proposals which integrate the feelings and philosophies of the various segments of the Suffolk University community."[71]

Suffolk students (early 1980s)

This new spirit not only helped to encourage participation by students during their sojourn at the University; it (and the habits of concern and involvement that it helped to develop in students) also went far to build the enthusiasm and vitality of the University's alumni. Their non-involvement during student days had built neither durable student institutions nor a strong sense of alumni identification.

A Law Alumni Association was founded in 1913, then again in 1920, 1925, and 1927. The 1927 effort even included purchase by Dean Archer of an Alumni Clubhouse at 73 Hancock Street, appointment of Archer's close friend and associate Alden Cleveland as part-time Alumni Secretary, and publication of the *Suffolk Alumni News*. By the mid-1930s, however, the *Alumni News* had vanished; and in September 1939 the Alumni Clubhouse (where Alden Cleveland had been resident caretaker since 1927) was vacated.

After the Second World War, the Trustees who had wrested control from the founder undertook a new initiative to mobilize the school's alumni.[72] University Treasurer and Trustee Frank J. Donahue led reorganization and revitalization of the Law Alumni Association after the war; by the early 1950s, the Association was regularly sponsoring fall, winter, and spring dinners at the Parker House, and providing funds for a number of Alumni Association scholarships at the Law School. Donahue's group even published (if somewhat sporadically) an *Alumni Bulletin*. College alumni, much less numerous in the late 1940s than their Law School counterparts, received proportionately less attention. After part-time Alumni Secretary Joseph Strain (who had been appointed by the Trustees in 1948) departed for service in the Korean War, they were left without leadership or support from the University.

Their number, however, grew rapidly during the early 1950s, as the large postwar classes graduated from the Colleges of Liberal Arts, Business, and Journalism. The opportunities offered to members of those classes for participation in an expanded program of undergraduate activities had also engendered in them a group dynamic and a continuing engagement in University affairs. Despite—in fact, because of—the University's neglect of them, a group of College alumni took the initiative into their own hands. They approached the Trustees in 1953 with a plan to reorganize the small and decentralized College alumni clubs (like the Accounting Club and the Suffolk University Club of Lowell) into a single College alumni association.[73] The group's leaders, however, began almost immediately to raise complaints that the Trustees were treating College alumni and students as second-class citizens, and that concern for the welfare of both groups was being subordinated to the Board's solicitude for the Law School and its graduates. The Trustees, for their part, became dismayed at the group's stridency, and suspicious of its motives; in 1954, the administration's paternalism was not reserved solely for students. As a result, the Board of Trustees withdrew its support from the new College alumni organization.

The organization's leaders then proceeded to petition the legislature for a charter independent of the University. There was adamant opposition by the Trustees before a legislative committee; but, ultimately, a charter was granted in July 1956 to the General Alumni Association of Suffolk University (GAASU). The school was then treated to the spectacle of its Trustees and a group of its alumni warily circling each other for the next eight years. Throughout this unpleasant interlude, student leaders in the Suffolk Colleges manifested steadfast support for GAASU and its demands, which included equal support from the University for College and Law alumni activities, the election of alumni Trustees, and the appointment of a full-time alumni secretary. Only when the Board's membership began to change and diversify in the early 1960s, however, was the way opened to a gradual rapprochement. By that time, the number of alumni from the Liberal Arts, Business, and Journalism Colleges had grown to a significant figure. As businessmen slowly gained parity on the Board with lawyers and judges, they expressed amazement at the long neglect of such a resource. The commitment made by the reconstituted Board to physical expansion of the University's facilities necessitated a growing reliance on alumni support and contributions. A reconciliation with the school's graduates—all of them—was imperative.

Thomas A. Fulham

The first step was taken in 1964, when Dorothy McNamara, a long-time supporter of GAASU within the University administration, was appointed full-time Alumni Secretary. Three years later, a University Development office was established. The real breakthrough, however, came under the Presidency of former business executive Thomas A. Fulham. One of Fulham's first acts after assuming office in 1970 was to engineer establishment of a Trustee Committee on Alumni Relations. Within three months after the new committee's creation, the Board had voted to encourage alumni participation in the affairs of the University, agreed in principle to the election of some Trustees by the alumni, and pledged to fund and coordinate all alumni activities through the Development office. The intractable College alumni, for their part, agreed to disband GAASU and to merge its members and resources into the new Suffolk University General Alumni Association (SUGAA). This new entity was to contain within it the alumni of the Liberal Arts College,[74] the Business School, and the Law School. It was a "department of the University"[75] in that it was funded from the University's budget, but it was administered by its own elected officers. Thus, the adversarial relation between Suffolk University and a segment of its alumni was to be ended, while regular consultation and coordination between alumni leaders and the University Development office were institutionalized. By the spring of 1972, SUGAA was functioning; to mark its debut, the new alumni organization launched yet another short-lived series of the *Alumni News*.

Within three years, however, both the *News* and SUGAA's original constitution had proved inadequate to their tasks. The Alumni Association was reorganized from a unitary body in which all University graduates were members—and with whose activities no individual academic unit's alumni were satisfied—into a much more flexible umbrella organization. Under the new constitution, SUGAA was restructured into three semi-autonomous divisions, each with its own elected governing body: the General Alumni Association, for holders of undergraduate or graduate degrees from the Liberal Arts College, and for holders of undergraduate Business School degrees; the MBA/MPA Alumni Association, for those who had received School of Management graduate degrees; and a Law School Alumni Association. Student representation was also included for the first time, on each of the three divisional governing bodies. The three divisions were linked, in turn, through an elected University Alumni Council. University funding for alumni activities continued, and the Development office's alumni relations staff was expanded (in part, to produce the new *Alumni Bulletin*). By 1976, the entire apparatus was in operation.[76]

Meanwhile, steady prodding from SUGAA and from student leaders helped impel the Board to apply the principle it had endorsed in 1971: election of some Trustees by the University's alumni. The first Trustee so designated was James Linnehan, who was elected to a three-year term on the Board in November 1976. Two other elected "Alumni Trustees" then joined the Board during the next year, fulfilling the Trustees' stipulation that three such representatives should serve on the Board at any given time.

By 1981, the Trustees' renunciation of paternalism, and their attempts to "integrate the feelings and philosophies of the various segments of the Suffolk University community," had yielded fruitful results. Channels of communication had been opened, and bases established for cooperation, among alumni, students, faculty, and the University administration.

The University's alumni, however, have contributed more to their *alma mater* than advice and cooperation. The record they have made in many spheres of endeavor provides, and has since 1906 provided, the best testimony to the institution's quality.[77] In 1981, there were over 8,500 living Law School graduates. By then, the number of alumni from the collegiate departments had surpassed that for the Law School; the College of Liberal Arts and the School of Management counted over ten thousand living graduates.[78]

General Alumni Association membership was evenly divided between Liberal Arts and School of Management alumni, while the MBA/MPA Alumni Association was growing at a rate of over three hundred members per year.

By 1981, the Law School had evolved to a point where its top administrators were trying to shed the University's traditional image as a path of upward mobility for ambitious poor people; Suffolk University Law School now presented itself primarily as a path of further mobility for qualified members of the middle class. On the other hand, the College of Liberal Arts and the School of Management (at least in its undergraduate division) still concentrated on offering to enthusiastic consumers the same commodity that Gleason Archer had purveyed seventy-five years before: a sound and practical education, independent of the state, that every working person could afford. Excellence was not overlooked; but the heritage of the University's social history was perhaps not so accurately preserved in the Law School as in the undergraduate departments. There, the dreams dreamed and the deeds done by Horatio Alger's heroes were not forgotten.

Chapter 7 *Suffolk University Sketches, 1906–1981*

Frank J. Donahue

Frank J. Donahue In 1921, Frank J. Donahue received his Bachelor of Laws (LLB) degree from Suffolk Law School, four years after he began part-time evening study, and three years after his admission (as a Suffolk Law freshman) to the Massachusetts bar. That time as a student at Dean Archer's law school instilled in the young lawyer a lifelong appreciation of and enthusiasm for the institution's potential. For the next six decades, Donahue never ceased his efforts to improve conditions and standards at Suffolk Law School, and to win increased respect and support for the school from its alumni and from the Boston community at large.

Born in Needham in 1881, Donahue—like many early Suffolk alumni—was the son of Irish immigrants. He attended Needham public schools, then studied journalism at Boston English High.

Attracted to politics at an early age, he was elected in 1902 Needham's Park Commissioner and Chairman of the local Democratic Committee. Young Donahue's interest in journalism temporarily won out, however, and he became a reporter for the newly formed *Boston American*. After three years, he left the paper to join the staff of a political magazine, *Practical Politics,* of which he eventually became managing editor.

His writing attracted the attention of state Democratic leaders, who soon reawakened his interest in a political career. In 1913, he became the first Democrat ever elected Massachusetts Secretary of State, and (at thirty-one) the youngest man ever to hold the position. He retained office for two years, then served between 1915 and 1928 as a member (and sometime chairman) of the Industrial Accident Board. From 1928 until 1932, Donahue was Democratic State Chairman; in 1931, he also became Chairman of the Fall River Finance Commission—and a year later, Democratic National Committeeman. In 1932, at the pinnacle of his political success, he abandoned politics for a judicial career, as a quarter-century earlier he had abandoned journalism for politics.

Donahue never ceased his efforts to improve conditions and standards at Suffolk Law School, and to win increased respect and support for the school from its alumni and from the Boston community at large.

On May 4, 1932, Donahue was appointed by Governor Ely to the Massachusetts Superior Court—the highest judicial office for which any Suffolk Law graduate had yet been chosen. For the next forty-one years, he remained a Superior Court Associate Justice; and in 1938 he became the first sitting justice ever named to the Massachusetts Judicial Council (on which he retained a seat until 1955). In addition, he wrote and sponsored the legislative act which created the Appellate Division of the Superior Court. A hard-nosed, law-and-order judge, Donahue was for four decades outspokenly critical of any legislators, penologists, or occupants of the bench whom he perceived to be "soft" on crime. He dismissed lenient juries, chastised convicted felons with high fines and stiff sentences, and filled the Deer Island House of Correction with the members of his "Daddy-Owe Club"—men who had fallen behind on their child-support payments. Yet he was also a cultured and widely-read man, whose controversial decision in 1948 prevented *Forever Amber* from being "banned in Boston." His forthrightness and trenchant wit earned Donahue a reputation as one of the state's most colorful jurists, and he served a judicial tenure that was the longest in Massachusetts history.

The prestige of Judge Donahue's position, his influence among Suffolk Law alumni, and his growing concern over conditions at his *alma mater,* combined with Suffolk University's wartime fiscal crisis to bring about his election as a Life Member of the Board of Trustees in 1945. At a time when a growing bloc of Trustees was challenging the political, economic, and educational policies of President Gleason L. Archer, Donahue became a leader of the anti-Archer faction.[1] Elected Vice-Chairman shortly after joining the Board, the Judge was chosen Board Chairman a year later. His rapid elevation was evidence of both the escalating severity of the University's financial crisis and the rising militancy of the Trustee rebellion against President Archer. Donahue retained the Chairmanship from 1946 until 1948. Then, after President Archer's resignation, Donahue assumed in 1949—and held for twenty years—the pivotal day-to-day responsibilities of University Treasurer.

The Frank J. Donahue Building, Law School

His first priority as Treasurer was to restore solvency and to liquidate the University's heavy debts. To do so, he clamped an iron hand on the school's finances. No payment, he insisted, was to be made or contracted without his scrutiny; no purchase—not even of library books—was to be made without his authorization; and no University check was to be valid without his personal signature. Donahue's tight management of University funds allowed him to use rising postwar tuition receipts from G.I. Bill-funded veterans in order to reduce the institution's onerous indebtedness, to see the University through what otherwise might have been a fatal financial crisis during the Korean War, and subsequently to accumulate the capital that ultimately made University expansion in the 1960s possible.[2] When the time came for that expansion, it was Judge Donahue who handled every aspect of the operation—from locating the site and acquiring the land, to supervising the construction of the new building, which opened its doors in September 1966. Appropriately, the new edifice was designated in 1971 the Frank J. Donahue Building.

Appropriately, too, the Donahue Building in the mid-1970s became the home of Suffolk University Law School. Frank Donahue served Suffolk University, but his first—and abiding—love was Suffolk Law School. His policies as Treasurer reflected this priority, permitting the Law School to remain throughout his tenure the "most favored" of the University's academic units. For twenty-seven years (1948-75), Judge Donahue chaired the Board's powerful Law School Committee, which exercised a nearly autonomous oversight of Law School affairs.[3] Simultaneously, he rebuilt, reorganized, and led the Suffolk Law Alumni Association—both for the increased financial support it could provide for the Law School and for the fillip it could give to the development of pride in Suffolk Law School among its graduates. As long-serving chairman of the Trustees' Honorary Degree Committee, as well, Donahue sought to increase public and professional awareness of Suffolk University by honoring each year leading members of the political and legal communities, in Massachusetts and nation-wide.[4]

Finally, Frank Donahue made himself a proud advertisement for his *alma mater.*[5] At a time when many Suffolk graduates were less than forthright about where they had obtained their education, he set himself the task of personifying—both to alumni and to the outside world—the achievements, eminence, and respect to which Suffolk Law School training could lead. For his efforts, Judge Donahue came to be nicknamed, and remained until his death in 1979, "Mr. Suffolk."

Dorothy M. McNamara

Dorothy M. McNamara When Dorothy M. McNamara joined Gleason L. Archer's office staff in 1927, Suffolk Law School was at the peak of its prosperity—the largest law school in the world. She served for twenty-one years under Archer's leadership, then for another twenty-six under the Donahue and Fenton regimes that succeeded him. Her career provides a common thread that ties together these eras of Suffolk University's history, and which binds many alumni from each of them loyally to their *alma mater.*

Dorothy Margaret McNamara was born in 1910 in Roxbury, and lived there until 1971, when she moved to the West End near Suffolk University. After attending Mission Hill Grammar School, Roxbury High, and Fisher Junior College, she came to Suffolk Law School in 1927 as a stenographer.[6] In 1935, she was promoted to Law School Recorder; then six years later was named Bursar by the Board of Trustees. She served twenty-five years in that capacity, during which time she acted not only as Treasurer Donahue's most trusted lieutenant, but also as a buffer between him and many financially beleaguered students. Her humanity provided a counterweight to Judge Donahue's fiscal stringency; and she managed for years after the fall of the Archer regime to preserve in practice the Archer era's leniency toward student tuition delinquencies. In so doing, she won for herself the lasting affection of countless graduates—and for Suffolk a lasting reputation as "the school with a heart."

University Life Trustee John Griffin, a Board member from 1937 until his death in 1987, recalled the "many, many successful alumni through the years who have told me that they would never have reached their positions in life if Miss Mac hadn't intervened when personal problems made them ready to quit school. Through her warm personality, she kept more people at Suffolk than any of our high-priced so-called experts."[7]

When the Bursar's duties were taken over in 1964 by a professional accountant—Donahue's newly-appointed Assistant Treasurer, Francis X. Flannery—the mutual affection between Miss McNamara and many Suffolk graduates made her the natural choice as the University's first full-time Alumni Secretary. In that capacity, she remained a friend, counselor, and advocate for both students and alumni. Even her retirement in 1974 did little to sever the bond between "Miss Mac" and the three generations of Suffolk alumni she had served.

Miss Mac won for herself the lasting affection of countless graduates—and for Suffolk a lasting reputation as "the school with a heart."

With her sister Evelyn (McNamara) Reilly, Dorothy McNamara endured many "payless paydays" during the difficult days of World War II. Her loyalty to the school and its students, however, saw her through this crisis, as it also saw her through the trauma of founder Gleason Archer's ouster in 1948. When most members of Archer's official "family" were turning their backs on Suffolk University out of loyalty to the fallen President, Miss Mac stayed on out of loyalty to the institution to which most of his life—and hers—had been dedicated. The administrative knowledge which she had gained in her wide-ranging duties as Bursar provided continuity of procedure and purpose (which might otherwise have been lacking) from the day-to-day operations of the Archer era to those of the Donahue regime.[8]

While serving as Bursar, Miss McNamara also oversaw Law School office and Bookstore activities. She became Veterans Coordinator when the G.I. Bill was enacted; was responsible for all payrolls, financial reports, equipment ordering, health and insurance benefits programs. Occasionally, she even helped place students and alumni in jobs. As Alumni Secretary after 1964, she organized and staffed the new office, played a key role in the ensuing Building Fund drive, and continued to develop alumni activities until her retirement ten years later.

During the 1950s and 1960s, Dorothy McNamara was lionized by all segments of the University community. There was hardly a gathering in which she wasn't publicly recognized—through a citation, trophy, plaque, bouquet, or standing ovation. Yearbooks were dedicated to her, and the *Suffolk Journal* never tired of writing features and editorials about her. The all-male Wig and Robe Law Society named her its first female life member, and undergraduate leaders inducted her into the Gold Key Honorary Society.

In 1954, the Board of Trustees awarded her an honorary Master of Arts degree, and two years later, at the University's Golden Anniversary celebration, Suffolk's founder Gleason L. Archer presented her with a huge trophy from an Alumni-Student Committee to honor her as Jubilee Queen.

Perhaps most fittingly, in 1967 the Trustees established a Dorothy M. McNamara Scholarship, to be awarded annually to two students "who have made a significant, lasting contribution to the quality of life at Suffolk University."[9] The dedication and service to Suffolk students which Miss Mac provided for forty-seven years could thus be nurtured in a new generation.

John Griffin

John Griffin In 1934, John Griffin was hired by Gleason Archer to assist him in establishing an undergraduate program which Archer envisioned as a "feeder" for Suffolk Law School. For the next five decades, Griffin's service to Suffolk was to be closely connected with the growth of the several undergraduate colleges that issued from this initiative, and with the establishment of a harmonious and equitable relationship between the parts of the University created by the integration of these new academic units with Suffolk Law School.

When he was appointed Archer's evening aide for undergraduate curriculum planning, Griffin was a Junior Master at Roxbury Memorial High School. Born in Roxbury, he had attended Dorchester High School and then gone on to Harvard, from which he had received a BS degree in 1925 and an MBA two years later.[10] In addition to his duties at Roxbury High and as Archer's aide, Griffin in 1934 was appointed to teach Economics at Archer's newly-founded Suffolk College of Liberal Arts. He was one of the school's original faculty members. Most of his colleagues were high school teachers; and, like them, he was able to serve on the Suffolk College faculty only because the fledgling institution offered instruction exclusively in the evening.

Griffin continued to teach in the College of Liberal Arts until 1937, serving also during this period as Student Advisor for Men (1935-37), and as Faculty Advisor on Athletics (1936-37). After the

Liberal Arts school was upgraded from junior college status by issuance of a 1935 charter conferring the right to grant bachelor's degrees, Griffin served for a year as the College's first Registrar (1935-36). When he was succeeded as Registrar in 1936 by Carrolla A. Bryant, Griffin's liberation from most administrative duties freed him to undertake the formative work of adding a College of Journalism and a College of Business Administration to Suffolk's undergraduate opportunities.

In 1936, Griffin played a key role in resolving the initial difficulties encountered by Dean Archer and Massachusetts Press Association Executive Secretary Paul A. Newsome in translating Newsome's proposed Suffolk College of Journalism from the drawing board to operational status. A year later, Harvard MBA Griffin again played a central part in implementing plans and organizing a curriculum for a College of Business Administration. This time, however, the conception as well as the execution was Griffin's. He was thus "in every sense the father" of the School of Management.[11]

Shortly after the incorporation of the three undergraduate "departments" and the Law School as Suffolk University in 1937, Griffin was elected to the University's Board of Trustees by members impressed by and grateful for his multi-faceted exertions on behalf of the Colleges during the preceding three years. Although he gave up teaching in 1937 to become a full-time executive in the tobacco distribution industry, Griffin remained closely identified with the College of Liberal Arts and the School of Management during more than five decades of service as a Suffolk University Trustee.[12] He was an active member of the Board's College Committee from its inception in 1938 until 1975, and retained in 1981 the Business School Committee membership he had held since that committee's initial meeting. From these two positions, Griffin maintained a close scrutiny over—and exerted a steady influence upon—the growth and development of the undergraduate, graduate Business, and graduate Education curricula at Suffolk.[13]

Griffin, however, did not limit his concern to the development of the Liberal Arts College and the School of Management. From the time of his election to the Board, he was a determined and skillful advocate of University policies favoring closer integration of the several academic units and parity between the Law School and the rest of the University. Although not always successful in his efforts, Griffin often won the ear—and consistently the respect—of his fellow Trustees. In 1957, he was elected Clerk of the Corporation;

Griffin, however, did not limit his concern to the development of the Liberal Arts College and the School of Management. From the time of his election to the Board, he was a determined and skillful advocate of University policies favoring closer integration of the several academic units and parity between the Law School and the rest of the University.

and nine years later, upon the death of senior Trustee Hiram J. Archer, was chosen by his colleagues to fill Archer's place as a Life Trustee of the University.[14]

A trusted advisor to every President of the University from Gleason Archer to Thomas Fulham, Griffin has been called "the conscience of the University."[15] For three decades, he chaired the Board's Auditing Committee; served three separate times as chairman of the Finance Committee; and in 1975 was elected a Trustee of the Suffolk University Endowment Fund.[16] It was certainly through his insistence on "fiscal integrity"[17] that a professional accountant (Francis X. Flannery) was first appointed Assistant Treasurer in 1964, that professional management was introduced in the University Bookstore in 1965, and that improved controls over the institution's marketable securities and Endowment Fund were instituted nine years later.

As an educational, business, civic, and Catholic lay leader, John Griffin served the Boston community for over fifty years.[18] When he died in April 1987, his forty-nine years on Suffolk University's Board of Trustees made him the longest-serving Trustee in University history. During that time, he worked tirelessly to make Boston a better place to live, and Suffolk University better adapted to serve Boston. In doing so, he played a principal role in shaping Suffolk University's tradition, its present structure, and its sense of purpose.

Robert S. Friedman

Robert S. Friedman When Robert S. Friedman was appointed Instructor in Biology at Suffolk in 1941, the department he joined offered only three courses and consisted solely of two part-time faculty members. In the succeeding three decades, the personal and financial contributions which this shy, modest, devout man was to make to the Natural Science program—and to the Biology department in particular—were to alter completely the scope, conditions, and approach of scientific instruction at Suffolk University.

Born in 1915 in Taunton, Massachusetts, he attended local schools until, after an accident following his freshman year in high school, he transferred to the Huntington School in Boston. He completed the three-year course in two, and went on to the University of Michigan. After two years, however, he left, because he lacked "purpose and orientation."[19] To support himself while trying to sort out his future career, Friedman became a Cape Cod boatyard apprentice. Finally, he decided to enter the teaching profession, hoping "to give others the guidance which he lacked."[20]

In 1936, he was graduated from Boston University with a BS degree in Education, and two years later B.U.'s Graduate School awarded him an MA in Biology. Even though his parents were financially quite well off, young Friedman insisted on playing in a band to pay for his own education. From B.U., he went on to Harvard, where he earned his second MA (1940) and a Ph.D. in Biology (1946). Meanwhile, he began to teach part-time at Suffolk.

When the U.S. entered World War II, Friedman tried to enlist, but his earlier injuries kept him out of the armed forces. Instead, he served the government by doing top secret work at the Radio Research Laboratory at Harvard. After the war, he received a full-time appointment at Suffolk University's College of Liberal Arts, where he also served one harried year (1946-47) as Director of Admissions. In 1947, he became Chairman of one of the three Divisions (there were not at that time separate departments) of the Liberal Arts College: the Division of Natural Sciences, which included faculty members drawn from the fields of Biology, Chemistry, Geology, Mathematics, and Physics.

Insisting on anonymity, Friedman purchased the land (twenty-two acres in 1968, eighteen more in 1971), on which a Marine Biology field research station was to be constructed.

The next year, when the Humanities and Social Sciences Divisions were reorganized into departments, Friedman's aggressive advocacy was instrumental in assuring the same type of restructuring for the Natural Sciences Division. He was appointed Chairman of the Biology department, and held that post for over two decades.[21] He remained on the faculty, however, until his untimely death in 1973. During his twenty-two years as Chairman, he succeeded in building a department seven times larger than it had been in 1948, in vastly improving the department's laboratory facilities (after years of foot-dragging by the administration), and in multiplying Biology course offerings from the three of 1941 to twenty-one in 1970. In 1960, he began a highly successful Medical Technology program which eventually led to the establishment of affiliations between Suffolk University and six New England hospitals where students undertook a year of clinical work after completing three years of on-campus training at Suffolk. The Biology department he assembled and led produced a number of students who went on not only to earn Ph.D.'s in Biology, but also to become prominent scientists in their own right. Two Suffolk graduates, Arthur West and Beatrice Snow, even joined Friedman on the Biology faculty.[22]

During the 1950s, when the University's fiscal situation called for strict austerity, Friedman personally paid for needed supplies and equipment for the Biology department. Always insisting on anonymity, he set up a special fund to aid Biology students, and also established the Albert K. Sheldon Student Loan Fund. In 1965, the largest single contribution by any faculty member to Suffolk's Building Campaign was his. ("If anyone finds out about this, I'll revoke it," he told the collector.)[23] Throughout most of his career at the Liberal Arts College, Friedman served without salary—consenting to accept only a small yearly honorarium.

Consistently an innovator, Friedman joined his Biology department colleagues in urging that Suffolk University offer a program in the new field of Marine Biology. To that end, a field-study site was chosen in the early 1960s on the shores of Cobscook Bay (an arm of the Bay of Fundy) near Edmunds, Maine. Again insisting on anonymity, Friedman purchased the land (twenty-two acres in 1968, eighteen more in 1971), on which a Marine Biology field research station was to be constructed. When he died in 1973, the station was nearly completed; six months later, the facility was officially dedicated as the Robert S. Friedman Cobscook Bay Laboratory.

Charles Law

That dedication, along with the Honorary Doctor of Science degree awarded him by Suffolk in 1965 and the Trustees' designation of him seven years later as the only Distinguished Service Professor in the University's history, acknowledged a debt of gratitude to Robert Friedman that could never be fully repaid. During thirty-two years as Suffolk University's professor-philanthropist,[24] he laid the foundation for subsequent development of the Natural Sciences at Suffolk, and especially for development of the Biology department. Today, the quality and variety of courses and programs available in both Division and department may well have grown beyond even Bob Friedman's expectations—if not beyond the hopes of his far-seeing imagination.

Charles Law When Charles Law came to Suffolk in 1946, the University had an athletic "tradition" spanning five years—all before the war, and with teams (tennis, golf, basketball, and baseball) composed primarily of law students. When he retired as Athletics Director thirty-two years later, what he had done defied all expectations. Even with the severe disadvantage caused by lack of on-campus athletic facilities, he had built up a strong tradition of undergraduate participation in intercollegiate athletics: his teams were consistently competitive, and frequently victorious. If Coach Law was not available to manage the 1969 Mets, it was only because he was busy performing bigger miracles back in Boston.

Born in Patrick, near Glasgow, Scotland, in 1913, Law grew up in Chelsea, Massachusetts. He graduated from Chelsea High, where he played football, basketball, and baseball, then went on to earn a BS degree in 1935 from Springfield College.[25] His small stature did not prevent him from lettering in football; nor did it keep him from making the basketball, lacrosse, and track teams. His first coaching job was at Melrose High, where he had charge of the football and basketball squads. He then moved on to Weston, and directed the high school basketball team to thirty-nine consecutive victories.[26]

"I guess I developed a love affair with Suffolk and its people—particularly the students. They worked a little harder than most students, and that kind of stuck with me."

In 1946, Law was persuaded to come to Suffolk University by Donald Fiorillo, who was then a young member of the faculty. "I never regretted it," Law later observed. "It not only presented me with a great challenge, but it also afforded me the opportunity to spend a career lifetime with down-to-earth kids and associates."[27]

Law's early years at Suffolk were extremely challenging. His assignment as Director of Athletics was to build an undergraduate intercollegiate athletics program from the ground up. He began in 1946 with baseball, basketball (both of which he coached himself), soccer, and ice hockey; golf (which he also coached) and tennis were added in 1948, and sailing in 1949. Many of his athletes were former World War II G.I.'s, frequently older than Law himself. Law admitted that this made discipline a bit touchy, but "they accepted the fact that I was the boss, and I appreciated the fact that they were men who had fought a war."[28]

Without Law's perseverance, it is possible that the undergraduate athletics program would not have survived those early years.[29] Only through the energetic support of University President Walter M. Burse, Trustee Athletics Committee Chairman William F.A. Graham, and Treasurer Frank J. Donahue were even an anemic athletics budget and a token scholarship program extracted from the Board from year to year. Hockey, soccer, and sailing were dropped in 1953, during the enrollment decline that followed the outbreak of the Korean War; and football, which had received sympathetic consideration from the Trustees since 1948, was rejected by the Board because of insufficient funds and inadequate facilities.[30]

Lack of facilities never seemed to discourage Charlie Law, however. He took his basketball nomads to the Charlestown YMCA

(1946-47), then to the old West End House on Blossom Street (1947-62), and finally to the Cambridge YMCA—which served as a home court for Suffolk basketball until the opening of the University's new Ridgeway Gymnasium in 1991. His baseball squads, likewise, had to move from diamond to diamond in greater Boston. From 1948 until 1972, Athletic Director Law also had the responsibility of running a compulsory Physical Education program for Suffolk freshmen; even when that program was discontinued in 1972, it was dropped only on condition that it be replaced by a much-expanded program of voluntary intramural competition. Not until 1966 did Law get his first full-time Assistant Director: James Nelson, who succeeded Law as basketball coach in 1976, and became Athletic Director upon Law's retirement in 1978. Despite major enrollment increases, it was 1972 before a second Assistant Director was added to supervise intramurals, and 1975 before a third—Ann Guilbert, for women's athletics—was hired.[31]

Nevertheless, Law's basketball teams won 295 games while losing only 258; and his last two teams were good enough to qualify for the NCAA Division III Regional Tournament. The 1974-75 squad reached the regional finals, and the 1975-76 quintet, with a 19-6 record, was ranked fifteenth nationally in their division.[32]

Everyone in regional athletic circles knew Charlie Law. His quiet wit enlivened many a sports luncheon. By 1969, when he received a distinguished service plaque from the National Association of Basketball Coaches, he was the dean of New England's basketball coaching fraternity. He was elected President of the New England Basketball Coaches Association in 1972; and three years later the Association voted him its highest award, the Doggie Julian Memorial Trophy, for his contributions to the sport.[33]

During his career, Law had a number of opportunities to move on from Suffolk. For twenty-two years, he served as an assistant football coach at Harvard. "But," he reflected, "I guess I developed a love affair with Suffolk and its people—particularly the students. They worked a little harder than most students, and that kind of stuck with me."[34]

Charlie Law worked more than a little harder than most Athletic Directors or coaches. His thirty-two years of persistence and extra effort gave Suffolk University an intercollegiate sports program and a tradition of undergraduate athletic competition where none had existed before.[35]

Donald W. Goodrich When Donald W. Goodrich came to Suffolk University, the Board of Trustees and founder-President Gleason L. Archer were conducting their own private war, which periodically engulfed other segments of the University community. Enrollments had plummeted during the Second World War, and the Colleges had been kept open by the narrowest of margins. By 1946, registrations were rising again, but the very speed of their increase was threatening to reduce to chaos the Colleges' skeletal and inexperienced administrative staff. In the midst of this turbulence, Goodrich took office as Registrar in February 1947.

Donald W. Goodrich

Goodrich was born in 1898 in Brooklyn, where he grew up. After being graduated from Phillips Exeter Academy in 1915, he entered Williams College, where he studied literature and the classics, was elected to Phi Beta Kappa, and received his BA *cum laude* in 1919. A year later, he earned an MA in English from Harvard. For the next two decades, he held teaching and administrative positions at several private secondary schools—eventually serving as Headmaster at the Buckley Country Day School on Long Island, and then at the prestigious Calvert School in Baltimore.

Just before World War II, Goodrich returned to Harvard for graduate study. There, he met Lester Ott, a history doctoral student who was then teaching part-time across the river at the Liberal Arts College of Suffolk University. When the U.S. entered the war, Goodrich joined the army as a captain. During five years of subsequent service at the Pentagon and in Germany, he rose to the rank of lieutenant colonel.

Just before his discharge, Goodrich heard from his old Harvard friend Lester Ott. In 1945, Ott had been appointed Dean of the Colleges at Suffolk, where he was struggling both to reorganize what had been predominantly a part-time night school into a full-time undergraduate institution, and to cope with the flood of new students generated by the postwar G.I. Bill educational benefits. Ott was desperate for experienced help, and he begged Goodrich—a seasoned educational administrator—to join his staff as Associate Dean and Registrar. In February 1947, Goodrich began over two decades of service which was to help steer Suffolk University toward the mainstream of American higher education.[36]

For the next two years, Registrar Goodrich was Ott's principal collaborator in giving Suffolk University's undergraduate programs—Liberal Arts, Journalism, and Business—the academic character and administrative shape they were to maintain into the 1960s and

1970s. A full-time (four-year) day undergraduate program was added to the part-time (five-year) evening program. Full-time faculty members, many with doctorates, were hired, and organized into full-fledged academic departments. A faculty committee structure was set up, and a core curriculum adopted.

When in 1949 Ott's Evening Division Director—Robert J. Munce—succeeded Ott as Dean, Goodrich continued in his role as Registrar and principal advisor to the Dean. Through Goodrich's influence, Dean Munce continued the academic and administrative policies of his predecessor At Goodrich's accession to the Deanship in his own right in 1956, most of the basic features of the Colleges remained those established by Ott and Goodrich nine years earlier.[37]

Goodrich's tenure represented a period of almost unbroken prosperity and expansion for the Liberal Arts and Business departments.

Not surprisingly, the major themes of Goodrich's thirteen-year Deanship were not reorganization and redirection, but development and strengthening. Goodrich expanded the faculty and pressed for higher salaries to improve its quality.[38] He supported facilities development, strengthened student services, improved library resources, and cultivated closer relations with College alumni. He endorsed the introduction of new courses and programs within the basic curriculum framework. He used and expanded the existing committee structure to involve the faculty in academic decision-making, while seeking to nurture a spirit of collegiality. To this latter end, Goodrich strove to know each faculty member personally, and for years made his home the scene of faculty social gatherings (for which there were no adequate facilities at the University).[39]

His tenure represented a period of almost unbroken prosperity and expansion for the Liberal Arts and Business departments. In 1966, a grateful Board of Trustees added to Dean Goodrich's title that of University Vice-President.[40] Three years later, on the occasion of his retirement from the Deanship, the Board also awarded him an honorary Doctor of Humanities degree.[41] The distinguished Dean Emeritus died, at 91, in July 1989.

Those who served under Goodrich unanimously attested to his salient character features: loyalty, decency, courtesy, and self-restraint.[42] He provided knowledgeable, sure-handed, and undramatic leadership that gained in effectiveness by its very contrast to the pyrotechnics of the late Archer era. His leadership style thus permitted him to cultivate Trustee confidence in the legitimacy of the Colleges in the post-Archer era; to foster faculty self-confidence, unity, harmony, and acceptance of the Colleges' academic and administrative structures; and to build a willingness among the

Trustees to take the risks and make the investments necessary to take advantage of the opportunities presented by the steadily-expanding student population of the 1960s.

The dominant themes of his two decades of influence in the Suffolk Colleges were stability and development; and his skillful melding of the two proved a remarkable restorative after the hyper-activity of the late Archer era and the fiscal lethargy of the early Donahue regime.

Edward G. Hartmann

Edward G. Hartmann As academic and fiscal order was restored at Suffolk after World War II, the University turned its attention to winning accreditation for the Law School and the undergraduate departments. To attain that goal, improved Library collections and an "accreditable Librarian"[43] were necessary. In September 1948, Edward G. Hartmann came to Suffolk University as Director of Libraries.

Hartmann was born in Wilkes-Barre, Pennsylvania, in 1912. He attended Bucknell University, receiving his AB in 1937 and his MA in History a year later. His studies for a Ph.D. in History at Columbia University were interrupted by World War II. From 1943 until 1946, Hartmann served as Combat Historian for the 90th Infantry Division with General Patton's Third Army, editing in the course of his duties a history of the 90th entitled *Tough 'Ombres* (1944) and another work, *A Short History of the 357th Infantry Regiment* (1945).

When the war ended, the young historian taught for a year at Wilkes College in his home town. He completed his Ph.D. at Columbia in 1947, and by the spring of 1948 he had also earned from Columbia a BS in Library Service.[44] That fall, he took charge of the College and Law School Libraries at Suffolk University, where he was also appointed an Associate Professor of History.[45]

Both Libraries were housed together throughout Hartmann's tenure as Director. By working with academics and administrators from all quarters of the University, he was able to strengthen the law and undergraduate collections, and to gain Trustee approval for Library budgets that made possible attainment of accreditation standards. These exertions permitted the University to pass the critical library inspection portion of the New England Association visitation that granted accreditation to the Colleges in 1952, and the more rigorous scrutiny in 1953 that resulted in American Bar Association accreditation for the Law School.

During Hartmann's ten years as Librarian, the law collection grew from ten thousand volumes to over twenty-five thousand—and was catalogued for the first time.[46] Meanwhile, the College (Liberal Arts and Business) collection expanded from five thousand volumes to nearly fifteen thousand. Perhaps most important, Hartmann trained a small professional Library staff, and imbued its members with pride in their work and in their Library. One of Hartmann's assistants, Patricia I. Brown, even went on to become Assistant Law Librarian at Suffolk.

Hartmann resigned as Director of Libraries in 1958 to devote full time to his duties as Professor of History. From his arrival in 1948, he had insisted on Suffolk's maintaining high academic standards. His appointment in 1956 as Chairman of the Colleges' Academic Standing Committee added authority to his advocacy. He retained the chair for twenty years, while also vigorously supporting academic excellence as a member of the Suffolk chapter of Phi Alpha Theta (the national History Honor Society) and of the University's Phi Beta Kappa Committee.

In order to assist students in adjusting to the academic challenges of college life, he wrote "Dr. Hartmann's Study Tips for Freshmen," a brief study guide which was distributed to incoming Suffolk freshmen for nearly twenty years.

In the classroom, Hartmann challenged his students. He was quick to praise quality, and to chastise mediocrity, in their work. The lower range of his grading scale—F, double F, triple F, and the dreaded Q (for "quit")—became a part of Suffolk folklore. On the other hand, it was widely rumored that an A in one of his courses was a ticket to Suffolk Law School. His students annually made him a leading candidate for the "Big Screw" award (bestowed in the mid-1970s by APO fraternity on the faculty member voted the toughest grader on campus). Many of them, however, also clearly appreciated his uncompromising demand for excellence: more than one *Beacon* yearbook was fondly dedicated to "Dr. Hartmann."

During the 1950s and 1960s, he worked closely with John Colburn, long-time Director of Student Activities, and was frequently asked by student class officers to serve as class advisor. He kept long office hours, and he took the time to know his students—to learn their names, their likes and dislikes, their school problems, and often their personal problems as well. In order to assist students in adjusting to the academic challenges of college life, he wrote "Dr. Hartmann's Study Tips for Freshmen," a brief study guide which was distributed to incoming Suffolk freshmen for nearly twenty years.

It was not only the Suffolk University community which recognized Hartmann's achievements. His writings on immigration and ethnicity were widely published and frequently cited; they included

The Movement to Americanize the Immigrant (1948, reprinted 1967), *A History of American Immigration* (1967), *Americans From Wales* (1967, reprinted 1978), and *American Immigration* (1978), the first textbook on American immigration history for secondary school students.[47] In 1966, he was awarded the Gold Medallion of the Welsh Society of Philadelphia for the contribution made by his works to the Welsh-American community. Subsequently, he also received the Hopkins Medal from the St. David's Society of New York (1970), and the Welsh-American newspaper *Ninnau*'s Citation (1978).

In 1978, after thirty years of dedicated service, Hartmann retired from teaching. As Emeritus Professor of History, however, he served as a member of the Heritage Committee's Editorial Board, and regularly updated his "Tentative Bibliography of Publications by Graduates of the Undergraduate Colleges of Suffolk University" (which he first compiled in 1976). After three decades at Suffolk, his goal was still the same: to win acceptance, both inside and outside the institution, of the importance of academic excellence to Suffolk University. Edward G. Hartmann died, at 83, on October 26, 1995.

John E. Fenton

John E. Fenton In 1924, John E. Fenton was graduated from Suffolk Law School. Twenty-five years later—in the stormy aftermath of the Archer era and in the midst of the University's campaign for accreditation—he joined the Board of Trustees. After sixteen years on the Board, during which he served as Trustees' Vice-Chairman, Board Chairman, University Vice-President, and Acting President, Fenton was elected in 1965 as Suffolk University's fifth President.

At the time, Fenton was sixty-seven, and had just retired from the Massachusetts Land Court after twenty-eight years of service. A bemused *Boston Globe* reporter asked him why he would accept such a new challenge at an age when most men were retired. "Retired?" replied Fenton. "Why, I'm just beginning. The main reason I took this job was to do some good for future generations."[48]

Thus began the five-year Presidency of John Edward Fenton. Born in 1898 in Concord, New Hampshire, Fenton lived most of his life in Lawrence, Massachusetts. While a student at Lawrence High School (from which he was graduated in 1916), he worked as a bobbin boy and cloth carrier in one of the local textile mills. In 1920, he graduated from Holy Cross,[49] and while teaching at Lawrence High, began to attend Suffolk Law School in the evening. After receiving his LLB, Fenton served eight years as Northern Essex

County Registrar of Deeds before his appointment in 1937 to the Land Court bench.

From the time of his election as a Suffolk University Trustee in 1949, he was one of the Board's most active members. No other Trustee in the institution's history has approached his record of long-term energetic participation on all of the Board's key committees. Most Trustees contented themselves with serving on the Law School Committee, the College Committee, or the Business School Committee (after it was created in 1965). Throughout much of his quarter-century on the Board, Fenton served on all three simultaneously—plus the Finance Committee and the Nominating Committee. He helped the fledgling Scholarship Committee (which he joined in 1949) build the school's financial aid resources from virtually nothing to an impressive level by the mid-1960s, and he served as a Trustee of the Suffolk University Endowment Fund from its creation until his death twenty-four years later.[50]

Fenton instituted an "open door" policy, which put him "within one day of any student."

His wide-ranging committee responsibilities gave him a comprehensive view of University affairs that few other Trustees could match. His colleagues acknowledged his unusual perspective by electing him Vice-Chairman of the Board between 1953 and 1960, a Life Trustee in 1957, and Vice-President of Suffolk University between 1957 and 1965.[51] While Vice-President, he twice served as Acting President of the institution (during the illnesses of Presidents Munce and Haley), and in 1966 he gave up the Board Chairman's seat (to which his fellow Trustees had elected him in 1964) to assume the Presidency.

He held office as University President during an era that was among the most turbulent in American educational history; campuses reeled from student demonstrations protesting the Vietnam War or demanding more participation in University decision-making. Yet, during Fenton's term of office, Suffolk was spared the worst excesses of this kind of agitation. In fact, the period 1965-70 was one of unparalleled growth for the University. During Fenton's tenure, enrollment and faculty membership doubled, while the qualifications of faculty members and the standards of instruction also advanced rapidly. The School of Management was first given autonomy, and the curricula offered there and in the other two academic units were significantly broadened. The Donahue Building was opened, and both 56 Temple Street and the original Ridgeway Building were purchased.

While President, Fenton used his influence on the Board to help remedy an important administrative problem that had been forcefully called to the Trustees' attention by his predecessor, Dennis C. Haley[52]: The President, who was nominally the University's chief academic officer, nevertheless had little authority. He was subject to the Board in all except trivial matters. This situation was the inevitable result of Judge Donahue's tight fiscal control, and also of the administrative machinery invented by the Trustees of the late Archer era to bring Gleason Archer and his successors to heel. Fenton fought to dismantle this machinery and to restore a significant degree of authority to the President. In doing so, he paved the way for subsequent strong Presidential leadership by men like Thomas A. Fulham (President 1970-1980) and Daniel H. Perlman (the first higher education professional to hold the office, 1980-1989). Although Fenton was something of a paternalist himself, his insistence that the Board give ear to the University's professional administrators proved to be the thin edge of a wedge: by the mid-1970s, the Trustees had expanded—well beyond the limits envisioned by Fenton—the variety of sources from which they sought advice, to include faculty, student, and alumni leaders.

Fenton remained what he had been since the early 1960s: the predominant figure in the most dynamic era of growth in Suffolk University's history.

Autocratic, traditional, and conservative as he sometimes was, Fenton was acknowledged by all elements of the University community to be a strong, shrewd leader with the jurist's sure sense of fairness. A large man whose white, shaggy hair often drooped over his forehead, he was a grandfather figure to many—a good listener with a soft spot in his heart for the students. He instituted an "open door" policy, which put him "within one day of any student."[53] When protests threatened, he called student leaders into his office to reach an understanding or compromise which would defuse the situation. When rallies took place in the Auditorium, Fenton took the stage to answer questions and reason with the protesters. He always took pride in the fact that, despite the charged political atmosphere of the late 1960s, Suffolk remained free of strikes during his Presidency.

Having shared power with Judge Donahue during the late 1950s and early 1960s, Fenton inherited it from him in the decade after 1964. Although, like Donahue, he came from a judicial background, he was better prepared—through his extraordinarily wide-ranging experience in civic affairs, fraternal organizations, charitable undertakings, and Catholic lay associations—to lead a Board which after 1960 was steadily being broadened beyond its traditional composition of lawyers and judges to include increasing number of prominent Boston-area businessmen.[54]

When Fenton stepped down as University President in 1970, the Board of Trustees reelected him to the Chairmanship that he had yielded in 1966 in order to assume the Presidency. He continued to serve on the Board's principal committees until shortly before his death in 1974, and he maintained a campus office where he was on hand most days to confer with President Fulham and Vice-President Flannery. Thus, Fenton remained what he had been since the early 1960s: the predominant figure in the most dynamic era of growth in Suffolk University's history.[55] In a fitting final tribute, the Trustees voted in 1974 to name the newly-completed Liberal Arts building at 32 Derne Street—the capstone on a decade of expansion—in honor of John E Fenton.

Chapter 8 *The Perlman Presidency, 1980–1989*

The Fulham Legacy In a world where necessity is the mother of invention, the year 1979 provides a pregnant pause. As Suffolk University rested ripe with success, the world around it ripened relentlessly with change. The University had prospered with the student surge of the 1970s, healing financial frailties that had dogged it since 1945. It had found an able and popular President in Thomas A. Fulham, who by 1979 was experienced and comfortable in his office—and so respected by his fellow chief executives that they had elected him to head the Association of Independent Colleges and Universities in Massachusetts (AICUM) for the current year. The Board of Trustees had approved a major building project to address Suffolk University's space deficiencies, and set into motion a capital campaign to underwrite it. The institution appeared poised

Thomas A. Fulham

for takeoff. Only habitual cynics would have pointed out, had they but known, that the country was about to begin a demographic toboggan-ride that would change the game, and the education market, completely—and which would initiate structural changes in the society and the culture more profound than anything that had occurred since World War II.

On September 12, 1979, Thomas A. Fulham informed the Board of Trustees of his decision to resign as the institution's sixth President, effective in the summer of 1980, concluding what was arguably the most successful and best-loved Presidency in Suffolk University's history. Although a non-academic who learned his trade as an academic chief executive on the job, Fulham was an experienced and knowledgeable business CEO who performed brilliantly as the University's helmsman. During Fulham's ten-year Presidency from October 1970 until the end of July 1980, longer than any other except that of founder Gleason L. Archer, Suffolk University experienced its greatest growth. As student enrollments rose to an all-time high (and institutional financial resources/stability with them), President Fulham was able to add three buildings to the University while keeping it debt-free. At the same time, he worked with the College of Business Administration/Graduate School of Administration (which was, thankfully, to become the School of Management in 1979) and the Law School to gain crucial professional accreditations from the National Association of Schools of Public Affairs and Administration (NASPAA, 1980) and the Association of American Law Schools (AALS, 1977).

During Fulham's ten-year Presidency from October 1970 until the end of July 1980, longer than any other except that of founder Gleason L. Archer, Suffolk University experienced its greatest growth.

Less observed, but probably far more important, President Fulham worked throughout his Presidency, with the incomparable constancy of what is fundamental to one's nature, to begin building a missing sense—and reality—of community and inclusiveness at all levels in a Suffolk University previously dominated by a Board of Trustees composed primarily of attorneys and judges. Fulham had been elected to that Board in June of 1961, coming to it directly from the newly-established (January 1961) Advisory Council of the College of Business Administration. In this circumstance, he was one of a small, vocal contingent of businessmen to whom the University's boardroom doors were cautiously being opened, whose creative energy and enthusiasm was enormous, and whose influence, over the short run, was carefully limited by their forensic colleagues. His associates in this commercial coterie included fellow CBA Advisory Council members George C. Seybolt, John P. Chase, Stephen P.

Mugar, and Joseph E. Sullivan, several of whom were to become, over the years, monumental figures in University history.

It was also on the recommendation of President Fulham (and the Development Committee which he had founded in 1962), that the University Development Office was reorganized in June 1974. In that configuration, it carried out the extraordinarily successful "Campaign for Excellence" (1979-82) which financed construction of the Sawyer Building at 8 Ashburton Place (opened in 1981, dedicated in 1982).[2] And it was after his enthusiastic endorsement in the spring of 1980 of the importance for the University to provide merit scholarships (not need-based scholarships alone) that an initial gift of $50,000 was contributed, in President Fulham's honor, by Cecil H. and Ida M. Green in October 1980 to establish the Thomas A. Fulham Merit Scholarship Endowment Fund.

At the same Board of Trustees meeting to which President Fulham submitted his resignation (September 12, 1979), Thomas J. Brown, John M. Corcoran, and Joseph B. Shanahan, Jr., Esq., were elected as Trustees, heralding, at least for the more sanguine, a new era (or at least a new direction) in the University's history. Brown was an African-American; Corcoran, a business leader in the building trade and in real estate; Shanahan, a former student, Student Government Association (SGA) President in 1971-72, and serving Alumni Trustee (elected in February 1977). All three filled longstanding needs on the Board. Their election not only brought much-needed skills and viewpoints into the University's camp; it also sent important signals of reconciliation and invitation to friends and alumni. At the same time, Shanahan was also embraced by the Board to relieve the aging John Griffin, who, having served as Clerk of the Board since 1957, was now succeeded by Shanahan.

At that moment (as in 1995), Suffolk University was a heavily tuition-dependent institution; it derived over 90% (somewhere between 92% and 97%, depending on the date) from tuition revenues. Nationally, the average private college or university was only 40% dependent on tuition and fees for its operating budget. Research institutions, such as Harvard and MIT, were about 30% tuition-dependent; institutions comparable to Suffolk University were generally about 75-80% tuition-dependent. As a heavily tuition-dependent institution, Suffolk University had a great need for significant philanthropic assistance from alumni and from corporate/foundation sources outside the University. Aware of the valuable help available, if appropriately solicited from such sources, Fulham and his colleagues in the small bloc of "business" Trustees consistently attempted to impress that priority on their forensic colleagues. One of the principal significances of John Corcoran's election as a Trustee in 1979 (besides the much-needed expertise on building and real estate which he brought to the Board) was that he was to be the first of a "second wave" of "business" Trustees—much more vocal and, eventually, with the aid of survivors from the "first wave," more influential than their predecessors—that joined the Board between 1979 and 1986. This "second wave" comprised, besides Corcoran, Thomas P. McDermott, Carol Sawyer Parks, and John C. Scully.

Daniel H. Perlman

Thus, the "renewal" of the Board at the end of the Fulham Presidency was Janus-faced, looking in two opposite directions at the same time. One face looked to the University's past, representing an initiative to bring reconciliation, concord, and inclusiveness to a University community whose constituent components (Trustees, faculty, students, alumni, and representatives from diverse ethnic and racial groups in each of these categories) had frequently, throughout the institution's turbulent and acrimonious history, regarded each others' interests as fundamentally incompatible. This face promised the University the capacity to mobilize, for the first time in living memory, its full internal energies and financial resources. The other face, that which presided with tentative benevolence over the election of businessman John Corcoran as a Trustee in 1979, looked toward the University's future, offering the prospect of enhanced access to corporate/foundation philanthropy, reduced vulnerability to tuition-dependence, and the capacity to mobilize in the institution's support, for the first time in its history, the full energies and financial resources of the external community. In this way, as in others, Suffolk University's growing openness to diversity in the last quarter of the twentieth century represented an effort simultaneously to reduce its insularity and its financial vulnerability.

President Perlman On July 31, 1980, Daniel H. Perlman, former Vice-President for Administration at Chicago's Roosevelt University, was elected by the Trustees as Suffolk University's seventh President. He was the institution's first Jewish chief executive, and he came directly from a campus where the majority of the students was African-American. Perlman was scheduled officially to assume the presidential duties on September 29, 1980; but he moved into his office and began work weeks early.[5] Within months of taking office, President Perlman had established a Long-Range Planning Committee (without Trustee representation) and initiated application for a $2 million federal Title III institutional development grant (without specific Trustee authorization).

In his eagerness, the new President startled some members of the Board, with its historic suspicion of presidential authority at Suffolk. But both he and his Trustees found considerable basis for optimism and self-congratulation. In the early days of the Perlman regime, the institution concluded a dazzlingly successful Campaign for Excellence, which, with a $2.7 million goal, produced $3.6 million in contributions. The 1982 dedication of the Frank Sawyer Building and Mildred Sawyer Library seemed to signal that the University had, at last, found a principal benefactor. Meanwhile, renovations continued to the Archer and Donahue Buildings, and future expectations were buoyed by the renewed teaming in the University's service of the pair who "made" the Campaign for Excellence: campaign chairman and corporate banker John S. Howe was elected Board Chair in June 1981, and Joseph M. Kelley, chief architect of the Campaign for Excellence, was appointed Suffolk's new Institutional Advancement Director six months later.

With no University indebtedness, and with freshman admissions at an all-time high in 1982, President Perlman's position was, ironically, a delicate one. As new President, he naturally wanted to cultivate the Board's confidence; but he was also faced with the unenviable responsibility of tempering the Board's enthusiasm and of delivering prudential and cautionary advice to its members regarding the institution's needs and prospects over the coming decade. As an education professional, Perlman saw much more clearly than many Board members that just ahead lay a demographic cataract, passage of which would clearly expose the vulnerability of the 94%–tuition-dependent institution.

Several factors were at work. The first was a precipitous drop in the number of projected high school graduates, beginning in the early 1980s and continuing into the 1990s. This was due, in turn, to a spectacular drop in the number of births from the early 1960s through the late 1970s. (By 1980, it was estimated that 65-70% of the individuals born in any given year would become high school graduates.) In Massachusetts, there had been 111,222 births in 1963; that number had fallen to a low of 65,947 in 1976—a decline of 40.7%. As a result, it was projected that the number of public secondary school graduates in Massachusetts would drop from a high of 79,400 in 1976-77 (and 75,820 in 1980-81) to a low of 43,357 in 1993-94, a 45.4% decrease. These Massachusetts figures were even more alarming than comparable ones for the Northeast region (34.3% decline in births, 36.9% drop in graduates) and the nation generally (23.5% decrease in births, 21% fall in graduates). The estimates for Massachusetts private secondary school graduates were less disturbing (a 16.5% decline). Even though Suffolk University in 1980 drew a higher percentage of its students from private schools than did most colleges, the majority of its students came from public secondary schools; so the private school projections could provide only cold comfort.

The second factor was an accelerating rate of change in the ethnic and racial composition of the population. In 1980, the City of Boston had a population that was 70% white; ten years later, it was 62.8% white (a decline of 8.4%). Over the same period, the percentage of African-Americans increased from 22.4% to 25.6% (a 16.4% increase); of Asians, from 2.7% to 5.3% (a 100.6% increase); and of Native Americans, from 0.2% to 0.3% (a 44.7% increase). By 1990, 10.8% of Bostonians (of any race) described themselves as Hispanic. The Commonwealth of Massachusetts dropped from 93.8% to 89.8% white between 1980 and 1990 (a 4.3% decline); the African-American percentage increased from 3.9% to 5% (a 28.2% gain); Asian, from 0.9% to 2.4% (a 166.7% gain); and Native American, from .15% to .2% (a 33.3% gain). By 1990, 4.8% of the Commonwealth's population was classified as Hispanic. Similar comparisons for the country as a whole (1980-90) showed whites as dropping from 83.1% to 80.1% (a 6% decrease), African-Americans as increasing from 11.7% to 12.1% (a 13.2% rise), Hispanics as growing from 6.4% to 9% (a 53% increase), Asians as rising from 1.5% to 2.9% (a 107.8% expansion), and Native Americans as increasing from .6% to .8% (a 37.9% growth).

Extrapolating from those figures, it was estimated that, for the country as a whole, the white percentage of the population would drop to 80% by 2010 and 72.8% by 2050; the African-American percentage would grow to 13.4% in 2010 and 15.7% in 2050; the Hispanic percentage would increase to 14% in 2010 and 23% in 2050; the Asian percentage would rise to 5.7% in 2010 and 11.3% in 2050; and the Native American percentage would expand to .9% in 2010 and 1.1% in 2050.

These figures portended a change from a buyer's to a seller's market from the point of view of Suffolk University and its fellow institutions of higher education in the U.S. The rapid decline in the traditional college-age population (18-24), as "Baby Boomers" postponed having children, confounded the marketing strategies of colleges that had come to focus more and more in the 1960s and 1970s on that particular group (as its designation implies) as their "prime" market. During this period, even Suffolk University, whose traditions pointed it away from "traditional" higher-education constituencies, had been seduced by the siren-song of numerical (and fiscal) prosperity to drift comfortably into an enhanced dependence on this "market segment." As that segment began to deflate in the early 1980s, the educational (and Suffolk University) community gradually awoke with a start to the precariousness of its position.

Law School classroom (1970's)

But there was more. In the seductive circumstances of the 1960s and 1970s, student-sated universities (including Suffolk) had subsided into torpid indolence regarding their outreach to "minority" groups. "Affirmative action" was fashionable, but not economically necessary: there were plenty of "traditional" (white) students to go around. So the sinews of racial and cultural outreach had grown flaccid; and when the terrain changed in the early 1980s, many of the runners found themselves badly out of shape. Having planted themselves into a stance of overdependence on "college-age," middle-class whites, many institutions appeared about to reap the whirlwind.

In Massachusetts, there were also the added disruptions caused by the emigration of job- and sun-seekers from New England to the Sun Belt and, especially in eastern Massachusetts, by expanding immigration from non-European sources.

Nor were all the challenges numerical. Other conditions were changing rapidly at the end of the 1970s as well. Worldwide, a significant growth of interest in international education was taking place in response to increases in multi-national ownership, the expansion of international business and commercial activity, and order-of-magnitude improvements in communication and travel facilities. The end of the Cold War and the multiplication of international trade/political associations (the European Union, NAFTA, GATT) also encouraged students in unprecedented numbers to consider the possibilities of study outside their borders. With English increasingly the international language, and given the number and variety of American educational institutions, these students offered, for those who knew how to attract them, at least a partial antidote to debilitation due to deprivation of "traditional college-age" Americans.

Finally, there was a subtle, challenging shift in student attitudes. Not all Americans prospered in the "Reagan prosperity" of the 1980s, but few were left untouched. The pervasive media and advertising emphasis on luxury, combined with a genuine augmentation of resources for many people, helped produce a "revolution of rising expectations" regarding university facilities among members of the "greed" generation, (sometimes unwitting) heirs of the Reagan legacy, and on the part of their children, accustomed to more affluent accommodation arrangements at home and at school. What had been good enough for their parents had become completely unacceptable to them. They demanded dormitories, student unions, lush campuses—and (by the way) comfortable classrooms. For a traditional "commuter" school, with a "workingman's" ethnic (and a matching decor), this quantum shift in expectations posed a perplexing problem. Economical was out.

President Daniel Perlman saw many . . . challenges, and their implications, with a clarity and vividness of vision which those around him often lacked.

New President Daniel Perlman saw many of these challenges, and their implications, with a clarity and vividness of vision which those around him often lacked. He took the role of Cassandra and embarked the University on a course of adaptation to and preparation for the coming changes that was sometimes controversial, and frequently unpopular with the Trustees. Perlman believed that major development of the University was necessary to make it viable. He called for new services, new facilities, the exploration of new markets, the wooing of new populations/constituencies, and above all for a major restructuring of the institution's finances and its Board, to permit the raising of the substantial endowment and capital funds that Perlman believed were necessary to keep the University afloat through the approaching exigencies. Such investments were far more than traditional Suffolk University Boards had been willing to contemplate, or than traditional Suffolk Trustees (mostly local, self-employed lawyers, judges, and small businessmen) were able to make.

Given these preoccupations, President Perlman embarked on a controversial campaign to change important historic realities of the University. Traditionally, the institution had eschewed government funding. To develop what he regarded as essential services, Perlman initiated application work for a federal Title III (Higher Education Act of 1965) grant without prior authorization from the Trustees. Partly using the resulting grant monies, he added support services, encouraged recruitment of new populations, flirted with internationalization, and introduced professional personnel and a professional system to a traditionally "lean" and flexible administration. His diversity initiatives, provoked by criticisms from the New England Association of Schools and Colleges (NEASC, the University's principal accreditation agency) and ramrodded by a newly-established Director of Minority Affairs—were not always popular with traditional Suffolk University community members and constituents, nor with some Trustees.

As President, Daniel H. Perlman challenged the historic preeminence of the Law School and the Trustees in University affairs. The "Perlman model" of institutional administration was, in fact, a fairly "traditional" one (though not at Suffolk), calling for an integrated University structure, with the College of Liberal Arts and Sciences as the intellectual center and for "unitary," centralized University governance. From this strong central administrative leadership, Perlman believed, there would result balanced development of institutional resources based on priorities established for the entire University by (his) "University" administration.

In this theoretical context, Perlman may fairly be characterized as a "uniformitarian," expecting joint strategic planning by a comprehensive all-University Long Range Planning Committee, and tactical coordination by an Administrative Council (where the institution's president, deans and vice-presidents regularly met to discuss policy and logistics), to produce relatively smooth and predictable modifications in the University's priorities and development. (Both the Administrative Council and the Long Range Planning Committee were, in fact, established by Perlman in 1981. On the latter, his principal collaborator was CLAS Associate Dean Joseph H. Strain, who was just completing his fourth decade of service to Suffolk University.)

Throughout his term in office, President Perlman consistently pressed for new buildings, new fund-raising campaigns, and substantial increases in Suffolk University-funded financial aid. On its side, the fiscally more conservative Board of Trustees generally inclined to satisfaction with the temporary triumphs and successes of the status quo. Perlman's tireless advocacy for his "causes" made enemies among traditionalists and others on the faculty, the administration, and the Board.

Whatever other crises the new President was fated to face during his tenure at Suffolk, his immediate challenge was an eminently practical one: With small spikes, CLAS and SOM enrollment decreased steadily from 1980 until 1988, principally because of a radical decline, a "precipitous drop," in the size of the college-age cohort (18-24 year-olds) in Massachusetts that was projected to continue throughout the decade 1983-93. From the largest freshman class in Suffolk history (613) in September 1982, freshman enrollments fell to 445 in September 1987. The decline began with a 22% drop in freshman applications from 1982-83 to 1983-84, and impacted the CLAS first. In the SOM, in turn, freshman admissions fell 40% (1983-88) and undergraduate enrollment decreased 31% (1984-88). The situation wasn't helped when, predictably, what had been the largest freshman class in Suffolk University history became its largest graduating class in 1986.

Dean Robert S. Lay

Such figures—and the population trends that threatened their long-term continuation—constituted critical issues for Suffolk University because of its abiding tuition-dependence. To address those issues, President Perlman pressed Institutional Advancement V-P Joseph Kelley for increases in alumni and corporate/foundation annual giving; importuned the Board of Trustees with urgent admonitions for another capital campaign (to offset operating costs, to improve facilities, to improve faculty salaries and support, to build endowment, and to decrease tuition dependence); and hired Robert S. Lay as Dean of Enrollment Management in March 1985 to confront the inescapable enrollment/tuition dependence issue and to formulate responses to "control" the problem of plummeting cohort numbers.

Although Dean Lay's "enrollment management" strategy (like much that President Perlman proposed) was new to Suffolk University, it consisted (like many of Perlman's proposals) of measures that most education professionals would have characterized as relatively conservative: internal institutional "restructuring," combined with careful analysis of the historical "patterns" of the University's traditional "prime" markets and of the reasons for the declining number of students Suffolk was attracting from them. Like the new President, who in 1982 established the University's first Office of Institutional Research, Dean Lay had profound faith in the importance and efficacy of data-gathering and analysis. Upon assuming office in 1985, Dean Lay (who had been Director of Enrollment Research at Boston College before being hired by Suffolk) established his own Director of Enrollment Research as part of his newly-created Division of Enrollment Management. His research dictated his tactics for "managing" enrollment shortfall: raise tuition, increase recruitment funds and financial aid to maintain "market share" in the University's decreasing "traditional" admissions pool, and retain a higher percentage of those students once they enrolled.

Despite the fact that the University's investment of its own funds into student aid had increased from $600,000 to $1.1 million since 1980, Lay argued, only 9% of tuition revenues in CLAS and SOM were committed to the financial aid budget; at comparable institutions, it was over 20%. To be competitive, in Lay's view, with the independent (private) colleges and universities that were its primary rivals for students, Suffolk had to increase institutional spending on need- and merit-based scholarships to that level. To achieve competitive status quickly, Lay recommended a 25% per year increase in the student aid budget for each of the next five years. Similarly, Suffolk needed to increase its budget for recruiting, on which, according to national studies, the University was spending only one-half to one-third the amount per incoming student that comparable institutions were investing. To fund these increases, Lay recommended that the University raise tuition 10% per year, "grandfathering" current students. Since Suffolk's tuition was "by a large margin the lowest of any independent university in Massachusetts" and, even with a 10% tuition increase, "lower than any independent university in the Commonwealth and approximately 30% below the average tuition of all the independent colleges and universities in Massachusetts," such tuition rises appeared well within the bounds of fairness and of prudence.[6]

The Frank Sawyer Building, at 8 Ashburton Place (1995)

Combined with facilities improvements, both Dean Lay and President Perlman argued, such a "scholarship strategy" could restore the "yield" percentage (which had dropped from 48% in 1985 to 41% in 1987) and numbers from traditional Suffolk sending constituencies. Such "irredentist" gains could then be consolidated, in the Perlman/Lay master plan, through an aggressive, comprehensive student retention program.

The institution responded smartly to the new leadership's initiatives. With the exception of the Fulham Merit Scholarships (established in 1980), all Suffolk University scholarships had been need-based since November 1977. In the year before Dean Lay's arrival, there had been a 16% increase in University scholarship funds (which, when combined with a decline of 4% in federal aid and an increase of 43% in state funds, represented a total overall increase in scholarship funds of approximately 6%). Beginning in 1985 the Trustees, under Lay's influence, expanded the outlay of University funds for financial aid (to support the financially needy as well as the academically meritorious) by 11% for 1986-87, then by 35% for 1987-88 (including new Trustee Loan/Grant and Minority Student

Scholarship programs), and by 23% for 1988-89. From 1986 on, the Dean of Enrollment Management also concentrated on ways to improve retention, presiding during the next two years over the expansion of the Cooperative Education program (98% retention) to 400 students and the introduction of a Continuing Orientation program, a Reading and Writing Laboratory, and a Math Help program.

Employing Suffolk's first TV advertising campaign in 1987 and the first experiments with a "modest residential component" (two small townhouse dormitories) at Lasell Junior College in 1988, the Lay/Perlman strategy had succeeded by the time of Lay's departure in June 1988 at least in slowing the rate of student loss. In the fall of 1988, the number of entering students actually rose, driven primarily by an increase of 20% (52% for CLAS) in transfer student enrollments that offset, at least for the moment, a discouraging drop of 5% in freshmen that confirmed long-term trend predictions. By 1988, undergraduates constituted 55% of total enrollment (compared to 45-50% a decade earlier), an increase comparable to that for full-time students over the same period. In the School of Management, graduate enrollments grew after 1986, partially offsetting persistent freshman declines and generating 40-42% of the SOM revenues.

President Perlman

As competition grew for the shrinking "college-age" cohort pool in the 1980s, Perlman and Lay stressed the need not only for more financial aid, but also for more support services and better facilities. These, they asserted, were required to address the demands of new student groups, but also to attract and retain higher percentages of traditional groups with rising expectations, in what was (from the students' point of view) a buyer's market.[7]

By the mid-1980s, not even the most sanguine at the University could ignore the changes in the surrounding environment and potential student population. Although tension continued to exist between the President and the Board, many came to acknowledge the validity of President Perlman's concerns, and to accept the wisdom and vision of his remedies.

The Perlman Administration Following completion of the "Campaign for Excellence" and occupation in the fall of 1981 of the Sawyer Building which it funded, the new President proceeded immediately with initiation of activities funded by the federal Title III grant that he had successfully obtained, with the appointment of Joseph M. Kelley as Director of Development (soon to be

Vice-President for Institutional Advancement in July 1982), and with obtaining Board authorization (granted in November 1982) to pursue development of a new "University Center" building on the site of the old Ridgeway Building at 148 Cambridge Street.

President Perlman was concerned about the well-being of students needful or desirous of expanded opportunities for academic preparation.[8] To expand, extend, and make more convenient for students the provision of such opportunities at Suffolk University, he initiated, in one of the earliest acts of his Presidency, preparation of an application for a U.S. Department of Education grant under Title III ("Strengthening Developing Institutions") of the Higher Education Act of 1965. Beginning in 1982, Suffolk University was awarded a grant totalling approximately $2 million over a four-year period (1982-86).[9]

The Geno A. Ballotti Learning Center

The Title III grant was an important seminal influence in several areas. It certainly gave initial impetus, mainly through course reductions and travel funds, to the School of Management's International Business course/exchange endeavors, which came to true fruition only in the early 1990s; and to the College's Integrated Studies freshman core course, which resided still in 1995 at the heart of the all-College curriculum, and its related faculty planning/background seminar. More directly, the Title III grant was clearly the point of origin for the College's Computer Engineering and Electrical Engineering programs, which, in the hands of Physics and Engineering Department Chair Walter Johnson, remained one of the College's most rapidly developing curriculum areas in 1995. Most important, the grant gave rise to the University's Learning Resource Center, which in subsequent years has affected so many students' lives. Established in November 1982 under the direction of Kevin M. Lyons, the Learning Center was absorbed for Suffolk University funding at the conclusion of the Title III grant in 1985. Almost immediately, under the Directorship of Susan Clark Thayer (who replaced Lyons in 1984), it received a $100,000 three-to-one challenge grant from the Boston Foundation in September 1985, which required that Suffolk University raise $300,000 to be added to the challenge grant in an endowment fund for the Center. Upon successful completion of the challenge, the Learning Resource Center was renamed the Geno A. Ballotti Learning Center, in memory of the late director of the Boston Foundation, and formally dedicated on October 19, 1988. Since that time, the Ballotti Learning Center has continuously provided exemplary academic support services in collaboration with the Mathematics Department's Math Support Center (established in 1986, shortly after introduction in 1985 of the mandatory all-College Basic Math Exam), the Continuing Orientation program (1987), the Dean of Students' office (established in 1966, but significantly strengthened in 1987), and the English Department's Remedial/Developmental Reading and Writing Program (1975).

In addition to the Title III grant, and also of considerable significance for the consolidation of educational support services at Suffolk, the University received during academic year 1982-83 a five-year federal grant of $234,000 to expand the Cooperative Education Program (which had originated in 1980 in the School of Management) and to extend its scope to include the College of Liberal Arts and Sciences. In the grant's first year, with Cooperative Education open for the first time (1983) to CLAS participants, there were more jobs than students to fill them; but by 1986, following a sensible and synergistic consolidation of the Coop and Career Planning/Placement offices in October 1985, there were over 400 SOM and CLAS students active in Cooperative Education. Most impressively, the Coop program retained 98% of its participants at Suffolk University.

Newly constructed Ridgeway Building at 148 Cambridge Street (1991)

In February 1986, within months of their merger, the Career Planning/Placement and Cooperative Education offices (now styled the Office of Career Services and Cooperative Education) moved to new quarters on the ground floor of the Massachusetts Teachers Association (MTA) Building at 20 Ashburton Place. It was rental space, however: the MTA Building was not for sale. Nonetheless, the problem of space, especially for student activities and student services, was once again becoming critical for the University, both internally and for its marketing/student recruitment credibility. President Perlman, whose portfolio at Roosevelt University had been for physical plant operations/development as well as administrative supervision, now undertook to address this problem directly.

Noting the "almost total" lack of athletic facilities, and recommendations from the 1982 NEASC accreditation team, the Board of Trustees voted in November 1982—only six months after the dedication of the new Sawyer Building—once again to authorize the administration to explore the feasibility of plans to replace the decaying Ridgeway Building at 148 Cambridge Street.[10] Four months later, with "the problem of available space at Suffolk University critical," the Trustees reviewed Beacon Hill architect

James McNeely's plan for development of the Ridgeway site and decided to seek city approval for a more adequate and attractive student center there—a decision that new President Daniel Perlman characterized as "critical to the future development of the University."[11] From 1983 on, President Perlman made the "University Center" project his touchstone, emphasizing the proposed facility's importance in enhancing the University's competitive position and working tirelessly to eradicate skepticism about it among Trustees, students, and Beacon Hill neighbors.

In June 1984, the Beacon Hill Civic Association's Board of Directors voted, 13-5, to rescind its opposition to new Ridgeway Building; and in February 1985 there followed a landmark settlement with the University. There still remained the problem of the immediate abutters; but when in 1986 an ingenious "linkage" arrangement was crafted for transfer of Student Activities (the abutters' bete noir) from Ridgeway to 28 Derne Street (plans for rehabilitation of which stood dead in the water), community opposition to both University development projects evaporated. Beacon Hill Architect James McNeely won general approbation with an inventive four-story, deep-basement Ridgeway design that presented the facade of two townhouses and completely concealed a full-sized gymnasium, and with a subtle plan for 28 Derne providing unobtrusive expansion and connection to the adjacent Fenton Building. By April 1987, formal accommodation had been made with the abutters.

The Ridgeway Gymnasium proudly displays the Suffolk school mascot—the Ram

Construction on the new Student Center at 28 Derne Street began in June 1988, and groundbreaking on the new Ridgeway Building took place a little more than a year later, in August 1989. By that time, both buildings were part of a comprehensive Facilities Development Project worthy of that which accompanied the renovation of the Sawyer Building in 1981: The Archer, Donahue, and 56 Temple (Goldberg) Buildings were all slated for 1991 rehabilitation in response to Law School accreditation concerns. There were even plans for a capital campaign, "Building the Future," on the model of the 1979-82 "Campaign for Excellence." The University's first real Student Activities Center opened, with abundant fanfare, in September 1989; and on February 5, 1991, the new Gymnasium cunningly hidden in the diminutive Ridgeway Building provided the setting for the first true "home game" in 56 years of Suffolk athletic history. The Ridgeway Gym's debut provided the occasion for an outpouring of euphoria that even a 75-70 loss to UMass (Boston) could do little to dampen. Like the students in the Student

Activities Center on Derne Street, the Rams basketball team—which, unremarkably, had more than once in its history borne the sobriquet of "Ramblers"—finally had a place on Beacon Hill to call their own.

Another aspect of President Perlman's passion to upgrade student services, student facilities, and "public space" at Suffolk University concerned the University Auditorium. It was part of Perlman's centralist vision of a university that there should be common space, "common ground," where representatives of the institution's respective academic units could meet one another, and representatives of the University's various "publics," on the soil of shared experience. The University's aging and dilapidated Auditorium was, from Perlman's point of view, a potentially vital forum for this interaction. His vision of the College as the legitimate "heartland" of the University, and of dramatic arts and the theatre as crucial constituents of the College's core, and of the Auditorium as a vital gateway for interaction between the University and the community, also strengthened the President's resolve that the long-neglected Suffolk University Theatre should be transformed into a very special space to address some very special possibilities.

Scene from the Suffolk Student Theatre production of The Threepenny Opera

Underwritten by a naming gift of $400,000 from Trustee Thomas Walsh, complete rehabilitation of the Suffolk Theatre took place during 1987. The first performance in the remodeled Auditorium at 55 Temple Street took place on February 1, 1988, and on April 30 the 600-seat facility underwent formal dedication as the C. Walsh Theatre at Suffolk University and the Anne Walsh Theatre Foyer.[12] On that occasion, President Daniel Perlman made perhaps his most eloquent characterization, describing the new C. Walsh Theatre as "our agora, the geographic and cultural center of the campus." In subsequent years, the refurbished Theatre provided the University with an outstanding facility where popular theatrical and cultural programs could be offered for the benefit and enjoyment of students, faculty, and the public at large; and which consistently provided Suffolk University with positive public relations.

Perhaps the two greatest beneficiaries of the C. Walsh Theatre renovation were the College's Theatre and Music programs. In 1978, the Suffolk University Theatre was established, with a full-time director who also served as a CLAS faculty member in the newly-reconstituted Department of Communications and Speech. To increase student participation in dramatic arts and in the Theatre, an interdepartmental Dramatic Arts major was approved in

April 1980. Since 1982, Marilyn J. Plotkins has served as Director of the Suffolk University Theatre; with the renovated C. Walsh facilities at her disposal, she has brought to Beacon Hill a truly bold and memorable combination of student and professional productions of every conceivable description. During her time at the University, Dr. Plotkins has won acclamation for her annual direction of student productions and admiration from those who have benefitted from the catholicity of taste with which she selects works to be presented in the C. Walsh Theatre. Beginning in 1988, the Board of Trustees also undertook to fund the hiring by the College's Humanities Department of a full-time music teacher whose principal responsibility it was to use the resources of the C. Walsh Theatre to attract to Suffolk University more musicians, more musical performers and programs, more people interested in music (especially Beacon Hill neighbors), and more affiliations with Boston-area music schools and musical institutions.

Under the Perlman administration, Suffolk University also adopted policies and established programs to end a tradition of "benign neglect" toward affirmative action issues. Between 1982 and 1989, Suffolk University made strides in increasing AHANA (African-American, Hispanic, Asian, and Native American) presence among its students and in strengthening its support for them. The University pledged resources to establish a centralized office to represent AHANA student interests and address their concerns. Increased financial aid and tailored academic outreach programs were among the other concrete steps which Suffolk took to attract and retain a "critical mass" of AHANA students. There was, by the end of the Perlman era, undeniably a heightened awareness of and sensitivity to the experiences and needs of people of color at Suffolk, which was attributable in part to co-curricular activities which reflected diverse cultures.

In response to the 1982 NEASC visiting team's observation (October 1982) that Suffolk University appeared to lack a clear commitment to affirmative action, President Perlman promptly announced (November 1982) that he had asked Trustees Dorothy A. Antonelli and Thomas J. Brown to co-chair a University-wide task force to address the issue; Task Force members represented all areas of the University. The charge of the Task Force was to address the affirmative action concerns noted in the NEASC report and to make specific recommendations relative to these issues.

In April 1983, the Affirmative Action Task Force recommended authorization of a new position of Assistant to the President and Director of Minority Affairs, with the purpose of increasing the number of AHANA students, faculty, and administrators at Suffolk University and of addressing all issues related to AHANA students and AHANA and women on the faculty and in the administration. In this capacity, the new Director superseded the efforts of part-time student Minority Student Advisors who had been appointed on a yearly basis since 1972. In September 1983, President Perlman appointed Carolyne Lamar Jordan, Associate Professor of Psychology and Music at Salem State College, to the new Director's position. Five years later, Dr. Sharon Artis from the staff of the Massachusetts Board of Regents, having replaced Dr. Jordan temporarily in 1986, succeeded her as Assistant to the President and Director of Multicultural Affairs.[13]

The ethnic and racial climate at Suffolk University improved substantially between 1983 and 1989. First, the numbers of American students of color and international students increased. Second, efforts were initiated to revise the undergraduate curriculum so that it was more reflective of cultural pluralism in U.S. and world society. Further, Suffolk sponsored several annual events in celebration of cultural difference and inter-cultural unity. These social events supplemented seminars, workshops, and other educational programs which provided forums for discussions on diversity. The Society Organized Against Racism, chartered at Suffolk in 1986, also sponsored programs on and off campus.[14]

The ethnic and racial climate at Suffolk University improved substantially between 1983 and 1989. First, the numbers of American students of color and international students increased. Second, efforts were initiated to revise the undergraduate curriculum so that it was more reflective of cultural pluralism in U.S. and world society.

The Collection of Afro-American Literature at Suffolk University was established in 1971, expanded in 1982, and rededicated with much fanfare in 1987 in connection with the reopening of the Museum of Afro-American History, with which the University had been affiliated since 1972. The Collection, comprising more than 3,000 titles, was permanently housed in the University's Mildred F. Sawyer Library, under joint custodianship with the Museum of Afro-American History and the National Park Service.

The Collection also regularly sponsored a speaker series funded through the College. A number of well-known scholars of African-American literature, black savants and artists, including Amiri Baraka, Ishmael Reed, and Derek Walcott, visited the University under these auspices. The audience at these presentations was frequently drawn not only from the University, but also from the greater Boston community.[15]

Financial and academic support for AHANA students increased as well. Introduced in 1987, the Maria Stewart Scholarships were doubled in amount in 1989, to renewable awards of $5,000 each for ten incoming freshman or transfer students of color per year. The Ballotti Learning Center's AHANA Peer Liaison program, which provided telephone and personal outreach to all incoming students of color, expanded steadily from its inception in 1987.

By 1989, African-American, Hispanic, Asian, and Native American (or AHANA) students at the University constituted 8.3% of the total. By comparison, American students of color comprised 6.3% of the total University enrollment in 1987 and 4% in 1982. In fall 1989, AHANA students in the Law School represented 5.9% of the total enrollment, compared to 4.6% in 1987 and 4.3% in 1982. In the College of Liberal Arts and Sciences and the School of Management, 10.8% of all students and 11% of undergraduate students enrolled in fall 1989 were AHANA. By contrast, AHANA student enrollment in these schools for fall 1987 and fall 1982 were 6.7% and 3.6% respectively. Note that the CLAS and SOM figures are conservative estimates, since students of color frequently omitted data about ethnicity from their admissions applications. International students comprised 4.5% of the total University enrollment in fall 1989.

As for Suffolk employees, the greatest diversity was found in the support staff, which by 1991 included about 22% AHANA members and 75% women. Diversity in faculty and administrative positions presented a challenge, however. In 1989, about 7% of all full-time faculty members were Americans of color. It is true that the proportion rose when adjunct and international faculty of color were counted, but the increase in AHANA faculty did not parallel that of students. Similarly, 7% of fall 1989 full-time administrators were AHANA.

Women were strongly represented in all employment categories. In fall 1990, the College of Liberal Arts and Sciences continued to employ the highest proportion of women faculty (34%), followed by the Law School (16%) and the School of Management (15%). Overall, women represented 24% of Suffolk's full-time faculty in 1990. The majority of full-time administrators were women, a pattern which had continued for several years. The proportion of women administrators grew from 52% in fall 1982, to 56% in fall 1987, to 62% in fall 1990.

From 1988 on, the Women's Studies Committee (established in 1984) oversaw and administered not only the Women's Studies

Minor (also established in 1984) that was its primary responsibility, but also the great bulk of activities related to women on campus. The chairperson of the Women's Studies Committee also played a significant role in shaping the University's Revised Policy Opposing Harassment (1991) and its associated Student Grievance Procedure. In 1982, the Suffolk University Women's Center established the Phyllis Mack Prize (in honor of Ms. Mack, who taught at the University for 18 years, retiring in June 1983), an annual award for the best undergraduate research paper in the field of Women's Studies. The Women's Center thereby continued to encourage the kind of work pioneered by the Faculty Colloquium for Research on Women from 1975 until the early 1980s. The Women's Studies Committee and the Women's Center also took over the responsibilities which, for thirty years after 1947, had been borne by a part-time faculty Advisor to Women.

Suffolk University established a free tuition policy for senior citizens in 1973. Beginning in 1978, the University also attached a senior citizen alumnus/alumna of the program to the Dean of Students' Office as Senior Citizen Program Advisor.[16]

In addition to his initiatives to redress the University's paucity of student services/facilities, and of certain classes of students, President Perlman also undertook widespread structural reorganization of the institution's constellations of administrative supervisory responsibility.

In addition to his initiatives to redress the University's paucity of student services/facilities, and of certain classes of students, President Perlman also undertook widespread structural reorganization of the institution's constellations of administrative supervisory responsibility.

Perlman began this enterprise with a restructuring of the University Development Office in 1982. Joseph M. Kelley, former Development Director at Boston College and "field general" (in a consulting capacity) of the extremely successful capital Campaign for Excellence (1979-82) was appointed to a newly-created Vice-Presidency for Institutional Advancement (November 1982). Over the next several years, the Division of Institutional Advancement was significantly expanded (as seemed eminently practical for a University audaciously reliant on tuition income) and the provinces of its satraps were redrawn and redistributed.

Next, the Admissions Office was reorganized in 1984 on a plan proposed by Dr. John Maguire, former Dean of Admissions at Boston College and a leading consultant on enrollment management. The new Office (later Division) of Enrollment Management brought within the gravitational well of a single coordinating authority what had previously been the semi-autonomous jurisdictions of the offices of Admissions (redesignated as Undergraduate

Admissions), Financial Aid, and the Registrar—and added that of a newly-created Graduate Admissions Office. In March 1985, Robert S. Lay, former Director of Enrollment Research at Boston College, was appointed to the new Deanship of Enrollment Management.

The third major administrative reorganization undertaken by President Perlman was a kind of Copernican Revolution in which he took the Dean of Students' Office (which, from the time of its creation in 1966 had become steadily more peripheral) and placed it at the center of a new solar system comprising the formerly autonomous (and disparate) responsibilities of Athletics, Campus Ministry, Career Services and Cooperative Education, Health Services, the International Student Advisor, Student Activities, and the Women's Program Center. To head (and identify a rationale for) this new Division of Student Services, Nancy Cadle Stoll from the New England Association of Schools and Colleges (and also previously associate dean of students at Brandeis University and Simmons College), was appointed Dean of Student Services in September 1987. In the years that followed, Dean Stoll spun straw into gold, so that these tattered, scattered fragments might be stitched together into a viable fabric.

Dean Nancy C. Stoll

Nancy Stoll added an Associate Dean (Elliot Gabriel, Director of Career Services and Cooperative Education) in October 1988 and an Assistant Dean (Harvard-trained Zegenu Tsige) in July 1990. In August 1988, she also appointed Donna L. Schmidt, who by 1995 had become one of the longest-serving Directors of Student Activities since the position became full-time in 1968. (Prof. John Colburn served sixteen years in a part-time capacity, 1952-68.) Under Ms. Schmidt's direction, the Student Activities Office—with its related student "umbrella" organizations (Student Government Association, Council of Presidents, Program Council)—became one of the most effective, and least acknowledged, promoters on campus of multiculturalism and student retention.

In addition, President Perlman collaborated with long-time University benefits consultant Judy Minardi in reorganizing the Personnel Office before she assumed the new Directorship of Human Resources in 1989. He worked closely with Director Christine A. Perry (appointed in February 1983) in giving the Financial Aid Office (separated from the functions of the Director of Student Activities only in 1977) its developed, definitive form. The President also played a similar role in supporting steps by new Director Paul F. Ladd (appointed February 1978) to develop and modernize the Data Processing Office into Management Information Services (1985). Likewise, he assisted Instructional Materials Center (IMC) Director Marilyn A. Wilcke (appointed in October 1982 as successor to founding Director Donald F. Mikes, 1979-81) in transforming her office into University Media Services (1988). Finally, Perlman aided new Director Elliot Gabriel in accomplishing the consolidation (October 1985) of the Career Planning/Placement and Cooperative Education Offices into the Office of Career Services and Cooperative Education.

Not surprisingly, given his faith in the positive influence of energetic administrative supervision, the University's administration grew significantly in numbers during the Perlman era, from 89 full-time administrators in 1982 to 118 in 1989, or 33%.

Not surprisingly, given his faith in the positive influence of energetic administrative supervision, the University's administration grew significantly in numbers during the Perlman era, from 89 full-time administrators in 1982 to 118 in 1989, or 33%.

As we have seen, President Perlman's attention to planning, repair, and maintenance, at Roosevelt University and then at Suffolk, extended beyond administration into the sphere of physical plant. As new President in 1980, Perlman immediately began work with Trustees Building Committee Chair John Corcoran to arrange for a "Facilities Audit," an inventory of the University's physical plant and the repairs/improvements necessary and desirable for each of its components. By the fall of 1982, the Facilities Audit, described enthusiastically by Corcoran as "an invaluable management tool," was completed and in the process of being refined into a six-year renovation schedule.

The elimination of "deferred maintenance" was a principal concern for President Perlman, and his campaign struck a resonant chord with the Trustees. Between 1979 and 1984, Suffolk University spent an average of $1 million a year to refurbish its physical plant. And in 1985, so enthusiastic was the Board about the success of the "Facilities Audit" concept, the Trustees commissioned the President to undertake, on the model of the "Facilities Audit," an "Insurance Audit" and a "Legal (or Policy) Audit."

One subject on which President Perlman, the Trustees, and Law School Dean David Sargent rarely disagreed was the value to the University—Law School, College, and School of Management—of external validations that called the attention of (especially) the general public to the "value added" and the "competitive edge" conferred by a Suffolk University education. One form of such "validations" was external accreditations, especially those with broad national recognition. Very much an education "professional"—an individual who set great store by the deliberations of the educational profession's "professional societies"—President Perlman was, in general, as enthusiastic about the University's successful pursuit of national accreditations as were the Deans of the institution's two "professional schools": the Law School and the School of Management. The Law School was accredited by the American Bar Association (ABA) in 1953 and the more prestigious Association of American Law Schools (AALS) in 1977. Retention of those accreditations was perhaps the highest single priority for the Law School, its Dean, and the Trustees. The School of Management was approved by the National Association of Schools of Public Affairs and Administration (NASPAA) in 1980, and throughout the remainder of the decade that corresponded to the Perlman Presidency, the School's highest priority—like Dean McDowell's and Trustee SOM Committee Chair Thomas P. McDermott's—was satisfaction of the requirements for accreditation by the American Assembly of Collegiate Schools of Business (AACSB). While President Perlman in theory endorsed the centrality of the College and its values to the University experience, his preoccupation with high-prestige external accreditation "validations," of the sort unavailable to undergraduate institutions, frequently made him an unreliable champion for the CLAS.[17]

Under these circumstances, it is not surprising to find that the reality about the University's Law School under Dean Sargent's guidance was its subjugation to and preoccupation with fulfilling American Bar Association (ABA) and Association of American Law Schools (AALS) accreditation requirements and dictates. This was not atypical for professional schools, which depend, in general, heavily for their success upon their place in the accreditation hierarchies.[18] Consequently, much of what Suffolk University Law School did between Dean Sargent's accession in 1973 and 1989 was done primarily to respond to or fulfill accreditation prescriptions.

The principal accreditation concern during the Sargent Deanship was with numbers: with the number of students, with the number of faculty members, with the student-teacher ratio, with the number of volumes in the Law Library, and with the number of credit-hours required for graduation. From 1975 on, even while the other two academic units struggled for admissions during the 1980s, the standing order in the Law School remained to reduce enrollments. The cause was not far to seek: a steadfast ABA directive to reduce student-teacher ratios. By cutting enrollments from over 2000 in 1975-76 to around 1600 within four years, and by adding 25 full-time instructors within two years, the Trustees and the Dean promised to reduce a 99-1 student-teacher ratio to 35-1 (with the great bulk of ABA-accredited schools between 20-1 and 25-1). Even by 1983, the Law School's student-teacher ratio was characterized by an ABA/AALS visiting team as "only marginally in compliance," and a caution was issued to draw enrollments down. The Law Library's progress—from 60,000 volumes in 1972 to 160,000 a decade later—was more satisfactory for the 1983 visiting team; but there was concern expressed that the number of credit-hours required for graduation by evening students was less than for day students, Equalization of the requirement was, of course, promptly attended to (1989), and, shortly afterward, a new full clinical experience for Evening Division students (which had been lacking) was also incorporated (1994).

What clearly was not driven by accrediting agencies' canons between 1973 and 1989, and what was obviously an indigenous (and persistent) characteristic of the institution, was the faculty's conservatism about the core curriculum.

What clearly was not driven by accrediting agencies' canons between 1973 and 1989, and what was obviously an indigenous (and persistent) characteristic of the institution, was the faculty's conservatism about the core curriculum. While many other Law Schools were becoming significantly less directive about curriculum in the 1980s, Suffolk University Law School's faculty was almost unanimous in its endorsement (and, in this, was in complete agreement with the faculties of the other two academic units) of a demanding, sizable core curriculum.[19]

This structured "core" was to be supplemented, as in the other two academic units, by a steadily growing variety of elective courses and by opportunities for experiential learning in many "learning laboratories" around Suffolk. A stronger center and a wider circle: that is the formula that seems to encompass the "family similarities" between approaches to education and curriculum across academic boundaries at Suffolk between 1979 and 1989.

One other notable "indigenous" initiative to come out of the Law School during the 1980s was the Center for Continuing Professional Education (renamed in 1992 the Center for Advanced Legal Studies), which was founded in 1982 by Professor Charles Kindregan as a locus at Suffolk University for Continuing Legal Education (CLE). It was Kindregan's belief that CLE (institutes and in-service advanced training for attorneys) would steadily expand in scope and significance in the profession and, consequently, at the institution.[20]

By 1989, the Law School was attracting students from more than 500 colleges and universities throughout the US (up significantly from 387 in 1986). Shortly after David Sargent resigned the

Deanship to accept the University's Presidency, an ABA inspectors' report (1990) summed up how far, and how fast, Dean Sargent had transformed the Law School, in its offhand observation that Suffolk Law had become "a regional school operating on the periphery of national status."[21]

As the struggle for national accreditation, and its attendant preoccupations, were associated primarily with the Sargent Deanship in the Law School, so they were in the School of Management indissolubly identified with the person and the decanal regime of Richard L. McDowell. Dean McDowell's background was in Public Administration and, having come to Suffolk in 1973 as Director of the newly-founded Center for State Management, one of his first accomplishments was to establish Master of Public Administration (MPA) and BS in Public Administration programs, giving reality, for the first time, to Gleason Archer's vision of thirty years before that the CBA might one day become a "College of Business and Governmental Administration." As Dean, McDowell created a Management Education Center (a descendant of the Center for State Management and the immediate forbear of the current Center for Management Development) in 1977. He also initiated an enormously successful Saturday-only Executive MBA program (the first of its kind in New England at its establishment in 1978, and the largest in the nation by 1990) and a companion Executive MPA in 1981; and in 1980 launched a Computer Information Systems bachelor's program, the first computer-related degree program to be offered by the University. In addition, under McDowell's stewardship, the College of Business Administration (or the School of Management, as it was renamed at his suggestion) inaugurated a graduate track in health administration and, during the 1980s, assumed the intellectual leadership (though not yet, at that epoch, the practical one) in the University's initial exploration of internationalization that accompanied and complemented the Perlman regime's much-heralded initiatives toward multiculturalism after 1983.[22] But, from the time that he assumed the Deanship in 1974, it was with the quest for national accreditations that McDowell primarily associated his fate, and that of the CBA/SOM.

Throughout the period 1974-89 (corresponding almost exactly to McDowell's tenure as Dean), the School of Management dedicated its efforts to satisfaction of the external accreditation criteria imposed by the National Association of Schools of Public Affairs and Administration (NASPAA) and the American Assembly of

Collegiate Schools of Business (AACSB). In 1980, the School first received approval of its Public Management programs by NASPAA's Peer Review Committee. In 1986, NASPAA was recognized by the Council on Post-Secondary Accreditation (COPA) as the official accrediting body for MPA programs, and its peer-review process was classified by COPA as conferring "national accreditation." Three years later, the SOM's undergraduate and masters business programs attained AACSB national accreditation. At the end of the "Quest" in 1989, Suffolk University was one of only five schools in New England (two in Massachusetts) accredited by NASPAA; one of a few schools in the nation (and the only New England institution) to receive both AACSB and NASPAA accreditation; and probably the only university in the country whose JD/MPA program was accredited by both the AALS and NASPAA.

Having entered the Promised Land, however, Dean McDowell promptly left it for another: California. When he resigned in 1991 to assume the deanship of the School of Business at Chapman College in Orange, California, Richard McDowell had served as SOM Dean for nearly 17 years. During that time, he had had a revolutionary impact on the School, having provided (as the Trustees' resolution upon his departure from Suffolk University noted):

" . . . distinguished leadership in the total transformation of the School from a regional to nationally accredited center for managerial education serving both private business and public administration and adhering to the highest national standards of professional excellence in teaching and research. . . . The SOM under his wise guidance has grown from the smallest to the largest among the student enrollments at SU [thanks to his] creative blending of tradition and innovation in the academic program."

In the College of Liberal Arts and Sciences the situation was somewhat different, both internally and externally, than in the other two academic units. Unlike the Law School and the SOM, the College of Liberal Arts and Sciences had no single professional accreditation standard around which fixedly to focus its energies. This circumstance conferred on the College simultaneously its greatest advantage (flexibility and creative autonomy) and its greatest disadvantage (lack of overriding external imperatives to leverage University attention to its needs). Lacking this central motor to propel it forward, College development depended for its motive power instead on the oars wielded, more or less in coordination, by its various academic departments in their respective struggles for program quality.

Despite this critical difference from the Law School and the SOM in structural positioning, the College of Liberal Arts and Sciences retained throughout the period 1979-89 some striking similarities to the other two academic units in educational philosophy and implementation strategies. Like the Law School (and the SOM), it committed (1982)—and then recommitted (1994)—itself to a comprehensive "core curriculum" constituting almost half of a student's undergraduate experience, while at the same time steadily expanding both a student's freedom to take self-selected specialization and practicum courses, and the opportunities for him/her to do so.

Like the University's other academic units, the College remained centrally committed during the Perlman era (and that of his successor) to good teaching and good teachers. In an institution characterized by low student-teacher ratios (approximately 28-1 in both the Law School and the School of Management), the College maintained the lowest (approximately 20-1). Effective teaching preparation and on-going research activity were both given significant support, as the teaching load in the College was reduced from 4/4 to 4/3 (1984), and then to 3/3 (1989). In 1990, the annual number of sabbaticals available to CLAS faculty members was increased from five to seven. Over the same period, steps were also taken to improve faculty salaries in the College relative to those at comparable area institutions.

Like the University's other academic units, the College remained centrally committed during the Perlman era (and that of his successor) to good teaching and good teachers. In an institution characterized by low student-teacher ratios (approximately 28-1 in both the Law School and the School of Management), the College maintained the lowest (approximately 20-1).

Under the University's senior dean, Michael R. Ronayne, who assumed office in 1972, the extension of varied opportunities for self-defined development remained, and was emphasized, as a characteristic feature of the College. The Archer Fellows all-College honors program (inaugurated in 1987) encouraged students to define for themselves the academic "challenges" they would undertake to fulfill program requirements. A new freshman Integrated Studies course, at the heart of the 1982 and 1994 CLAS core curricula, attempted to orient students early to the particular opportunities and challenges of university education. The introduction of Cooperative Education to the College (1983) opened numerous development options, as did the multiplication of internships, international (1984) and otherwise. The InterFuture study-abroad program (1983) likewise offered multiple-country opportunities for student-designed research projects that went well beyond the limited options envisioned by the older SAFARI program (1971). With the introduction of double major and departmental minor programs, the CLAS attempted to indicate to students the multiplicity of options available to them in "classroom" studies as well.

During the Perlman era, several CLAS centers of dynamic activity emerged. The new Economics Department, separated from Government in 1983 and chaired by new arrival David G. Tuerck, introduced the first International Economics program in the greater Boston area (1984). The Communications and Speech Department, under new chair Edward J. Harris, achieved a series of successes in debate that placed the Suffolk team among the top five in the region; and, through newcomer Marilyn J. Plotkins' work with her Suffolk University Theatre and the new interdepartmental Dramatic Arts major (1980), gained plaudits for the institution comparable to those gleaned through forensics. The Physics Department, under new chair Walter H. Johnson, introduced new programs in Computer Engineering Systems Technology (1983) and Electronic Engineering Technology (1984). By 1988, these programs had become Computer Engineering and Electrical Engineering, respectively, and the Department that offered them became Physics and Engineering in 1989. The Physics and Engineering Department also offered a five-year (3-2) Engineering program in cooperation with Notre Dame (1982-86), Boston University (1983-94), and Case Western Reserve University (1983-). In the Mathematics Department, Chair Paul Ezust and Dr. Eric Myrvaagnes had been detailed since 1976 to analyze the College's computer needs, but progress toward a department-centered program was slow. In April 1979, "computer science" tracks were established within the Biology, Chemistry, Physics, and Mathematics majors, and in June 1979 a CLAS Physical and Computer Science Applications Certificate Program was introduced. It was not until 1981, however, that a Computer Science major was approved in the College. At that time, the Math Department was renamed the Department of Mathematics and Computer Science, and Myrvaagnes was appointed as CLAS Director of Academic Computing.[23]

To help communicate the quality of Suffolk University to its various "publics," the University inaugurated two new annual public lecture series during the Perlman administration. The initial presentation in the first year of the Lowell Lecture Series at Suffolk University, sponsored by the Lowell Institute, took place on December 8, 1982. The Dwight L. Allison International Lecture Series was established in 1986 in memory of Dwight L. Allison, noted trial practitioner and 1922 graduate of Suffolk Law School, under a grant from the Dwight L. and Stella Allison Fund administered by the Boston Foundation (Dwight L. Allison, Jr., President). The first lecture in the Allison Series took place on April 23, 1986. These two series added to and complemented a third Suffolk University-sponsored public lecture series: the Frank J. Donahue Lecture Series, first offered in 1979 and sponsored by the *Law Review*.[24]

To advertise, attract, retain, and recognize the excellence about which President Perlman was so enthusiastic, several "merit-focused" initiatives were taken under his regime. In 1987, an Archer Fellows all-College honors program was established in the College of Liberal Arts and Sciences. Within three years, participants in this program were receiving merit scholarships funded by the University. This was part of a movement during the Perlman administration to "adjust" the University's financial aid policy, which since 1977 had stipulated that all scholarships be based on financial need, to make room for at least some merit-based scholarship programs (on the model of the Fulham Merit Scholarships introduced in 1980). One of Perlman's leading Trustee supporters on this matter was John Corcoran, who advocated repeatedly with the Board in favor of fund-raising for merit scholarships, convinced his Trustee colleagues to set aside matching money for merit scholarship donations, and personally donated funds to establish a Corcoran Merit Scholarship program.[25]

The Perlman Record The changes during President Perlman's nine years in office were impressive. Suffolk University's operating budget, which had been $14 million in 1980 (and $1.5 million in 1964), had grown by 1989 to $38.7 million—an increase of 176%. Plant assets had grown from $13.4 million in 1980 (and $1.8 million in 1964) to $40 million in 1989—a 199% expansion. Likewise, the institution's Endowment grew from $7.6 million in 1980 (and $245,000 in 1964) to $16.4 million—a rise of 116%.

In nine years, the total financial aid offered to Suffolk University students had risen from $12.9 million to $20.7 million, or 60%; and, more significantly, institutional (Suffolk University) funds invested in financial aid had grown from $665,000 in 1981 (and $8,500 in 1964) to $2.8 million in 1989—an increase of 321%.

Under President Perlman's administration, total University enrollment fell from 6,198 (4,728 full-time equivalent, or FTE, students) in 1981 to 5,551 (4,395 FTE) in 1989, a headcount decrease of 10% and an FTE decrease of 7%. In the College of Liberal Arts and Sciences, overall enrollment fell from 1,854 (1,491 FTE) in 1981 to 1,717 (1,452 FTE) in 1989—a headcount decline of 7% and an FTE drop of 2.6%. Over the same period, CLAS undergraduate enrollments dropped by only 30 students (from 1,682 to 1,652); but graduate enrollments fell by 64%, from 182 to 65. In the School of Management, total headcount enrollments fell from 2,673 to 2,177 (a 19% decline) and total FTE enrollments dropped by 16%, from 1,748 to 1,460. School of Management undergraduates decreased from 1,585 to 1,235 (22%), while SOM graduate enrollments fell from 1,088 to 942 (13%). Throughout the Perlman era, the MBA program retained by far the SOM's largest graduate enrollment, with 771 students in 1981 and 739 nine years later (a decrease of only 4% over the course of a difficult decade). Between 1981 and 1989, Law School enrollments held up better than those in the two other academic units. Over that period, the number of students enrolled in the Law School decreased, much more as a matter of policy than was the case in CLAS or SOM, from 1,673 (1,489 FTE) to 1,657 (1,483 FTE), a headcount decline of under 1%. In 1981, 43.2% of the University's total credit hours had been offered in the College, 24.5% in the School of Management, and 32.3% in the Law School. A decade later, the distribution was College 44%, SOM 20.9%, and Law 35%. Overall, the percentage of part-time and evening students in the University dropped from 46% to 43% between 1981 and 1989—in the College, from 34% to 29%; in the School of Management, from 61% to 57%; and in the Law School, from 44% to 42%.

Not surprisingly, given the demographic changes underway during the 1980s, the Perlman era saw the beginning of some significant changes in the University's student population. First, by 1990 women for the first time constituted a majority of Suffolk students. Women made up 47% of enrollments (47% FT, 47% PT) in 1981; nine years later, 52% of all students were female (52% FT, 51% PT). Combined enrollment in the College and the School of Management in 1981 was 50% female (53% among undergraduates, 39% among graduate students); but this combined figure masked a considerable disparity between the two academic units. In the College, women in 1981 constituted some 60% of total enrollment, over 55% of undergraduates, and around 70% of graduate students. In the SOM, however, the percentage of women was closer to 40%—

slightly over for undergraduates, slightly under for graduate students. By 1990, the combined CLAS/SOM enrollment was 53% female (54% among undergraduates, 48% among graduates). College enrollments were 61% female (60% among undergraduates, 77% among graduate students), while SOM enrollments were 47% female (49% among undergraduates, 45% among graduate students). In the Law School, 40% of students in 1981 were women (43% in the Day Division, 36% in the Evening Division). By 1990, Law School enrollments were 49% female (51% in the Day Division, 46% in the Evening Division). Clearly, by 1990, Suffolk University was definitely no longer simply "A Man's School," as founder Gleason Archer described it in 1925.[26]

Not surprisingly, given the demographic changes underway during the 1980s, the Perlman era saw the beginning of some significant changes in the University's student population.

Enrollments of AHANA (African-American, Hispanic, Asian, and Native American) and international students also grew steadily, if slowly, during the Perlman era. In 1981, overall Suffolk University enrollments were 4% AHANA (3.4% CLAS, 4.7% SOM, 4.3% Law). By 1989, the overall University AHANA enrollment had risen to 8.3% (10.8% CLAS, 7.8% SOM, 5.9% Law). In 1984, international students made up 2.3% of the overall University enrollment (3.5% CLAS, 2.9% SOM, 0% Law). In 1989, overall international student enrollment had grown, very slightly, to 3% (3.1% CLAS, 4.5% SOM, 1.1% Law). Combined CLAS/SOM AHANA and international student enrollment in 1984 was 7.4%; by 1989, it had grown to 13%.

Suffolk's principal undergraduate feeder schools remained substantially unchanged throughout the Perlman administration. These were concentrated in Boston, the inner suburbs, and northern South Shore communities. Among the top ten feeder schools from 1978 through 1989 were Revere, Medford, Somerville, Boston College High School, Boston Latin, North Quincy, Malden Catholic, Catholic Memorial, and Pope John XXIII. A smaller, but regular contribution of undergraduate students also came, between 1981 and 1991, from high schools in communities situated further from Boston, notably Arlington, Weymouth, Milton, Melrose, and Saugus. Principal suppliers of undergraduate transfer students during the Perlman era were Bunker Hill Community College, Northeastern University, Quincy Junior College, Massachusetts Bay Community College, Massasoit Community College, UMass (Boston), North Shore Community College, and Newbury Junior College. After 1985, Roxbury Community College also became a prominent feeder institution. For the Law School, major contributors of students during the

1980s were Boston College, Boston University, UMass (Amherst), Suffolk University, Harvard, Middlebury, Brandeis, and Tufts.

Enrollment declines and population changes were met not with cutbacks, but rather with efforts to strengthen and improve the University's faculty and staff, and to make them more compatible with new and expanding student ethnic, racial, and cultural groups. The University's central emphasis on good teaching and low student-teacher ratios was maintained, as demonstrated by the institution's willingness to increase the size (and quality) of its faculties at a time of declining student enrollments. By 1990, the CLAS faculty had grown to 112 full-time and 102 part-time members (compared to 107 and 92, respectively, in 1980); the SOM faculty had expanded to 55 full-timers and 30 part-timers (compared to 33 and 61, respectively, in 1980); and the Law School faculty had increased to 58 full-time and 81 part-time members (compared to 48 and 58, respectively, in 1980). As faculty numbers increased and student numbers declined, student-teacher ratios improved, and average class sizes dropped. By 1991, the average class size in the College was 20; in the School of Management, 29; and in the Law School, approximately 30. What had been a young University faculty in 1981 had by 1991 become a seasoned faculty of veteran teachers: 51% of the CLAS faculty was tenured in 1991, compared to 43% a decade earlier: 40% was tenured in the SOM, compared to 8%; and 73% in the Law School, compared to 7%.

The credentials of faculty members improved, even as their numbers and their skills increased. By 1990, 84% of CLAS full-timers and 36% of part-timers had doctorates (compared to 78% and 30%, respectively, in 1980); in the School of Management, 91% of full-timers and 23% of part-timers had doctorates (compared to 61% and 10% in 1980); and in the Law School 100% of full-timers and 97% of part-timers had JD degrees (compared to 100% and 98% in 1980). In 1991, 31% of the CLAS faculty had national or international reputations, and 23% had published books or their equivalent during past 10 years. At that time, 62% of the SOM faculty had published during the past four years (compared to 47% in 1981). As of 1991, 67% of the total University faculty had published recently, and 86% belonged to professional associations (compared to 51% and 75%, respectively, in 1981. In the College, 62% of faculty members had published recently in 1991, and 85% belonged to professional associations (compared to 47% and 82% in 1981); 87% of SOM faculty members had published recently, and

85% belonged to professional associations (compared to 52% and 80% in 1981); and, likewise in 1991, 75% of Law faculty members had published recently, while 95% belonged to professional associations (compared to 56% and 50% a decade earlier).

The University also took steps to attract and retain faculty members who would help make the faculty more reflective of the gender, ethnic, and racial "mix" of the new, more diverse generation of students that was appearing in the institution's classrooms. By 1990, 34% of the College's full-time faculty, and 37% of its part-time faculty, was female (compared to 28% and 28%, respectively, in 1980). In the School of Management, 15% of full-time faculty members were women in 1990, and 17% of part-timers; in 1980, the comparable percentages had been 3% and 2%. Women constituted 16% of the Law School's full-time faculty in 1990, and 20% of its part-time faculty; in 1980, the figures had been 10% and 16%, respectively. Similarly, AHANA faculty members made up 9.9% of the CLAS full-time faculty (and 10% of its combined full- and part-time faculty) in 1990, compared to 7.4% and 14% in 1983. In the School of Management, AHANA constituted 7.8% of the full-time, and 13% of the combined full- and part-time faculty, in 1990 (compared to 8.6% and 10% in 1983); and in the Law School, 1.6% of the full-time faculty was AHANA, and 5% of the combined full- and part-time faculty (compared to 1.8% and 2% in 1983). The AHANA percentage for all full-time University faculty members in 1991 was 7%, and for all full-time and part-time University faculty members, 9%; in 1983, the equivalent AHANA percentages had been 6.3% and 10%, respectively.

The University also took steps to attract and retain faculty members who would help make the faculty more reflective of the gender, ethnic, and racial "mix" of the new, more diverse generation of students that was appearing in the institution's classrooms.

As with the faculty, the University's administration grew significantly in numbers during the Perlman era, from 89 full-time administrators in 1982 to 118 in 1989, or a 33% increase. Among University administrators, 8% were AHANA and 62% were female in 1989, compared to 0% and 52% in 1982. By 1991, it was in the support staff, however, that the University's highest percentages of both women and AHANA individuals were to be found, at 75% and 22% (compared to a 1982 AHANA percentage of 6.4%).

Historically, retention had not been either a principal goal or a principal achievement of Suffolk Law School: between its foundation in 1906 and June 1937, approximately 10,600 young men attended the Law School, of whom 2,887 eventually graduated—constituting a hair-raising retention figure of 27.2%. Under the Perlman regime, the University first explicitly proclaimed student retention to be one of its priorities. The motive was to shore up crumbling enrollments; but the results produced by a skilled faculty, a supportive administration, and a steadily increasing openness to diverse students, faculty members, and administrators were impressive. In 1980-81, 38% of Suffolk University freshmen graduated in four years, and 46% in six years (compared to a national median of 35%-40% in four years); for classes beginning in 1985-87, 54% of full-time undergraduates graduated in six years (57% in 1985, 53% in 1986, and 52% in 1987).

Joseph M. Kelley

Successful job placements (the ultimate measure of a University education's utility) also increased markedly under the Perlman administration. Between 1982 and 1989, placement figures for CLAS undergraduates increased from 74% to 89%; and for SOM undergraduates, from 79% to 97%. Over the same period, placement percentages for CLAS graduate students improved from 87% to 91%; for MBA graduates, from 93% to 94%; for MPA graduates, from 87% to 100%, and for Law graduates, from 84% to 90%. The great majority of Law School graduates, in 1981 (64%) and 1989 (59%), went into private practice or small business ventures—not into corporate law or government.

Between 1982 and 1990, the total number of Suffolk University alumni increased from 28,306 to 39,023 (living alumni, from 25,805 to 36,324). Law School alumni grew from 10,491 to 16,184; CLAS alumni, from 7,409 (including 864 master's graduates) to 11,523 (including 2790 master's-level graduates); and SOM alumni, from 7,906 (including 2989 master's graduates) to 13,266 (including 5921 master's-level graduates). In 1982, Law School graduates had constituted 41% of the University's living alumni, CLAS graduates 29%, and SOM graduates 30%; by 1990, those percentages were 39%, 28%, and 33%, respectively. Alumni of the graduate programs (including the JD and LLM programs) had increased from 56% in 1982 to 61% in 1990.[27]

Under the influence of Perlman's Vice-President for Institutional Advancement, Joseph M. Kelley, alumni contributions (as well as corporate/foundation contributions) increased dramatically during the Perlman administration. Even in Kelley's first year in office (1982-83), on the heels of the exceptional success of the Campaign for Excellence (1979-82), there was a 45% increase in the number of alumni donors (with donors totaling 25% higher than in any previous year), and SUMMA, a new donor recognition group introduced by Kelley for those giving over $1,000 annually, attracted 115 members. Between 1982 and 1990, these figures climbed steadily, with alumni donations increasing from $609,000 in 1983 to as high as $976,000 in 1987; alumni donor numbers, from 3100 in 1983 to 5800 in 1990; and SUMMA members, from 115 in 1983 to 241 in 1990. Over the same period, corporate/foundation contributions grew from $116,000 in 1983 (compared to $30,000 in 1979) to a high of $527,000 in 1986 (and $462,000 in 1990). Such figures encouraged and emboldened both Vice-President Kelley and the Board with which he was finding favor. In September 1988, on Kelley's assurances that its goal was "reasonable and achievable," the Trustees authorized a $15 million, multi-year "Building the Future" capital campaign, which was designed as a worthy successor to the "Campaign for Excellence." Unfortunately, Kelley was prevented by illness (which ultimately resulted in his untimely death, at 58, in 1992) from ever fully implementing his campaign plans, and "Building the Future" came to naught.[28]

When, in April 1989, Daniel Perlman reflected retrospectively on his Presidency, he found much to be proud of as he described its principal achievements:

"The transformation of Suffolk University's facilities, the stronger links with the community, the increase in scholarship support, the increased attention to supplemental instruction and study skills, the new academic programs in engineering and international economics, the increased pluralism and diversity in the student body and the curriculum, the increase in student services and in opportunities for experiential learning, and the increased attention to student retention and success."[29]

Suffolk University's reputation in the community, President Perlman asserted, was at an all-time high for providing both opportunities for working students and academic quality, both access and excellence.

On February 8, 1989, Daniel Perlman resigned (effective June 30) as Suffolk University's President. The next day, John S. Howe, Chairman of the Board for the bulk of the Perlman Presidency (1981-87), resigned as a Trustee. The Perlman era was at an end. Perlman himself returned to the Midwest to become President of Webster University in St. Louis and to die, tragically young, at 58 in 1994.

Chapter 9 *The Sargent Era, 1989–1995*

David A. Sargent

President Sargent Past President Thomas A. Fulham, by 1989 a Life Trustee (1987) and the institution's "eminence grise," chaired the Presidential Advisory Committee that worked with the Board of Trustees to select President Perlman's successor. Predictably, the Trustees, having despatched an imported President, now turned to a domestic breed. David Sargent was the consensus choice. He had been a member of the Suffolk University community for 38 years, as a student, as a highly-respected member of the Law School faculty, and then (from 1973) as Law School Dean. During his tenure, Dean Sargent had transformed the Law School from marginal compliance with ABA canons to full membership in the prestigious Association of American Law Schools (AALS), and from a regional law school to one "operating on the periphery of national status."[1] At the moment of his elevation, he was the longest-serving Law Dean in the country. Board Chairman James F. Linnehan even appropriated for the new President a title that, until his death in 1979, had been reserved for the venerable Judge Frank J. Donahue, when he described David Sargent as

" . . . truly Mr. Suffolk University, who knows [the school] as well as anyone associated with the institution and is prepared to lead the Law School, the College of Liberal Arts and Sciences, and the School of Management into the nineties with vigor, clarity, and strong direction."[2]

Borne aloft on a cloud of approbation, David J. Sargent ascended to the Presidency on August 22, 1989.

Not surprisingly, from the beginning of his Presidency (and even before), David Sargent found in Board Chair James F. Linnehan (as President Perlman had found in Board Chair John S. Howe) his principal partner, advocate, collaborator, and champion. Linnehan, a 1956 graduate of Suffolk University Law School, had been elected to the Board in 1976 as the first Trustee nominated directly by University alumni. In June 1978 he was elected a "regular" term Trustee, and in June 1987 was elected as Board Chair.[3]

Like his predecessor, President Sargent also inherited an in-progress facilities development project and a capital campaign.[4] As construction work on the Sawyer Building through 1981 was really an inertial remnant of the Fulham Presidency, so completion of the Student Activities Center at 28 Derne Street (September 1989) and of the "University Center" Building and Gymnasium at 148 Cambridge Street (January 1991) was truly a vestige of the Perlman era. The exploration of dormitories as a residential option for Suffolk University students was also a Perlman initiative.[5]

Among President Sargent's goals, as he articulated and refined them in October 1989, Perlmanesque echoes still predominated: to strengthen the physical facilities of the institution, to attract more AHANA and non-traditional students, to continue expansion of academic programs, to be an active force in the upcoming capital campaign, and to be an accessible president. These goals would remain as his Presidency proceeded, but they would be supplemented and complemented by several others that would, through their reprioritizing and restructuring influence, propel him to formulate and embrace a program that was clearer, more relevant, and more compelling for the new President—a genuine "Sargent agenda."

Among President Sargent's goals, as he articulated and refined them in October 1989, Perlmanesque echoes still predominated: to strengthen the physical facilities of the institution, to attract more AHANA and non-traditional students, to continue expansion of academic programs, to be an active force in the upcoming capital campaign, and to be an accessible president.

The Sargent Administration The "Sargent" agenda was shaped and implemented under the dynamic influence of Dean of Enrollment and Retention Management Marguerite J. Dennis, one of the last and most influential legacies of the Perlman era.[6] Enrollment Management was much more consciously acknowledged by 1989 to be playing an initiating, shaping, dominant, hegemonic, and vital role in 94%-tuition-dependent Suffolk University compared to traditional academic centers. Ms. Dennis' cleverness and vision kept the University increasing in students at a time when other institutions were suffering double digit declines. They also won her the unswerving loyalty of President David Sargent.

Marguerite J. Dennis

Like Perlman and Lay, Sargent and Dennis had to face the dangerously volatile combination of rapidly changing "college-age" cohort numbers and heavy tuition dependence. Dean Dennis' approach emphasized outreach to new, and often shifting, markets rather than dependence on a single, fixed, limited-capacity reservoir of students. The strategy led in the direction of diversification, internationalization, and ultimately dormitories. It also led to unprecedented and accelerating changes in the face of the institution.

Marguerite Dennis continued, and expanded, some of the initiatives originally undertaken by Dean Lay. Lay's modest increases in University advertising were succeeded under Dean Dennis by a series of prize-winning campaigns.[7] The Lay/Perlman residential housing experiment at Lasell Junior College in Newton was expanded, under Dennis, into a high-profile "marquee" program, at first featuring two rented Back Bay dormitories reserved for Suffolk University students; then highlighted by the University's purchase in December 1995 of an eleven-story building facing the Boston Common at 150 Tremont Street for conversion into a 400-bed urban dormitory by the fall of 1996.[8] In addition, the retention experiments of the Lay/Perlman era were succeeded by an integrated, nationally-honored retention/advising program under Dean Dennis.[9]

Dean Dennis also built on Dean Lay's scholarship-expansion policy, although here, too, her efforts eclipsed those of her predecessor. Under Dennis' influence, total financial aid offered to Suffolk University students rose from $20.7 million in 1989-90 to $37.7 million in 1993-94, an increase of 82% (compared to an increase from $12.9 million to $20.7 million, or 60%, between 1981 and 1989). During the same period, Suffolk University institutional aid rose from $2.8 million in 1989-90 to $6.1 million in 1993-94, an increase of 118% (again, compared to an increase from $665,000 to $2.8 million, or 321%, between 1981 and 1989). By 1995, approximately 80% of Suffolk University's student population held jobs while pursuing their education; 50% received financial aid.[10]

Even in the relatively conservative tactic of recruitment/retention through financial aid, Dean Dennis went beyond Dean Lay's measures, emphasizing merit, service, and excellence. Dennis' initiatives included: continued expansion of the Fulham and Corcoran Merit Scholarship Programs; Merit Scholarships for Archer Fellows (approved in February 1990) and for Griffin Scholars after this "sister" program was inaugurated in the School of Management (February 1992); a "Grandfathered Tuition" Program for Meritorious Students, i.e. those students maintaining a prescribed grade point average (February 1990); full-tuition scholarships for applicants who received the highest quality rating from the Admissions Office (November 1989); ten "Trustee Ambassador" Scholarships, for outstanding students to assist Enrollment Management in recruiting (April 1989); a Ballotti Learning Center Retention Scholarship Program for ten students who would each receive $2,500 in exchange for ten hours of academic support work per week (November 1989); and an Orientation/Scheduling Assistantship Program, to attract top-quality students to assist in critical Enrollment Management functions (February 1990).[11]

Applications for 1990-91, the year when the most precipitous decline in the number of 18-year-old high school graduates was anticipated, ran 41% ahead of 1989-90, as the University remained (as it had for several years) one of the largest recipients of transfer students in the region.

Applications for 1990-91, the year when the most precipitous decline in the number of 18-year-old high school graduates was anticipated, ran 41% ahead of 1989-90, as the University remained (as it had for several years) one of the largest recipients of transfer students in the region. In 1991, fall semester enrollments at Suffolk showed a net gain of 9% over fall 1990, with an increased percentage of women and AHANA students, despite a severe demographic downturn in graduates from the University's traditional public and parochial feeder high schools. The following fall (1992), the CLAS and SOM combined had 150-200 more students than they had in 1991, even though their 20 leading feeder schools were down 25% in their graduating classes. Rather than attempt to cling to traditional, diminishing "sender groups," Dean Dennis explained to the Trustees in defending one of her numerous "focused" scholarship proposals, she was directing Enrollment and Retention Management efforts

"To attract applicants from new markets, such as non-traditional students like adult learners and international students; also to move toward common Suffolk University goals, i.e. increasing the number of AHANA (African-American, Hispanic-American, Asian, and

Native American) students, enhancing the academic profile of Suffolk University's student population, [and] improving retention rates."[12]

Her efforts drove forward changes that others could only advocate. The cultural diversity of the student body changed with unaccustomed speed as recruitment proceeded with unprecedented energy in the Boston Public Schools, as an English as a Second Language program (which targeted U.S. inner-city students) was inaugurated in September 1989, and as, two months later, the stipend for Maria Stewart Scholars (ten outstanding AHANA students) was increased from $2,500 to $5,000. Internationalization similarly benefitted, both from her promotion of international exchange/articulation agreements and from her establishment of a need-based employment program for international students (November 1989).[13]

After 1989, Suffolk University was one of a handful of colleges and universities in New England experiencing enrollment increases. By the spring of 1995, Dean Dennis' tireless ministrations had brought eleven consecutive semesters of increasing enrollments, with no decrease in quality. Indeed, the evidence on quality pointed in the other direction.

In Dean Dennis' recruitment activities, as in her financial aid innovations, diversity concerns were closely allied with quality enhancement/retention. Her Enrollment Management Division maintained an acceptance rate of approximately 80%, compared to 89% for Northeastern and 76% for UMass (Amherst). Statistically, this was comparable to the 75% of the nation's colleges that admitted more than 70% of their applicants, and to the 80% of New England colleges which were essentially open-enrollment institutions. But beneath the surface of these statistics lurked some interesting developments. In the Lay era, a simultaneous increase in the percentage of students being recruited from the top high school quintile and from the bottom two quintiles posed serious challenges for CLAS and SOM faculty members, as they attempted to accommodate both more top students and increasing numbers of less well prepared high school graduates. After Dean Dennis' arrival, this "bi-polar" distribution pattern began to dissipate, as the percentage of top-quintile students rose from 19% in 1989 to 30% in 1993, and the percentage of bottom-quintile entrants dropped from 9% in 1989 to 5% in 1993. Interestingly, as Dennis reported to the Trustees that 82% of all students accepted to the University's undergraduate programs had a "B" or better high school average, and that 14% had an "A" high school average, she was also reporting a substantial increase in enrollments from the Boston Public Schools and an increase in AHANA enrollments approximating 50%. As the number of international students attracted by the University rose from 128 (4.5% of total enrollment) in 1989 toward 357 (8% of total enrollment) in 1994, their quality rapidly manifested itself: of the 214 international students who had come to Suffolk University by February 1992 as graduate or transfer students, 128 (or 60%) maintained GPAs of 3.0 or better. Such developments did not go unremarked; in the early 1990s, 70% of the potential students who visited the University enrolled.

Law School admissions, of course, were another matter, handled by a separate Law Admissions office. In the 1990s, as in the 1980s, Suffolk University Law School maintained an admissions posture that called for a slow, intentional decrease in Law School enrollments toward 1,600 to improve compliance with ABA/AALS student-teacher ratio and square-foot-per-student guidelines. Under these conditions, and with the demand for law degrees retaining surprising strength nationally despite demographic trends, competition for seats in the Law School remained intense, producing slow, but steady, increases in average LSAT scores and GPAs among entering students. By 1990, applications came from over 350 colleges and universities throughout the country, with more than 500 institutions represented among registered students. In general, there were at least ten candidates for each seat in the first-year class.

Under the Sargent/Dennis dispensation, the emphasis even in discussions regarding improved support services and facilities was expansive—always focusing on those required primarily to serve the academic (and other) needs of new constituencies. Such programs introduced after 1989 included expanded Ballotti Learning Center services, an English Department Writing Laboratory, refinements of Math Competency tutoring services and the introduction of Mathshop (a basic math skills non-credit offering), English as a Second Language, intensive English language workshops, and a Center for International Education to serve the needs of international students. In 1995, the Cooperative Education program placed more than 250 students in positions of paid employment, and continued to record retention rates of 90% and above.[14]

The University Counseling Center, originally accredited by the International Association of Counseling Services, was scheduled in 1995 to undergo a site visit (its fourth, over twenty years) for reaccreditation. The Counseling Center, which in 1978 began to offer pre-doctoral internship training to advanced doctoral candidates, received approval of its internship program from the Association of Psychology Internship Centers (APIC) in 1982. To enhance its already enviable reputation as a training site and to make it more attractive to national candidates for advanced training, the Counseling Center planned to seek American Psychological Association (APA) accreditation during 1995-96.[15]

Sharon Artis-Jackson

One of the most public priorities of the Perlman regime had been to restore to the University something of the racial and cultural diversity that had slipped away from it during the 1960s and 1970s. In practice, however, progress was slow. But under the Sargent Presidency, Suffolk University underwent between 1989 and 1995 a "cultural revolution" of unprecedented proportions. This "revolution" was due primarily to the work of Dr. Sharon Artis-Jackson, appointed in October 1988 as Assistant to the President and Director of Multicultural Affairs, and it promised to restore the relevance of Gleason Archer's 1923 vision of the "Cosmopolitan Character of the School," as

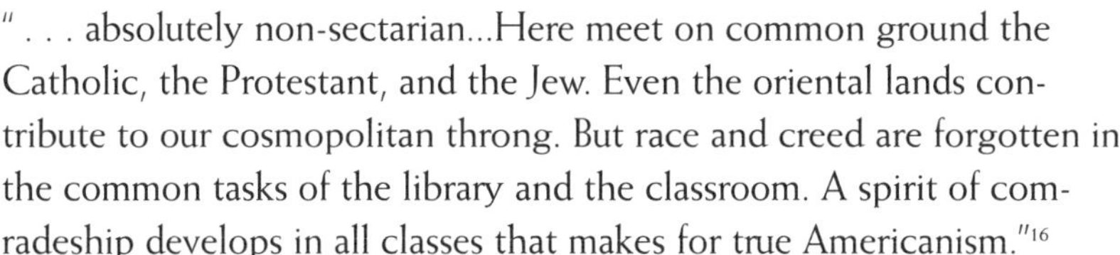

" . . . absolutely non-sectarian...Here meet on common ground the Catholic, the Protestant, and the Jew. Even the oriental lands contribute to our cosmopolitan throng. But race and creed are forgotten in the common tasks of the library and the classroom. A spirit of comradeship develops in all classes that makes for true Americanism."[16]

Most notably, President Sargent responded forcefully, in the very first days of his Presidency, to the October 1989 posting on campus of a flyer which many people deemed racist and particularly hurtful to African Americans and other students of color. Institutional response was swift, clear, and comprehensive. In his statement issued the day after the flyer appeared, President Sargent denounced the racist message and announced short- and long-term plans for more dialogue and education on diversity issues. A cultural awareness forum held two weeks later was planned by a large group of student and employee volunteers. Most significantly, the University resolved that its response would be on-going and institutionalized, not a one-time occurrence. Suffolk's handling of the crisis was so exemplary that other campuses subsequently consulted the University for assistance.[17]

The new University Strategic Planning Committee's efforts from the time of its appointment by President Sargent in 1990 included a central focus on enhancing diversity. In June 1991, the University's mission statement was revised to reflect conspicuously the institutional commitment to cultural, ethnic, and racial diversity. At the same time, the University Strategic Planning Committee that revised the mission statement also adopted, as one of only five all-University goals for 1991-96, a mandate for increased University diversity to enhance the comprehensiveness and quality of the educational experience offered by the institution.[18]

In 1976, the University's By-Laws had been revised to prohibit discrimination, but a proposed new Diversity Policy was designed to articulate a much more affirmative approach. On November 30, 1993, President Sargent announced that the Board of Trustees and the Administrative Council had approved a Diversity Policy Statement, based on that contained in the University's 1991 revised Mission Statement, and modified as suggested by the Presidential Diversity Task Force chaired by Dr. Sharon Artis-Jackson. The announcement also charged the Diversity Task Force to formulate suggestions to make the Statement's professions effective in practice.

Under the Sargent regime, a high priority was consistently given to efforts to create in the University a multi-cultural, multi-racial, gender-balanced community and an atmosphere highly receptive to cultural diversity. In these efforts, recruitment, retention, and cultural diversity initiatives were interdependent and inseparable, as the University struggled to attract and accommodate a "critical mass" of individuals from traditionally disempowered "minority" groups. It is important to note that efforts to make the campus a more welcome environment for AHANA students also enabled other underrepresented groups to feel more comfortable at the University. The definition of cultural diversity at Suffolk was broadened to include not only race or ethnicity, but also gender, socio-economic class, nationality, religion, age, sexual orientation, and physical disability.[19]

In the 1991 administration of the Institutional Functioning Inventory attitude survey, Suffolk University, which ten years earlier had scored well below a comparison group of schools in the category of "cultural diversity," was rated by all participating groups in the Suffolk University community (students, faculty, administrators) significantly higher in "cultural diversity" than the 1991 group of comparison schools. As President Sargent himself asserted: "The future vitality of Suffolk and other urban universities depends on [their] ability to be responsive to . . . [and provide] a welcoming campus climate for people of many cultures."[20]

In addition to the obvious diversity benefits of internationalization, very significant strides were taken toward multi-cultural understanding in the University community through an ambitious program of course content modification, curriculum broadening and reform, forums, conferences, co-curricular activities, and publications around cultural diversity.[21] One of the most notable cultural contributions to multicultural understanding was a powerful 1995 student production of *Fires in the Mirror*, a play about neighborhood conflict between African-Americans and Jews; staged and directed by C. Walsh Theatre Director Marilyn J. Plotkins, it featured a multiracial, multiethnic international cast and created such a sensation that numerous area schools subsequently requested performances to focus multicultural discussion among their own students. Another significant change was implemented in the orientation program for all entering freshman and transfer students. Beginning in 1990, it included sessions designed to reduce prejudice and to increase appreciation of racial and other differences.

By the fall of 1994, AHANA and international student enrollments in the University, and in its respective academic units, were higher than they had ever been: AHANA students constituted 14.8% of Suffolk University's total enrollment (undergraduate, 20.3%; graduate, 7.1%; combined CLAS/SOM, 16.0%; CLAS, 17.5%; SOM, 14.6%; Law, 11.7%), compared to 7.4% (8.3% CLAS/SOM, 5.4% Law) in 1988 and 4% in 1982. By 1994, AHANA and international students constituted 24% of combined CLAS/SOM enrollment, compared to 12% in 1989 and 6.2% in 1984.[22]

Shortly after taking office in 1989, President David Sargent appointed a University Strategic Planning Committee. In June 1991, that committee, chaired by CLAS Dean Michael R. Ronayne, approved a Five-Year University Strategic Plan for 1991-96 that strongly endorsed internationalization as an effective means of promoting excellence through cultural diversity. Under the impetus of that Strategic Plan, and the relentless creativity of Dean Marguerite Dennis, unprecedented initiatives were undertaken to internationalize the University's educational experience. In the fall of 1994, there were nearly 400 international students at Suffolk University from over 80 countries; this cohort had increased by 15% since the fall of 1993. The CLAS/SOM class of 1994 included graduates from 29 countries, and a total of over 100 international students. For academic 1993-94, there were 130 international students enrolled in the College of Liberal Arts and Sciences, compared to 104 in academic

1992-93, or an increase of 25%. Eighty-two U.S. students from Suffolk University (the overwhelming majority of them from the College of Liberal Arts and Sciences) took part in study-abroad programs during academic 1993-94. This number represented approximately 2% of the University's enrollment; but it comprised a very respectable 4-5% of the College's FTE enrollment.

By 1995, the University's international educational agreements included exchange programs with: Suffolk University's new Madrid Campus (Spain), the Stilwell School for International Studies at Sichuan International Studies University (the first college involving foreigners to be established in China), the International University in Moscow, the University of Aix-Marseille and the Ecole Supérieure de Physique de Marseille (France), Charles University and Czech Technical University (Czech Republic), and University College, Cork/Portobello College, Dublin (Ireland).[23] In conjunction with Dean Dennis and the Kuwaiti government, the Departments of Education/Human Services and Psychology established a master's degree in Mental Health Counseling program in Kuwait, beginning in November 1994.[24]

Suffolk University's Madrid campus

One of Suffolk University's most visible public commitments to international studies was the establishment in 1986 of the Dwight L. Allison International Lecture Series as a companion and complement to its two other "marquee" annual speaker events: the Donahue Lecture Series, established in 1979 and sponsored by the *Law Review*; and the Lowell Lecture Series (sponsored by the Lowell Institute), which was first presented at Suffolk University beginning in December 1982. The initial speaker in the Allison Lecture Series (April 1986) was former French minister of reform Jean-Jacques Servan-Schreiber; among his successors was future Czech Prime Minister Vaclav Klaus, the Allison Lecturer for 1991.[25]

During the period between 1988 and 1996, five Suffolk University faculty members and two undergraduate students also succeeded in the competition for Fulbright Scholarships, funded by the U.S. government under legislation originally proposed by Senator J. William Fulbright. The successive student Fulbright Scholars, Susanne Gruber (1988-89, United Kingdom) and Helen Protopapas (1989-90, Federal Republic of Germany), were the first Suffolk University undergraduates ever so designated.[26]

Internationalization helped the University avoid enrollment, retention, and staffing problems; and it also provided a powerful fillip for efforts to improve quality. Equally important, internationalization was a powerful instrument in attracting and holding high-quality faculty members, foreign and domestic.

As the number of international students on campus, and the institution's financial reliance on them, rose from 1989 on, many constituencies in the University became steadily more concerned about two subjects that had previously been regarded as marginal to the institution's agenda: dormitory housing and international support services. Principally because of the influx of international students, the University energetically pursued the expansion of its dormitory facilities (whatever their other advantages) after 1989, with University purchase of its own residence hall (inconceivable less than a decade earlier) regarded as an acceptable option. In addition, the Center for International Education at Suffolk University was created in September 1993 to coordinate all of the University's international activities and services. An English Language for International Students (ELI) program, for college-bound international students, was also established in 1994.[27]

President Sargent (left) and Dr. Lan Renzhe at the Stilwell School for International Studies at Sichuan International Studies University

The Sargent era also saw an unprecedented multiplication and diversification of graduate programming, which brought a modest expansion in the graduate student population in the College and the School of Management. In the College, the Department of Education and Human Services had conducted graduate programs in education and counseling since 1948.[28] The EHS graduate programs remained without siblings until 1990, when, in conformity to guidelines approved for prospective graduate initiatives by the CLAS Educational Policy Committee, the Department of Communication and Journalism introduced a master's degree in Communication, "to strengthen and supplement the undergraduate offerings that will continue to constitute the College's area of primary focus." When it was approved in 1990, planning was already underway for two other new CLAS master's programs, both of which were approved in 1993 and inaugurated in 1994: a Master of Science in International Economics (MSIE) and an M.S. in Political Science, concentrating on Professional Politics (the only such program in New England). In 1990, the Psychology Department, under new chair Jack Demick, built on existing programming to create (in close collaboration with the Department of Education and Human Services) a Five Year Combined Bachelor's and Master's Degree Program. Five years later, the Psychology Department (once again working through interdepartmental cooperation, this time with EHS and the University Counseling Center) formulated the first Ph.D. program ever offered at Suffolk University, a "Boulder Model" Ph.D. in Clinical Psychology, to be implemented in September 1995.[29]

In the early 1990s, the School of Management also struck out in new directions with its graduate programs. The School's two "old reliables" were the MBA and the MPA programs (1948 and 1973, respectively), with their Executive cousins (1978 and 1981). In April 1991, a major MBA curriculum revision was approved, in which courses were restructured into "functional areas," and a new track in Health Administration was introduced into the Executive MPA program. These two changes, combined with the approval in February 1991 of a specialized Master of Science in Finance (MSF) degree program, at least partially designed to appeal to the growing market of international students, signaled the opening of the floodgates. In short order, the "old reliables" were joined by a host of new master's degree programs and program peripherals. Two close relatives to the MSF program, a Master of Science in Accounting (MSA) and a Master of Science in Taxation (MST) were introduced in 1992, along with a Graduate Diploma in Public Accounting (GDPA). A year later, an Advanced Accounting Certificate, an Intermediate Accounting Certificate, and an Advanced Certificate in Taxation (ACT) were first offered, along with a selection of new "concentrations" within the MPA program, modelled in the MPA/Health Administration concentration successfully introduced in 1982-83 by Dr. Eric Fortess. These new MPA "concentrations" included Disability Studies, Finance and Human Resources, and State/Local Government, with the addition in 1994 of a concentration in Non-Profit Management. Also inaugurated in 1993 was a Master of Health Administration (MHA) program. This cornucopia of new offerings drew new classes of graduate students, some from outside the Greater Boston area, to Suffolk University—and promised to attract more.

By that time, there were important factors beyond graduate program expansion and international recruitment at work. To advertise, attract, retain, and recognize the excellence about which President Sargent, like his predecessor, was so enthusiastic, several "merit-focused" initiatives were taken under his regime. In 1992, a Griffin Scholars program, a "sister" enterprise equivalent to the Archer Fellows all-College honors program in the College, was established in the School of Management. From its beginning, participants in this program received merit scholarships (identical to those that had been introduced for Archer Fellows in 1990) funded by the University. This was one of a number of measures sponsored by the Sargent regime that carried on work begun in the Perlman era to "adjust" the University's financial aid policy to accommodate more merit-based scholarship programs.[30]

With Dean Dennis's help and encouragement, *Barron's Best Buys in College Education* recognized Suffolk University, in 1992 and again in 1994, as one of an exclusive group of only 300 colleges nationwide combining educational excellence and affordability. In 1993, *US News and World Report*'s guide to *America's Best Colleges* listed Suffolk in the first quartile for northern colleges and universities, *Barron's Profiles of American Colleges* upgraded the University's rating from "nonselective" to "competitive." The following year, *Money* magazine named Suffolk as one of the ten best private commuter colleges in the U.S. In this environment, Suffolk University undertook in 1993, for the first time in its history, active out-of-state, in-country undergraduate recruitment, in Connecticut, New Hampshire, New York, New Jersey, Rhode Island, and Florida.

Suffolk University was recognized as one of Barron's Best Buys in College Education

The result was a cascade of applications, over 300 of them from the new recruiting markets outside the Greater Boston area, a 111% increase over 1992-93. These, combined with applications for the rapidly-multiplying SOM and CLAS graduate programs—and from international students representing over 40 countries—validated the judgment of those who had steered the new course. The University's challenge was to find appropriate methods of accommodating these new applicants, and the other out-of-state and international students who were rapidly joining them. Its response was the 1995 purchase of the eleven-story future urban dormitory building at 150 Tremont Street.

In the midst of these innovations, however, the Sargent Presidency also represented, in other ways, a reaction, a return to the traditional administrative style of a Suffolk University descended from Suffolk Law School. Under Sargent, Suffolk University was once again (or still) to be "Triad University," the only major university in the U.S. without a Provost, in which the three Deans enjoyed the unparalleled autonomy of reporting directly to the President—as well as to their own respective (and largely autonomous) sub-committees of the Board of Trustees. CLAS Dean Michael R. Ronayne, a Suffolk University "veteran" like Sargent with even longer tenure as Dean (1972), had no problems with this "counterrevolution." His decanal colleagues, new Law Dean Paul R. Sugarman (1990) and new SOM Dean John F. Brennan (1991)—"new hands" from outside the

University environment—tended to have more; and, in this sense, the replacement of Sugarman after only four years as Law Dean in 1994 by John E. Fenton, Jr., may be viewed as the same sort of "traditionalist reaction."

In January 1990, Paul R. Sugarman, one of the nation's most respected trial lawyers, past President of the Massachusetts Bar Association and of the Massachusetts Academy of Trial Lawyers, former chairman of the Massachusetts Board of Bar Overseers, and the unanimous choice of the Trustee Search Committee, succeeded President Sargent as Dean of the Law School. Sugarman, the Law School's first Jewish Dean, was a brilliant, dynamic, energetic, and restless figure. He headed the Law School for four years (January 1990 to June 1994) before returning to the legal practice which he so enjoyed.

Dean John E. Fenton, Jr.

In July 1994, the Trustees settled on Dean Sugarman's replacement. Their choice, the Hon. John E. Fenton, Jr., Chief Justice for Administration and Management of the Trial Court of Massachusetts, was as much a Suffolk "insider" as was David Sargent. Dean Fenton's father, Judge John E. Fenton, Sr., had served one term (1965-70) as Suffolk University's President, and two (1964-66, 1970-74) as Chair of the Board of Trustees. Throughout his judicial career, Judge Fenton, Jr., had continued to teach at the Law School, and had 37 years of faculty service when he assumed the office of Dean in September 1994. Upon his appointment, he was hailed by President Sargent as "a man who is ideally suited to lead the Law School into the next century. He has earned an outstanding reputation as a lawyer, teacher, judge, and administrator."[31]

After 1990, the accreditation priority in the Law School became physical space. Once the ABA accreditation team announced in September 1990 that Suffolk ranked last among the 193 accredited ABA institutions in square feet per student, alarm spread rapidly through the Law School's constituencies. The Sugarman administration, in particular, spread the alarm, and it found attentive ears in the office of the University President. Guided by President Sargent, the Trustees were immediately responsive.[32] In June 1992, the Board voted to construct a new home for the Law School. Toward that end, the University committed itself to acquire two abandoned buildings at 110-120 Tremont Street, immediately opposite the Park Street Church and the Old Granary Burying Ground. Dating from the 1890s and vacant for four years, the two structures were purchased for $5.5 million from Olympia and York, a Canada-based real estate empire. As soon as feasible following demolition of the extant edifices, the University planned to erect a new Law School Building of eight stories and 250,000 square feet, at a total cost of $50-60 million.[33]

Richard L. McDowell was succeeded as SOM Dean in July 1991 by John F. Brennan, truly a horse of a very different color. Dean Brennan's background comprised, in an impressive and diversified career, a rich and varied combination of the worlds of business and academics. With a BA from Williams College (English, 1954) and an MBA (1958) from the Harvard School of Business Administration, Brennan had, during the previous two decades, served as president and CEO of a number of companies, taught at Wake Forest University and the University of Tennessee, chaired the Board of Trustees of Webb School of Knoxville, and been a member of the University of Tennessee Development Council. In 1984 he had been appointed the first F. William Harder Professor of Management at Skidmore College in Saratoga Springs, New York, whence he came to the Deanship of Suffolk University's School of Management.

Dean Paul R. Sugarman

To a significant extent, the new Dean's concerns were different from those of Dean McDowell. Dean Brennan was also relieved of many external-accreditation-standard pressures that had preoccupied his predecessor when the AACSB in 1990, virtually on the morrow of Suffolk University's accession, fundamentally altered the nature of its accreditation standards. The new criteria no longer emphasized the inflexible, externally-imposed "uniform criteria" whose satisfaction had made the pursuit of AACSB accreditation such an ordeal for the School of Management under Dean McDowell's leadership, but rather on institutionally self-defined mission. With these Jovian perturbations eliminated, Dean Brennan was left free to pursue his natural orbit: a renewed focus on teaching, on the crafting of an undergraduate core curriculum that addressed the particular needs and interests of Management students, and on the rationalization and restructuring of course offerings within the MBA curriculum into "functional areas."

In a planning process initiated by Dean Brennan upon his arrival in 1991, the School of Management faculty significantly modified the School's mission statement to reemphasize teaching as of equal importance with research. By 1995, under Brennan's leadership, the faculty had instituted a complete revision of the MBA curriculum (1992), introduced a cluster of new SOM core courses for undergraduates (1993), and initiated new specialized Master of Science in Finance (MSF), Master of Science in Taxation (MST), and Master of Science in Accounting (MSA) degrees aimed at international students. In addition, the faculty governance structure had been entirely recast, and a Griffin Scholars honors/merit scholarship program (1992) had been added. Equally important was the fact that in 1991 the SOM had been accepted as a member of the Beta Gamma Sigma National Honor Society in Business and Management, the highest national recognition that a student could receive in an undergraduate or master's program in business or management.[34]

Dean Brennan also had a pressing practical problem to solve: how to "stop the bleeding" in enrollments, where SOM undergraduate numbers (and, consequently, overall SOM figures) had dropped steadily from 1983-84 on. To address this problem, Brennan and his faculty were obliged to put into energetic practice many of the ambitious (but often unimplemented) professions of the McDowell era regarding the need for "internationalization." Their solution, to compensate for the continuing undergraduate enrollment shortfall, was to attract international students, in unprecedented numbers, into new graduate programs specifically designed for them (MSF, MST, MSA)—and, as an unavoidable consequence, to give endorsement to some international support services previously regarded by the bulk of SOM administrators and faculty as unacceptable. Particularly to address international possibilities in non-credit programming, Dean Brennan also resurrected the SOM's moribund Center for Management Development. In 1994, the AACSB delivered a ringing endorsement of the SOM's (and Dean Brennan's) accomplishments, by enthusiastically reaccrediting the School under its new mission-driven criteria. Less than a year later, in February 1995, Trustee Carol Sawyer Parks presented Dean Brennan with a $1 million naming gift to rededicate his academic unit as the Frank Sawyer School of Management.

Dean John F. Brennan

In the Sargent as in the Perlman regime, the absence of a single professional accreditation standard (like those in the Law School and SOM) diminished the College's "competitive advantage" in the vital struggle for temporary priority access to University resources. The College's response to this problem was a rising tide of appeals by individual CLAS academic departments to the authority of accrediting agencies for their specific disciplines or programs. Since 1989, application for outside accreditation, to provide "objective validation" for the excellence of their programs and externally-imposed "imperatives" for institutional support, has been made by a number of CLAS departments. The Chemistry Department had been accredited by the American Chemical Society (ACS) in 1973, and retained its approval. Suffolk University's "special relationship" in its Cooperative Agreement with the Center for International Studies, Madrid, was reviewed and approved by the New England Association of Schools and Colleges (NEASC) in 1992. In February 1994, the Paralegal Studies program at Suffolk University won American Bar Association (ABA) approval, making it one of only three accredited programs in eastern Massachusetts. The Department of Education and Human Services also won "reaccreditation," during 1994 and 1995, for all of its graduate secondary education programs under the Interstate Certification Compact (ICC). In April 1995, the Interior Design program at the New England School of Art and Design (NESAD), with which Suffolk University was a partner in a joint Bachelor of Fine Arts degree arrangement approved in 1990, sought and gained reaccreditation from the Foundation for Interior Design Education Research (FIDER). The Physics and Engineering Department planned to seek, in 1995-96, accreditation for its Electrical Engineering program (to be followed shortly by the Computer Engineering program) from the Accreditation Board for Engineering and Technology (ABET). In addition, the Physics and Engineering Department also planned to seek in 1995-96 (with the help of its collaborators, the Biology Department, and the Department of Radiation Oncology at Massachusetts General Hospital) approval from the Joint Review Committee on Education in Radiologic Technology (JCERT) for its joint B.S. program in the Medical Sciences.

The New England School of Art & Design at Suffolk University

Similarly, new graduate programs in Communication (1990), International Economics (1993), Professional Politics (1993), and Computer Science (1995) were initiated, and plans were made to seek appropriate accreditation for them in their turn. In 1990, the Psychology Department and the Department of Education/Human Services created a Five Year Combined Bachelor's and Master's Degree Program. Five years later, the same two departments, in cooperation with the University Counseling Center, established Suffolk University's first Ph.D. program, a "Boulder Model" Ph.D. in Clinical Psychology.

The College of Liberal Arts and Sciences also took the practical lead in internationalization, with a consequent position on the point in the battle for dormitories to maintain/increase numbers, quality, and diversity, and in the struggle to provide needed new international/intercultural support services. In addition, the College maintained a strong emphasis (like the SOM and the Law School) on effective teaching and a strong core program revised in 1994 to add an upper-division third-semester natural science capstone course and (as the SOM added to its undergraduate core curriculum in 1993) computer literacy and cultural diversity requirements. By 1995, the College had its keystone Archer Fellows all-college honors/merit scholarship program (1987/1990) in place, along with departmental honors programs in all but four academic departments and affiliation with national/international academic honorary societies in all but five (compared to 5 of 14, and 7 of 14, respectively, in 1980).[35]

Under the Sargent regime, two departments in the College remained centers of dynamic influence as they had been in the Perlman era. Foremost among them was the Communication and Journalism Department, whose exceptional successes in debate and in theatre continued unabated, and whose master's program proposal in 1990 broke trail for other new CLAS graduate offerings. Second, by a head, was Physics and Engineering, whose Engineering programs continued to grow, and to add new international, internship, coop, and scholarship features; and whose new joint program in Medical Sciences, in collaboration with the Biology Department and the Department of Radiation Oncology at Massachusetts General Hospital initiated two attractive new B.S. degree programs (in Medical Biophysics and in Radiation Biology) and added significantly to the University's prestige. Important new centers were Jack Demick's Psychology Department, with its Five Year Combined Bachelor's and Master's Degree Program (1990), its participation in the master's degree in Mental Health Counseling program in Kuwait (1994), and its first-ever-at-Suffolk "Boulder Model" Ph.D. in Clinical Psychology (1995), all in close and constructive collaboration with the Department of Education and Human Services. Glen Eskedal's EHS Department, in turn, produced not only the conspicuous collaborations with Psychology (and the University Counseling Center), but also, in its own right, implemented (1992) and gained ABA accreditation (1994) for its Paralegal Studies program. The Humanities and Modern Languages Department, under Margaret Weitz, contributed considerable cultural enrichment to the Sargent era at Suffolk through its championship (in the person of Dr. Raymond Kelton) of music study/performance programs at Suffolk, its development of fine/studio arts minors and subsequent cultivation of audiences for them, and its ingenious elision of these latter to its joint BFA degree program with the New England School of Art and Design.[36]

Several spheres of support services indispensable to Suffolk University developed during the period 1979-95 with substantial immunity from the politics and personalities of the Perlman and Sargent eras: computer services, library services, language services, and media services.

The growth in magnitude of the first is literally incalculable, since it started from zero: there were no university-owned computers at Suffolk in 1979. The central figure in this development is that of Paul F. Ladd, who in February 1978 became the University's first full-time Director of Data Processing. (In 1981, Ladd changed his title to Director, Management Information Services; and in 1985 the office he headed officially became Management Information Services.) It was on Ladd's recommendation that Suffolk University in November 1979 undertook to lease two PRIME 750 computers, one for administrative and one for academic use. By November 1980, the new equipment was completely installed on campus.[37] In April 1984, again on Ladd's advice, the Trustees approved acquisition of two PRIME 9950s (to replace the 750s as the institution's principal administrative and academic computers) and extension of the lease on the two older (750) machines. Installation of the 9950s was completed in November 1984. By 1995, Suffolk's computer center housed two PRIME 6350 supermini computers, with over 600 microcomputers, 200 terminals and printers available to academic and administrative users. In August 1995, the 6350s were replaced by two new state-of-the-art IBM RS6000s, very significantly upgrading the University's computer services.[38]

In 1977, Edmund G. Hamann was appointed Director of what then bore the altogether misleading title of "the College Libraries"—that is, of the library that served the College of Liberal Arts and Sciences and the School of Management. Hamann's title changed in 1982 to Director, Mildred F. Sawyer Library, when the facility he managed moved from the Archer Building to the renovated edifice at 8 Ashburton Place which was named for Frank Sawyer at the same time that the recently-arrived library was named for his wife (April 29, 1982). In 1995, Hamann remained Director of the Sawyer Library. Over the same period, the Law Library, consisting of the Stephen P. Mugar Library (in the Donahue Building) and the E. Albert Pallot Library (in the Archer Building, on the pre-1982 site of the College Library), had only two directors. Edward J. Bander became Law Librarian in September 1978 and served though June 1990; he was replaced in July 1990 by Michael J. Slinger, former Associate Director for Public Services at the Notre Dame University Library.

Between 1972 and 1982, the Law School Library grew from 60,000 volumes to 160,000, and by the latter date was already considered one of the finest law school libraries in the area. In 1979, it was designated a Government Depository Library by the U.S. Government. The Sawyer Library received in 1966 the donation of the Irving Zieman Poetry Collection, and in 1971, upon affiliation of Suffolk University with the Museum of Afro-American History, also received what became known as the Afro-American Literature Collection. That collection, permanently housed at the Sawyer Library and in the joint custody of the Museum, the University, and the National Park Service, had grown to more than 3000 titles by 1987, when it was officially (re)dedicated in connection with the reopening of the Museum of Afro-American History. The Sawyer Library joined the Fenway Consortium in 1976.

Between 1972 and 1982, the Law School library grew from 60,000 volumes to 160,000

By 1995, Suffolk University's Libraries were ranked in the top 20 of 111 college and university libraries in Massachusetts by the American Library Association. At that time, the Mildred F. Sawyer Library contained 107,000 volumes (compared to 90,000 in 1980), 171,000 microtext volumes (compared to 24,000 in 1980), 1,350 periodical subscriptions (compared to 2,100 in 1980), and 15 CD-ROM titles; while the Law School Library held 173,620 volumes (compared to 102,500 volumes in 1980), 44,923 microtexts, 5,628 serial subscriptions, and 11 CD-ROM titles. In addition, the Collection of Afro-American Literature had grown, by 1995, to 4000 volumes (compared to 2500 in 1980 and 3000 in 1987); and the Fenway Library Consortium, of which the Sawyer Library was a member, had expanded its total holdings to over 2 million volumes (compared to 660,000 in 1989).[39]

Under the leadership of Director Ted Hamann, the Sawyer Library committed itself whole-heartedly to computer technology and to electronic data management. The operative word for Library materials, he insisted, was "access," not "acquisition." In his view, service was the key; the quality of its staff was the bedrock of the Library, and the primary service responsibility of staff members was to guide students to information resources and databases.

According to Hamann, the "new technologies"—powerful desktop computers, sophisticated software, networks, and a proliferation of data in electronic formats from compact disks to telecommunication linkage to remote databases—meant that even small libraries were able to provide access to vast quantities of information. This heralded significant changes in the way that libraries would do business. Spending priorities would shift from periodical subscriptions to services that access the articles themselves. The article would become the basic unit of information for users. The packaging and delivery of articles would be on-demand and rapid ("just-in-time," in the jargon of business). Instead of subscribing to a handful of expensive scholarly and technical journals ("just-in-case"), the library would "subscribe" to services that electronically search and retrieve specific articles from thousands of journals. Patrons, said Hamann, would soon be able to walk up to a public terminal, perform their own search of a variety of relevant index databases, and request articles with or without the mediation of reference librarians.

In March 1994, the Sawyer Library, the Law Library, and Management Information Services contracted with Innovative Interfaces, Inc., to automate the Law and Sawyer Libraries' operating systems. By December 1994, the Sawyer Library and the Law School Library jointly started up their sophisticated new automated library system. The new catalog displays the book and periodical holdings of both libraries at any computer linked to the University's network, and allows the libraries to order, catalogue, and circulate books and to check in individual periodical issues and volumes in "real time." It will also eventually provide the major platform for patron-access online databases.[40]

A University Language Laboratory was completed in 1965; after over two decades of use, it was renovated in two stages, 1987 and 1990, with a satellite TV antenna added in 1990 to allow world-wide reception.

Finally, under the supervision of Marilyn A. Wilcke, who was appointed Director in October 1982, Instructional Media Services (renamed University Media Services in 1988) has steadily grown in personnel and resources throughout the Perlman and Sargent eras. Its most recent outgrowth (1993) is Creative Services, the newly created UMS unit responsible for publications.

The Sargent Record David Sargent remained President of Suffolk University in 1995, so no "final" evaluation of his administration can be offered here. Nevertheless, the changes during his six years in office were impressive. Suffolk University's operating budget, which had been $38.7 million in 1989, had, by 1994, grown to $59 million—an increase of 52%. Plant assets had grown from $40 million in 1989 to $43 million in 1994—a 7.5% expansion. Likewise, the institution's Endowment grew from $16.4 million in 1989 to $31 million—a rise of 89%.

In five years (1989-94), the total financial aid offered to Suffolk University students had risen from $20.7 million to $37.7 million, or 82%; and, more significantly, institutional (Suffolk University) funds invested in financial aid had grown from $2.8 in 1989 to $6.1 million in 1994—an increase of 118%.

Under President Sargent's administration, total University enrollment rose from 5,551 (4,395 FTE) in 1989 to 5,984 (4,844 FTE) in 1994, a headcount increase of 7.8% and an FTE increase of 10.2%. In the College of Liberal Arts and Sciences, overall enrollment rose from 1,717 (1,452 FTE) in 1989 to 2,182 (1,819 FTE) in 1994—a headcount growth of 27.1% and an FTE rise of 25.3%. Over the same period, CLAS undergraduate enrollments rose by 18.6% (from 1,652 to 1,959); and graduate enrollments rose by 243%, from 65 to 223. In the School of Management, total headcount enrollments fell from 2,177 to 2,141 (a 1.7% decline), but total FTE enrollments rose by 3.6%, from 1,460 to 1,512. School of Management undergraduates decreased from 1,235 to 1,064 (13.8%), while SOM graduate enrollments rose from 942 to 1,077 (14.3%). Under the Sargent administration, as in the Perlman era, the MBA program retained by far the SOM's largest graduate enrollment, with 739 students in 1989 and 613 five years later (a decrease of 17.1%). Between 1989 and 1994, the number of students enrolled in the Law School increased slightly, from 1,657 (1,483 FTE) to 1,682 (1,513 FTE), a headcount growth of 1.5% and an FTE rise of 2%. Overall, the percentage of part-time and evening students in the University rose slightly from 43% to 44% between 1989 and 1984—in the College, from 29% to 32%; and in the School of Management, from 57% to 59%. In the Law School, however, the percentage of Evening Division students fell from 42% in 1989 to 40% in 1994.

By 1994, women constituted 55% of Suffolk University students.

The Sargent era saw the acceleration of very significant changes in the University's student population. By 1994, women constituted 55% of Suffolk students. Women made up 52% of enrollments in 1990; four years later, 55% of all students were female. Combined enrollment in the College and the School of Management in 1990 was 53% female; by 1994, the combined CLAS/SOM enrollment was 56%. College enrollments were 65% female in 1994 (compared to 61% in 1990), while SOM enrollments were 37% female (compared to 47% in 1990). In the Law School, 49% of students in 1990 were women (51% in the Day Division, 46% in the Evening

Division). By 1994, Law School enrollments were 52% female (53% in the Day Division, 50% in the Evening Division).

Enrollments of AHANA (African-American, Hispanic, Asian, and Native American) and international students grew much more rapidly under the Sargent administration than during the Perlman era. In 1989, overall Suffolk University enrollments were 8.3% AHANA (10.8% CLAS, 7.8% SOM, 5.9% Law). By 1994, the overall University AHANA enrollment had risen to 14.8%% (17.5% CLAS, 14.6% SOM, 11.7% Law). In 1989, international students made up 3% of the overall University enrollment (3.1% CLAS, 4.5% SOM, 1.1% Law). In 1994, overall international student enrollment had grown significantly to 8% of total CLAS/SOM enrollment (6.7% CLAS, 9.7% SOM). Combined CLAS/SOM AHANA and international student enrollment in 1989 was 13%; by 1994, it had grown to 24%.

Enrollments of AHANA (African-American, Hispanic, Asian, and Native American) and international students grew much more rapidly under the Sargent administration than during the Perlman era.

Substantial ethnic shifts also took place in Suffolk University enrollments between 1980 and 1995. In 1980, four principal groups had predominated in all categories of enrollments, from CLAS/SOM undergraduate and graduate to the Law School: Irish-Americans (generally around 35% of enrollments), "Yankees" (or Anglo-Americans, 27%), Italian-Americans (16%, but slightly lower in the Law School), and American Jews (10%, but slightly higher in the Law School). Other groups in 1980 included Portuguese-Americans (3-4%), French surname (3-4%), Greek-Americans (2%), Asian-Americans (.5%-1%), and Armenian-Americans (.5%-1%). By the 1990s, Irish-Americans and Anglo-Americans combined constituted only 30% of enrollments of all CLAS/SOM enrollments; Italian-Americans, 20%. The percentage of Portuguese-Americans (15%), Spanish surname students (15%), and Asian-Americans (10%) in CLAS/SOM had increased dramatically. Another 5% of CLAS/SOM enrollments were French surname students (including, by the 1990s, a significantly higher percentage of Haitians than in 1980). Among CLAS/SOM enrollments, there were many less Greek-Americans in the 1990s than in 1980, and very few identifiable American Jews. Slavic surname students increased to 2% of CLAS/SOM enrollments in the 1990s; Muslim/Arabic names constituted approximately 1%, as did Armenian-Americans. During the 1990s, ethnic enrollment patterns were notably different in the Law School than in CLAS/SOM; this was a different situation from 1980, when, as noted, the patterns were quite similar. In the 1990s, ethnic enrollment patterns in Suffolk University Law School were: Anglo-Irish 50%. Italian-Americans 10%, American Jews 10%, Spanish surname

5%, Portuguese-Americans 5%, French surname (few Haitians) 5%, Slavic 2%, Asian-Americans 2%.

The number of students entering Suffolk University from the Boston Public School System grew significantly after 1989: throughout the 1980s, it had hovered around 35; by 1994, it was 74. Boston Tech and Boston English joined the list of Suffolk's major "feeder" secondary schools in the early 1990s, along with Matignon and Mt. St. Joseph Academy. By 1994, approximately 75% of the University's undergraduate students were being recruited from public secondary schools and 25% from private institutions, compared to 60% and 40%, respectively, in 1989. Suffolk's largest geographic market in 1994 was Boston-Cambridge, from which 56% of incoming CLAS/SOM freshmen were drawn in 1991, compared to 49% in 1988. The University's second-largest undergraduate market in the 1990s was Quincy/Plymouth. For CLAS/SOM transfer students, the Center for International Studies (Madrid) became the second-largest "feeder" institution in the early 1990s, second only to Bunker Hill Community College. The New England School of Art and Design, with which the University concluded a joint Bachelor of Fine Arts degree collaboration in 1991, also joined the list of leading "sender" colleges from that date.

By 1994, the CLAS faculty had grown to 120 full-time and 121 part-time members (compared to 112 and 102, respectively, in 1990); the SOM faculty had expanded to 63 full-timers and 67 part-timers (compared to 55 and 30, respectively, in 1990); and the Law School faculty had increased to 61 full-time and 109 part-time members (compared to 58 and 81, respectively, in 1990). In 1994, 66% of the CLAS faculty was tenured, compared to 51% in 1991; 40% of the SOM faculty and 73% of the Law School faculty were tenured in 1994, as had been the case in 1991. By 1994, 86% of CLAS full-timers and 44% of part-timers had doctorates (compared to 84% and 36%, respectively, in 1990); in the School of Management, 87% of full-timers and 31% of part-timers had doctorates (compared to 91% and 23% in 1990); and in the Law School 100% of full-timers and 100% of part-timers had JD degrees (compared to 100% and 97% in 1990).

Under the Sargent regime, the University continued and intensified steps to attract and retain faculty members who would help make the faculty more reflective of the gender, ethnic, and racial "mix" of the new, more diverse generation of students that was appearing in the institution's classrooms. By 1994, 38% of the College's full-time faculty, and 36% of its part-time faculty, was female (compared to 34% and 37%, respectively, in 1990). In the School of Management, 24% of full-time faculty members were women in 1990, and 31% of part-timers; in 1990, the comparable percentages had been 15% and 17%. Women constituted 20% of the Law School's full-time faculty in 1994, and 31% of its part-time faculty; in 1990, the figures had been 16% and 20%, respectively. Similarly, the AHANA percentage for all full-time University faculty members in 1994 was 10.5%, compared to 7% in 1991.

In the Sargent era, the University's administration actually decreased in numbers between 1989 and 1994, from 118 full-time administrators in 1989 to 101 in 1994, or 14%. Among University administrators, 11.4% were AHANA and 60% were female in 1994, compared to 8% and 62% in 1989. By 1994, 17% of support staff workers were AHANA, compared to 22% in 1991.

During President Sargent's tenure, the University reinforced the importance that had been attached to retention activities under the Perlman regime. President Sargent formally declared that retention should be a first-priority concern, and, as an important symbolic manifestation of this priority, the Office of Enrollment Management was renamed the Division of Enrollment and Retention Management in 1990. For classes beginning in 1985-87, 54% of full-time undergraduates graduated in six years (57% in 1985, 53% in 1986, and 52% in 1987). By 1993-94, the overall CLAS/SOM graduate and undergraduate retention figure from semester to semester was 86.3%.

Successful job placements continued as a "real-world" validation of Suffolk University's educational activities during the Sargent Presidency. Between 1989 and 1994, placement figures for CLAS undergraduates decreased slightly, from 89% to 79%; and for SOM undergraduates, from 97% to 92%. Over the same period, placement percentages for CLAS graduate students improved from 91% to 100%; and for MBA graduates, from 94% to 99%. For MPA graduates, placement figures dropped (how could they not) from 100% in 1989 to a "mere" 97% in 1994; and for graduates of the new SOM Master of Science in Finance (MSF) program, the placement record was unblemished, at 100%. The great majority of Law School graduates, in 1994 (65%) as in 1989 (59%), went into private practice or small business ventures—not into corporate law or government.

By 1995, the number of active Suffolk University alumni stood at 31,803; of these, 39% were Law School graduates (the same percentage as in 1990), 26% were CLAS graduates (compared to 28% in 1990), and 35% were SOM graduates (compared to 32%

in 1990). The Law School boasted one of the largest law alumni in the nation, numbering approximately 13,000 and representing every aspect of the profession in the judiciary as well as the bar, the legislature, and governmental service.[41]

In April 1994, Richard M. Rosenberg (BSJ 52), Chairman and CEO of BankAmerica, was the featured speaker at a Suffolk University-sponsored symposium on the banking industry, which was attended by most of the leading banking officials and regulators in New England. Mr. Rosenberg had also served as speaker at the CLAS/SOM Commencement on May 26, 1991. In May 1994, Congresswoman Olympia J. Snowe (R-Maine), a Law School alumna, delivered the CLAS/SOM Commencement address.

The Law School boasted one of the largest law alumni in the nation, numbering approximately 13,000 and representing every aspect of the profession in the judiciary as well as the bar, the legislature, and governmental service.

In the Office of Institutional Advancement, an interregnum existed from January 1991 until November 1993, during and after the final illness of Joseph M. Kelley.[42] Only in November 1993 was James A. Campbell, former Director of Major Gifts at the College of the Holy Cross, appointed as Vice-President of Development. Campbell's immediate and pressing task was the planning and preparation of a $25 million capital campaign projected by the Trustees in June 1992 as a partial solution to the problem of financing the University's projected new $50-60 million Law School building at 110-120 Tremont Street. Upon Campbell's departure in December 1995, that responsibility fell to his successor, Marguerite J. Dennis. After six years as Dean of Enrollment and Retention Management, Dennis was named Vice-President for Development and Enrollment, becoming the first female Vice-President in Suffolk University's history. She was succeeded as Dean of Enrollment and Retention Management by her deputy, Barbara Ericson.

In February 1984, the Trustees authorized the Development Committee and Vice-President Kelley to proceed with establishment of an estate planning council. New Trustee Thomas M. Mawn, Jr., assumed the lead role in the undertaking, which concentrated on the development of publications and seminars on estate planning. Over the next decade, the Council continued its work, bolstered in November 1992 by President Sargent's announcement that he and the institution's other senior administrators had all pledged to make testamentary provisions for Suffolk University in their estate plans and that he was requesting the Trustees to make similar pledges as an example for the alumni.

Since 1981, the lot on Temple Street behind St. John's Church, opposite the Donahue Building, has served as a Suffolk University Alumni Memorial Park. In June 1979, in the immediate aftermath of the University's very successful collaboration with its neighbors to create the Temple Street Mall (1974-77, dedicated December 16, 1977), the Trustees proposed, in the interest of further improving the quality of the environment and the neighborhood, to enter into an agreement with the St. John's Church to rent the lot for park purposes, and to expend up to $7000 on improvements. Board Chairman Vincent Fulmer suggested in September 1979 that it be designated an Alumni Memorial Park, and on September 13, 1981, the new park received its dedication.

Temple Street, home of Suffolk University Law School

The Temple Street Mall and Alumni Memorial Park projects were only two examples of the University's sincere, energetic—and often underappreciated—efforts to build and maintain good relations with its urban neighbors. As early as 1969, Suffolk University was a pioneer among educational institutions in extending Payments in Lieu of Taxes to the City of Boston, and the University's PILOT relations with its host city remained in 1995 among the most amicable in its category. In 1990, and again in 1991, Suffolk was cited by the City of Boston as the City's Best Collegiate Neighbor—initially for keeping its properties clean and free of sanitary violations and in the following year in the Urban Landscaping category, for its Ridgeway Building.

Like these "good neighbor" initiatives, President Sargent's boldness in committing Suffolk University to Law School expansion and student dormitory construction in the heart of downtown Boston was part of an unprecedented expansiveness in his vision of the University's proper profile and responsibilities in the community—and, indeed, regarding the very scale of the "community" of which Suffolk University constituted a part.

As early as November 1986, President Perlman had suggested affiliations and mergers with other institutions as potentially constructive possibilities; but it was President Sargent's unequivocal assertion that Suffolk University "should expand" that definitively carried the Trustees and the institution with him down this road.[43] His "building plan" comprised far more than construction; it represented, as well, an "adjustment," upward and outward, of the University's appropriate scope and field of action, from the local and regional to the national and international, and in ways that committed the institution in a "high-profile, high-visibility" fashion, publicly and energetically, to cooperation, consortium, and even affiliation with any willing compatible institutions, great or small.

This new expansiveness called for new, "high-visibility" University accommodations. In the first days of the Sargent

Presidency, long before the floating of the Law School or downtown dormitory projects, the University's administrative offices were transferred to corporate-standard rental space on the twenty-fifth floor of One Beacon Street. Shortly thereafter, the University made a bold (and ultimately rebuffed) offer to purchase and refurbish the prominent Women's City Club building, a historic four-story brick townhouse built in 1818 overlooking the Boston Common at 40 Beacon Street, as a University Club and administration building.[44]

Characteristic of this new approach, this new "University image," as well, was an affinity for the inception, both within and reaching outside the University, of educational "joint ventures" of many types. At the most basic level, these included a number of collaborative degree programs within the University, all modeled on a five-year BA/JD program established (at the insistence of Dean Ronayne) in 1979 between the College and the Law School, and of a joint JD/MPA program inaugurated (on the instigation of Dean McDowell) in 1984 between the School of Management and the Law School. A BSBA/MBA program was approved in 1990, BSBA/JD and JD/MBA programs in 1992, a JD/MSIE in 1993, and an MBA/GDPA a year later.[45]

At a second level, this widening of the University's self-definition involved the establishment/development of a number of centers at Suffolk University which would encourage and facilitate interaction with broadening publics. Certain tentative steps had been taken in this direction under Presidents Fulham and Perlman: the housing of the Collection of Afro-American Literature in the College Library (and the concurrent affiliation with the neighboring Museum of Afro-American History) in 1971, the creation of the Suffolk University Theatre in 1978, a short-lived experiment with a Center for Management Education (for non-credit professional and training activities) by the School of Management between 1977 and 1980, its reanimation as the Center for Management Development in 1988, and the formation of a Center for Continuing Professional Development (renamed the Center for Advanced Legal Studies in 1992) as a locus for continuing legal education. Upon President Sargent's accession, activity around these outreach centers intensified, with, for example, the foundation of the Beacon Hill Institute for Public Policy Research (with an emphasis on state government issues) in June 1991, the revitalization and redirection of the Center for Management Development in 1992, escalating levels of artistic achievement and prominence for the C. Walsh Theatre under the direction of Marilyn J. Plotkins, and organization of the Center for International Education at Suffolk University in 1993.

At a third level, the University committed itself to an unprecedented extent to affiliations and joint programs with various Boston-area institutions. Before 1989, there existed an emaciated remnant of academic cooperation with Emerson College (greatly reduced from the original program of 1968), the Afro-American Museum connection (from 1971), and a five-year (3-2) joint Engineering program with Boston University (as well as with Case Western Reserve University and Notre Dame). Shortly after David Sargent's assumption of the Presidency, the number of collaborations began to multiply. A Cooperative Agreement with the Center for International Studies in Madrid was signed in 1990, a joint Bachelor of Fine Arts degree program was concluded with the New England School of Art and Design (NESAD) in 1991, an academic collaboration/exchange arrangement with the Northeast School of Broadcasting was implemented in 1993, and a joint Medical Sciences program between the Physics and Engineering Department, the Biology Department, and the Department of Radiation Oncology at Massachusetts General Hospital was inaugurated in 1994 to offer bachelor's degrees in Radiation Biology and Medical Biophysics. In 1995, the University established its own Madrid Campus, and a full merger agreement was concluded with NESAD, by which it became the New England School of Art and Design at Suffolk University.[46]

Francis X. Flannery, Vice President and Treasurer, who arrived in 1964 as Assistant Treasurer, played a central role in facilitating the overall progress of the University.

President Sargent had come to a point where the exigencies of Law School accreditation and University development were creating for Suffolk (and for him) a challenge, and an opportunity, of unprecedented scale. To confront that challenge, he accepted a second seven-year term as President of Suffolk University. Then, in the fall of 1995 he convinced the Board of Trustees to expand the size of its membership and to modify the by-laws concerning its meeting schedule and the way in which it conducted University business. Board meetings (and meetings of the Board's principal subcommittees) would no longer take place on mid-week evenings, but rather one weekend every two months—a change that would permit high-ranking corporate officers and other Trustees from outside the New England area to join the Board with a reasonable expectation of participation in its deliberations. Sargent's success in carrying the Trustees with him on these reforms (as on the new Law School and urban dormitory projects) marked a major shift in direction for a Board that historically had been local, insular, and conservative.

As Suffolk University approached the second millennium and its second century, the inner tension that has characterized the institution throughout its history—between "access" and "excellence," between "diversity" and "quality"—persisted. By 1995, experience with the iron realities of demographics had added a new relevance to multiculturalism, and thereby constructively moderated the historic tension. That tension, however, remained a central defining characteristic of the University and of the University's identity: not by its mere existence, but by its creative role throughout the institution's history.[47]

What, then, is Suffolk University as the end of the twentieth century rapidly approaches? Aristotle, in one of his efforts to illumine the nature of identity, invokes the case of what has since been denominated "Aristotle's boat." Imagine, says the philosopher, a boat which, for whatever reasons, has all of its constituent materials entirely renewed. Is it still the same boat? Well . . . Now take the case of Suffolk University. In many ways, it is "Aristotle's University," consisting of entirely renewed constituent matter, but still itself, retaining its unique identity, still in essence what founder Gleason Archer wanted it to be—changed, but not "changed utterly." In recent years—typically, independently and in practice (not theory)—all three academic units of the institution have been developing a common manifestation of the University's identity, a means of providing the community service that President Archer saw as the primary mission of the University while transcending the historically divisive dichotomy between "access" and "excellence." That reconciliation, little noted nor long remembered, which allows Suffolk University to be itself, is to be found in the unique combination of theory and practice that is coming to exist in all academic units of Suffolk University, in which the highest quality of careful, attentive, personalized classroom teaching is being fused with the widest possible access to experiential learning in the many "laboratories" with which the University must necessarily link itself in the cause of service to its students and to the community, the city, the state, the country, and the world around it.

Suffolk University has long professed, and demonstrated, an affinity for small business—in its programs, in the disposition of its graduates, in its selection of Trustees, and even in its approach to the "business" of education. The University's historic concentration has always been on service to its "customers," on providing a high-quality, reasonably-priced "product" in a straightforward way to a constituency inured to condescension—on running the university, in fine, like a small business, not a monastery. Suffolk, thereby, has consciously and carefully avoided drawing its alumni and students into the "mystique" of education with which many more "prestigious" institutions regale their postulants and draw them into a sense of incorporation into a mystical, eternal "body collegiate," to which they owe a spiritual (and financial) loyalty that is more than lifelong. On the contrary, Suffolk University has been (and continues to be) characterized by its emphasis on unencumbered service, its historic restraint from rhetoric and tactics primarily promoting self-perpetuation and monumentalization instead of "product." The School of Management's graduate program description emphasizes small business advisorship; the School maintains a Small Business Incubator Program and an association with the Small Business Institute of the Small Business Administration, through which students work with local small businesses in need of assistance. This solicitude for small businesses is, evidently, a simple matter of elective affinity. There is clearly something of the small business, and the small town, about Suffolk's core values: the personal attention, the personal politics, the tight-fisted economizing, the emphasis on service (and personal service in particular), the eyeball-to-eyeball interactions, the sense of purpose, the sense of scale, the sense of worth, of being taken seriously, of being conferred dignity as a human being.

In a world where economies of scale are assuming colossal importance, and are growing steadily more economically significant, Suffolk University's core values are becoming an endangered species. There is clearly a strong incentive to "grow," to change the scale of the institution for the economic benefits that the change might confer. But the consequences that skulk in the shadows of "bigness" are themselves treacherous—and potentially fatal—to what "scrappy" little Suffolk represents. The problems (and the threats) are those inherent in changing a small business into a large business, a small town into a large town.

Suffolk University strives to help every individual member of its learning community (students and faculty) identify, cultivate, and mobilize her or his own "special excellence"—just as the University itself is constantly attempting to do. Personal dignity and personal responsibility lie at the core of the Suffolk University education, in all three academic units. The institution's "small business" mentality, its gruff "don't tread on me" defense of individuals and individual enterprise, combines incongruously with its (equally real) high-Renaissance veneration of human autonomy and human scale to shape the Suffolk academic experience: small classes; personal attention, but with a focus on preparing the student to shift from dependence to autonomy (the "success skills" component in the College, the LPS program in the Law School, the SOM core experience); a high level of personal responsibility for each student in determining his or her own educational (and life) direction; preparation, then voluntarism.[48]

Ultimately, the common University goals outlined in June 1991, as part of the revised Mission Statement requested by President David Sargent, go far to define Suffolk University in 1995. The University is characterized as "a genuine community of student and faculty learners, mutually supportive and mutually respectful," strong emphasis is laid on "the University's historic mission to provide education of the highest possible quality and the greatest possible richness to a population of the greatest possible diversity, " a central commitment is confirmed "to the complementarity of quality...and of diversity," and a pledge is made (in very significant language) that

"[In] the University's efforts...to improve quality by increasing diversity. . . . 'Opportunity' and 'excellence' are not contradictory or opposing terms; they are 100% (and necessarily) compatible and complementary."[49]

In January 1939, President Gleason L. Archer offered to his Trustees the cautionary appeal that Suffolk University continue, after years of committed effort, to be engaged in "a great pioneer work that can succeed only if we exercise courage and vision similar to what has characterized the Suffolk of the past."[50]

President Archer would have been the first to admit, upon his involuntary retirement nine years later, that truths and deep ironies were indissolubly mixed in this pronouncement, as were courage, wisdom, pettiness, and folly in the history of the University which it invoked. Yet, even so, with all the appropriate caveats admitted, Archer's dictum holds today at Suffolk University, as does his purpose.

Endnotes

Chapter 1

1 Boston 200, *Boston: The Official Bicentennial Guidebook* (New York: E.P. Dutton, 1975), pp. 159-70.

2 Walter Muir Whitehill, *Boston: A Topographical History,* 2nd edition (Cambridge: Belknap Press, 1968), p. 8.

3 All population figures are from Whitehill, *Boston*; for the growth of the city, see Bonner's maps (1722-69) and Whitehill's discussions based on them, pp. 22-46.

4 The Hancock house was not demolished until 1863.

5 The land which the Tays and the Minots were subdividing had originally belonged, as early as 1648, to a family named Scottow. Faced with financial difficulties, the Scottows had been forced to sell the land; it was divided in 1691 between the Tay family, which received the eastern half, and the Minot family, which received the western half. Both families then continued to use their portions of the Scottow land for pasture until the boom times of the 1730s. Tay Street was renamed Temple Street in 1769 to honor Sir John

Temple, a slick commissioner of customs who played both sides before and during the Revolution, and his wife, the daughter of Governor James Bowdoin. Derne Street received its name from the 1804 American victory at Durna in the Tripolitan War. Allen Chamberlain, *Beacon Hill* (Boston: Houghton Mifflin, 1925), pp. 13, 237, disagrees with A.H. Thwing, *The Crooked and Narrow Streets of Boston* (Detroit: Singing Tree Press, 1970), p. 211, about the date in which Tay Street became Temple Street; Chamberlain is correct, however: it was 1769. On Derne Street, see Christina Robb, "Names," *Boston Globe Calendar,* May 19, 1977, p. 13.

6 George Street was renamed Hancock Street in 1788.

7 Chamberlain, *Beacon Hill,* p. 58; Thwing, *The Crooked and Narrow Streets,* pp. 210-11. On this and the preceding lot information, Chamberlain is an invaluable source; on street names, Thwing is good, though not infallible; on Hodson, see Chamberlain, p.31.

8 The farmhouses, located at 44 and 46 Temple Street, were demolished in 1952; see Boston Historic Conservation Committee (W.M. Whitehill, Chairman), *Beacon Hill: The North Slope* (Boston: By the Committee, 1963), pp. 11-12, and Chamberlain, *Beacon Hill,* pp. 236-39.

9 Chamberlain, *Beacon Hill,* p. 215.

10 Eliza Susan Morton (later Mrs. Josiah Quincy), 1795, quoted in Whitehill, *Boston,* p. 52.

11 Thomas Bulfinch, 1815, quoted in Whitehill, *Boston,* p. 70.

12 Today, the Longfellow Bridge occupies the former site of the West Boston Bridge.

13 The Bulfinch Building at Massachusetts General Hospital still stands: there, in an amphitheater known today as the Ether Dome, the first public demonstration of the use of ether in a surgical operation was performed on October 16, 1846.

14 Chamberlain, *Beacon Hill,* p. 216; Whitehill, *Boston,* provides valuable information on the shearing of the peaks.

15 Boston Historic Conservation Committee (henceforth B.H.C.C.), *North Slope,* p. 4.

16 Another aspect of the neighborhood's movement toward respectability was the rebuilding of the Athenaeum (founded 1807) in 1847-49 at 10½ Beacon Street. On the Northeast Slope churches and their religious rivalries, see the chapters on Boston's religious communities in the nineteenth century in Volume III of Justin Winsor, ed., *The Memorial History of Boston,* 4 volumes (Boston; James P. Osgood, 1881); on the Bowdoin Street Church, see Lyman Beecher, *Autobiography,* 2 volumes, ed. Barbara M. Cross (Cambridge: Belknap Press, 1961), Volume II, pp. 171-84, and A. McVoy McIntyre, *Beacon Hill: A Walking Tour* (Boston: Beacon Hill Civic Association, 1975), p.107.

17 On the activities of the abolitionist party, see the chapter in Volume III of Winsor, ed., *Memorial History;* and on their residences, see Boston 200, *Bicentennial Guidebook,* pp. 164-70.

18 B.H.C.C., *North Slope,* pp. 4, 12; Whitehill, *Boston,* pp. 110-11; on the extension of Temple Street, see Chamberlain, *Beacon Hill,* p. 28.

19 Oscar Handlin, *Boston's Immigrants 1790-1880,* revised and enlarged edition (New York: Atheneum, 1977), pp. 94-98.

20 Peter Roger Knights, *The Plain People of Boston 1830-60* (Ph.D. Dissertation, Wisconsin, 1969), p. 59; on the Beacon Hill Reservoir, see Carl Seaburg, *Boston Observed* (Boston: Beacon Press, 1971), pp. 293-94, and Winsor, ed., *Memorial History,* Vol. IV, p. 483; on both the reservoir and the earlier discussion of ropewalks, see McIntyre, *Beacon Hill,* pp. 105-06.

21 B.H.C.C., *North Slope,* p. 5; on what follows (including the store fronts), see *North Slope,* p. 12.

22 During this same period, however, a Catholic church (St. Joseph's, opened 1862) was established in the West End near Cambridge Street. The congregation, drawn from the new Irish and, later, Italian residents, increased steadily throughout the last half of the nineteenth century and the first half of the twentieth. St. Joseph's Church stands today, immediately behind Charles River Plaza, having survived the destruction of the West End in the early 1960s.

23 The monument discussion is based on Chamberlain, *Beacon Hill,* p. 29. The replacement of the monument had been voted in 1865, but was not carried out until 1898; the new monument incorporated Bulfinch's original eagle and tablets, which had been stored in a State House garret since the removal of the first monument in 1811.

24 Boston 200, *Bicentennial Guidebook,* pp. 32-35.

25 Suffolk Law School catalogue, 1936, p. 11.

26 The school had been Archer's Evening Law School in 1906-07; but from the time it became clear that a move into downtown Boston would be necessary, Archer had begun to cast about for a new name. He rejected "Boston Law School" as being too easily confused with Boston University Law School; but he gave active consideration to a number of other names such as Bay State, Massachusetts, Atlantic, New England, and Suffolk. Good Yankee and "true" (Anglo-Saxon) American that he was, Archer chose Suffolk as the "most appropriate of all." "To be sure," he said, "it was the name of a county in Massachusetts, but it was also an old English name derived from the more ancient 'South-folk'." It was also "alliterative, clear cut, and sonorous." From the summer of 1907 on, Archer's Evening Law School became the Suffolk School of Law. Gleason L. Archer, *Building A School* (Boston: By the Author, 1919), p. 59.

27 *Ibid.,* p. 78.

28 Everett C. Marston, *Origins and Development of Northeastern University* (Boston: Northeastern University, 1961), pp. 1-25; Edward R. Speare, *Interesting Happenings in Boston University's History* (Boston: Boston University Press, 1957), pp. 37-39. While they were both law students at Boston University, Gleason and Hiram Archer shared a room on Myrtle Street. It probably should be mentioned—if only for the sake of symmetry—that the Boston College Law School was founded in 1929.

29 The sign remained until 1937, when it was replaced with one which read "Suffolk University." That one stayed in place until 1946. Archer also had a plan in 1920 to pay for the new building partially out of revenues obtained by showing motion pictures in the school auditorium during the day. When that plan proved less lucrative than hoped for, daytime classes were inaugurated in 1924.

30 The General Court of Massachusetts created the Historic Beacon Hill District by Chapter 616 of the Acts of 1955, which also set up the Beacon Hill Architectural Commission as a watchdog group for the District. The area included in the Historic District has been expanded several times by acts of the General Court; Temple, Derne, and Hancock Streets were added in 1963.

Chapter 2

1 Suffolk Law School catalogue, 1923-24, p.17.

2 Archer's name disappeared from the Law School catalogue in 1947-48, and from the College catalogue in 1955-56; it was restored to the College catalogues in 1978-79, but, other than the listing of a Gleason L. Archer Scholarship after 1969, it did not reappear in the Law School catalogue until 1995-96.

3 A student initiative in the spring of 1968 began the rehabilitation of Archer's reputation. Led by Business School junior Lou Farina, a group of "interested students" petitioned the Trustees to have the "old" building (20 Derne

Street) named for Gleason Archer, and to have a repository established for Archer's "books, papers, and other relevant materials." The Board voted to grant the latter request in September 1968—although it was not actually implemented until eleven years later. The former request was satisfied when the "old" building was named "in honor of the Archer family" in September 1971. A Gleason L. Archer Law Scholarship was established by the Board in September 1968. The portrait of President Archer now hangs—unshrouded—in the Munce Conference Room, Archer Building.

4 Sam Smith, "Dean Archer's Career a Horatio Alger Story," *Boston Post,* February 6, 1927. Archer stood six feet, one and a half inches tall; his weight fluctuated between 175 and 200 pounds. His hair had turned gray by the time he was forty.

5 Horatio Alger was born January 13, 1834, and died July 18, 1899. He was the author of more than a hundred books, among the better known of which were *Ragged Dick, Tattered Tom,* and *Luck and Pluck.*

6 Gleason Archer, "Lumber Camp to College" (unpublished autobiography), p. 2 1/2. For material on Archer's life prior to his departure for Sabattus, see "Lumber Camp to College," pp. 1-325, and two other unpublished autobiographies by Archer: "Rainbow Trail," pp. 1-268, and "Lumber Jack Land," pp. 202-386.

7 "Lumber Camp to College," p. 2 1/2; see also Gleason Archer, *Ancestors and Descendants of Joshua Williams* (Boston: By the Author, 1927). Archer was Counselor-General of the American Society of Mayflower Descendants from 1933 until 1939; he was also a life member of the Massachusetts Society of Mayflower Descendants, an honorary life member of the National Society of Puritan Descendants, and a member of the Sons of the American Revolution.

8 The Archer children were: Clifford, 1876-1926; Hiram 1878-1966; Gleason, 1880-1966; Perley, 1883-1903; Ella, born and died 1885; Maurice, 1886-1899; unnamed male infant, born and died 1888; Maude, 1889-1962; Harold, 1891-1968; and Claude, 1892-1910. Archer's mother lived from 1857 until 1905; his father was born in 1851 and died in 1931.

9 During his senior year, Archer stayed with the Williams family; on his time at Sabattus High School, see "Lumber Camp to College," pp. 326-461, and "Rainbow Trail," pp. 269-371.

10 During the remainder of his college and law school career, Gleason roomed successively at 70 Pinckney Street, 4th floor (summer 1903); 48 Pinckney Street, 2nd floor (fall 1903); 66 Myrtle Street (October 1903-summer 1904; owned by Mr. and Mrs. Jesse Dean); 63 Myrtle Street (fall 1904-spring 1905); and 66 Myrtle Street again (spring 1905-summer 1906). On his school days in Boston, see "Lumber Camp to College," pp. 462-632, and "Rainbow Trail," pp. 371-497.

11 "Lumber Camp to College," pp. 514-42; "Rainbow Trail," pp. 412-43; Gleason Archer, *Fifty Years of Suffolk University* (Boston: By the Author, 1956), pp. 1-2. The hotel name appears as "Cotocheset" in "Lumber Camp to College," p. 514.

12 "Rainbow Trail," p. 507; *Fifty Years of Suffolk University,* p. 2. On the general events of the summer of 1906, see "Lumber Camp to College," pp. 632-34, and "Rainbow Trail," pp. 498-509.

13 Archer also taught at the Durham, Maine, school in the spring of 1902, after he had taught at Great Pond in the spring of 1901. On his 1905 law tutoring, see Archer's manuscript history of his "Evening Law School": also "Lumber Camp to College," pp. 612-13, and "Rainbow Trail," pp. 489-90. Archer appears to have been personally fond of the Horatio Alger tales: his son, Gleason, Jr., recalls that Dean Archer made numerous books by Alger available to him and his siblings as they were growing up.

14 Gleason Archer, *Building A School* (Boston: By the Author, 1919), pp. 48-49: the "flat topped mission office desk"at which Archer sat (p. 45) was donated to the Suffolk University Archives in 1974. In his search for an apartment, Archer had been drawn to Alpine Street because "Uncle" John Hanson, widowed husband of Lucy Archer, his father's sister, lived there.

15 A defense by Archer of "true Americanism" first appeared in the Suffolk Law School catalogue, 1923-24, p.18; it was reprinted more often than any other material in that catalogue, and was not eliminated until 1944-45.

16 On Archer's Progressivism, see Chapter One, pp. 10-12. For an excellent general discussion of American responses to immigration, see John Higham, *Strangers in the Land: Patterns of American Nativism 1860-1925* (New Brunswick, N.J.; Rutgers University Press, 1955).

17 *Building A School,* pp. 51-97; see also Archer's scrapbooks of newspaper clippings from this era. The prototype Suffolk Law School ring, designed by Archer at this time and bearing the seal he created, was worn by the Dean until it passed to his son many years later. It was donated to the Suffolk Archives by Gleason L. Archer, Jr., in 1980. Gleason, Sr., changed the name of "Archer's Evening Law School" to "Suffolk School of Law" when it moved to the old Suffolk Savings Bank Building in the fall of 1907; the name was changed to "Suffolk Law School" when the institution received its charter to grant degrees in 1914.

18 For a chronological list of Archer's publications, see Chapter Two, note 44.

19 *Building A School.* pp. 108-11. The old Suffolk Savings Bank Building at 53 Tremont Street had been gas-lit.

20 Archer married Elizabeth Glenn Snyder on October 6, 1906; they had met as students at Boston University. Four children were born to them, of whom three survived infancy: Allan Frost Archer (named for Archer's friend Allan Gleason and for George Frost), born in 1908; Marian Glenn Archer (named for one of her mother's sisters), born 1910; and Gleason Leonard Archer, Jr., born in 1916. Norman Bradley Archer was born, and died, in 1912. After their marriage, the Archers lived at 6 Alpine Street, Roxbury, until June 1909, when they moved to a house on Mishawum Road, Woburn. They remained there until removing to the top floor of the school building in September 1914.

21 *An Important Message* (1919) was produced by Archer as publicity for this expansion campaign; it was reprinted in 1978 as the first number in the Suffolk University Historical Pamphlet Series. On this period, see Gleason Archer, *The Impossible Task* (Boston: Suffolk Law School Press, 1926). The Law School grew from 14 students in 1906, to 135 in 1914, to 761 in 1920, to a peak of 2604 in 1927. In the face of continued growth after 1920, a Temple Street Annex was added (also under Dean Archer's supervision) to 20 Derne Street in 1923-24.

22 Archer purchased a bungalow on Stetson Road in Norwell in 1916; five years later, he bought a larger house across Stetson Road from the bungalow. Although living most of the year at the law school, the Archers spent their summers and holidays in the "country" at Norwell. The bungalow was finally sold to Catharine Caraher in 1933. On the Archer family and its occupations in the school, see *Ancestors and Descendants,* as well as Suffolk catalogues and Trustee minutes for this period. An interview with Gleason Archer, Jr., also provided insight. Not to be outdone by her relatives, Elizabeth Glenn Archer composed a school song, "Hymn to Suffolk."

23 Both Hiram Archer and the Reverend Leonard Williams married Stinchfields: John F. Stinchfield served as Librarian at Suffolk from 1910 until 1912. On Archer's relatives, see *Ancestors and Descendants:* on their occupations and on the "Maine mafia," see the Suffolk catalogues and Trustee minutes for the period 1921-30. Useful information was also provided in interviews with Catharine (Caraher) Finnegan, Kenneth B. Williams, and Dorothy McNamara. In

addition, Archer maintained until his resignation a pension list of needy individuals who had helped or befriended him during his early struggles at the school.

24 Alden Cleveland lived at 73 Hancock Street until 1939, when it was given up by the Alumni Association: he had managed the Suffolk Bookstore before being drafted by Archer as Alumni Secretary. At Norwell, Archer constructed with his own hands a log cabin and a screened, open-air dining platform. They were christened, respectively, the "Reverie" and the " Air Castle." Both were located well away from the main house, beside a bubbling spring. Archer also dug a trout brook and pond there, using the run-off from the spring for water. He stocked the pond with trout and trained them to bite on hamburger, so that only his guests could successfully fish the pond. Ultimately, he even constructed a net over the pond to repel predatory birds. It was an extraordinary complex, and it provides an excellent indication both of Archer's manual dexterity and of the lengths to which he would go to provide hospitality for his guests. Interviews with Catharine (Caraher) Finnegan and Gleason Archer, Jr., afforded me some indication of why an invitation to Norwell was so highly valued; and Elizabeth Archer's first book, *Poems on Nature and Human Nature* (Boston: By the Author, 1930), also contains a revealing set of verses on "The Air Castle."

25 Gleason Archer, *The Educational Octopus* (Boston: By the Author, 1915), p. 278; *Building A School,* p. 78; Gleason Archer, *How Suffolk University Was Captured* (Boston: By the Author, 1956), p. 1.

26 "Rainbow Trail," p. 39.

27 Gleason Archer, "Journal II" (1920-32, unpublished), p. 384. Half of Suffolk's students were of Irish descent throughout Archer's tenure (for example, see survey in Suffolk Law School catalogue, 1925-26, pp. 21-22).

28 "Archer Refuses to Serve Curley," *Boston Traveler,* July 25, 1936. Among other civic offices to which Archer was appointed were: chief state arbiter for the Springfield Street Railway strike, 1914; special assistant to Massachusetts Commissioners on Uniform State Laws, 1926-28; Conference Committee on Unemployment, 1930; State Utilities Commission, 1935; and Shoe Industry Committee, 1935. In addition, he was a Trustee of the First Methodist Church, one of the first presidents of the Park Street Men's Club, on the Advisory Council of the Committee for Constitutional Government, a member of the Bostonian Society, and a Rotarian. Throughout his life, he was also an active supporter of temperance organizations and prohibition.

29 "Dean Archer Lauds Solons," *Boston Evening American,* March 29, 1932; "Archer Joins New Deal Foes," *Boston Traveler,* August 13, 1936; "Archer Declines Governor Curley Appointment," *Boston Evening Transcript,* July 24, 1936. All of Suffolk's charters (1914, 1935, 1937) were challenged by the State Board of Education: on the other conflicts, see Chapter Two, notes 31 and 39.

30 "Dean Archer Lauds Solons," *Boston Evening American,* March 29, 1932; Gleason Archer, "Equality of Opportunity Demanded," *Boston Evening American,* April 4, 1932; Gleason Archer, " Dean Archer Checks on Bar Test Correctors," *Boston Evening American,* April 5, 1932; "Journal II," pp. 121, 248. Archer refers to the "juggernaut of monopoly" in "Journal III" (1932-34, unpublished), p. 1.

31 "Archer and Law School Scored," *Boston Herald,* February 18, 1930; "Journal II," pp. 120, 125-26; "Journal III," p. 1. Archer was attacked as a "reactionary" not only because he opposed compulsory college training for lawyers, but also because he denounced the case method in favor of black-letter law. The National Association of Law Schools was still alive, if only on paper, in 1945-46; that was the last year in which the Suffolk Law School catalogue identifies Suffolk as a member. Archer's honorary degrees came from Atlanta Law School (LLD, 1926) and John Marshall Law School, Chicago (LLM, 1944). When Archer became convinced in 1932 that the Massachusetts Board of Bar Examiners was discriminating against evening

law school candidates, he opened a full-scale attack on the Board, its members, and the "monopolists" with which it was "conspiring." Archer not only appealed to the General Court to curb the Bar Examiners' power; he also carried his case to the general public in spirited newspaper columns and radio broadcasts. On the significance of this and the "college monopoly" fight, see Jerold S. Auerbach, *Unequal Justice: Lawyers and Social Change in Modern America* (New York: Oxford University Press, 1976).

32 The account of Archer's radio career is based on "Journal II," pp. 274-79, 298-325.

33 For a list of the books based on Archer's broadcasts and broadcasting experience, see Chapter Two, note 44.

34 Suffolk College of Liberal Arts catalogue, 1934-35, p. 4; "Journal II," p. 348.

35 Archer had purchased 32, 34, 59, and 73 Hancock Street, and 2 Myrtle Street, by 1927. He brought 5 Hancock Street in December 1927, and sold it again in 1928. He then purchased 40 Hancock Street in the spring of 1928. According to Dorothy McNamara, his plan was that Suffolk should one day expand northward from 20 Derne Street in the block bounded by Derne, Temple, Hancock, and Cambridge Streets—much as it has done many years later. Archer was also counselor to a real estate operation in Duxbury run by Carrolla Bryant (see Chapter Two, note 39).

36 After Marian Archer's marriage in 1935, her mother lived mainly in Norwell, while Dean Archer continued to reside at the school. He moved to 40 Hancock Street in 1937, when reconstruction of the University Building began, and remained there until 1948.

37 On these conflicts, see Trustee minutes and the transcripts of Board meetings that were taken from 1946 until 1948. See also Gleason Archer's "Status of Suffolk University, January 16, 1939" (reply to Hiram Archer's memorandum to the Board), President Archer's "Program for Accreditation of Suffolk University (April 10, 1947)," his "In re the Evans Bill—Senate 433 (Remarks before Joint Committee on Education, January 26, 1948)," and *How Suffolk University Was Captured.* Interviews with John Griffin, Kenneth B. Williams, Donald Goodrich, and Gleason Archer, Jr., have also been very helpful.

38 "Dean Archer Heads Anti-Roosevelt Drive," *Boston Herald,* August 14, 1936; "House Probes Dean Archer's Organization," *Boston Traveler,* October 7, 1944; "Archer Group Probe Shifts to Dallas, Texas," *Boston Traveler,* October 10, 1944; Gleason Archer, *On the Cuff* (Boston: Suffolk University Press, 1944), back jacket; see also Otis L. Graham, Jr., *Encore for Reform: The Old Progressives and the New Deal* (New York: Oxford University Press, 1967). As head of the American Democratic National Committee, Archer found himself with some unsavory bedfellows; the organization (and *On the Cuff*) received enthusiastic support from both the Reverend Charles E. Coughlin's Christian Front and Gerald L.K. Smith's America First Party. The subsequent Congressional investigation of the ADNC did nothing to raise Archer's standing in the eyes of his Trustees.

39 The attempt to attract financial support during Suffolk's wartime crisis had brought to the Board ambitious, strong-willed men. Tension quickly developed between them and Carrolla Bryant. Archer had hired Miss Bryant, a former radio executive at WEAF in New York, as Registrar of the new "collegiate departments" in 1936. When Suffolk became a University one year later, she became Executive Secretary of the University. By 1939, she had replaced Catharine Caraher as Archer's right hand. A number of Trustees blamed her influence over the President for his obduracy. During the postwar crunch, a proposal was floated in the Board to retrench financially by abolition of the fledgling colleges. Miss Bryant, chief administrative officer of the colleges, steeled Archer against the Trustees' plan; by using his own money, he was able to keep the colleges open in the fall of 1945. Over opposition by the Board of Collegiate Authority, President Archer appealed to the state legislature, so that the Suffolk colleges could receive accreditation and the students there become

eligible for G.I. Bill funding. Accreditation was granted in March 1946; the colleges were saved. The Trustees, however, dealt harshly with the defiant saviors. Miss Bryant was summarily dismissed; Archer was deposed as Treasurer, and most of his authority as President was stripped from him. It was at this point that he petitioned both the courts and the legislature for suspension of the Trustees' authority. The internecine struggle became a public brawl.

40 Hiram Archer, however, remained; he had outspokenly criticized his brother and Miss Bryant since before the war, and he was instrumental in organizing opposition to them. Hiram continued to serve the University, as Police School Director, Alumni Director, and finally as Suffolk's first Archivist, until his death in 1966. His "defection" in 1948 left a wide family rift: it was years before the two brothers were reconciled. Also see Chapter Two, note 37.

41 During the confrontation of 1945-48, irresponsible accusations were hurled by both sides. The one which receives most notoriety, however, was the charge by one Trustee that President Archer had, over the years, siphoned some two million dollars from the school. Since indictment always receives larger print than exoneration, I feel constrained to dignify the charge by noting that an independent audit conducted by order of the Trustees in 1947 found Gleason Archer free from any financial wrongdoing. Stories have since circulated at Suffolk (from what source, I cannot ascertain) about Archer's loose handling of school monies—as, for instance, his having grabbed (literally) handfuls of tuition money at registration to take his staff to dinner. Catharine (Caraher) Finnegan, who maintained the scrupulous financial records which gained Archer a clean bill of health in 1947, indignantly denied that any such thing could have taken place. It would have disrupted her accounts, she asserted, and she would not have permitted it.

42 Archer and his first wife, Elizabeth, had been separated for years by the time she died in 1961. Archer had moved in 1948 from 40 Hancock Street to the ten-acre farm he purchased on Old Washington Street in Pembroke. Elizabeth Archer continued to live at the Norwell complex until 1955, after which she lived with relatives until moving, two years before her death, to a Hanover, Massachusetts, nursing home. Polly Clark, a singer and radio-TV personality, was an old friend of Archer: her husband was John Clark, the WBZ Program Director who had launched Archer's broadcasting career. The Clarks had lost touch with Gleason Archer, but, after John Clark's death in 1959, Polly Clark's career brought her back to Boston—where contact was reestablished by the widowed Dean. After their marriage, Gleason Archer and his new wife moved to 222 Hollis Avenue, North Quincy, where they remained until Archer's death. He was buried in Centre Cemetery, Pembroke. An interview with Polly Archer proved very helpful, as have materials contributed by her.

43 *Fifty Years of Suffolk University,* p. 8: "Journal II," p. 385.

44 Chronological List of Writings by Gleason Archer

Published

1889 *Ellsworth (Maine) American:* "Battleship Maine," May 3, 1899: "The Labor Problem," May 31, 1899; "The Story of a Stone," July 19, 1899; "The Forest," August, 1899.

1901 *Lewiston (Maine) Journal* and *Webster (Maine) Herald* (Volume I, Number 1, October 18, 1901 - December, 1901): various articles. Also edited the latter. *Maine High School:* edited magazine and wrote various articles.

1907 Suffolk University catalogues: Law School catalogue through 1945-46 edition and fall, 1946, flyer; College catalogue through 1947-48 edition. Also wrote Suffolk flyers, brochures, and program announcements until 1948.

1910 *Law Office and Court Procedure.* Boston: Little, Brown, and Company. *Ethical Obligations of the Lawyer.* Boston: Little, Brown, and Company. *Suffolk Law Student* (Volume 1, Number 1, December, 1910 - March, 1911): various articles.

1911 *The Law of Contracts.* Chicago: T.H. Flood and Company. Second edition, 1916. Chicago: T.H. Flood and Company; then reprinted by Suffolk Law School Press, 1920.

1915 *The Law of Agency.* Chicago: T.H. Flood and Company. Reprinted by Suffolk Law School Press, 1926. *The Educational Octopus* (first 57 chapters of *Building A School*). Boston: By the Author. *Suffolk Law School Register* (Volume 1, Number 1, October, 1915 - June, 1921): various articles.

1916 *The Law of Torts.* Boston: Suffolk Law School Press. Second edition, 1920. Boston: Suffolk Law School Press.

1918 *Principles of Equity and Trusts.* Boston: Suffolk Law School Press. Second edition, 1927. Boston: Suffolk Law School Press.

1919 *The Law of Evidence.* Boston Suffolk Law School Press. Second edition, 1929. Boston: Suffolk Law School Press. *Introduction to the Study of Law in Suffolk Law School.* Boston: Suffolk Law School Press. *Building A School.* Boston: By the Author. *An Important Message. Boston:* Suffolk Law School Press. (Fund appeal for expansion campaign).

1923 *Criminal Law.* Boston: Suffolk Law School Press. *The Law of Real Property.* Boston: Suffolk Law School Press. Second edition, 1927. Boston: Suffolk Law School Press.

1925 *Wills and Probate.* Boston: Suffolk Law School Press. *Boston Traveler:* "Leniency Due to Several Factors," March 28, 1925.

1926 *The Impossible Task.* Boston: Suffolk Law School Press.

1927 *Ancestors and Descendants of Joshua Williams.* Boston: Wright and Potter Printing Company. *Suffolk Alumni News* (Volume 1, Number 1, April, 1927 - March/April 1931): numerous articles; editor during 1927.

1928 *The Law of Private Corporations.* Boston: Suffolk Law School Press. *History of the Law.* Boston: Suffolk Law School Press. Forward, Chronology, and Historical Sketch in *Suffolk Law Alumni Directory.* Boston: Suffolk Law Alumni Association. *American Law School Review,* December, 1928: "Address to Section on Legal Education, July 26, 1928" (offprint).

1929 *Digest of Criminal Law Cases.* Boston: Suffolk Law School Press. "Remarks before Executive Committee of American Bar Association at Miami, Florida, January 16, 1929." "Facts and Implications of College Monopoly of Legal Education (Address to Section on Legal Education, American Bar Association, at Memphis, Tennessee, October 22, 1929)." "What is Wrong with the Section on Legal Education?"

1930 *Digest of Evidence Cases.* Boston: Suffolk Law School Press. *First Essentials of Law Study.* Boston: Suffolk Law School Press. *Boston Sunday Herald.* April 13 - June 1, 1930: Transcripts of Archer's Boston Tercentenary historical radio broadcasts.

1931 *Mayflower Heroes.* New York and London: The Century Company. (First half of Archer's radio broadcasts on the history of Plimoth Plantation). *Laws That Safeguard Society.* Boston: Suffolk Law School Press. (First thirty-six broadcasts of Archer's NBC radio series on law).

1932 *Radio Digest:* "Education by Radio," January, 1932. NBC radio broadcasts published verbatim in *Radio Digest* after 1932. "Amazing Conduct of Bar Examiners, February 15, 1932" (to the General Court). "Analysis of Bar Exam Bills of 1932, Second Edition, March 18, 1932" (date of first edition uncertain). "Bar Exam of January, 1932 (Radio Address, WBZ, March 20, 1932)." "Control of Admission to Bar by Supreme Court or Legislature? March 30, 1932." *Boston Evening American,* April 4-8, 1932: Four articles on Bar Examiners. "First Thanksgiving" for United Press (1300 papers), November 7, 1932. *RudyMents* (Rudy Vallee fan paper): article in December, 1932, issue.

1934 "Notes on Motor Vehicle Law" (?); included in list of Archer's works in several Law School catalogues. Forward to an article in Carrolla A. Bryant, *Pilgrim Homes and How They Were Built* (brochure for Duxbury Realty Company; Miss Carrolla A. Bryant, Director, and Gleason L. Archer, Counsellor).

1935 *Americana* (magazine of lhe American Historical Society): serialized articles that were published in 1936 as *With Axe and Musket at Plymouth.*

1936 *With Axe and Musket at Plymouth.* New York: The American Historical Society, Inc. (Second half of Archer's radio broadcasts on the history of Plimoth Plantation). *Suffolk Journal* (Volume 1, Number 1, September 19, 1936-May, 1940): numerous articles.

1937 "In re House Bill 477 - An Act to Establish Suffolk University (Letter to the Committee on Education)."

1938 *Americana:* serialized articles (six parts) beginning in April, 1938: nine copies bound in book form in March, 1947, under title *Pioneers of the Rock-Bound Coast. History of Radio to 1926.* New York: The American Historical Society, Inc.

1939 *Big Business and Radio.* New York: The American Historical Company, Inc.

1941 "Data for Joseph F. Dineen - In re: Gleason L. Archer, President, Suffolk University (September 19, 1941)."

1944 *On the Cuff.* Boston: Suffolk University Press.

1947 "Program for the Accreditation of Suffolk University (Special Report to the Board of Trustees, April 10, 1947)." "Letter to the Legislature of Massachusetts, May 6,1947." "Letter to the Legislature of Massachusetts, May 12,1947" (supplement to May 6,1947 letter). "Letter to the Hon. Joseph W. Martin, Jr., November 26, 1947" (letter to the Speaker of the U.S. House of Representatives on the treatment of Suffolk University law students by the Veterans Administration).

1948 "In re the Evans Bill — Senate 433 (Remarks before Joint Committee on Education, January 26,1948)." "The Rowell Audit of Suffolk University, January 27,1948." "Harmony Vitally Essential, January 28, 1948." "A Valentine from Stoneman. February 15, 1948 (Letter to the Joint Committee on Education)."

1956 *Fifty Years of Suffolk University.* Boston: By the Author. (Address given before the Alumni of Suffolk University, April 5, 1956). *How Suffolk University Was Captured.* Boston: By the Author. (Address before Wig and Robe Society of Suffolk University, April 30, 1956).

1961 *Robert, Duke of Kragcastle.* New York: Pageant Press, Inc.

Unpublished (Book-length Manuscripts and Typescripts)

"Archer's Evening Law School: History and Statistics" (ca 1907).

"Journal II" (1920-32), personal journal.

"Laws That Safeguard Society" (typescript of thirty-seventh broadcast, April 4, 1931, to seventy-first broadcast, December 5, 1931).

"Laws That Safeguard Society" (Typescript of seventy-second broadcast, December 12, 1931, to one hundred and twenty-fourth broadcast, June 4, 1933).

"Journal III" (1932-34), personal journal.

"Weekly Broadcasts on the History of the Massachusetts Bay Colony" (roughly two years' worth; these broadcasts followed the two years of broadcasts on Plimoth Plantation which were published in *Mayflower Heroes* and *With Axe and Musket at Plymouth*).

"Lumber Camp to College," 1947 (1880-1906 autobiography, with addenda).

"America 1620-1932" (2 copies); also part of same entitled "New England in America" ("Brewster, Bradford, Winslow, and Co."), dated 1950-51.

"Lumber Jack Land" (autobiography, 1889-April 17, 1896; second half of first part of 1880-1906 autobiography of which "Lumber Jack to Lawyer" is the second part).

"Lumber Jack to Lawyer" (autobiography April 17, 1896-1906); dated February, 1959. Chapter 1 is Chapter XXX in "Rainbow Trail."

"Rainbow Trail" (autobiography, 1880-1906); ca. 1959.

"The Tudor Dynasty" (1961).

"Princess Magda's Embattled Trout Brook" (1962).

"More Than A Man" (biography of George Washington), n.d.

"The New England Colonies 1628-92." n. d.

"Plymouth Pioneers" (1628-29), n. d.

Radio

Sunday afternoon, September 29, 1929: "Equality of Opportunity." WBZ-WBZA.

Beginning November 12, 1929, Tuesday afternoons, 4:15-4:35 (moved to 7:15 PM shortly thereafter): "Crime" ("Criminal Law"), WBZ-WBZA.

March 17, 1930. Monday, 4:45-5:00 PM: Inaugural Boston Tercentenary broadcast, WNAC; also later Tercentenary broadcasts (WEEI, WBZ-WBZA, WLOE, WLEX).

Beginning April 11, 1930, Fridays, 11:45 AM: NBC network Tercentenary historical broadcasts, WEAF (New York); after end of historical series, began (July 15, 1930, Tuesdays, 7:15 PM) "Laws That Safeguard Society," WEAF/NBC. Moved to Saturdays, 7:15 PM. from January 10, 1931 until series ended June 4, 1933; also aired on WBZ on Thursday evenings from January 19, 1933.

Beginning January, 1931, Tuesdays, 7:45 PM: "Colonial History" (first Plimoth Plantation, then Massachusetts Bay Colony), WBZ-WBZA; moved to Sundays, 3:00-3:15 PM in February, 1931. Still broadcasting this series (Sundays, 4:15-4:30 PM) in April, 1934.

January 31-February 12. 1932: eight broadcasts on "Bar Exam Abuses in Massachusetts," WBZ-WBZA; also March 20, 1932 broadcast on the "Bar Exam of January, 1932," WBZ-WBZA.

December 3,1939-February 4, 1940, Sundays, 3:45-4:00 PM: "New Series" of nine broadcasts, on various topics, for Suffolk University, WBZ-WBZA.

Beginning March 4, 1940, Mondays, 7:30 PM: "Pioneers of Essex County," WESX. Still broadcasting this series in April, 1940.

Chapter 3

1 Suffolk University Law School, 1938 catalogue, p. 2. On the Law School's early history, see Chapter Two and David L. Robbins, "Opportunity's Haven: The Ambiguous Heritage of Suffolk University Law School" (*Advocate,* 75th Anniversary Issue, 1981). Some material in the present chapter first appeared in that *Advocate* article.

2 Suffolk University Law School, 1939 catalogue, p. 6.

3 Suffolk University's 1979-81 capital funds drive was designated the "Campaign for Excellence."

4 Dean Archer experimented briefly with a full-time day program between September 1911 and May 1915; daytime classes were reinaugurated in

September 1924 and have been offered continuously (excluding the war years 1942-45) ever since.

5 High school equivalency was required by the Massachusetts bar examiners after March 1910; in 1916, attendance at the Summer Preparatory Department was required by Dean Archer of all Suffolk Law students who lacked a high school diploma.

6 Many students came to Suffolk not to become lawyers, but to acquaint themselves with certain areas of law for business careers; they attended only until their needs, or curiosity, had been satisfied, and then dropped out—thereby swelling the attrition rate to a misleading level. Between September 1906 and June 1937, 10,600 students attended Suffolk Law; of these, 2887 (or 27.2%) received degrees.

7 A moot court program was instituted in September 1907; it was discontinued in 1914.

8 Suffolk Law School, 1929 catalogue, p. 33.

9 Director Hiram J. Archer thus became the first full-time member of Suffolk's instructional staff; until 1943, the school's only full-time faculty members (a maximum of four) were Research and Review Department personnel.

10 Suffolk's competitors were Harvard Law (founded 1817), B.U. Law (1872), the YMCA (later Northeastern) Law School (1898), and Portia Law School (1908); B.C. Law was founded in 1929.

11 Arthur W. McLean (1907-22), Webster A. Chandler (1907-18), Frederick O. Downes (1907-31), A. Chesley York (1907-41), Thomas R.P. Gibb (1909-18), Wilmot R. Evans (1911-13, 1923-35), Walter R. Meins (1911-18), and Leon R. Eyges (1912-17).

12 George A. Douglas '09 (1910-25), Karl G. Baker '16 (1918-27), Joseph A Parks '17 (1915-41), Leo Wyman '18 (1921-41, 1953-59), John L. Hurley '18 (1919-45, 1951-57), William H. Henchey '21 (1921-38), George H. Spillane '21 (1921-34), Arthur V. Getchell '22 (1922-62), Harry Bloomberg '25 (1926-35), Thomas J. Finnegan '26 (1927-41), and Kenneth B. Williams '27 (1929-59).

13 The new College was co-educational; in 1937, the Law School formally opened its doors to women as well. In 1938, a combined degree (BA/LLB) program was instituted, which allowed Suffolk College upperclassmen to satisfy their last year of BA requirements with the first year of Suffolk Law School credits.

14 The Law School, the College of Liberal Arts, the College of Journalism (1936), and the College of Business Administration (1937) were chartered as Suffolk University on April 29, 1937; the next day, Gleason Archer became the University's first President, while also retaining (to the consternation of many) the Deanship of the Law School.

15 Suffolk Law offered both day and evening students only a four-year (part-time) program until 1943. Evening classes for the part-time program continued throughout the war; day classes, however, were suspended in September 1942 to make room for wartime WAACS training. When the expected WAACS contract fell through, a full-time program of day classes was begun, and day classes for the part-time program were restored, in September 1943.

16 Parke served on the Suffolk Law faculty from 1943 until 1964; Donald R. Simpson, 1945-55 and 1959-72; Pray taught part-time at the institution until 1952.

17 A practice court had been inaugurated in the Graduate School of Law on January 29, 1940; a leading figure in the movement for its adoption was Professor John L. Hurley.

18 Judges and lawyers remained dominant on the Board for the next twenty years; by the late 1950s, Land Court Judge John E. Fenton had emerged as Donahues's only serious rival for Trustee leadership. Fenton, also an alumnus, served as University Vice-President (1957-65), President (1965-70), and Board Chairman (1964-66, 1970-74).

19 Donald Simpson thus described his father, in an interview on December 1, 1979.

20 Thomas Reed Powell served on the Law School faculty from 1950 until 1956; Hurley, who had already served from 1919 until 1945, returned in 1951 and remained until 1957. O'Brien had taught English in the College of Liberal Arts, served as Dean of the College of Business Administration, and obtained an LLB from Boston University before his appointment to the Suffolk Law School faculty in 1948.

21 To help him with his decisions as interim Dean, O'Brien set up a Faculty Administrative Committee (consisting of all full-time faculty members) in 1952; it was the first real organ of faculty governance in the Law School's history, and it continues to function today.

22 In 1953, the ABA (and Suffolk Law School) adopted a three-year college requirement for admission; thirteen years later, both raised requirements to call for possession of a bachelor's degree.

23 Suffolk University Board of Trustees, Minutes of the November 7, 1956 meeting.

24 McDermott added Malcolm M. Donahue (1956); John J. Nolan, John E. Fenton, Jr., and David J. Sargent (1957); Alfred I. Maleson (1959); Clifford E. Elias (1962); Alvan Brody and Brian T. Callahan (1963).

25 Northeastern's Law School closed in May 1956, and did not reopen until 1968; in 1965, B.C. Law terminated its evening program. These events left Suffolk with the only accredited evening law program in the Boston area.

26 Hollingsworth served on the full-time faculty until 1975.

27 The *Law Review*'s first advisor was John E. Fenton, Jr.; he was succeeded by Alexander J. Cella. David Sargent and Richard Pizzano were the *Advocate*'s advisors at its inception in 1968; Charles P. Kindregan succeeded them in 1971. Previous Suffolk Law School review publications had included the *Suffolk Law School Register* (1915-21) and the *Jurist*.

28 Newsome served 1936-48; Hartmann, 1948-58. Sullivan had authority over the law collection from 1958 until 1967, when John Lynch became Law Librarian. Edward J. Bander succeeded Lynch in 1978.

29 Donald Simpson increased the number of full-time faculty members to twenty-one. Besides Hollingsworth and Garabedian, his additions included Herbert Lemelman (1965); Charles P. Kindregan and Richard G. Pizzano (1967); Richard M. Perlmutter, Richard Vacco, and Basil Yanakakis (1969); and Joseph D. Cronin (1970). Hollingsworth, Pizzano, Vacco, and Yanakakis were Suffolk Law graduates.

30 The Evening Division program was expanded in 1964 from three nights a week to five, while mid-year Evening admissions were halted entirely four years later. After 1965, the Law School's graduate program was formally divided into LLM (degree) students and Continuing Legal Education (CLE, non-degree) students; this vestigial graduate program was terminated in 1973.

31 Upon Dean Simpson's retirement in July 1972, the Law School Committee of the Trustees deadlocked over a replacement. One bloc backed Judge Donahue's son; the other, Judge Fenton's. For six months, Trustee Joseph A. Caulfield acted as interim Dean; when Caulfield relinquished the position in January 1973, he was replaced—also on an interim basis—by law professor David Sargent. Very shortly thereafter, the Law School Committee evolved a compromise settlement whereby both Malcolm Donahue and John Fenton, Jr., became Associate Deans, while an outsider, Francis J. Larkin, was named

Dean. Larkin, 39, had served previously as associate law dean at Boston College. His term at Suffolk, however, was brief; in July 1973, he resigned to devote his full time to a judicial appointment. His departure opened the way for the immediate appointment of Professor Sargent as the new Dean.

32 The proportion of female students, however, increased between 1972 and 1980 from 7% to 35%; during the same period, the proportion of women on the full-time faculty rose from 5% to 11%.

33 Sargent's additions to the full-time faculty included R. Lisle Baker, Valerie C. Epps, Charles M. Burnim, Gerald J. Clark, Thomas F. Lambert, Jr., Crystal C. Lloyd, and Joseph P. McEttrick (1973); Louise Weinberg, Thomas J. O'Toole, and John R. Sherman (1974); Cornelius J. Moynihan (1976); Stephen C. Hicks, Marc G. Perlin, and Anthony B. Sandoe (1977); and Milton Katz (1978). Alexander J. Cella, Karen Blum, and Bernard M. Ortwein were among the six alumni appointed full-time by Sargent. Under Donald Simpson's Deanship, the proportion of Suffolk graduates on the full-time faculty had reached one-third.

34 SULAB's Charlestown office (opened in 1976) replaced a 1974-76 Gloucester site.

35 Earlier SBA newspapers had included the *Suffolk Law Reporter* (spring 1960) and the *SBA Briefcase* (March 1962–December 1967); David Sargent, as SBA advisor, was also advisor to both of these publications. The later *Suffolkate* (also SBA–published, 1971-72) was mainly inflammatory in content. An International Law Society, founded early in 1976, published the first number of its *Transnational Law Journal* (Karen Blum, advisor) later that year; Stephen C. Hicks was advisor to subsequent *TLJ* volumes.

Chapter 4

1 Suffolk College of Liberal Arts, 1934 catalogue, p. 4; Hiram J. Archer and a high school principal named Foss had attempted in 1908-09 to establish a "Suffolk College," but the effort was abandoned after one year.

2 "Equality of Opportunity" was the title of the broadcast which, in 1929, launched Gleason Archer's radio career; the phrase, however, was often employed by Archer.

3 Gleason L. Archer, "Journal III" (1932-34), p. 1.

4 "Journal II" (1920-32), p. 244; Archer's resolution was passed.

5 "Journal II," pp. 348-49.

6 Suffolk College of Liberal Arts, 1936 catalogue, p. 4.

7 Gleason L. Archer, "Status of Suffolk University, January 16, 1939" (special report to the Board of Trustees), p. 6.

8 Gleason L. Archer, Annual Report to the Board of Trustees, June 8, 1934.

9 Gleason L. Archer, "Program for the Accreditation of Suffolk University (Special Report to the Board of Trustees, April 10, 1947)," pp. 5-6.

10 "Status of Suffolk University," p. 15; "Program for Accreditation," pp. 5-6.

11 Gleason L. Archer, Annual Report to the Board of Trustees, June 7, 1935; "Status of Suffolk University," p. 15.

12 "Status of Suffolk University," p. 16; many of these trade school teachers were graduates of three-year normal schools who sought to complete four-year college degrees.

13 Suffolk Law School, 1934 catalogue, p. 11; "Status of Suffolk University," p. 26.

14 "Status of Suffolk University," p. 16.

15 Interview with John Griffin, June 18, 1979; Griffin was a Harvard MBA.

16 Miller took office as Liberal Arts Dean in July 1937.

17 By 1938, every student in the Colleges was required to take at least half of his or her credits in the College of Liberal Arts. This stipulation guaranteed good-sized classes for Liberal Arts instructors and minimized the number of faculty members necessary by eliminating duplication of effort, but it also confirmed the College of Liberal Arts in the role of senior partner. After 1938, all undergraduate classes met in the enlarged "University Building" at 20 Derne Street.

18 The Liberal Arts College's first "scholarships," established in 1934, had involved tuition reductions in proportion to the grades a student attained.

19 Twenty-three percent of the Liberal Arts students were women, compared to 39% in Journalism and 22% in Business Administration; less than a quarter of all undergraduates attended the day division. The Liberal Arts College presented its first honorary degree to Governor James Michael Curley shortly after he signed the 1935 charter.

20 "Status of Suffolk University," p. 6.

21 "Status of Suffolk University," p. 23.

22 In July 1945.

23 Hanson was succeeded by Dennis C. Haley (1965-66), Thomas A. Fulham (1966-75), and Vincent A Fulmer (1975-76), among others.

24 In January 1947.

25 Ten percent of the full-time faculty members were women; and four, including Joseph Strain and Laurence Rand, were Suffolk alumni.

26 Suffolk University Board of Trustees, Minutes, May 13, 1948. Leo Lieberman established the Guidance department in 1948 and remained its head until 1973.

27 Dean Ott and his faculty designed a curriculum compatible with Archer's pre-war insistence that the number of electives available should not be allowed unduly to multiply; the set of "core" requirements which Ott established on the Williams/Colgate model was, in fact, even more restrictive than pre-war requirements. It was well suited to the small, compact full-time faculty that characterized the Suffolk Colleges until the mid-1960s. The Ott-Goodrich core curriculum, major and minor field requirements, and BA and BS requirements remained the basic undergraduate academic framework for twenty years.

28 Ott's faculty did yeoman service during these early years. Neilson Hannay, Ella Murphy, William Sahakian, and Donald Goodrich laid the foundations of programs in English and the Humanities, George McKee, Catherine Fehrer, and Stanley Vogel did the same in Modern Languages; Norman Floyd, Israel Stolper, and Frank Buckley, in History and the Social Sciences. Meanwhile, Robert Friedman and Nelson Anderson took charge of developing a Natural Sciences and Mathematics program. A Teacher Training program was organized in 1948 by Harold Copp, and a Speech department, headed by Edgar DeForest, was added in the spring of 1949. Charles Law also inaugurated a compulsory Physical Education program during this period. Both the College of Journalism and the College of Business Administration continued to be administered by Ott as departments of the Liberal Arts college. Edith Marken headed post-war reorganization efforts in Journalism, and her counterpart in Business Administration was John Mahoney. As with the All-College requirements evolved by the Dean and the Registrar during this period, the programs developed by these faculty members defined the academic orientation of the various departments well into the 1960s.

29 A summer-long, three-division summer session, similar to that of 1946, was held in 1947 to accommodate the demands of returning veterans for accelerated academic progress; after that, the Colleges returned to a traditional academic-year schedule and a short summer session similar to those of the pre-war period. Attendance, however, remained high even with this return to relative normality. Of those enrolled in 1949, over three-quarters were veter-

ans, and only 3% were women; this latter figure contrasted sharply with the 25% female enrollment of 1940. A further contrast lay in the fact that while 75% of the pre-war students attended the evening division, now less than 15% were enrolled in evening programs.

30 In the first flush of postwar success, there was even a brief experiment with dormitory facilities; subsidized accommodations for undergraduate students were provided at the Boston City Club from 1947 until 1949, but the arrangement ended when the City Club's building was sold to the Community Fund. The Community Fund later became the United Way of Massachusetts Bay, which sold this Ashburton Place building to Suffolk University in 1978. With the exception of the 1947-49 experiment, Suffolk University, like Suffolk Law School before it, remained entirely a commuter institution until 1988.

31 Most regular evening courses in 1948 met three nights a week and offered exact equivalence to daytime courses. The majority of Adult Education courses met two nights a week (instead of one) after 1957, and after the abolition of the Adult Education program in 1960, a two-nights-a-week schedule was adopted for most evening classes. After 1968, double-period, one-night-a-week scheduling gradually replaced the two-nights-a-week format.

32 Master of Arts (MA) degrees were offered in Economics, English, Government, and History from 1948 until 1954.

33 Robert J. Munce succeeded Ott as Dean in June 1949. Munce became University President in 1954, then served as the first and only Chancellor in the University's history between 1960 and 1964. Of all the University's Deans and Presidents, none was more beloved by the students than Munce.

34 By that time, Munce had added an Extension Division (primarily graduate education courses for in-service teachers), the Harry Bloomberg Police School, and the Colleges' first academic honorary society, Phi Beta Chi. The Police School, named for a pre-war Suffolk Law School teacher, operated from 1952 until 1964; its director was Hiram Archer. Phi Beta Chi was a natural science honorary fraternity. Dean Munce also experimented with several social service programs, but they withered quickly during the student drought of 1953-56.

35 Suffolk University Board of Trustees, Minutes, May 12, 1954. The Colleges' low-point in attendance after World War II came in 1953, by which time enrollment had fallen to 589; the 1949 figure had been twice that number. (All statistics cited for the period before 1969 are, unless otherwise noted, for all three Colleges combined; for the period after that date, separate figures are presented for the Liberal Arts College—including Journalism—and for the newly autonomous Business School.)

36 Suffolk University Board of Trustees, Minutes, November 7, 1956. Women now constituted 7% of the student body (double the 1949 figure), and the percentage of veterans had decreased dramatically (to fifty percent).

37 The proportion of full-time women teachers had doubled since 1949 (although it was still only 17%), but the proportion of alumni on the faculty (14%) remained unchanged. Many faculty members were quite elderly. Neilson Hannay, for example, retired at age 80; Ella Murphy, at 76; George McKee, at 73. Israel Stolper received his Ph.D. from Harvard at 68; he continued to teach at Suffolk well into his seventies, as did Frank Buckley, Nelson Anderson, and a number of other full-time teachers.

38 He was helped by many young faculty members, as well as by more experienced professors loyal to Dean Ott's vision. During Goodrich's tenure, newcomers Arthur West and Richard Maehl teamed with veteran Robert Friedman to revolutionize conditions and programs in the Natural Sciences division; Dion Archon and John Sullivan combined with Donald Fiorillo to increase the relevance of offerings in the Social Sciences; while Stanley Vogel and Florence Petherick introduced new programs and approaches in the Humanities divi-

sion. Donald Unger replaced Harold Copp as head of the Education department, and Harold Stone superseded John Mahoney in Business.

39 It involved affiliation with the Newton-Wellesley Hospital to provide practical training for fourth-year students; and as the program expanded, so did the number of affiliated hospitals, until their number reached six.

40 On October 7, 1973, the Cobscook Bay Laboratory was named for Robert S. Friedman, the long-time champion of science in the College; Friedman had donated most of the laboratory's forty-acre site.

41 The Master of Science degree programs survived from 1968 until 1973, when they were discontinued on the recommendation of the 1972 NEASC reaccreditation team.

42 The Extension Division offered graduate education courses at area high schools until 1973; after 1980, an In-Service Institute at Suffolk offered workshops for teachers.

43 Under Vogel, the English department introduced the Liberal Arts College's first departmental honors seminar, established the first departmental scholarship (the Ella Murphy Scholarship), and in 1968 created *Venture,* a student-edited literary magazine. Catherine Fehrer was instrumental in developing the school's first interdisciplinary honors seminar, and in obtaining the first Fulbright Scholarship for a College student.

44 Veterans constituted only a small minority of students in the Colleges in 1969, while the proportion of women had risen to twenty-three percent.

45 The percentage of Suffolk graduates on the faculty also remained at its 1956 level (14%). By 1969, women constituted 25% of the full-time Liberal Arts teaching staff (compared to 17% in 1956), and Ella Murphy had become in 1959 the first woman in the undergraduate departments to attain the rank of full professor.

46 Nonetheless, a number of faculty members published extensively in the 1950s and 1960s, including Edward Hartmann, Ella Murphy, William Sahakian, and Stanley Vogel.

47 In 1967, the confluence of faculty and student demands produced a liberalization of All-College requirements. Most "core" courses were replaced by Option Groups made up of courses in several departments from which a student could select one. Similarly, the minor field requirement which limited students to a single discipline was replaced by a system of "related electives' in which students could choose courses in several disciplines related only by their relevance to the student's major field.

48 Under Goodrich's regime, the Scholastic Aptitude Test (SAT) was first required of all applicants. Catherine Fehrer proposed a Trustee Graduate Scholarship, to send a Liberal Arts graduate to the master's or doctoral program of the recipient's choice. It was established in 1960, and one of the first beneficiaries, Robert Bates, joined the Liberal Arts faculty several years afterward. In 1963, the Martin J. Flaherty Scholarship was instituted for the outstanding student in the College of Journalism; three years later, eight Graduate Fellowships were set up—four for graduate Education students and four for those in Business Administration post-graduate programs. During Goodrich's administration, submission of the Parents' Confidential Statement (on their financial circumstances) by scholarship applicants was first required. National Defense Student Loans, full-tuition Trustee Scholarships, Work-Study, and scholarships for disadvantaged students were also begun while Goodrich was Dean. By the time he left office, financial aid funds had increased ten-fold (to $157,000) over what they had totaled when his Deanship began. There were 134 academic scholarships awarded in 1969, compared to only 34 thirteen years earlier. (The figures used here—and throughout this chapter unless otherwise noted—represent only scholarship funds contributed directly by the University, and do not include Work-Study, state, or federal scholarship funds.)

49 Conditions also improved significantly for the faculty. Before 1966, the Liberal Arts faculty was housed in the "bullpen," a large second-floor room in the Archer Building, where they shared one telephone and one typewriter. Expansion into the Donahue Building permitted the Dean to provide his teaching staff with individual office space for the first time. Goodrich's administration also established the first elected organs of faculty governance in the history of the Colleges. On the initiative of Assistant Dean Joseph Strain, a Faculty Assembly and the institution's first elected faculty committee, the Educational Policy Committee, were set up in 1962; six years later, an elected Promotion, Tenure and Review Committee was inaugurated. With the support of President Dennis C. Haley, Strain and Neilson Hannay also secured Trustees' approval in 1962 for a pension plan and a tenure system.

50 The proportion of women on the full-time Liberal Arts faculty remained at 25% in 1972, and women comprised 39% of Liberal Arts undergraduate enrollments.

51 Grunewald extended the liberalization of degree requirements begun by his predecessor; he introduced a new, loosely-structured BS degree in 1972, and initiated work on a more flexible BSGS degree that was adopted a year later. Compulsory Physical Education was abolished, and voluntary participation in an expanded program of intramural athletics substituted. Pass-Fail grading was made an option, and an unlimited cuts policy was adopted on class attendance. In 1969, student representatives were accredited to the Trustees' College Committee. Scholarship funds increased from $157,000 in 1969 to $200,000 three years later, and the number of programs oriented toward AHANA (African-American, Hispanic, Asian, and Native American) members of the University and greater Boston communities was steadily expanded. An affiliation, for example, was established in 1972 with the Museum of Afro-American History.

52 To house the University's growing administrative staff, the 56 Temple Street building was opened in 1971, and space was rented at 100 Charles River Plaza after 1973.

53 Improved administrative efficiency also resulted from Grunewald's understanding and application of computers as management tools. As Dean of the College of Business Administration, Grunewald had initiated computerization at Suffolk; when he moved over to the Liberal Arts College, he took the lead in emphasizing the importance of computers for effective administration there, as well. He thus laid the groundwork for the dramatic expansion in computer facilities, staff, and programs that took place after his departure.

54 During 1973, a Health Careers Committee was set up to help undergraduates obtain access to graduate programs in the health field. In 1975, a Chemistry-Business program was inaugurated, and an affiliation was established with the New England Aquarium as part of the Environmental Technology program.

55 Kenneth Garni succeeded Leo Lieberman as head of Psychological Services (as the Guidance office had been renamed) in 1973; two years later, Psychological Services received accreditation from the International Association of Counseling Services, and in 1978 was renamed the University Counseling Center.

56 An informal exchange of faculty between Suffolk and Emerson College took place as early as the 1950's; Stanley Vogel, Ella Murphy, Florence Petherick, and Arthur West gave courses at Emerson, while Dean Richard Pierce and other members of the Emerson faculty taught Humanities and Speech courses at Suffolk. In 1968, Dean Goodrich established a formal affiliation, which opened Suffolk's science facilities to Emerson students in exchange for Emerson's assumption of responsibility for training Suffolk students in Speech, Communications, and Dramatic Arts; the affiliation was scaled down—and a separate Suffolk Speech and debate program reestablished—after 1973. The College administration had demonstrated a particular solicitude toward Speech programs since the early 1950s, sponsoring a High School Speech Contest from 1952 on, and adding a High School Debate

Tournament after 1965. The quality of undergraduate forensics, however, jumped dramatically with Kennedy's move from Emerson to Suffolk in 1974; within seven years, the school's debaters were invited to participate in the national championship tournament. Kennedy also revived an undergraduate dramatics program that was first offered at Suffolk in 1936, and which had flourished during the 1950s under Ella Murphy's direction. In 1978, a Suffolk Theater Company, made up primarily of professional actors-in-residence, was established as a stimulus for this rebuilding effort.

57 A Greater Boston High School Awards Day, complete with scholarships to the editors of the winning high school newspapers, was instituted; and in 1975 a program of Hearst Foundation scholarships was initiated for Suffolk undergraduates in Journalism. A closed-circuit television station (WSUB) was set up in 1974, and a radio station (WSFR) in 1976. By 1981, the *Suffolk Journal,* one of the region's leading student papers, had been joined by the Evening Voice (founded in 1970 as the Evening Shadow).

58 Federally-supported Economic Opportunity Grant programs (BEOG, SEOG), along with HELP loans, provided additional funds to Suffolk students; the conditions attached to the growing volume of governmental assistance helped bring about the adoption of a needs analysis for all financial aid after 1977.

59 In 1976, 69% of Liberal Arts College students were day students, and 31% were evening (part-time) students. By 1980, the Colleges' summer session had grown to two day and two evening semesters, with a total enrollment of 2400.

60 By 1980, more than half of the College's students were women, compared to 39% in 1972, and non-white representation had also increased (to 5.5%). The undergraduate community's diversity in the 1970s, however, did not equal that simultaneously being cultivated in the Law School; most College students still came from the greater Boston area, whereas nearly 40% of law students by 1979 came from outside Massachusetts.

61 The total teaching staff, however, grew by 29%, from 144 to 186. Part-time instructors had played a vital role in the Liberal Arts College since Gleason Archer's time; under Dean Ronayne's regime, the number of part-time instructors increased dramatically, from 44 to 86. The proportion of full-time women teachers rose only slightly, from 25% to 29%, while the proportion of Suffolk graduates on the full-time faculty was halved, from 14% to seven percent. In 1977, the Trustees instituted a seven-year up-or-out rule for untenured faculty members. Dean Ronayne vigorously supported faculty governance: a Faculty Life Committee (authorized by Dean Grunewald in 1971 to represent the faculty in discussions about salaries, fringe benefits, and working conditions) was made elective in 1972; and in 1976 faculty representatives were accredited to the Trustees' College Committee.

62 A sabbatical leave program was established in 1974, and a formal policy authorizing load reductions for research purposes was instituted seven years later; in 1980, a Grants office was set up.

63 A free tuition program for senior citizens, for example, was established in 1973. Liberal Arts faculty assistance was provided to Boston's Magnet School project, and a solar energy project was undertaken in 1980 at both the Beacon Hill and Cobscook Bay campuses.

Chapter 5

1 Suffolk University College of Business Administration, 1937 catalogue, p. 6; in 1995, the School of Management was renamed the Frank Sawyer School of Management, in honor of the late University benefactor Frank Sawyer.

2 Suffolk University College of Business Administration, 1937 catalogue, p. 4.

3 Suffolk University College of Business Administration, 1976 catalogue, p. 54.

4 Suffolk University College of Business Administration, 1937 catalogue, p. 4; Suffolk College of Liberal Arts, 1934 catalogue, p. 4.

5 Interview with John Griffin, June 18, 1979. Griffin, who was to play a critical role in Suffolk University's development for the next half-century, was among the first high school instructors recruited by Gleason Archer to teach at the College of Liberal Arts. Beginning in the summer of 1934, he also served as Archer's evening aide for undergraduate curriculum planning. He was appointed the College's first Registrar in 1935, and during the next year played an important role in founding the College of Journalism. He was elected to Suffolk University's Board of Trustees in 1937, and remained a member until his death in April 1987.

6 Gleason L. Archer, "Status of Suffolk University, January 16, 1939" (special report to the Board of Trustees), p. 6.

7 Interview with John Griffin, June 18, 1979.

8 In 1940, there were 843 students and 23 faculty members in the Law School. Women constituted 22% of the Business School's students at that time, compared to 23% in the College of Liberal Arts and under 1% in the Law School.

9 O'Brien was also appointed Dean of the Liberal Arts College in 1944; he thus, in effect, served as "Dean of the Colleges" during the 1944-45 academic year. In 1948, he was appointed to the Law School faculty, and served as Acting Dean of the Law School from 1952 until 1956.

10 Suffolk University Board of Trustees, Minutes, May 8, 1947.

11 Sklar served as chairman from 1946 until 1948, and was succeeded for one year by Dalton Pilcher. John Mahoney became chairman in 1949.

12 In 1948, there were 413 students in the Law School. At that time, more than three-quarters of the Business students were veterans, less than one percent were women, and ten percent attended evening classes. This was a substantial change from 1940, when women constituted 22% of Business enrollments and over 75% of Business students attended courses in the evening.

13 Two full-time Business faculty members were Suffolk alumni, and no full-time member of that faculty held an MBA or a higher Business degree. There were no women on the Business faculty until 1970. A Marketing Club was established in 1950; it affiliated with the American Marketing Association (AMA) in 1951. A year later, the Marketing Club was the largest undergraduate student organization. An Accounting-Business (Alumni) Club was founded in 1948, and remained active until 1952; four years later, it merged into the newly-organized General Alumni Association of Suffolk University.

14 Less than 50% of Business students were now veterans; 36% attended at night (more than three times the 1948 figure); and the proportion of women had risen to between one and two percent.

15 Twelve of these Business graduate students attended during the day, sixteen at night.

16 In 1958, there were 34 full-time members of the Liberal Arts faculty; at that time, there were seven full-time faculty members and 255 students in the Law School.

17 MBA's constituted 29% of the full-time faculty, compared to zero in 1948; and 43% of the Business School's full-time faculty members were Suffolk graduates, compared to 50% a decade earlier. Archon served on the full-time Business faculty from 1954 until 1961; Diamond, 1956-93; Donahue, 1956-91. William O'Connor was a member of the full-time faculty from 1957 until 1972; and Frederick Sullivan, from 1959 until 1969.

18 Chase chaired both the Trustees' School of Management Committee and the School of Management Advisory Council until 1986; he continued to serve on the Board of Trustees until his death in April 1994.

19 The faculties of the College of Business Administration and the Graduate School of Administration were congruent; they were composed of identical personnel.

20 In 1975, the Business School also established a lecture series named in Bloomfield's honor.

21 The examination's name was changed in 1968 to the Admission Test for Graduate Schools of Business (ATGSB), and in 1975 to the Graduate Management Admission Test (GMAT); in 1962, the Scholastic Aptitude Test (SAT) was required of applicants for undergraduate admission. In 1960, the Business School's first professional fraternity, Delta Sigma Pi, was founded; it was the first non-honorary undergraduate fraternity permitted on campus.

22 The number of graduate Education students doubled (to 93) over the same period. By 1967, veterans constituted a small minority of Suffolk undergraduates. Of the Business undergraduates, 26% were evening students (down from 36% in 1958), while the proportion of women stood at 4% (double the 1958 figure). Between 1958 and 1967, Law School enrollment rose from 285 to 1294.

23 Over the same period, the proportion of MBA's on the full-time Business faculty increased from 29% to 64%, and the proportion of alumni declined from 43% to 27%. Between 1958 and 1967, the full-time Liberal Arts faculty grew from 34 to 65, and the full-time Law faculty from 7 to 14.

24 In 1969, Grunewald resigned to become Dean of the College of Liberal Arts and Sciences.

25 Although Management and Marketing majors had nominally been introduced in 1948, these programs remained undeveloped until the Deanships of Donald Grunewald and his successor, Robert Waehler.

26 The Raytheon Extension program survived only until 1968. That same year, Joel Corman joined the full-time Business faculty, as did Howard Aucoin (the University's first computer specialist) and Stanley Dennis.

27 Business School faculty members could now work out some proposals before submitting them to the joint Liberal Arts/Business committees which had final governance jurisdiction over them.

28 Management, Marketing, Finance, and a General Business Administration program were under the supervision of the Business Administration department.

29 Before Grunewald's arrival, however, John Mahoney had attended an AACSB convention in San Diego during the spring of 1966.

30 The proportion of MBA's grew from 64% of the full-time Business faculty in 1967 to 81% in 1969. The proportion of full-time Business faculty members who were Suffolk graduates also rose, from 27% to 38%.

31 Liberal Arts attendance rose from 1200 to 1500 between 1967 and 1969; Law attendance, from 1294 to 1467. By 1969, evening students constituted 34% of Business undergraduates and 81% of Business graduate students (compared to 26% and 68%, respectively, two years earlier), while women made up seven percent of Business undergraduates (nearly double the 1967 figure) and one percent of Business graduate students.

32 A Trustee Graduate Scholarship was established for the College of Business Administration in 1971, to send a graduating senior to the master's or doctoral program of the recipient's choice; a Liberal Arts equivalent had been initiated in 1960. An MBA Association was founded in 1969 as a structure for student government and professional development for graduate Business students. In March 1972, the *Memorandum,* the MBA Association's newsletter, began publication. Within a year, an MBA activities fee was approved. A full scholarship was also granted to the Association's president, who, along with several undergraduate student representatives, was accredited to meet with the Trustees' Business School Committee. The MBA Association was in

the forefront of efforts to expand the School of Management's placement resources and physical facilities.

33 The proportion of evening Business undergraduates rose from 34% to 47%, and of evening Business graduate students from 81% to 88%. By 1974, the proportion of women among Business undergraduates had risen to 15% (double the 1969 figure), and among graduate Business students to five percent (a five-fold increase).

34 The first female member of the full-time Business faculty was Jo Ann Renfrew. The proportion of MBA's and of Suffolk alumni on the full-time Business faculty remained constant, at 81% and 38% respectively.

35 The 45 Mount Vernon Street building had housed Suffolk Law School from 1914 until 1921. It was sold to Portia Law School (later New England School of Law) in 1922, and was reacquired in 1972 when the New England School of Law moved to Newbury Street.

36 The Business School had offered an IRS Tax Seminar since 1964; its subject matter was of great utility to the accountants and accounting students who constituted the Business School's primary academic constituency in the pre-Grunewald era.

37 An MPA activities fee was approved in 1975, a Public Administration Society (a Public Management equivalent to the MBA Association) was founded in 1976, and a charter chapter of Pi Alpha Alpha (the Public Administration honorary society) was established later in that year.

38 The Search Committee which recommended McDowell to the Board of Trustees was composed of faculty members, students, alumni, and Trustees. The Center for State Government Management became in 1975 the Center for Public Management. Donald Levitan replaced McDowell as director in 1974, and David Pfeiffer was appointed Levitan's assistant. In 1975, Pfeiffer transferred to the full-time faculty. Pfeiffer, Levitan, and Frances Burke (who also joined the full-time Business faculty in 1975) formed the nucleus of the Public Management department.

39 In 1976, the Business School issued a catalogue separate from that of the Liberal Arts College for the first time since 1944.

40 A Business School Educational Policy Committee and a Business School Promotion, Tenure, and Review Committee were both established in 1974; the next year, a Business School Faculty Life Committee was created. Most of the Business School's appointive faculty committees had been separate from their Liberal Arts counterparts since 1967.

41 The proportion of alumni on the full-time Business faculty, meanwhile, dropped from 38% to 24%. Emma Auer served between 1976 and 1978 as the Business School's first female chairperson, and in 1979 Frances Burke became the first woman in the Business School's history to attain the rank of full professor. By that time, Burke was one of two women on the full-time Business faculty.

42 Between 1974 and 1981, the School of Management's professional administrative staff trebled, from three to nine. The School, however, still depended in 1981 on staff shared with the Liberal Arts College for Admissions, Placement, Alumni Activities, and Financial Aid, and on staff shared with the Liberal Arts College and the Law School for Development and Counseling. In addition, 40% of the courses taken by students registered in the School of Management were taught by members of the Liberal Arts faculty.

43 During that same year, the School's first fund-raising effort was undertaken: a Development Committee, chaired by Peter Volpe, raised over $30,000. This money financed establishment of a Business/Government Forum and planning for a Cooperative Education program.

44 Suffolk University College of Business Administration, 1976 catalogue, p. 50.

45 Suffolk University Board of Trustees, Minutes, November 13, 1974.

46 Suffolk University College of Business Administration, 1978 catalogue, p. 95. The operations of the Management Education Center were suspended in June 1980, to be resumed once facilities became available in the Sawyer Building.

47 By 1981, the College Library's Management holdings had increased to the point where student and faculty work could be supported mainly by on-campus collections. The Merrimack Valley Satellite (transferred from Western Electric to Bradford College in 1975) survived until 1977. The Swampscott Center was opened in 1974, and closed two years later. Public Welfare Office courses and Boston City Hall courses began in 1973; they were discontinued in 1978 and 1981, respectively.

48 During Dean McDowell's tenure, graduate service scholarships and teaching assistantships were added to the four Graduate Business Fellowships that had been established in 1966; all were awarded on a merit basis, and were specifically exempted in 1978 from the Financial Aid Office's shift to a needs analysis. In 1976, a Visiting Committee for the Business School was established by the Trustees; three years later, an Accounting Advisory Committee was also created.

49 Suffolk University College of Business Administration, 1976 catalogue, p. 54.

50 The Small Business Institute program was directed by Professor Joel Corman.

51 During the 1970s, Suffolk's student chapter of the American Marketing Association became a regular participant in the American Advertising Federation's annual marketing competition. A Suffolk University Forum was organized in 1976, and the Business School began publication of a newsletter (*CBA/GSA Today*, which by 1981 had been renamed the *Update*) and a Working Paper/Reprint Series. A Business sorority, Phi Chi Theta, was founded in 1975 as an alternative to the male-dominated Delta Sigma Pi. In 1978, the national business honor society Delta Mu Delta was brought to the campus by Professor Roger Shawcross. He also established the Financial Management Society, a Finance department honorary organization, in 1971. By 1981, the School of Management had four academic honorary societies.

52 Evening (part-time) students now constituted 41% of the School of Management's undergraduate enrollments (compared to 47% in 1974) and 77% of its graduate student body (compared to 88%). Executive MBA enrollment peaked at 160 in 1977, and stood at 105 three years later. In 1980, part-time students constituted 60% of the School of Management's enrollments, compared to 32% for Liberal Arts (23% undergraduate, 87% graduate) and 42% for Law. Fifteen percent of those who received BSBA or BSPA degrees in 1980 were women, a figure little changed since 1974. At the MBA/MPA level, however, the proportion of women among degree recipients was 19% in 1980, compared to only 5% six years earlier.

53 In 1974, the Business School's enrollment was 1,643, or 72% of the Liberal Arts College's enrollment of 2,268; in 1980, the Liberal Arts College enrolled 2,018 students, or 73% of the 2,758 students enrolled by the School of Management. Between 1974 and 1980, meanwhile, the Law School reduced its enrollment from 1,939 to 1,680. In 1974, Business School enrollment was 85% that of the Law School; by 1980, Law School attendance was 60% that of the School of Management and 26% of total University enrollment (compared to 43% for the School of Management and 31% for the Liberal Arts College).

54 Suffolk Law School, 1934 catalogue, p. 11; "Status of Suffolk University," p. 26.

55 Full-time School of Management faculty members came not only from Harvard, MIT, Tufts, Suffolk University, and Boston University, but also from the University of Pennsylvania, New York University, the University of Rochester, Ohio State University, the University of Wisconsin, and the University of Southern California. Research contacts were also established with a number of sister institutions. During 1980, faculty members were invited to participate in seminars at Harvard, Sloan, and a number of other

leading business schools. By 1981, the faculty and staff were active participants in the American Accounting Association, the American Institute of Certified Public Accountants, the American Society for Public Administration, the American Institute of Decision Sciences, the Academy of Management, the Financial Management Association, the Institute of Marketing Sciences, the Massachusetts Society of Certified Public Accountants, the Massachusetts Association of Public Accountants, the National Association of Schools of Public Affairs and Administration, the National Conference on Teaching Public Administration, and the New England Association for Business Administration.

56 The 1979 Mission Statement also represented a response to increased competition from other schools for students from the School of Management's traditional constituencies. In 1981, the School's students still came, as they had come throughout its history, primarily from the greater Boston area; and its historic role in Boston area business training still constituted part of the School of Management's broadened regional mission.

Chapter 6

1 Suffolk Law School, 1923 catalogue, p. 16.

2 "Archer's Evening Law School: History and Statistics" (unpublished, ca. 1907), pp. 3, 14-15; Suffolk Law School, 1908 catalogue, p. 3.

3 Suffolk Law School, 1923 catalogue, p. 17; 1932 catalogue, p. 13.

4 Suffolk Law School, 1931 catalogue, p. 14; "but by a natural process of elimination to sift the wheat from the chaff" (p. 14).

5 *Luck and Pluck* was probably Alger's best-known book.

6 Suffolk Law School, 1931 catalogue, p. 15.

7 Twenty million people—a number equal to the entire American population in 1850—arrived in the United States from Europe between the Civil War and 1906; half of these entered the country after 1890. In 1870, Boston's population was 25% foreign-born; the country's, 9%. By 1906, the figures were 36% and 14%, respectively.

8 Gleason L. Archer, "Status of Suffolk University, January 16, 1939" (special report to the Board of Trustees), p. 26; Suffolk Law School, 1923 catalogue, p. 17.

9 "Status of Suffolk University," p. 23. Day students constituted 14.6% of Suffolk Law School's student body in 1924, and 25% of the Liberal Arts College's enrollment in 1938. By 1980, day students made up 68.1% of Liberal Arts attendance. In the School of Management, the figure was 40%; and in the Law School, 57.7%. Scholarships specifically designed for Evening Division students were introduced briefly at the Colleges in 1948, then revived in 1966.

10 Suffolk Law School, 1923 catalogue, p. 17.

11 Suffolk University Law School, 1939 catalogue, p. 6; Suffolk Law School, 1923 catalogue, p. 17. "Bankers, brokers, and businessmen" (1923 catalogue, p. 17), with no interest in obtaining a law degree, also took individual courses at Suffolk to provide themselves with a background in certain legal areas. Their presence added variety to the student body, but their departure after taking only one or two courses lowered the proportion of students registered at Suffolk Law School between 1906 and 1937 who eventually graduated to a misleading 27.2%. By 1980, 38% of the undergraduates who entered Suffolk University as freshmen graduated in four years (compared to a national median of 35-40%), and 46% within six years.

12 Archer himself had risen from poverty through the providential philanthropic aid given him by Boston businessman George A. Frost; for details, see Chapter Two, pp. 20-21.

13 Suffolk University College of Liberal Arts, 1937 catalogue, p. 14.

14 Suffolk University College of Liberal Arts, 1937 catalogue, pp. 14-15.

15 Gleason L. Archer, *Building A School* (Boston: By the Author, 1919), p. 301.

16 After 1937, Archer's alumni gradually captured his school. By that time, ninety percent of the Law School teaching staff were Suffolk graduates; and in the next decade more and more Irish Catholic alumni were elected to the Board. They presented a striking contrast to the small band of Yankees who had constituted Dean Archer's Board of Trustees during Suffolk's first thirty years. Apart from an office staff of Irish Catholic women, Archer and his Trustees maintained an administrative team composed predominantly of Yankee men; it was staffed primarily by the Dean's relations and his "Maine mafia" of part-time assistants. The students, of course, were mainly Irish Catholic men. By 1948, the ethnic composition of the Board of Trustees had become approximately what that of the student body had been during the 1920s—a composition which the Board retained for three decades.

17 Suffolk University College of Liberal Arts and Sciences, 1971 catalogue, p. 115.

18 Suffolk Law School, 1923 catalogue, pp. 17-18. In 1925, 81.5% of the students at Suffolk Law School had been born in the U.S.; 71% of the total student body were Massachusetts-born (Suffolk Law School, 1925 catalogue, pp. 21-22). In 1938, 93.6% of Suffolk's Liberal Arts students were American-born, and 80% were natives of Massachusetts.

19 Suffolk Law School, 1923 catalogue, pp. 17-18.

20 There was this manipulative element in the Progressive approach itself; Archer was not unique among Progressivism's adherents in desiring to teach immigrants the "true American" values held by himself and his fellow Progressives, in an effort to rally those immigrants to the side of the Progressive campaign to protect "equality of opportunity" against well-to-do "monopolists." For more details, see Chapter One, pp. 10-11, and Chapter Two, pp. 21-22.

21 Because of Suffolk Law School's location and its provision of opportunities for West End residents, local ward boss Martin Lomasney long evinced a paternal solicitude for the institution's well-being. In a ward run by Irish politicians, who depended on a population of Jewish and Italian immigrants for election, Suffolk Law School constituted an almost universal source of hope. The school's sociology mirrored that of the ward, and West End Democratic leaders worked diligently to protect such an institution from the outside "quality control" which might destroy it or alter its symbiosis with the West End community. The large Irish representation at Suffolk guaranteed Irish domination of class elections at the school; it also insured the continuing loyalty of Lomasney's Irish colleagues in the Democratic leadership at the city and state level.

22 Immigration quotas were imposed in 1920; as a result, the foreign-born proportion of the American population dropped from 14% in 1910 to 12% in 1930. However, 70% of Boston's population in 1930 was either foreign-born or belonged to the first generation born in the U.S.

23 In Europe, the comparable figure remained at 10% throughout the 1930s.

24 Between 1930 and 1950, the foreign-born proportion of the American population fell from 12% to 7%.

25 In the late 1940s, three times more Suffolk Law School entrants came from the Suffolk Colleges than from any other undergraduate institution; and, despite a two-year college requirement for admission, only 25% of all entering law students had completed a bachelor's degree. By 1956, that figure had risen to 87%; but it was not until the early 1960s (by the time it had reached

97%) that Boston College, Boston University, and Northeastern surpassed Suffolk's Colleges as suppliers of entering Suffolk Law School students. By that time, even Harvard sent several students each year. The University of Massachusetts had, by the early 1970s, joined B.C., B.U., and Northeastern in sending more students each to Suffolk Law than did the Suffolk Colleges.

26 Students from Massachusetts towns west of Worcester formed 3% of the Law School's student population after 1970; in no previous era did they constitute more than a trace. By 1980, Suffolk Law School was enrolling students from Brown, Tufts, Smith, Mount Holyoke, and Harvard, as well as from its traditional reservoirs: B.C., B.U., the University of Massachusetts (Boston), Holy Cross, Providence, and the Suffolk Colleges.

27 Of Suffolk undergraduates between 1976 and 1980, 26.2% were Boston residents; 51.1% lived in the greater Boston area; 9.1%, between Routes 128 and 495; and 2.2%, in Massachusetts communities outside Route 495. In all, 95.4% came from Massachusetts; 3.2%, from other states; and 1.4% from abroad. Thirty percent of undergraduates entered Suffolk from Catholic high schools. By 1980, the Liberal Arts and School of Management graduate student bodies had a third of their membership composed of students from Irish backgrounds, and a quarter of Yankee students. In the School of Management, however, graduate students from Italian backgrounds outnumbered Jewish graduate students by 16% to 12%; while in Liberal Arts those two ethnic groups composed equal proportions (11% each) of the graduate enrollment. In addition, 5% of the Liberal Arts graduate population was composed of students from Portuguese backgrounds—twice the proportion they constituted in the School of Management. Although suburban representation was growing, more Liberal Arts graduate students still came to Suffolk in 1980 from traditional recruiting centers (like Medford, Boston, Lawrence, Cambridge, and Winthrop) than from any other communities. In the School of Management, more graduate students came from Boston than from any other city; but the size of the graduate student delegations from suburban communities like Andover, Brookline, and Newton followed closely behind that of Boston—displacing a number of the School's traditional urban recruiting areas.

28 Until the late 1960s, less than one percent of students in the Suffolk Colleges came from abroad.

29 The respective proportions of undergraduate students from Italian and Jewish backgrounds had remained virtually equal until 1970.

30 It is difficult to assess the impact of demography on these figures; only 4.7% of the U.S. population was foreign-born in 1970, compared to 5.4% in 1960 and 6.9% in 1950. Equally hard to assess is the impact of social and geographic mobility, as is that of Suffolk's improved academic standards and changing reputation.

31 Jones is the earliest graduate thus far confirmed as having been African-American. There were, however, a number of other black students (clearly shown in a 1911 photograph) during the Law School's first decade of existence. They remain unidentified; but one or more of them could have graduated before 1915.

32 Shichiro Hayashi.

33 Law student participation was also authorized (and funded) in the Council on Legal Education Opportunity (CLEO) minority student program. Undergraduate courses in black and third world history and literature were established, as was a special Law School AHANA admissions program. A Suffolk University Afro-American Club was founded in 1969; BALSA (the Black American Law Students' Association), in 1973; and HALSA (the Hispanic American Law Students' Association), two years afterward. In 1976, the Suffolk Student Coalition against Racism was organized. The first AHANA members joined the School of Management Advisory Council in 1974, and five years later Thomas J. Brown became Suffolk University's first black

Trustee. That same year (1979), the Law School engaged the services of a Consultant on Minority Admission.

34 One provision of the affiliation was that the College Library would hold the Museum's 2500-volume collection of Afro-American literature, which was designed to serve as the nucleus for a permanent center in Boston for the study of African-American literature.

35 The remaining one-fifth was composed predominantly of Asians.

36 The number of foreign students grew so fast that in the fall of 1971 the University's first Foreign Student Advisor, Professor Vahe Sarafian, was appointed. Establishment of an International Students Club followed in the fall of 1976, preceded slightly by the founding of a Latin American Club (1975). In 1980, students representing twenty-six countries were enrolled at Suffolk.

37 *Boston Journal,* May 20, 1908. Several other newspapers also picked up the story, which outraged Boston feminists and women's suffragists. A battle in the letters columns of the local press ensued which dragged the then-obscure name of Suffolk repeatedly into the popular consciousness, as Archer knew it would. Attendance increased, and, not incidentally, the way was paved for the founding—in the fall of 1908—of Portia Law School. Portia was open only to female students, and was run by Archer's law partner, Arthur W. McLean. Many years later, Portia—by then co-educational—was to become the New England School of Law.

38 Catharine Caraher, Dean Archer's secretary and right hand, attended Suffolk Law School classes briefly in 1927, but soon abandoned the undertaking.

39 Combined with the fact that Portia Law School had broken the "gentlemen's agreement" between the two school by admitting men.

40 Suffolk College of Liberal Arts, 1934 catalogue, pp. 7, 10. This stipulation appeared in Suffolk's undergraduate catalogues from 1934 through 1941.

41 In 1939, Harriet M. Kandler and Agnes S. Blyth became the first women to receive Bachelor of Science (BS) degrees from the Liberal Arts College, and a year later Theresa M. Bodwell became the first of her sex to be awarded a Bachelor of Arts (BA) degree. The first female graduates of the Journalism and Business Colleges received their degrees in 1948, and Mary F. McLaughlin in 1954 was the first woman to receive a Master of Science in Business Administration (MSBA) from Suffolk.

42 In 1955, 24% of Liberal Arts graduate students were women, compared to only 4% in Business. Five years later, the figure among Liberal Arts graduate students was 26%, while there was not one female graduate Business student. Beginning in 1948, Suffolk attempted to use scholarships to attract female students (especially undergraduates) to a University where 97% of those enrolled were men.

43 Marian Archer served as Advisor to Women in the Liberal Arts College from 1934 until 1937. After World War II, there was a suggestion that a Dean of Women be appointed (Suffolk University Board of Trustees, Minutes, May 8, 1947); instead, the post of Advisor to Women was revived—and filled successively by Ruth C. Widmayer (1947-48), Catherine Fehrer (1948-50, 1953-56, 1957-58), Edith Marken (1950-53), Renee Hubert (1956-57), Florence Petherick (1958-72), and Elizabeth Williams (1972-77, after which the position was abolished). One of the principal organizations through which the Women's Advisor operated was the Women's Association of Suffolk University (WASU), founded in 1947 as the school's first women's organization. WASU became Gamma Sigma Upsilon service sorority in 1959, and affiliated with the national service sorority Gamma Sigma Sigma in 1966. In addition to its service functions, the organization ran a "Miss Suffolk" contest from 1947 through 1969, and sponsored a series of mother-daughter luncheons (beginning in 1959) and dinners (after 1965). Despite their relatively small numbers at Suffolk before 1960, women clearly came into their own as University student leaders in the 1950s. The first woman had been elected to

student government in 1940, but it was not until 1958 that Jeanne McCarthy was elected the first female SGA president. During that same year, Kuni Kreutel served as the *Suffolk Journal*'s first female editor-in-chief, while three years earlier Jeanne Hession had become the first woman ever elected class president in the Law School.

44 In 1965, women constituted 45% of Liberal Arts graduate students and 17% of graduate Business students, compared to 26% and zero percent, respectively, in 1960.

45 The proportion of Liberal Arts graduate students who were females grew from 40% in 1970 to 70% in 1980; in the School of Management, the figure decreased over the same period from 21% to 19%. For the 775 women who had graduated in the Law School's history (as of 1981), the median year of graduation was 1978.

46 As the proportion of female students grew, so did the proportion of female faculty members. Mary Frances Pray, who taught part-time in the Law School from 1942 until 1952, was the University's first female faculty member. Two part-time Liberal Arts instructors, one of whom was Ruth Widmayer, were hired in 1947; and the University's first female full-time teachers—Ella Murphy, Catherine Fehrer, and Edith Marken—joined the Liberal Arts faculty in 1948. Eleven years later, Murphy became the first woman at Suffolk to be appointed a full professor; she was followed one year afterward by Catherine Fehrer. Edith Marken served from 1948 until 1953 as Suffolk's first female department chairperson; in 1963, Fehrer became the second. The Law School's first full-time woman teacher (1967), and its first female full professor (1972), was Catherine Judge. The proportion of women on the Law faculty, which stood at 5% in 1970 compared to 25% on the Liberal Arts faculty, rose during the next decade to 11% (compared to 29% in the Liberal Arts). The first woman to join the Business faculty (Jo Ann Renfrew) did so only in 1970; Emma Auer became its first female department chairperson in 1976, and it was 1979 before Frances Burke was appointed the School of Management's first female full professor. By 1980, Burke was the only woman on the Management faculty, constituting 3% of the full-time teaching staff in the School of Management. Women composed 47.1% of the University's professional administrative staff in 1937; the proportion in 1980 was 48.1%. The number of organizations focused on women's lives and concerns also multiplied as female enrollment expanded. Suffolk's first social sorority, Phi Sigma Sigma, was established in 1969—the same year in which the "Miss Suffolk" contest was discontinued. Equal Opportunity/Affirmative Action officer Judy Minardi was hired in 1972, and in the same year a President's Committee on the Status of Women was formed. Under the leadership of Professor Maria Miliora, the committee produced during its eight years of existence a "Report on the Status of Women at Suffolk" (1975) and a later addendum, "Sexism in the University Curriculum" (1978); both called attention to various areas of sex discrimination at the institution. In 1973, Jeanne Hession was elected the University's first woman Trustee, followed a year later by Dorothy Antonelli. The Business School Advisory Council's first female member was also named in 1974. A Women's Program Committee was set up that same year, to assume the responsibilities for obtaining speakers, monitoring library acquisitions, and the like, which had originally been envisioned for the Committee on the Status of Women (but which the Committee of the Status of Women had left unaddressed while preparing its report); three years later, the Program Committee created—and merged into—the Women's Program Center. In 1973, a branch of Women in Communications, a national professional organization, had also been established for Journalism and Communications students; and two years later a Committee for the Continuing Education of Women was set up, primarily to serve those women who were returning to college after an extended interval—of which there were about 400 at Suffolk at that time. (The next year, it became the Continuing Education Committee, serving the needs of returning men as well as women.) By 1975, Ann Guilbert had been added to the

Athletic Department staff to introduce a program of women's athletics. As female enrollment grew in the Law School and the Business School after 1970, feminist activity spread there from its early center in the College of Liberal Arts. The Suffolk Women's Law Caucus, for example, was founded in 1973, and a business professional sorority, Phi Chi Theta, two years later.

47 Many faculty members, in both the Law School and the Colleges, continued during the 1950s and 1960s to teach into their seventies—and, in several cases, even into their eighties.

48 As participation in the program grew, Niles was appointed Senior Citizen Advisor in 1978; two years later, Warren succeeded him in the position.

49 A Debating Society, originally founded in 1907, was refounded in 1916; it survived less than a year. In 1910, the school's first newspaper, the *Suffolk Law Student,* published only three issues before dissolving. The *Suffolk Law School Register,* a student magazine, was the most successful; it first appeared in October 1915 and continued publication until 1921. Like the others, however, it was finally killed by lack of student time. Even ambitious men in search of opportunity had physical limits.

50 Thus, some activities—which Archer had for years tried, unsuccessfully, to cultivate in the Law School—flourished, temporarily, when hijacked from the Colleges. Debate was the oldest extra-curricular activity at Suffolk, and perhaps the closest to Gleason Archer's heart. Even when his successive attempts to found forensics programs faltered in the school's early decades, the Dean made certain that there was always a course in public speaking available to his students; when the College of Liberal Arts was founded, Archer insisted that a speech course be among the earliest offered at the new institution. The third attempt at establishing a Law School Debating Society took place in January 1936; the first president of the new organization was Paul Smith, and after 1939 the society was coached by the ubiquitous John F. X. O'Brien. In 1937, a College Debating Society was set up. The two clubs regularly debated one another, and those identified as the best speakers in these confrontations were pooled into a "Suffolk University Debating Team," which engaged after 1938 in intercollegiate competition. The second-oldest extra-curricular activity was journalism, as indicated by the short-lived *Suffolk Law Student* (1910) and the *Register* (1915-21). With the establishment of a College of Journalism, Archer helped to arrange the foundation of a new student newspaper, the *Suffolk Journal,* in September 1936. Student dramatics, an activity previously unrepresented at Suffolk, was begun in November 1936 by establishment of the Suffolk Players. The moving force behind the Players was Esther Newsome, Archer's new Librarian, whom he also appointed to be his first Director of Student Activities. Edith R. Doane succeeded Newsome as head of Student Activities in 1938, and served in that capacity until the virtual suspension of the extra-curricular program four years later because of the war. During Doane's tenure, Professor Frank Pizzuto founded in 1938 the University's first foreign language club, the *Circolo Italiano*; in 1938, as well, a Recreation Room (designated Hall 6) was opened in the University Building.

51 Suffolk University College of Liberal Arts, 1937 catalogue, p. 20.

52 The same period also saw a foundation laid for an athletics program. John Griffin was appointed first Athletics Advisor for the Colleges in 1937, and an Athletics Committee was set up the following year. A men's tennis team was established in the spring of 1938; it practiced on the roof of the reconstructed University (20 Derne Street) Building—Archer's so-called "sky campus" (Suffolk University College of Liberal Arts, 1937 catalogue, p. 16)—until leaks caused by pounding feet, combined with the clear and present danger posed to passer-by five stories below by misdirected lobs, forced alteration of the arrangements. A golf program was begun the following autumn, and in the fall of 1939 practice began for men's—and women's—basketball. The men's team, coached by law student John Sexton, practiced two nights a week at the English High School gymnasium; while the women's team, under Sargent

College senior Mary Pratt, was allowed on Saturday mornings to use the gym at the Bulfinch Memorial Chapel near the University. In the spring of 1940, a baseball program was also launched. Most of these initial athletic efforts were modest, but, like the other extra-curricular activities begun during the same era, they stood the test of time; forty years later, they were still part of the University's student activities program.

53 Extra-curricular options for law students narrowed considerably; in an attempt to fill the void, Suffolk's first law fraternity—Wig and Robe—was founded in 1948. It survived until the early 1970s.

54 Rand also served as first editor of the *Beacon* yearbook, the first issue of which was published in 1948. Student dramatics was revitalized, as was the Suffolk University Debating Society—known as SUDS until 1950, when it was renamed to honor the contributions made to the forensics program by President Walter M. Burse. After World War II, a basement Recreation Room replaced Hall 6. Publication of the *Journal* recommenced in November 1946, and three sister societies (Spanish, German, and French) were added to the *Circolo Italiano.* All of the foreign language organizations eventually merged, in 1964, into the Modern Language Club. A number of other organizations were founded to bring together students in particular disciplines—among them a Psychology Club (founded in 1948) and a Science Club (1952), both of which were still active in 1981. A Business Club, founded in 1950 and affiliated with the American Marketing Association a year later, quickly became one of the largest organizations on campus; its vitality remained intact three decades later. The election of Suffolk students active in extra-curricular activities to *Who's Who in Colleges and Universities* began in 1948, while the Colleges' first academic honorary society. Phi Beta Chi (for science) was chartered in 1952.

55 College athletics underwent a similar boom. Tennis, golf, basketball, and baseball were revived after the war, with Charles Law taking over as coach of the latter two. Law soon became head of the Physical Education department and Director of Athletics, as well. Under Law, the basketball team played first at the Charlestown Army and Navy YMCA, then—after 1947—at the West End House on Blossom Street, which remained the squad's home until 1962. Soccer (coached at one time by Harvard star Malcolm Donahue) and hockey were both introduced, while the first women's varsity letter (for women's sailing) was awarded in 1950. Twenty full-tuition athletic scholarships were made available by the Trustees; a cheerleading squad and a Varsity Club were organized in 1948. In April 1950, a contest run by the Varsity Club and the *Journal* dubbed Suffolk athletic teams (previously known as the "Royals" or the "Judges") the "Rams." To celebrate the change, a University mascot—Hiram the Ram—was acquired; and for an entire year the *Suffolk Journal* was renamed the *Rambler.* In 1953, Law's program received its "athletic accreditation": membership in the New England College Athletic Conference. National Collegiate Athletic Association (NCAA) membership followed within a year.

56 Hockey, soccer, and sailing were eliminated as varsity sports, and athletic scholarships were cut to a bare minimum.

57 *Suffolk Journal,* November 9, 1951; December 12, 1951. The student activities fee, which had been introduced in 1936, was discontinued in the early 1950s for both the Law School and the collegiate departments; also, fraternities were formally barred from the Colleges.

58 Colburn, like his predecessors and all his successors, served the Colleges, not the Law School.

59 In 1948, a Law School Student Relations Committee was set up; it was composed of law students nominated by the Dean and elected by faculty members. Three years later, it was replaced by a Law School Student Council appointed by the Dean. By 1967, Evening Division student members of the Student Bar Association were represented by an Evening Division Board of Governors, headed by a Chairman; Day Division members were represented by a separate slate of Day Division officers, headed by a President. In 1960,

the SBA began publication of its own newspaper: the *Suffolk Law Reporter* was born (and died) in the spring of that year. In March 1962, it was succeeded by the *SBA Briefcase,* which survived until December 1967. *Dicta,* which began publication in 1972, was still in existence twenty-four years later.

60 Before 1971, membership in EDSA was limited to twelve; it was completely reorganized in 1971, and opened to all evening and part-time students in Liberal Arts and Business. EDSA's first elections were held in the spring of 1972. The *Evening Shadow,* first published in 1970, provided the constituencies served by EDSA with a newspaper of their own. Renamed the *Evening Press* in 1975, and the *Evening Voice* in 1976, it was by 1981 the only evening student newspaper in Massachusetts. An active and long-lived Humanities Club was founded in 1958, while the similarly durable Political Science Association began operation the following year. In the College of Business Administration, the American Marketing Association ceased to be the only student organization in 1959 with the foundation of the Society for the Advancement of Management (SAM) and the chartering of Delta Sigma Pi, the first non-honorary fraternity permitted in the collegiate departments. Within eight years, the business professional fraternity was joined by two others; Alpha Phi Omega, a service fraternity, in 1963; and Phi Alpha Tau, for communications, arts, and journalism, in 1967. Five academic honorary societies had also been established by 1967.

61 Colburn's tenure also witnessed several significant developments in athletics. As enrollments rose after 1956, athletic scholarship funds were restored to—and eventually surpassed—the levels of the late 1940s. This made Law's job slightly easier, but it was almost immediately complicated by another problem. When the West End was leveled to make way for Charles River Park, the basketball team lost its gymnasium at the West End House; Coach Law was forced to find new quarters for his team. He finally settled on the Cambridge YMCA, where Suffolk basketball teams practiced and played their home games for the next twenty-nine years. Finally, in 1966, Director Law was permitted to have his first full-time assistant: James Nelson, the man who eventually succeeded Law as basketball coach (1976) and Athletic Director (1978).

62 Sullivan had served as Director of Admissions since 1960. From that position, he worked hard to win creation of a Dean of Students post. He resigned as Admissions Director in 1966 to assume the new Deanship, in which he served until 1987.

63 Student agitation during the 1960's and early 1970s also helped expedite Trustee approval for a strengthened Public Relations office, an expanded Placement office, a full-time Alumni Secretary, cooperation with the General Alumni Association, a new firm for the Cafeteria, Sunday Library hours during exams, and restoration of an Activities Period shortly after the Board had abolished it.

64 *Suffolk Journal,* November 21, 1968; December 20, 1968.

65 In 1970, law student representatives were accredited to the Law School Committee of the Trustees.

66 *Suffolk Journal,* May 1967 ("Special Issue: Student Union"); March 14, 1969; September 22, 1969.

67 Lewis' successors were James O. Peterson (1971-75), Kenneth E. Kelly (1975-77), Bonita Betters-Reed (1977-79), Duane R. Anderson (1979-88), and Donna L. Schmidt (appointed in 1988).

68 An MBA Association was founded in 1969 in the Business School to give its graduate students a measure of the representation and self-government that had been established among Suffolk's other student constituencies. An Accounting-Finance Club was organized in 1974, and, to accommodate students interested in the Business School's newest program, a Public Administration Society was set up in 1976. Student-run organizations multiplied and diversified in the Law School, particularly under the Deanship of

alumnus (and first SBA advisor) David J. Sargent. A *Law Review* had been founded in 1967, and the *Advocate*—a student-run legal magazine and journal—the following year. An Environmental Law Society, established in 1970, was also in existence when Sargent took office three years later. By 1980, Law School student activities had expanded to include BALSA, HALSA, the Suffolk Women's Law Caucus, *Dicta* (the new SBA newspaper, founded in 1972), the Suffolk Lawyers Guild (1975), the Suffolk Law Forum (1976), the International Law Society and its *Transnational Law Journal* (both founded in 1976), as well as three law fraternities to replace the long-lived but finally defunct Wig and Robe. In the Liberal Arts College, *Venture*—an undergraduate literary magazine founded by Professor Stanley Vogel—was first published in 1968. New Directions, a center to help students resolve their problems, opened its doors two years later, while student TV station WSUB and radio station WSFR began broadcasting in 1974 and 1976, respectively. In the spring of 1975, a History Society was founded; and the era's interest in ethnic roots manifested itself in foundation of Afro-American, Latin American, International Students, Hellenic, Irish, and Italian-American undergraduate organizations. A twenty-year ban on social fraternities was ended in 1969 when Tau Kappa Epsilon (TKE) was permitted to establish a chapter at Suffolk; later the same year, Phi Sigma Sigma, the University's first social sorority, was founded. The first Springfest, which with the support of Mrs. Thomas Fulham and the leadership of Professor Ilse Fang soon became an annual all-University end-of-classes festival, was held in 1971. Two years later, Gold Key—an undergraduate service society which owed its name to the gold keys that had been given to SGA members since the late 1940s—was established to honor (as did *Who's Who in American Colleges and Universities*) those students who distinguished themselves by their contributions to extra-curricular activities. Academic recognition was also available from a growing number of honorary societies; by 1980, there were nineteen at Suffolk, including Alpha Sigma Lambda (chartered in 1975 for evening undergraduates) and four School of Management honoraries. During the 1970s, Suffolk's intercollegiate athletic teams scored a number of signal successes. The golf team, for example, three times won the Little Four Golf Tournament, while the basketball team participated in the NCAA Division 3 regional tournament from 1975 through 1978—reaching the regional finals in 1975. When compulsory Physical Education classes for undergraduates were discontinued in 1972, the University offered students in their stead an expanded and strengthened program of voluntary intramural competition, including basketball, flag football, and co-ed softball. Arrangements were concluded with the Boston Young Men's Christian (BYMC) Union gymnasium to provide facilities for the indoor portions of the intramural program. Suffolk's commitment to intercollegiate athletics was also expanded, as ice hockey was reintroduced as a varsity sport in 1980, and varsity competition was begun in cross country (1972), women's tennis (1977), and women's basketball (1977). The regeneration of the women's sports program at Suffolk was the work of Ann Guilbert, who joined Director Law's staff in 1975 as an Assistant Director of Athletics for women. By 1978, Suffolk University had joined the Massachusetts Association of Intercollegiate Athletics for Women and the Metropolitan Women's Intercollegiate Athletic Council.

69 So complex, in fact, had the job of student government become that the SGA was forced to create two new bodies under its jurisdiction to handle specialized functions: the Council of Presidents, in 1973, to deal with the coordination and funding of the rapidly-increasing assortment of undergraduate clubs and societies; and the Program Board and Council, in 1980, to concentrate on the planning of social events.

70 Suffolk University Board of Trustees, Minutes, November 13, 1974. Publication of the *Suffolk University Newsletter* (*SUN*) began in 1971, to provide better communications between the administration (including the Trustees) and the rest of the University; the *SUN*'s editor was University Public Relations Director Louis Connelly. Faculty participation in University

governance also increased. The Law School had had a Faculty Administrative Committee (composed of all full-time faculty members) since 1952. Ten years later, the Liberal Arts College and the Business School obtained Trustee approval for a similar body, a joint Liberal Arts-Business Faculty Assembly. Three elective faculty governance committees were established to report to the Faculty Assembly: an Educational Policy Committee (EPC) in 1962; a Promotion, Tenure and Review Committee (PTR) in 1968; and a Faculty Life Committee, which was set up in 1971 and made elective in 1972. Separately elected Business School governance committees were established in 1974 (EPC and PTR) and 1975 (Faculty Life), to serve a newly autonomous Business School Faculty Assembly. In 1972, a Joint Council on University Affairs was founded; it included Trustees, administrators, and elected faculty representatives from the Law School, the Liberal Arts College, and the Business School. Four years later, Liberal Arts faculty representatives were accredited to the Trustees' College Committee.

71 Trustee Student Affairs Committee reports for meetings of April 2, 1979 (in Suffolk University Board of Trustees, Minutes, April 11, 1979) and March 27, 1980 (in Suffolk University Board of Trustees, Minutes, April 9, 1980).

72 Gleason Archer resigned as President of Suffolk University in 1948. That same year, Hiram Archer was appointed the University's first Director of Alumni Relations, and Joseph Strain was assigned to assist him as Alumni Secretary. Early on, a division of labor emerged; Archer took primary responsibility for Law School alumni affairs, while Strain (himself a College of Liberal Arts graduate) assumed administrative responsibility for alumni of the collegiate departments. Despite the Trustees' repeated professions of support, however, neither man was permitted to devote his full time to alumni work.

73 The leaders of the group were George Karavasiles '49, Michael Linquata '49, John L. (Jack) McCarthy '49, and Arthur West '51. Dorothy McNamara, under the watchful eye of Judge Donahue, was authorized to work with the organizers; the *Alumni News* was revived, and arrangements were made to have the *Suffolk Journal*—in which a regular alumni news page was instituted—sent to all graduates of the collegiate departments.

74 Including Journalism.

75 Suffolk University Board of Trustees, Minutes, April 14, 1971.

76 A number of Alumni Fellow Awards were presented in 1974; and beginning in 1976, several Outstanding Alumni Awards were given annually. The first Annual Fund drives, one for the Law School and the other for the Colleges, were held in 1975. Four years later, a School of Management Development Committee, chaired by Peter Volpe, undertook that school's first separate fund-raising effort.

77 There were already twenty-nine Law School alumni in the Massachusetts Legislature when, in 1929, F. Leslie Viccaro became the first Suffolk graduate appointed to the bench. Three years later, Frank J. Donahue retired as Democratic State Chairman and received an appointment to the Superior Court of the Commonwealth; he was the first alumnus to serve in either capacity. Suffolk Law graduates numbered fourteen judges by 1937 (including Viccaro, Donahue, John E. Fenton, C. Edward Rowe, Daniel J. Gillen, Frankland W. L. Miles, David G. Nagle, and Edward T. Simoneau), as well as thirty Massachusetts legislators, twenty-two state government members, and nine clerks of court. Twenty years later, the Law alumni boasted three Superior Court justices (Donahue, Nagle, and Eugene A. Hudson), sixty other judges, Massachusetts Attorney-General George Fingold, and the Mayor of Boston—John B. Hynes. John F. Collins '41 replaced Hynes as Mayor. In 1972, sixteen percent of the Massachusetts judiciary, including Superior Court Chief Justice Walter H. McLaughlin, had graduated from Suffolk, as had ten percent of the state's legislators. Charlotte Anne Perretta was named in 1978 to the Massachusetts Appeals Court; her designation constituted the highest Massachusetts state judicial appointment yet granted a Suffolk graduate. Two

years later, alumna Linda S. Dalianis received designation as the New Hampshire Superior Court's first woman justice. Finally, in March 1979, Martin F. Loughlin became the first Suffolk Law alumnus to sit on the federal bench when he was appointed to the Federal District Court, First Circuit (New Hampshire). Congressman John J. Moakley and long-time Suffolk County District Attorney Garrett H. Byrne were Suffolk Law graduates, as were respected Massachusetts legislators John A Brennan, Jr., and W. Paul White.

78 Among them were college presidents, doctors, scientists, eminent scholars like Harry Zohn and Nicholas Perella, banking executives like Irene Grzybinska and John R. McDonald, business leaders, legislators, mayors, journalists, and professional athletes like Raymond "Sugar Bear" Hamilton. Hollywood comedy writer Mike Marmer and actor Paul Benedict graduated from the Suffolk Colleges, as did Coast Guard captain Eleanor L'Ecuyer and novelist Nancy Pierce Zaroulis. In 1980, Suffolk alumni constituted 59% of the University's Board of Trustees and 14% of its total full-time faculty (25% in the Law School, 7% in Liberal Arts, and 24% in the School of Management).

Chapter 7

1 Other leaders of the anti-Archer faction were Hiram J. Archer, the founder's brother, and David Stoneman, proprietor of the Bretton Woods Hotel. Suffolk University would never have survived World War II had it not been for the forbearance of Thomas F. McNichols, Manager of the West End Branch of the First National Bank of Boston, which held the mortgage note on the University Building.

2 Treasurer Donahue also established a Suffolk University Endowment Fund in 1950, and served as one of its three Trustees until his death twenty-nine years later.

3 Donahue also served extended terms on the Finance Committee (1945, 1948-76; Chairman 1969-75), the Business School Committee (1965-75), and the By-Laws Committee (1949-65), as well as shorter stints on the Nominating Committee, the Endowment Fund Committee, the Development Committee, the New Building Committee, the Committee to Acquire Property on Beacon Hill, and the Committee to Investigate Administrative Operations at Other Academic Institutions. In addition to his University duties, he was a Trustee of the Boston Public Library from 1948 until 1956.

4 Donahue served on the Honorary Degree Committee from 1948 until 1978, and chaired it after 1954. Under his direction, the committee displayed an uncanny knack for singling out individuals for honorary degrees who would later make headlines in the political or judicial world. Notable examples include Edmund S. Muskie (1955), Hon. William J. Brennan, Jr. (1956), Samuel J. Ervin, Jr. (1957), John F. Kennedy (1957), Thomas F. Eagleton (1958, 1970), Hugh D. Scott, Jr. (1959), and Leon Jaworski (1971).

5 Judge Donahue taught part-time in the evening division at Suffolk Law School from 1921 until 1926, then served as a Visiting Lecturer between 1943 and 1957. He received two honorary degrees from Suffolk University: a JD in 1942, and then in 1952 the University's first LLD degree. He was also the recipient in 1976 of an Outstanding Alumnus Award from the Suffolk University General Alumni Association.

6 Interview with Dorothy McNamara, May 1, 1979.

7 Interview with John Griffin, June 18, 1979.

8 The dedication and self-sacrifice of administrators like Dorothy McNamara, Evelyn Reilly, and McNamara's long-time assistant Alice DeRosa contributed much to the University's success through the years. Their willingness, along with the faculty members, to accept low pay and voluntarily to place themselves on long hours, permitted the institution to grow and prosper.

9 Suffolk University Board of Trustees, Minutes, February 6, 1974.

10 Interview with John Griffin, June 18, 1979. Griffin also received an MA degree in History from Boston University in 1936.

11 Resolution to honor John Griffin, Suffolk University Board of Trustees, Minutes, November 9, 1977.

12 After marrying Virginia Manning in 1936, Griffin became Treasurer, then President (1961), of his father-in-law's business, the Joseph P. Manning Company. In 1969, he became President of the Virginia Investment Company of Boston. He also served for some time as chairman of the directors of the national and Massachusetts associations of tobacco distributors.

13 Griffin also served a long term (1963-81) on the Building Committee, chairing it from 1973 until 1979. It was during his Chairmanship that the Fenton Building was opened for the College of Liberal Arts and Sciences, and that the Sawyer Building was acquired to provide a new home for the School of Management.

14 Griffin served as Clerk until incapacitated in 1979.

15 Resolution to honor John Griffin, Suffolk University Board of Trustees, Minutes, November 9, 1977.

16 Griffin served on the Auditing Committee from 1951 until 1981, and chaired it after 1953. His years of service on the Finance Committee (1944, 1948-50, 1964-80; Chairman 1948-50, 1964-65, 1966-68) made him a natural choice to chair the Salary Sub-Committee of the Finance Committee when it was created in 1976. He also served on the Nominating Committee (1946-48, 1965-69; Chairman 1946, 1948, 1966-69), the Honorary Degree Committee (1969-75), the Endowment Fund Committee (1958-81), the Insurance Committee, the Accreditation Committee, and as Vice-Chairman of the Development Committee. He received an honorary DCS degree from Suffolk in 1952, and in 1979 the Suffolk University General Alumni Association designated him the recipient of an Outstanding Alumnus Award.

17 Suffolk University Board of Trustees, Minutes, February 6, 1963.

18 Griffin was President of the Jamaica Plain Cooperative Bank, a Corporator of the Faulkner Hospital, a Knight of Malta, Vice-President of the St. Thomas Aquinas Conference of the St. Vincent de Paul Society, Chairman of the Tobacco and Allied Industries Division of the American Jewish Committee's Appeal for Human Relations, and an active worker in the National Conference of Christians and Jews and in the Massachusetts Committee of Catholics, Protestants, and Jews.

19 Interview with Arthur West, March 12, 1981.

20 Interview with Arthur West, March 12, 1981.

21 In 1970, Friedman stepped down as Chairman to devote more time to the family textile business left by his late father.

22 The seven hospitals affiliated with Suffolk's Medical Technology program were: the Newton-Wellesley Hospital (1960-96); the Henry Heywood Memorial Hospital, Gardner, Massachusetts (1964-86); St. Francis Hospital, Hartford, Connecticut (1967-76); the Veterans Administration Hospital, Jamaica Plain (1968-78); the Cambridge Hospital (1971-95); the Norwood Hospital (1984-86); and the Bon Secours Hospital, Methuen (1972-76). Besides Arthur West (BS '51, MA in Ed. '56) and Beatrice Snow (BA '62), alumni of Friedman's Biology department who went on to earn Ph.D.'s and recognition as distinguished scientists or scholars included Kenneth Sherman (BS '54, D. Sci. '79; oceanographer, ecosystems specialist, authority on plankton, and Director of the National Marine Fisheries Service Laboratory), Joseph Geraci (BS '59; a widely-published authority on marine mammals, and Professor of Veterinary Medicine at the University of Guelph, Ontario), and Frank O'Brien (BA '63; Professor of Biology and Chairman of the Biology department, University of Massachusetts, North Dartmouth, Massachusetts.)

23 Interview with Arthur West, March 12, 1981.

24 Friedman was a member of numerous organizations, including the American Association for the Advancement of Science; the Technion Society; the Textile Research Institute; the American Friends of the Hebrew University; the Zionist Organization of America; and B'nai B'rith, where he was a charter member of the Dr. Joshua Loth Liebman Lodge. He was very active in the affairs of Temple Emmanuel in Newton, and served on the national board of the American Association for Jewish Education.

25 Law also received an Ed.M. degree from Boston University in 1955.

26 During one of Law's seasons at Weston, his football team also went undefeated.

27 Interview with Charlie Law, June 10, 1975.

28 Interview with Charlie Law, June 10, 1975.

29 Baseball, basketball, tennis, and golf were still varsity sports at Suffolk when Law retired in 1978.

30 Ice hockey was reinstated as a varsity sport in 1980.

31 In 1972, arrangements were made with the Boston YMC Union to provide facilities for indoor intramural competition. Cross country was introduced as a varsity sport in 1972. Assistant Director Ann Guilbert introduced varsity women's tennis and varsity women's basketball in 1977; four years later, a separate women's cross country team was established.

32 Among the outstanding basketball players Law developed were: a pair of Division III All-Americans, Pat Ryan and Donovan Little; Jack Resnick of Boston's West End; Art Mellace, now a well-known college basketball official; Bill Vrettes, whom Law called the best player he ever coached; Allan Dalton, a former Celtic draft choice; Jay Crowley; Kevin Clark; Chris Tsiotos; and John Howard.

33 In 1978, the New England Athletic Conference presented Law with a citation recognizing three decades of devotion and service.

34 Interview with Charlie Law, June 10, 1975.

35 Charlie Law died in April 1981.

36 Goodrich was also appointed Professor of Humanities. In addition, he served as Director of Admissions from 1947 until 1949.

37 Dean Robert Munce was appointed Acting University President in 1954 to succeed Walter M. Burse. After he was formally designated as President in 1955, Munce retained the College Deanship as well. Only in 1956 was the Dean's title removed from the President and added to that of Registrar Goodrich.

38 Interview with Donald Goodrich, June 27, 1979. A faculty tenure system and a TIAA-CREF retirement program were both introduced during Goodrich's Deanship (1962).

39 As Professor Stanley Vogel pointed out at a testimonial upon Goodrich's retirement from the Deanship in 1969: "[Goodrich] took the trouble to entertain the whole faculty, for many years at his own expense in his own house, and came to know each of us personally. Many of us will never forget the garden parties, cocktail parties, and dinners at One Boulder Brook Road. This was important for a college that had no campus or regular social gatherings for its faculty."

40 When Goodrich became Vice-President in 1966, he gave up the Registrar's position—which he had retained, at least nominally, after assuming the Deanship in 1956. A separate College Registrar, Mary Hefron, was then appointed. Also in 1966, a new Deanship of the College of Business Administration was created—releasing Goodrich from his supervisory responsibilities over that academic unit, and permitting him to devote more time to

his duties as Vice-President and Dean of the College of Liberal Arts and Sciences. The new Business School Dean was Donald Grunewald.

41 Emerson College had already awarded Goodrich an honorary Litt.D. degree in 1958. After retiring from the Deanship, he continued to teach in the Humanities Department at Suffolk until 1974.

42 Interview with Donald Unger, January 19, 1981. Always active in civic and professional affairs, Goodrich served as President of the Private School Association of Baltimore, and held memberships in the American Conference of Academic Deans, the National Education Association, Phi Beta Kappa, the State Club, the Schoolmasters' Club of Massachusetts, the Publicity Club of Boston, and the Boston Rotary Club. He belonged to the Wellesley Hills Congregational Church, where he served as a Deacon and as a member of the Religious Education Committee.

43 Suffolk University Board of Trustees, Minutes, May 13, 1948.

44 While working on his BS in Library Service at Columbia, Hartmann served as a lecturer in History and a Library Fellow at City College, New York.

45 Interview with Edward Hartmann, February 15, 1981.

46 It was Patricia I. Brown who, under Hartmann's supervision, catalogued the law collection. The College collection had been catalogued as it was accumulated, beginning in the mid-1930s.

47 Other published works by Hartmann included: *A Centennial History of the Welsh Baptist Association of Northeastern Pennsylvania* (1955), *History of the Welsh Congregational Church of the City of New York, 1801-1951* (1969), and *The Welsh Society of Philadelphia, 1729-1979* (1980).

48 *Boston Globe,* December 13, 1965.

49 Trustee William F.A. Graham, a Holy Cross alumnus, had helped to win the election of Fenton to Suffolk University's Board of Trustees, Fenton, in turn, worked successfully to win election to the Board—and ultimately to the Presidency—for two other Holy Cross graduates: Dennis C. Haley, Fenton's predecessor as University President, and Thomas A. Fulham, Fenton's successor as President.

50 Fenton served on the Law School Committee (1949-74), the College Committee (1952-74), the Business School Committee (1965-74), the Finance Committee (1950-74; Chairman 1956-57, 1961-64), the Nominating Committee (1952-69, 1970-74; Chairman 1957-59, 1965-66), the Scholarship Committee (1949-64), the Athletics Committee (1958-74), the Honorary Degree Committee (1950-74), the By-Laws Committee (1950-65), the Building Committee (1969-74), the Development Committee (1969-74), the Endowment Fund Committee (1950-57), the New Building Committee, the Committee to Acquire Property on Beacon Hill, and the Committee to Investigate Administrative Operations at Other Academic Institutions.

51 The Board of Trustees, under the By-Laws adopted in 1937, annually elects its Chairman, Vice-Chairman, Treasurer, and Clerk, along with the President and Vice-President of the University.

52 Dennis C. Haley, who retired as Boston's Superintendent of Schools in 1960 to become Suffolk University's fourth President, played an important role in gaining Trustee acceptance for many demands put forward by faculty representatives. Haley's background in academic administration made him sympathetic to a number of the faculty's proposals, and his reputation gave him the influence necessary to reconcile the Trustees to the changes—an influence lacked by Presidents Burse and Munce. Haley (President 1960-65) also succeeded in convincing the Trustees to trust his expertise on the issue of expansion, as he had on a number of other issues; he thus played a leading role in the building campaign that led to construction of the Donahue Building—a campaign which began a new era, mentally as well as physically, at Suffolk. Steadily increasing Trustee reliance on Haley's experience and

judgment finally began a process of restoring to the President some of the powers which the Board's struggle with Gleason Archer had led it to arrogate to itself—a process that was subsequently encouraged by Haley's successors John E. Fenton (1965-70) and Thomas A. Fulham (1970-80), and which was continued under their administrations.

53 Interview with John Fenton, February 16, 1968. Fenton was preceded as Chairman of the Board of Trustees at Suffolk University by Thomas J. Boynton (1911-45), James M. Swift (1945-46), Frank J. Donahue (1946-48), and George B. Rowell (1948-64). Between Judge Fenton's two terms (1964-66, 1970-74) as Board Chairman, that position was filled by George C. Seybolt (1966-70). After Fenton's death in 1974, his successors as Chairman were C. Edward Rowe (1974-76), Vincent J. Fulmer (1976-81), John S. Howe (1981-87), and James F. Linnehan (elected in 1987).

54 Like most of the University's top leaders after 1948, Fenton came from an Irish Catholic background. He was a friend and advisor to both Cardinal Cushing and to Cardinal Medeiros; and he was a Knight of the Grand Cross of the Holy Sepulchre. The social and charitable applications of his religious convictions, however, were ecumenical; he worked easily with those of other faiths and backgrounds. He served in high regional, state, and national offices in the Elks, the Knights of Columbus, the United Fund, the Boy Scouts, the American Legion, the Ancient Order of Hibernians, and the National Conference of Christians and Jews. In addition, he was President of Bon Secours Hospital, Methuen; a Director of St. Ann's Orphanage and Home; and Chairman of the Board of the Paul A. Dever School for Exceptional Children in Taunton.

55 Fenton held honorary degrees from Suffolk (1949), Holy Cross, Emerson, and Merrimack. He was also voted the Frederick A. McDermott Award in 1966 by Suffolk's Student Bar Association, and the Administrator of the Year Award in 1974 by the University's undergraduate student leaders.

Chapter 8

1 Suffolk University Board of Trustees, Minutes, January 13, 1971; March 10, 1971; November 10, 1971; April 11, 1973; February 14, 1979; and April 11, 1979.

George C. Seybolt, President of the William Underwood Company, Watertown, was appointed Chair of the CBA Advisory Council on November 8, 1961; Thomas A. Fulham was, at the time of his appointment to the CBA Advisory Council, Chairman of the Board, Fulham Bros., Inc., Boston; John P. Chase was Chairman, John P. Chase, Inc., Boston; Stephen P. Mugar was President, Star Market Company, Cambridge; and Joseph E. Sullivan was Treasurer, Sullivan Brothers Printers, Lowell.

From the time of his election to the Board, Fulham was active on the College Committee, chairing it from Dennis Haley's death in 1966 until well into his own Presidency (1975). Almost immediately, as well, the Trustees called upon Fulham's special expertise to chair a committee established in 1962 to prepare a University Development program—what was to become the pivotal University Development Committee. But, as became apparent over time, Fulham's unique talent was for creating consensus and community, for coalition-building—and for paideia, cultural and spiritual healing/reconciliation. It was upon Fulham's recommendation in September 1971 that the symbolically crucial step was taken by the Trustees of naming the "old" building the "Archer" Building "in honor of the Archer family," and the "new" building the "Donahue" Building "in honor of Judge Frank J. Donahue." Fulham it was, too, who convinced the Trustees:

1) To accept accreditation for student representatives to his College Committee (1969, with students accredited, on the same model, to the Law School Committee in 1970 and to the Business School Committee in 1971);

2) To establish a Committee on Black Student Affairs and an historic affiliation with the Museum of Afro-American History (February 1972);

3) To constitute a President's Committee on Women in the University (November 1972);

4) To "encourage alumni participation in the affairs of the University" (January 1971) and to approve an arrangement "whereby members of the General Alumni should be granted the right to elect [three] Trustees from the Alumni" (November 1975, with the first Alumni Trustee, James F. Linnehan, elected in November 1976);

5) To consider establishment of a Trustee Committee on Faculty to provide a "direct access route between the Faculties and Trustees" (April 1973);

6) To create a Trustee Student Affairs Committee "to provide for more effective student participation in the governance of Suffolk University and to develop a systematic basis for improved communication between students and Trustees" (February 1979); and

7) To vote, upon the recommendation of that committee, to approve the "Shanahan Motion" that the Board "encourages and endorses an effort to improve the communication by and between the Suffolk University Board of Trustees and the Suffolk University community, and will welcome proposals, which integrate the feelings and philosophies of the various segments of the Suffolk University community, aimed at this goal." (April 1979).

Above all, it was President Fulham's particular contribution, to the University of his time and to its posterity, to set as an individual (as chief executives are inescapably called upon to do) a remarkable tone for the institution, embodying what historically had proven best in it and what, among educational institutions, it had best, uniquely, and significantly to contribute to the future.

At the end of the day, then, President Fulham's legacy remains Suffolk University's present and future. His was the Renaissance ideal of human beings being made more human by their habitation of an institution that offers a physical, emotional, and intellectual landscape of human scale; and by their treatment, within that institution, always with personal attention, individual concern, and human dignity. True education, he believed, could take place only in a setting where the asking of an individual question, or the expression of a personal opinion, commands attention and is dignified by the common expectation of a serious and humane response; only where gatherings of people are small enough for individuals to see, when they look at others, "the whites of their eyes," with the subtleties of personal expression and feeling therein. Only thus, he insisted, could occur the interconnected, indispensable expansions of our understanding of other human beings, of our understanding of ourselves, and of our conception of what it means for us (and others) to be human. In the simple human dignity which Thomas A. Fulham afforded to all those engaged, like him, in the search that is living, lies his indispensable legacy, educational and otherwise, to Suffolk University.

2 In November 1977, Suffolk University agreed to purchase the 12-story United Way Building (Mason Memorial Building), 14 Somerset Street, Boston, from the United Way of Massachusetts Bay, Inc., for $605,000. Built in 1913 for the Boston City Club, it had been occupied by the City Club until 1950; since 1960, it had been home to the United Way of Massachusetts Bay, Inc. On September 1, 1978, the building was officially conveyed to Suffolk University. Assured by architectural engineer Henry Portnoy that "the architecture of the building . . . has character and quality that enhances the area and . . . it fits in well with the environment," the Board of Trustees voted later that month to remodel, not demolish, the building, relocating the main entrance from 14 Somerset Street to 8 Ashburton Place.

On April 11, 1979, the Board of Trustees voted to proceed with a $9.9 million Facilities Development Project, leaving the Law School in Donahue Building and undertaking a total renovation of the 12-story building at 8 Ashburton

Place, along with substantial alterations to the Donahue and Archer Buildings and the property at 56 Temple Street. The project, it was decided, would be financed through tax-exempt bond issues, Suffolk University funds, and a capital campaign for which a goal was established (in April 1980) of $2.7 million. The "Campaign for Excellence," as it was designated, was chaired by Suffolk University Trustee John S. Howe, retired Chairman of the Board and CEO of the Provident Institution for Savings. Between its initiation in 1979 and its successful conclusion in February 1982, the Campaign for Excellence exceeded its goal by one-third, or nearly a million dollars: in all, $3.6 million was collected, $884,595 beyond the projected goal of $2.7 million. The funds raised through the Campaign for Excellence enabled Suffolk University to renovate the Sawyer Building and the E. Albert Pallot Library, establish the John P. Chase Computer Center and the Thomas Fulham Merit Scholarship Program, and achieve other objectives which enabled the University to advance the quality of its academic programs. The $10 million invested in the Sawyer Building was completely paid off by November 1987, within five years of the building's dedication. In June 1981, successful Campaign chairman John S. Howe (a Trustee since 1974) was elected Chairman of the University's Board of Trustees, succeeding Vincent A. Fulmer. In July 1982, Joseph A. Kelley, who directed the Campaign for Excellence, was appointed Suffolk University's Director of Development.

In January 1980, the Trustees authorized Vappi Co. to begin construction for renovation and conversion of the Ashburton Building. Demolition work began on February 8, and work on the building proceeded on schedule and on budget. Administrative offices, classrooms, and faculty offices were completed for the opening of classes in the fall of 1981; the move there actually began in mid-July 1981 from rental space at 100 Charles River Plaza, third floor (University Development, Alumni, Public Relations, Financial Aid) and from 56 Temple Street (Instructional Media Center and College Admissions), with the School of Management faculty following from 45-47 Mount Vernon Street in August, and the students in September.

The Ashburton Building was officially opened on Founder's Day, September 19, 1981, with formal dedication postponed until spring 1982 to await completion of the library and the cafeteria. On January 16, 1982, the new Mildred E. Sawyer Library (so designated thanks to a $200,000 naming gift from Frank Sawyer, her husband) opened. Three months later, on Charter Day, April 29, 1982, the University dedicated the Frank Sawyer Building at 8 Ashburton Place, named in honor of the Co-Chairman of the Board of Avis, Inc., a self-made businessman who started the Checker Taxi Company, and who was the largest individual donor to the Campaign for Excellence.

With the completion of the 8 Ashburton Place Building, the Board of Trustees voted to proceed with Phase II of the rehabilitation of the University's physical space with an expenditure of approximately $750,000 to be made during the summer of 1981 and $700,000 during the summer of 1982, to implement the Board's unfinished commitment to the Law School that the Donahue Building be occupied by the Law School only, the use of 56 Temple Street as Law Faculty offices, the acquisition by the Law School of the College Library space in the Archer Building, and the conversion of the Donahue Building cafeteria into Law School space. Phase II of the Facilities Development Program called for conversion of the one-time College Library into the E. Albert Pallot Library, a new wing of the Law Library, to enhance what was already considered one of the finest law school libraries in the area, having grown from 60,000 volumes to 160,000 between 1972 and 1982. In addition, Phase II Archer Building construction was planned for the new Edward I. Masterman Law Student Lounge; new amphitheatre classrooms; a Law School faculty lounge; new offices for the *Law Review* and *Transnational Law Journal*; new computer science laboratories; additional Biology labs; and new classrooms. Phase II work in the Donahue Building work entailed renovation and expansion of the University's Instructional Media Center and its existing studio, and faculty and library offices. These renovations of the Archer,

Donahue, and Fenton Buildings were carried out during the summers of 1981 and 1982. On October 21, 1982, dedication took place of the E. Albert Pallot Library, the large third-floor reading room in the Archer Building, formerly the site of the College Library; four months later, on February 17, 1983, the John P. Chase Computer Room was dedicated.

3 Thomas J. Brown, at the time of his election to the Board, was Assistant to the Chairman of the Board, Polaroid Corporation, Cambridge; John M. Corcoran, was President, John M. Corcoran Co.; and Joseph B. Shanahan, Jr., Esq., was a serving Alumni Trustee, elected on February 9, 1977.

4 Thomas P. McDermott, CPA, at the time of his election to the Suffolk University Board of Trustees Managing Partner, Arthur Young and Company, served as a Trustee June 4 1986-June 30, 1993; Carol Sawyer Parks, Vice-President/Treasurer, Checker Taxi Company, was elected a Trustee on June 4, 1986; John C. Scully, Executive Vice-President of Marketing, John Hancock Mutual Life Insurance Co., and a member of the Board of Directors of that corporation, was elected a Trustee on November 12, 1986.

Two of the new "business" Trustees, John Scully and Thomas McDermott, spoke for the others when they encouraged the Trustees to be optimistic about the potential of raising funds from the business community for projects and objectives for which the University could present a strong case. Throughout the Perlman era and into the Sargent administration, Corcoran, McDermott, and Scully repeatedly urged—at first with limited impact, but with gradually growing consequence—the addition to the Board of more, and more powerful, representatives of business, corporations, banking institutions, and foundations. Corporations, they emphasized, patiently and persistently, would play a significant role in fund-raising efforts and a successful corporate campaign would require an expanded representation of business leaders on the Board.

5 The new President was inaugurated on Charter Day (April 29), 1981, at the John Hancock Hall, attended by 700 guests, representatives from more than 100 colleges and universities, and all due pomp and circumstance. In his Inaugural Address, he chose his text for the day from among the most orthodox verses in the Suffolk Gospel: "Education for Opportunity."

6 Suffolk University Board of Trustees, Minutes, November 11, 1985; the statistics cited on previous pages concerning demographic changes in the 1970s and 1980s were drawn from the National Center for Education Statistics, *Projections of Education Statistics to 1997-98* (Washington: U.S. Government Printing Office, 1988) and from the Western Interstate Commission for Higher Education, *High School Graduates: Projections by State, 1986 to 2004,* Northeast Region (Boulder, CO: By the Commission, 1988).

7 As President Perlman put it, in one of his "President's Reports" to the Trustees:

Suffolk University increasingly faces competition from area universities through increased grants and merit-based scholarships, increased student services, improved facilities (including student unions and recreational facilities), and expensive advertising. Suffolk is also competing against subsidized state-supported schools and a strong economy which encourages families to borrow for schools with more amenities. In this environment, institutions unable or unwilling to upgrade their scholarship programs, curriculum, services to students, and facilities stand to lose their market position when the number of students increases again in the 1990s. To compete more favorably, Suffolk University needs additional support staff for new student services: Computer Center, Financial Aid, Cooperative Education, Placement, Learning Center, etc. The University also needs increased alumni and corporate/foundation giving, which is especially necessary in a tuition-dependent institution in a time of declining enrollments. (Daniel H. Perlman, President's Report to the Board of Trustees [in Suffolk University Board of Trustees, Minutes, November 18, 1987]).

8 Suffolk University had a long history of providing additional assistance for its (frequently) educationally—as well as financially—needy students. Almost from the opening of the Suffolk School of Law in 1906, founder Gleason Archer made faithful and persistent efforts to arrange and underwrite the provision of high-school equivalency (and other necessary/appropriate) instruction at nearby locations convenient to the Law School. Hiram Archer, the founder's brother, taught courses in a "Suffolk College" established briefly for this purpose in 1908-09, and for two decades in the Law School's own Department of Research and Review. In addition, there was, in and around Suffolk Law School, a Preparatory or Summer Preparatory Department from 1923 until 1931, when Dean Archer's ambitious plans to provide expanded preparatory services through a Suffolk takeover of the Wheeler Preparatory School at 59 Hancock Street set in motion a train of events that led to establishment there of the Suffolk College of Liberal Arts in 1934.

9 The various activities funded by "Perlman's grant" included:

1) Establishment of a Computer Engineering Technology program (which by 1986 enrolled 70 students), one aspect of which was to focus on and promote Emerging Careers for Women and Minorities in Science;

2) Creation of an Office of Institutional Research;

3) Institution of a program of office automation (word-processing equipment);

4) Expansion of Career Planning and Placement services to students, especially evening students, and to increase the number of students participating in internship programs;

5) Establishment of a Learning Resource Center;

6) Support for faculty development, including reduced loads for a new Integrated Studies faculty seminar, travel funds, released time for preparation of new courses, and on-campus speakers and workshops;

7) Development of courses, seminars, and exchange activities in the field of International Business in the School of Management; and

8) Initiation of a competency-based assessment and advising project in the School of Management.

10 Within months of the opening of the Donahue Building in the fall of 1966, the Trustees were negotiating with the Stop and Shop grocery chain to purchase its disused market at 148 Cambridge Street. At least partially in response to a student request for a Student Union (April 1967), the Board of Trustees actively pursued from that time purchase of the building, with the aim of tearing it down and erecting in its place a planned 7-story building (reduced in December 1967 to 5 stories plus a basement and sub-basement in an attempt to mollify neighbors). From April 1967 on, future President Fulham (chairman of the College Committee) became the Trustees' point man in discussion with the Beacon Hill Civic Association and other Beacon Hill neighbors (as chair of a special Trustees' committee to meet with Beacon Hill neighbors from April 5, 1967). In June of 1967, the Trustees approve purchase of both 148 Cambridge Street and 56 Temple Street, resolving to sell University properties at 32 and 34 Hancock Street to cover the purchase cost. Shortly after purchase of 148 Cambridge Street, the University filed for a variance from the zoning code to construct the proposed 7-story academic building. The Board of Appeals subsequently approved a 5-story building on the proposed site, and the decision was upheld in Superior Court; however, upon appeal to the Supreme Judicial Court, the Beacon Hill Civic Association prevailed, thus killing the project for some years. Fulham, by then President of Suffolk University, continued to negotiate desultorily, in general terms, on Suffolk University "policies and expansion" with the Beacon Hill Civic Association through the late 1960s and early 1970s.

Then, in April 1975, the Trustees approved an urgent, accreditation-driven resolution calling for the Law School to take over the Donahue Building, with rental space and new construction on the Ridgeway site to accommodate the needs of the Colleges. This emergency resolution reenergized discussion with the University's Beacon Hill neighbors. After the dedication of the Fenton Building on October 25, 1975, Fulham undertook negotiations with the Beacon Hill Civic Association and the Northeast Slope Neighborhood Association (NESNA) about the proposed Ridgeway plans. They were still talking, and Fulham was optimistic, when the Mason Memorial Building (8 Ashburton Place) became available (November 1977) and took him and the Trustees off in another direction. At about the same time (April 1978), the building at 28 Derne Street that had long housed Conda's Restaurant also became available and, after unsuccessful negotiations to purchase the building, the Trustees approved (September 1978) a proposed lease agreement by which, after purchase of the building by Suffolk alumnus John Bennett, Esq., as a "straw" for the University, Bennett would temporarily "manage" (read: "hold") the property as an unofficial agent of the University. Throughout much of the preceding negotiation and maneuvering, President Fulham was a Director of the Beacon Hill Civic Association, a position to which he was reelected in June 1979.

11 Suffolk University Board of Trustees, Minutes, September 14, 1983.

12 In the campaign to renovate the Auditorium, the President's concern for regular facilities maintenance—and the Trustees' clear awareness of it—was his first ally. The old Auditorium provided a classic example of "deferred maintenance." By 1984, with President Perlman's establishment of a University Facilities Audit in 1982 and with the progressive routinizing of its workings, the Trustees' attention was thereby guided, rather undramatically, to Dramatic Arts and their vestibule. Originally, renovation of the Archer Building's science labs and of the Auditorium over several years was planned; but the necessity for joint HVAC work forced its consolidation into the summer of 1986, at a cost of $2.2 million.

13 Pervasive and energetic work by many members of the University community in support of multiculturalism yielded clear dividends. In April 1987, for example, after endorsements from the CLAS Faculty Assembly and from the Trustees' Students Affairs Committee, the Board of Trustees—after a year of debate and three votes on the matter—finally voted to divest its holdings in companies doing business with South Africa.

14 University-wide initiatives complemented those of individual schools. In 1990 Suffolk launched an annual "Cultural Unity Week," a combination of educational and social activities sponsored by a broad coalition of student groups, faculty, and administrators. In that same year, a University-wide Intercultural Affairs Committee was established and presented its first annual awards to students, faculty members, and administrators for their contributions to intercultural understanding. Other intercultural annual events that became favorite traditions included the Chinese New Year celebration, the Martin Luther King, Jr., luncheon, and the Hispanic Culture Week, which included Noche Latina. The Black Student Union sponsored events throughout the year, but particularly during Black History Month. Typically, that February celebration of the African-American heritage featured speakers, a gospel concert, a play, films with discussions, a family banquet, and an all-day community reading of African-American literature. Co-sponsored by the History Department, the latter event attracted a large and enthusiastic audience from inside and outside the University.

The University's establishment in 1987 of a Minority Student (later called the Maria Stewart AHANA Student) Scholarship program, which provided for ten incoming or transfer students a renewable stipend of $2,500 per year plus an employment option, sent a clear signal to the community about the institution's commitment to recruit AHANA (African-American, Hispanic, Asian, and

Native American) students. The Maria Stewart Scholarship Program proved to be an effective vehicle for AHANA recruitment.

15 Collection curators H. Edward Clark (1971-85), Robert E. Fox (1985-91), and Robert Bellinger (appointed in 1991) also maintained a close relationship with the neighboring Museum of Afro-American History and the National Park Service. Henry Hampton, president of Blackside, Inc., producers of the award-winning civil rights documentary "Eyes on the Prize," and chairman of the Board of the Museum of Afro-American History, was awarded an honorary degree at the CLAS/SOM Commencement on June 5, 1988, and Suffolk was honored to host the Reverend Jesse L. Jackson in March 1992 as a result of this collaboration.

16 From 1978 until 1980, Charles L. Niles filled the position; his successor, from 1980 until 1988, was Rosalie L. Warren.

17 During his nine years in office, President Perlman had numerous opportunities to call attention to landmark successes by Suffolk University students. These included:

1) The winning in 1984, by Sociology major Matthew J. Buckley, of the University's first prestigious Harry S. Truman Scholarship (one of 105, established in 1977).

2) The winning in 1988, by English major Susanne Gruber, of the University's first undergraduate Fulbright Scholarship, in this case to the United Kingdom, the fiercest country competition; followed in 1989 by a similar success for History major Helen Protopapas in the Fulbright country competition for the Federal Republic of Germany.

3) Suffolk University was ranked #1 in forensics competition in 1984-85 for institutions its size. According to a study by Dr. Steven Hunt of Lewis and Clark College, the accomplishments of Suffolk University's CLAS Forensics program in the decade 1979-89 entitled it to be recognized as one of only four New England programs (Suffolk, Dartmouth, Emerson, and Harvard) among the top fifty nationally during that period.

4) Moot Court Teams from Suffolk University Law School won national championships in the 1983 Patent/Intellectual Property Law Giles S. Rich Moot Court Competition, the 1985 Anti-Trust Moot Court Competition, and the 1985 Constitutional Law Moot Court Competition.

5) Between 1983 and 1988, the Law School's National Moot Court Competition team advanced to the national finals four out of five years (the best record in the region over that period).

6) Suffolk Law School individuals or teams won honors for "Best Brief" for the entire 1986 and 1987 Stetson Tax Moot Court Competition, Best Oral Advocate for the entire 1987 Irving R. Kaufman Securities Moot Court Team Competition, Best Brief in the 1987 F. Lee Bailey Team Competition sponsored by the National University in San Diego, and Best Government Brief in the national finals of the 1989 Tax Moot Court Competition.

7) A recent SOM graduate won the Silver Medal in the May 1985 CPA Exam; on that exam, over 44% of Suffolk University's first-time takers passed all four parts, the best percentage of any Accounting program in the Commonwealth.

8) Suffolk University Law School graduates distinguished themselves on the July 1986 administration of the Massachusetts Bar Exam: 88.3% of the 302 first-time candidates from Suffolk University succeeded, second only to Harvard.

9) One CLAS student was accepted in 1985 by the Fletcher School of Law and Diplomacy directly out of the College's undergraduate program (with InterFuture experience); another CLAS student was admitted to Harvard Law School in 1986; and an SOM undergraduate was accepted by the Harvard Business School in 1989.

18 The degree of the Law School's preoccupation with externally-imposed accreditation requirements was vaguely disturbing to some at Suffolk, given founder Gleason Archer's (and the institution's) long-standing concern about the "hidden agendas" of accreditation processes and about the dangers of enforced conformity/submission.

19 Charles P. Kindregan, Jr., Suffolk University Law School ABA/AALS Reaccreditation Self-Study, 1989.

20 In 1985-86, the University's townhouse at 56 Temple Street (henceforth called the Goldberg Building) was renovated through a gift from the Ethel Goldberg estate, and the Center was installed there. In November 1987, after additional alterations to 56 Temple, it was joined there by the National Board of Trial Advocacy, founded in 1977 by noted trial attorney Theodore I. Rostoff to certify the quality of attorneys throughout the nation in civil and criminal trial advocacy, which relocated from Washington, D.C. for a period of three years in response to a proposal from Suffolk University.

In 1973, the Law School faculty spent the better part of a summer considering the curriculum. At that time, the faculty made a determination that the core curriculum was educationally sound, but that more opportunities for electives and clinical courses should be permitted. In order to increase opportunities for elective studies, a summer session was created. Credit-hour requirements for evening students were increased. In order to improve the writing ability of students, a new first-year legal writing requirement was added to the curriculum. Legal Practice Skills, a three-credit course (to acquaint students with the basic tools by which a practicing attorney advocates his/her client's cause, and to develop practice skills through closely supervised exercises in legal research, writing, and oral advocacy) was initiated in its present form in September 1973 and became a well-established part of the Law School curriculum. The stability and continuity of the LPS program was enhanced by the appointment of a full-time faculty member as Director. The exclusive use, after 1979, of full-time instructors also provided a major improvement in the LPS program.

Between 1983 and 1989, the LPS Tutorial program was added and strengthened; it was ultimately conducted by the full-time LPS instructors, not (as originally) by law faculty volunteers. All LPS instructors were required to teach full-time and to teach only in the LPS program. They worked under the supervision of a full-time tenure-track faculty member as Director. Prof. Joseph Glannon served as LPS Director from 1983 until 1987; he was succeeded by Prof. Kate Nace Day (1987-89), Prof. Steven M. Eisenstat (1989-92), and Martha Siegel (appointed in 1992).

The number of elective courses offered in the Law School increased from 105 in 1981 to 139 fourteen years later. Elective courses added between 1981 and 1995 included: Alternative Dispute Resolution (complementing Arbitration Seminar, which had been part of the elective curriculum since the early 1980s); Chemical Health Hazards and Corporate Liability; Computers and the Law; Human Reproduction and the Law; Law and Economics; Law and Psychology; two electives in Law Practice Management (taught by a full-time Law School faculty member and an adjunct with an MBA degree); Law, Science, and Medicine; Using Computers to Enhance Legal Skills; and Mass Media Law. Additional elective courses (such as Intellectual Property) were also being developed to address new legal problems.

A Summer Day Division was added in 1992 to the Summer Evening Division that had existed since 1974. In September 1994, the opportunity for a full clinical experience for Evening Division students was also introduced, when an evening component (S.U. Clinica Legal Evening Clinic) was inaugurated in the S.U. Clinica Legal Landlord-Tenant Clinic in Chelsea.

Between 1974 and 1981, the Law School faculty continued to review and make changes in the curriculum. The most important of these involved the creation of a substantial legal writing requirement as a condition of graduation. Between 1981 and 1995, the Writing Requirement matured and developed under the direction of a faculty committee. By 1995, students could satisfy the writing requirement in a number of ways: publications in various Law School periodicals; preparation of briefs in various moot court competitions; participation in seminars requiring papers; and individual projects under the supervision of a resident faculty member.

During the tenure of Dean Sargent, and those of his successors, the Law School demonstrated substantial progress in fostering the scholarly research and writing of its faculty. The Law faculty recognized its responsibility to engage in legal scholarship, and the Law School undertook various measures to provide an atmosphere which was conducive to accomplishing that objective—including the establishment of a Faculty Publications Committee in 1983, creation of a Summer Research Stipend program, reductions in teaching loads and additional time-release for faculty members engaged in scholarship, strengthening of the sabbatical program, and availability of student research assistantships for academic credit. By 1989, a Law School Self-Study Task Force concluded that scholarly writings by Law faculty members had increased substantially, both in quantity and quality, since the previous self-study in 1983.

A formal tenure policy was adopted in the Law School in April 1976; in 1983, a seventh-year up-or-out tenure policy was approved by the Law faculty and the Board of Trustees.

In April 1989, the Law School introduced a pilot loan forgiveness program for two Law School graduates per year who were employed full-time as public interest legal service providers, as public interest attorneys, or as advocates for a cause or concern commonly understood to be in the public interest.

In 1989, a Law School Long-Range Planning Report recommended appointment of a Development officer to work exclusively on Law School alumni relations. That position was created in April 1990. Subsequently, the 1994 Law School Long-Range Plan urged the engagement of a public relations specialist for the Law School.

On November 18, 1987, the Trustees voted to change the emphasis of the student aid program in the Law School by awarding most of the University funds available for financial aid to law students as no-interest loans rather than as grants.

The Center for Continuing Professional Development was founded in 1982 to provide the Law School with a locus for Continuing Legal Education. In 1992, it was renamed the Center for Advanced Legal Studies. Its spiritual father and first Director was Prof. Charles P. Kindregan (1982-88); he was succeeded by Prof. Anthony B. Sandoe (1988-92) and Carole A. Wagan (appointed in 1992).

The Law School's newly founded International Law Society (established in early 1976) published the first volume of the *Transnational Law Journal* (Prof. Karen Blum, advisor) later that year; Prof. Stephen C. Hicks served as faculty advisor for all subsequent volumes. In April 1979, the *Transnational Law Journal* was recognized by the Trustees as an official publication of Suffolk University Law School.

At various times during the period 1976-83, there were active chapters at the Law School of the Hispanic Law Student Association (HALSA), the Asian-American Law Student Association (AALSA), and the Black American Law Student Association (BALSA); at least in part because of the very limited number of Asian and Hispanic students at the school, the most active organization was BALSA.

An Environmental Law Society, founded in 1969 by Prof. Charles P. Kindregan, was by 1995 one of oldest student organizations at the Law School; Prof. R. Lisle Baker, whose teaching specialty lay in this area, became its faculty advisor in 1974.

The Suffolk Women's Law Caucus has remained active since its foundation in the early 1970s.

The Suffolk Equal Justice Foundation was established in 1981.

The Suffolk Chapter of the National Lawyers Guild was inaugurated in 1974.

The Lex, which appeared sporadically between 1946 and 1995, presented itself as the student yearbook of the Law School.

Organizations listed in the Law School's 1989 Self-Study included: the Asian Law Society (ALSA), BALSA, the Catholic Lawyers Guild, the Consumer Law Society, the Entertainment and Sports Law Society, the Environmental Law Society, the Gaelic Law Society, HLSA (Hispanic Law Student Association), the International Law Society, the Jewish Law Student Association, Phi Alpha Delta, the Real Estate Law Society, the Suffolk Law Democrats and Republicans, the Suffolk Lawyers Guild, and the Suffolk Women's Law Caucus. By 1995, an Intellectual Property Law Society had been added; the Simpson Chapter of Delta Theta Phi International Law Fraternity had been revived (1990); and HLSA had been renamed the Latino Law Students Association (LALSA).

21 Exactly how Gleason Archer would have reacted to this "endorsement," it is very difficult to say.

22 These initiatives ultimately resulted, once the School's—and the Dean's—overriding accreditation concerns had been satisfied—in establishment of SOM International Business minor and International Business double major programs in 1990, an International Business Studies major in 1991, large-scale recruitment of international students into the SOM's MBA program, and introduction in 1991 of a Master of Science in Finance degree (the first of several specialized master's programs designed specifically to attract international participants).

23 In 1984, the College implemented a Women's Studies minor, and established a Women's Studies Committee to oversee and administer it. By 1988, the Committee had beneficially brought within its purview the great bulk of activities related to women on campus. Dr. Agnes S. Bain was the first chair (and Director of Women's Studies from 1986), succeeded by Alexandra D. Todd (1989-92) and Krisanne Bursik (appointed in 1992). It was, in all probability, encouraging to their Women's Studies colleagues that both Dr. Bain and Dr. Todd resigned the Directorship in favor of the chairperson's responsibilities in their "home" departments.

From 1990 until her departure from the University in August 1993, Doris M. Clausen served as Advisor to the Women's Studies Program Center.

In the spring of 1985, the CLAS Educational Policy Committee and the College's Faculty Assembly created a CLAS Committee on Cultural Diversity in the Curriculum, which was charged to work with EPC and the Department chairs to create a culturally diverse curriculum and to create a minority studies minor. Dr. Donald R. Morton served as the committee's first chair. In January 1988, Dr. Morton, still Chair of the CLAS Committee on Cultural Diversity in the Curriculum, submitted a resolution to the CLAS Faculty Assembly calling for cultural diversity in all courses, which was endorsed by the Faculty Assembly and referred to the College's academic departments for implementation.

24 Two particularly notable public events were also hosted by Suffolk University in the mid-1980s: these were two international conferences sponsored by the English Department and organized by its chair, Dr. Frederick Wilkins, and his colleagues. The first, on "O'Neill: The Early Years," took place on March 22-25, 1984, and its sequel, "Eugene O'Neill: The Later Years," occurred on May 29-June 1, 1986. Both were enormously successful; and a third in the "series," entitled "O'Neill's People," followed on May 11-14, 1995.

25 In addition to this "adjustment" in financial aid policy, the Perlman era also saw the establishment of numerous small privately-funded endowments for departmental academic prizes, several of which (in English, History, and, later, Philosophy) were gifts from the family of Rosalie L. Warren. The redoubtable Mrs. Warren received a BS degree from Suffolk in 1980 and an M.Ed. in 1983—both when she was well over seventy years old—and was still an active CLAS student in 1995.

26 The sobriquet "A Man's School" first appeared in the Suffolk Law School catalogue in 1925-26; it was placed on the cover of the Suffolk Law School catalogue in 1931; and it was removed entirely from the Suffolk Law School catalogue in 1937.

The entry in the Suffolk Law School catalogue read as follows: "A Man's School: Suffolk Law School is distinctly a man's school. It does not admit women, not because of a desire to discriminate but because the school believes that the few women who would have the hardihood to attend night classes with a great multitude of men would add greatly to administrative problems without corresponding benefit to the institution. We now have the largest attendance of men students of law in any institution in the world." (1925-26 Suffolk Law School catalogue, p. 12). During the time that this description was included in the Suffolk Law School catalogue, Dean Archer's secretary Catharine C. Caraher was attending classes there in 1927. The Dean's daughter Marian Archer began to take classes at Suffolk Law School in the fall of 1933, and graduated in the spring of 1937.

A related entry also appeared in the Suffolk College of Liberal Arts catalogue from the time of its first publication in 1934-35. That entry read as follows: "Suffolk College of Liberal Arts is open to students of both sexes on equal terms, except that the college reserves the right to limit the number of young women who may enter in any one year. In these days of financial distress the educational ambitions of the girls of a family are even more likely to suffer than those of boys of the same family. Young women may therefore find in Suffolk College of Liberal Arts an answer to an otherwise unsolvable problem." (1934-35 Suffolk College of Liberal Arts catalogue, pp. 7, 10). The potential limit on the number of women in the College continued to be included in the catalogue of the Suffolk Colleges through 1941-42. No statement regarding potential numerical limits was inserted in the Suffolk Law School catalogue after the total prohibition of women's attendance was removed in 1937.

27 Total Suffolk University alumni 1906-1982, 28,306; living alumni 25,805; 49AA, 20 ABA, 10AS, 2780BA, 2986BS, 4877BSBA, 146BSGS, 574BSJ, 20BSPA, 10,421JD, 70LLM, 301MA, 563MAE, 2521MBA, 468MPA.

Total Suffolk University alumni 1906-1990, 39,023; living alumni 36,324; Total degrees 1906-90, 96 Associates (51AA, 20ABA, 25AS); 15,982 Bachelor's (3272BA, 4371BS, 7301BSBA, 177BSGS, 837BSJ, 24BSPA); 8,711 Master's and Advanced Certificates (308MA, 578MAE, 5114MBA, 1298MED, 9MEC, 791MPA, 444MS, 50MSB, 17MCO, 33MSC, 4MHR, 16APC, 49CAGS); 16,184 Law (15,582JD, 15JDP, 587LLM).

First Asian graduate: Shichiro Hayashi, 1922.

First Native American graduate: Nelson D. Simons, 1925.

First female graduate: Marian G. (Archer) MacDonald, 1937.

28 Alumni giving:

Suffolk University's Campaign for Excellence was concluded in 1982.

Gift Income (in thousands of dollars)

	Alumni	Friends	Corpor-ations	Founda-tions	Total	Alumni Donors	Total Contri-buted	SUMMA
79	134	31	21	9	195			
80	304	45	36	88	473			
81	291	297	93	270	951			
82	333	885	54	265	1537			
83	437	34	26	90	587	3100	609.2	115
84	347	140	82	220	789	3630	363.3	181
85	381	168	180	34	763	4444	381	169
86	858	276	172	355	1661	4718	858	156
87	976	789	130	126	2021	4904	976	215
88	490	336	203	308	1337	4939	490	232
89	697.5	394	86	49	1227	5487	697.5	229
90	623.6	396.3	129.1	333	1482	5800	623.6	241

29 Suffolk University Board of Trustees, Minutes, April 12, 1989.

Chapter 9

1 ABA Inspectors' Report, 1990.

2 James F. Linnehan, Memorandum to the Suffolk University Community, August 1989.

3 Linnehan's predecessor, John S. Howe, retired Chairman of the Board and CEO of the Provident Institution for Savings, had been elected to the Board in October 1974, filling the seat vacated by the death of the legendary Judge John E. Fenton, Sr. From 1979 to 1982, Howe served as chairman of the Campaign for Excellence, and its supererogatory success propelled him in June 1981 to election as Chairman of the University's Board of Trustees. He ceded the gavel to Linnehan in 1987, As Chairman of the Board, Howe himself succeeded Vincent A. Fulmer. Fulmer, who was elected to the Board in November 1972, served as its Chair from June 1976 until 1981. While not so closely associated with the Fulham Presidency as Howe with Perlman's or Linnehan with Sargent's, Fulmer played pivotal roles at that time in impelling the Board into the Campaign for Excellence, in bringing the University to terms with its history through the Heritage Project, and in the creation of the Trustees' Student Affairs Committee as an ingenious solution to the problem of student participation in University governance. After stepping down from the Chair, Trustee Fulmer continued to serve on the Board until June 1994, consistently throughout that period providing University affairs with the dedicated and energetic scrutiny which is indispensable to their appropriate conduct.

4 During his final years in office, President Perlman relentlessly urged on the Board of Trustees a new capital campaign to finance:

1) Improved facilities; 2) Faculty and staff development; 3) Endowment funds and scholarship support; 4) Program development and library enrichment. (Suffolk University Board of Trustees, Minutes, June 4, 1986)

In his first appearance before the Board, on September 13, 1989, the newly elected President Sargent asserted that the University's principal priority remained "the capital campaign," in preparation for which he intended:

To focus attention toward obtaining funds from alumni, corporations, foundations, and friends of the University for capital improvements, scholarships, faculty enrichment, and program enhancement. (Suffolk University Board of Trustees, Minutes, September 13, 1989)

President Sargent's inaugural manifesto recapitulated, word for word, the Perlman program.

Due to the illness of Vice-President Kelley, the "Building the Future" capital campaign was much more amorphous, much less definitively formulated, when Sargent assumed office in September 1989 than was the "Campaign for Excellence" when Perlman came to it in 1980. As Kelley's condition worsened in 1990 and 1991, his "Building the Future" campaign was eventually abandoned.

5 And, as with a number of other recent "additions" to the University, the original conception can be found with Suffolk founder Gleason L. Archer. Under Archer's Presidency (specifically, in 1947) the need for dormitories was readily acknowledged, and students were housed by the Boston City Club for several years. Archer similarly (fore)saw the value and advantages of Cooperative Education when he envisioned, in February 1931, a College of Liberal Arts which would:

offer to ambitious boys in far off places an opportunity to earn their education by placing them in positions in or near Boston. (Gleason Archer, "Journal II," Volume II, p. 351 [February 4, 1931])

More surprisingly, and dramatically at odds with his attitudes regarding Law School accreditation, Archer firmly endorsed efforts (like those which enjoyed top priority in the School of Management throughout the Perlman Presidency) to obtain validating accreditations for CLAS and SOM programs, As early as 1939, in fact, the founder was "looking toward accreditation of the colleges." (Gleason L. Archer, "Program for Accreditation of Suffolk University, April 10, 1947," p. 9)

6 When President Perlman's initial choice as Dean of Enrollment Management, Robert S. Lay, departed in June 1988, the President turned for an interim replacement to CLAS Associate Dean Joseph H. Strain, one of his few close and trusted collaborators. Strain loyally assumed the vital and intimidating responsibility, serving creditably from June 1988 until January 1989. Meanwhile, a nation-wide search was launched for Lay's replacement. To his credit, the often enigmatic Perlman was adamant on this subject, asserting (perhaps in part because of his experience with Dean Lay) that what the University needed was "an energetic, imaginative, optimistic, and experienced enrollment manager who has knowledge, insight, and experience in college marketing, advertising, and financial aid." That was what he got. In December 1988, President Daniel Perlman announced the appointment of Marguerite J. Dennis, former Associate Dean of the Dental School at Georgetown University, as the new Dean of Enrollment Management. Typically, within eighteen months Dean Dennis had expanded her mandate, and therefore was, from July 1990, Dean of Enrollment and Retention Management. At the same time, her Office of Enrollment Management became the Division of Enrollment and Retention Management; and by January 1993, she had added an Associate Dean, Barbara K. Ericson.

7 In 1995, for example, the University garnered top honors in the 10th Annual Admissions Advertising Awards, a national competition recognizing excellence and achievement in admission advertising.

8 The building was constructed in 1908 to house Chandler's department store, was later used as office space, and was substantially renovated in 1982 for use by the Massachusetts Department of Health. The Health Department occupied the building until December 1994. Suffolk University purchased the building from the Aetna Insurance Company, which held it after foreclosure on a mortgage, for $5 million.

As College Dean, Michael R. Ronayne had long been one of the strongest advocates in the University for the introduction of student dormitory facilities. On this matter, he and Dean Dennis were in complete accord. Very committed to multiculturalism, diversity, and internationalism, the Dean of Enrollment Management argued that expanded University commitment to dormitory facilities was essential for the recruitment and accommodation of AHANA and international students.

Ironically (although probably no participant in the brewing debate over residential housing knew, or remembered), Suffolk University founder Gleason Archer had endorsed dormitories, and the University had actually established one, in 1947. What makes the irony more delicious is the fact that the elusive dormitory was located—where else?—at 8 Ashburton Place, in what was then the Boston City Club Building, and is today the University's Frank Sawyer Building. Suffolk University's "residence hall" was maintained there until the Boston City Club decided in 1949 to sell the building—and Suffolk's Board of Trustees, in another palpable irony, declined to purchase it.

The Board had voted in the mid-1980s flatly to disregard the option of a "modest residential component." But by 1988, with the tide of "college-age" students ebbing fast, the Trustees agreed in June 1988 to lease from Lasell Junior College two Victorian townhouses on the school's Newton campus, to provide housing for a total of 25 undergraduate students. The leased dormitory space quickly filled up, and, hesitantly, the Board renewed the agreement with Lasell in April 1989.

In the fall of 1989, Marguerite Dennis and David Sargent suggested to the Board that the University replace its distant Lasell residences with space rented from Newbury College in the Back Bay, within easy walking distance against the arcadian backdrop of the Common and the Public Garden. It was a difficult proposition to contravene, and in April 1990, Suffolk University duly contracted with Newbury College for 35 spaces in the residence at 138 Marlborough Street. That arrangement was renewed in November 1990—early enough, for the first time, that the Division of Enrollment and Retention Management could confidently market the dormitory space to prospective students, foreign and domestic. Over the next five years, all "residential component" discussions were over how much more space was necessary to accommodate the rapidly-increasing number of international (and other) students recruited by Dean Dennis and her minions. Even former enemies of the dormitory project became enthusiastic proponents. In this environment, the University's first Residential Life Committee was convened in the fall of 1993. By 1995, two Back Bay dormitories owned by Newbury College had been reserved for Suffolk University students, and the University had purchased the eleven-story building at 150 Tremont Street for conversion into a dormitory.

9 Suffolk University's Retention Management Program was nationally honored by Noel-Levitz's Outstanding Retention Management Award as the best overall retention program for 1993; the National Academic Advising Association selected Suffolk's Special Advising Program as the Outstanding Institutional Advising Program for 1994.

10 Of the tuition revenues received by Suffolk University, about half came from student savings and earnings; the other half, from borrowing. To a remarkable degree, Suffolk University still served well the same constituency (more broadly defined) that it had been founded to serve in 1906: "ambitious [people] who are obliged to work for a living while studying." (Suffolk Law School catalogue, 1936, p. 11) Founder Gleason Archer had been righter than he knew (although in many ways he could not imagine) when he prophesied that "Suffolk's mission is and probably always will be to minister to the . . . employed student." (Gleason L. Archer, "Status of Suffolk University, January 16, 1939," p. 23)

11 Several touches particularly exhibiting Dean Dennis's instinct for "public relations" were a "Family Discount" plan, reducing tuition for families with more than one child at Suffolk (April 1989); the awarding of a full four-year scholarship to Zakia Cox, a 9-year-old homeless student from Boston (February 1991), plus simultaneous institution of an annual scholarship to a homeless student meritorious of scholarship support (February 1991); and the granting

of one tuition-free semester and counseling assistance to six Suffolk University students serving in the Gulf conflict (February 1991).

12 Suffolk University Board of Trustees, Minutes, November 8, 1989.

13 In general, however, international students had much less need of financial assistance than Suffolk's domestic students, making their recruitment all the more desirable from a pecuniary standpoint.

14 Reflecting the University's continuing commitment to its mission, substantial expansion took place during the Sargent era in academic support services for Suffolk University students. The hub around which the entire network of academic support services revolved was the Geno A. Ballotti Learning Center. Collaborating closely with the Learning Center, and complementing its general academic support coverage, were several additional subject- and audience-specific academic support service centers: the English as a Second Language Program (established 1989), the Mathematics Department's Math Support Center (1986, shortly after introduction in 1985 of the mandatory all-College Basic Math Exam), the English Department's Remedial Program in English (1975), and the English Department's Writing Center (1990). All Academic Support Services reported to the Dean of the College of Liberal Arts and Sciences.

15 Beginning in 1947, Suffolk University had offered in-house Guidance (counseling/psychological) services to its students; but after Dr. Kenneth F. Garni took over as Chair of the Psychological Services Department in July 1973, that office undertook notable diversification and professionalization. (A similar development in the Education Department's Counseling/Counselor Training program also took place from July 1973, when Glen A. Eskedal took over as Program Director.) In 1975, the Psychological Services Department was accredited by the International Association of Counseling Services; and from 1978 on (renamed the University Counseling Center) it offered pre-doctoral internship training to advanced doctoral candidates. Although the internship program was approved by the Association of Psychology Internship Centers (APIC) in 1982, the Counseling Center did not choose at that time to seek for this program the more prestigious accreditation of the American Psychological Association (APA).

16 Suffolk Law School catalogue, 1923-24, pp. 17-18.

17 To manifest unity, solidarity, and mutual support among members of the Suffolk University community in the face of that misguided individual's dissemination of racial hate literature on campus, an unprecedented all-campus forum was convened on cultural awareness and intercultural understanding on November 8, 1989, in the C. Walsh Theatre. Day classes for Suffolk University's School of Management, College of Liberal Arts and Sciences, and Law School were moved to the Theatre for the event; the Theatre's 525 available seats were not enough for the audience, which included students, faculty, and administrators. Many had to stand. Organized by Sharon Artis, Assistant to the President and Director of Multicultural Affairs, with the help of the Black Students' Union, the event featured an agenda that included a consultant team from the National Coalition Building Institute to discuss issues of cultural difference and discrimination in general, followed by small group sessions to discuss ideas and solutions, and an intercultural party, which included food, music, and some feedback from the group sessions. In addition, all CLAS full-time and adjunct faculty members were strongly encouraged to build into their course sections, in whatever discipline, during the week of November 8 components and exercises that would help students to prepare for, and then to react to and apply what they had discovered at, the forum. These components and exercises included writing assignments, special class and individual projects, guest speakers, and classroom discussions that focused on multicultural awareness and interethnic support. A follow-up session on November 14 offered students and faculty members an opportunity to make comments and give feedback on the Forum.

In furtherance of Sharon Artis's credo that progress toward true cultural diversity at Suffolk University could never come by chance, but only through persistent planning and advocacy for multiculturalism, a second significant step toward systematic change occurred in January 1990, when the University administration hosted a conference entitled "Suffolk University 1990: Deadline for Diversity." It was attended by approximately sixty people, including President Sargent, a representative of the Board of Trustees, administrators, faculty, student leaders, and other interested students, who were invited from across the University to identify strategies for addressing discrimination which might exist on campus and to recommend steps for increasing diversity on an on-going basis. A set of recommendations was developed for each academic unit and for the institution as a whole.

18 To assist in this planning effort, and to carry forward preparations for implementation of the recommendations formulated at the "Deadline for Diversity" conference, Dr. Artis established a working group of students, faculty, and administrators. That working group, established in 1991 to collaborate with the University Strategic Planning Committee by producing a document on diversity at Suffolk University which, like similar documents being prepared on other campuses nation-wide, would provide timelines and points of accountability for each recommendation. Under Artis' guidance, the working group also organized a September 1992 planning conference entitled "Suffolk University: Rebuilding a Diverse Community." From that planning conference, and the working group that prepared it, there emerged a Diversity Task Force (headed by Artis), which continued work on the diversity plan and collaboration with the University Strategic Planning Committee. Meanwhile, the Diversity Task Force also worked directly with President Sargent in the final crafting of a landmark University Diversity Policy Statement.

19 For example, after years of meeting at non-publicized times and places, the Gay and Lesbian Alliance at Suffolk began to invite all University community members to its events. The group was chartered by the Student Government Association in 1992 and subsequently received SGA funding for its programs. Another example of change was to be found in greater appreciation of religious differences. Although the Jewish population at Suffolk was quite small, Chanukah and Passover celebrations became annual events open to the entire campus.

In 1989, there were fifteen student organizations functioning in the Law School (not counting the moot courts or the clinical programs) compared to only eleven in 1980. By 1995, that number had risen to seventeen. In the College and the School of Management, meanwhile, there were by 1989 thirty-eight student organizations (31 CLAS, 7 SOM) compared to forty-six (38 CLAS, 8 SOM) in 1980. There remained 38 CLAS/SSOM student organizations in 1995; by that time, 32 were College of Liberal Arts and Sciences organizations and only six were associated with the School of Management. Most notable in the configuration of student associations during the period 1980-95 was the multiplication of ethnic and culturally diverse organizations. A Black Student Union and an International Student Association had both been founded before 1980. In addition to them, there were established between 1980 and 1995 all of the following: the Asian-American Association; the Caribbean-American Student Alliance; the Emerald (Irish Cultural) Club; the Gay and Lesbian Alliance at Suffolk University; the Haitian-American Student Association; the Hispanic Association; the Republic of China Student Club; and the Suffolk University Society Organized Against Racism (SOAR). During the same period in the Law School, already-extant Asian, Black, and Hispanic Law Student Associations were complemented by the foundation of a Gaelic Law Society and a Jewish Law Student Association.

20 David Sargent, Call to January 1990 Conference on "Suffolk University 1990: Deadline for Diversity."

21 In January 1988, Donald Morton, Chair of the CLAS Committee on Cultural Diversity in the Curriculum (established in 1985), submitted a resolution to

the CLAS Faculty Assembly calling for cultural diversity in all courses, which was endorsed by the Faculty Assembly and referred to the College's academic departments for implementation. Two years later, in 1990, the Committee, chaired by Dr. Maria Miliora, submitted a proposal for establishment of a Cultural Diversity requirement in the all-College core curriculum. That proposal was finally adopted by the CLAS Faculty Assembly in 1994 and incorporated in the new all-College curriculum introduced in the fall of 1994. Similarly, as part of the new SOM undergraduate core curriculum implemented in September 1993, Dean Brennan and his faculty had also introduced a Cultural Contacts in World History course, to satisfy the newly-adopted SOM cultural diversity requirement. A long-awaited Black Studies minor program, of which the CLAS Cultural Diversity in the Curriculum Committee had been charged to facilitate development in 1985, was finally approved by the CLAS Faculty Assembly in 1994.

22 The University established the Minority Student (later called the Maria Stewart AHANA Student) Scholarship program in 1987. In 1989, on the proposal of Dean Dennis, the Stewart Scholars' stipend was doubled from $2,500 to $5,000.

23 Suffolk University was the first institution of higher education in the greater Boston area to offer a major in International Economics (1984), and in November 1993 the Trustees also approved a new CLAS master's degree program in International Economics and a combined MSIE/JD with Suffolk University Law School.

In July 1990, the College of Liberal Arts and Sciences introduced a Certificate in U.S. Studies program, which provided, over the next few years, a nucleus around which to build an American Studies program designed for international students.

Each year, students from various departments were given modest no-interest loans for study overseas under the SAFARI (Study at Foreign Academically Recognized Institutions) program, established by the University in 1971.

24 The program, scheduled to extend through the fall of 1996, was designed to train Kuwaiti students in clinical psychology generally and in post-traumatic stress disorder more specifically. It consisted of courses parallel to those offered in the Education and Human Services Department's master's degree program in Counseling; clinical psychologists affiliated with the Department of Education and Human Services/Psychology visited Kuwait on three-week "locale assignments" to serve as course instructors.

25 The Allison Lecture Series, named in memory of Dwight L. Allison, noted trial practitioner and 1922 graduate of Suffolk Law School, was funded through a grant from the Dwight L. and Stella Allison Fund administered by the Boston Foundation (Dwight L. Allison, Jr., President). Under the Sargent regime, the Allison Lecture became an annual event.

26 Suffolk University Faculty Fulbright Scholarship recipients, 1989-96: Law Prof. Eric D. Blumenson, Pakistan, 3 months, spring 1989; SOM Prof. Edward L. Bubnys, Finance, Lithuania, 11 months, fall 1990-spring 1991; Law Prof. Robert P. Wasson, Jr. (African-American), Kenya, fall 1991-spring 1992; CLAS Prof. David L. Robbins, History, Czech Republic, fall 1994; CLAS Prof. Thomas Connolly, English, Czech Republic, fall 1996.

27 ELI classes began in September 1994, with a group of students from Kazakhstan prominent among their participants.

28 Master of Arts (MA) degrees were also offered in Economics, English, Government and History between 1948 and 1954; followed by a brief, unedifying dalliance with master's programs in Chemistry and Physics beginning in September 1967.

29 Formal authorization for Suffolk University to grant the Ph.D. degree was given by the Massachusetts General Court in July 1995.

30 On this front, Sargent's generalissima was Dean Marguerite Dennis, whose merit/quality funding initiatives after 1989 (beyond funding Archer/Griffin merit scholarships) included: efforts to continue expansion of the Fulham and Corcoran Merit Scholarship Programs; a "Grandfathered Tuition" Program for Meritorious Students, for students maintaining a prescribed grade-point average (February 1990); full-tuition scholarships for applicants who received the highest quality rating from the Admissions Office (November 1989); and ten "Trustee Ambassador" Scholarships, for outstanding students to assist Enrollment Management in recruiting (April 1989).

In addition to this "adjustment" in financial aid policy, the Sargent era also saw the establishment of a privately-funded Sears Roebuck Foundation Teaching Award, to honor (to a degree that reflected its priority within the institution) top-quality teaching.

Signal successes scored by Suffolk University students under the Sargent regime included:

1) In the 55th Putnam Mathematical Competition, held on December 3, 1994, the Suffolk University team (Anna Petrovskaya, Ivan Bulyko, and Vitaly Vanchurin, coached by Jack Hajj) finished 34th in a field of 409 teams from around the U.S., improving on their exceptional performance of the previous year, when Suffolk University placed third among Commonwealth of Massachusetts competitors, behind only Harvard and MIT.

2) In 1991, the University's novice debate team placed two pairs in the top ten at their national competition, and one of their number, CLAS sophomore Allison Hazen, was honored as the best novice speaker in the nation.

3) In January 1992, the Debate Team, having successfully made the transition from two-person to one-person—or Lincoln-Douglas—debate, won the first-ever Boston Debate Beanpot Tournament. Also-rans in the competition included Boston College, Boston University, Emerson College, Harvard University, and Northeastern University. The Suffolk debaters also won the Eastern Region Championship, and at the nationals, the team of Guy DiGrande, Linda DiGrande, John Forde, and Kristy Guarnieri captured third place honors.

4) In 1993, the Lincoln-Douglas debate team improved upon its third-place national standing in 1992 by winning the National Championship. Seniors Guy DiGrande, John Forde, and Kristen Ciolkosz all reached the championship rounds, with DiGrande and Forde tying for ninth and Ciolkosz finishing fifth. The combined scores for these three performances clinched the overall team title for Suffolk, which also had strong preliminary performances from Kathy Fitzpatrick and Kristy Guarnieri. Suffolk's effort overcame strong showings by the University of Wisconsin, Western Kentucky University, Ohio State, and Wayne State, and dethroned reigning national champion Ohio University.

5) In 1995, the Lincoln-Douglas debate team again won the National Championship, this time with CLAS junior Mary Cunningham capturing honors as the #1 speaker in the country.

To help communicate the quality of Suffolk University to its various "publics," the University hosted several notable public events following President Sargent's accession in 1989. These included:

1) An International French Revolution Bicentennial Symposium on Human Rights, organized by Humanities and Modern Languages Department Chair Margaret C. Weitz and conducted at Suffolk University on November 6, 1989. The proceedings, edited by Dr. Weitz and with an introduction by CLAS Associate Dean David L. Robbins, were subsequently published in 1992 as *Celebrating Human Rights,* featuring contributions from Stanley Hoffman of Harvard, Valerie Epps of Suffolk University Law School, and several scholars from the University of Strasbourg.

2) A Conference on Women and the French Resistance, funded by a grant from the French Cultural Services, which was coordinated and conducted at Suffolk University on October 13-16, 1992, by widely respected French Resistance and women's history scholar Dr. Margaret C. Weitz, Chair, Department of Humanities and Modern Languages.

3) A Bioethics Symposium: "Law and Science at the Crossroads," hosted by Suffolk University Law School and the University of Massachusetts Medical School, on October 21-22, 1993, at the Hotel Meridien, Boston, which was attended by 150 professionals from 24 states and 5 foreign countries.

4) An international conference sponsored by the English Department and organized by its chair, Dr. Frederick Wilkins, and his colleagues, on May 11-14, 1995, entitled "O'Neill's People." This was the third in an enormously successful series, which began, on March 22-25, 1984, with "O'Neill: The Early Years," and continued with its sequel, "Eugene O'Neill: The Later Years," on May 29-June 1, 1986.

31 Shortly before his death in 1974, John Fenton, Sr., had made his son a prime candidate for the vacant Deanship of the Law School; however, when another of the Board's power brokers, Judge Frank J. Donahue, also pushed his son, Malcolm, for Dean, the resulting standoff ultimately forced the Trustees to name a compromise candidate, David Sargent, as Dean. Both Malcolm Donahue and John Fenton, Jr., were already members of the Law School faculty, and both were designated in 1973 to serve as Sargent's Associate Deans. Fenton, however, served for only one year, resigning in May 1974 to accept appointment to the seat of Associate Justice of the Land Court formerly occupied by his father. There he served until 1992, when he was appointed by Supreme Court Chief Justice Paul J. Liacos to the key position of Chief Justice for Administration and Management of the Trial Court.

32 As enquiries were made regarding the precise amount of additional space actually required by the Law School, estimates steadily grew. Dean Sargent's November 1988 estimate of 10,000-20,000 was expanded in a November 1990 facilities report prepared by a faculty committee to 51,255; then, in June 1991 the Trustees raised the figure to 80,000, and finally, in June 1992, to 160,000 additional square feet. By November 1990, it was clear to the Board (as it had already been to then-Dean Sargent when he made his November 1988 appeal for Law School expansion) that space requirements of this magnitude could not be accommodated in existing University facilities, and in February 1992 the Law School Committee recommended to the Board that "all practical steps be taken to secure a new facility for the Law School other than its present physical site, but in reasonably close proximity to the present site."

The Law School had had space problems before, particularly in the early 1970s, which had led to precipitous and potentially disruptive action: an "emergency" (accreditation-driven) decision in April 1975 to evict non-Law personnel from the Donahue Building and to reserve that structure solely for Law School use.

33 To help finance the new Law School, the Trustees envisioned a $25 million capital campaign and a federal grant. There was, the Board agreed, "no better site available" for the endeavor. (Suffolk University Board of Trustees, Minutes, June 3, 1992)

The Law School's March 1994 Long-Range Plan called for further expansion of student opportunities for community service, especially through internships in the "learning laboratories" which surrounded Suffolk University Law School, and for the provision of formal and informal recognition of such student activity, as well as volunteer community and public service by law students.

Wilbur G. Hollingsworth directed all clinical, internship, clerk, and defender programs in the Law School from his arrival at Suffolk in January 1970 until his retirement in 1975. He was then succeeded as supervisor of the criminal clinical programs by Prof. Eric D. Blumenson, who served in that capacity from September 1975. In 1990, Prof. Stephen J. Callahan was appointed as Coordinator of Clinical Programs.

The Law School's oldest criminal clinical program, the Voluntary Defenders, was established in 1967. By 1995, it was structured as a full-year six-credit course for students in their final year, providing experience in the Commonwealth's district courts, whose jurisdiction included misdemeanors and minor felonies. Each student was assigned several indigent defendants, and all were supervised by experienced criminal defense attorneys (6-7 students per supervisor). The students obtained cases through appointments at arraignment in the Boston Municipal Court and District Courts in Quincy, Somerville, Malden, and Dorchester. In 1995, the director of the Voluntary Defenders program was Prof. Eric D. Blumenson (appointed in 1975).

The Prosecutors Program, established in 1970, provided a six-credit full-year course to students in their final year. These students represented the Commonwealth in criminal cases in several district courts in the Boston area, in cases assigned to them by District Attorneys' offices. In 1995, the program was directed by Prof. Sarah Landis (appointed in 1990), who coordinated with the DAs and District Judges, and supervised the Assistant DAs involved in program. The majority of students in the Prosecutors Program were in the District Courts of Suffolk County (Boston Municipal Court, Chelsea, Brighton, South Boston, Charlestown, East Boston); a smaller number served in Plymouth County (Hingham, Brockton, Plymouth).

The Law School's civil clinical program, the Suffolk University Legal Assistance Bureau (SULAB), was introduced in 1973. Initially directed (1973-76) by Prof. Charles B. Garabedian, it was by 1995 a separate and distinct law practice working in affiliation with Greater Boston Legal Services (GBLS), the largest local provider of free legal services to indigent clients in civil cases. During the 1970s, SULAB offices had been established in Beverly (1973) and Charlestown (1976); during the 1980s and 1990s, it maintained offices at GBLS (68 Essex Street) and at the Law School (56 Temple Street). In 1995, SULAB consisted of two components, for students only in their final year at the Law School: the Family Unit and the Housing Unit. In the Family Unit, the students generally represented clients seeking a divorce in the probate courts of Suffolk and Middlesex counties. The students in the Housing Unit typically represented tenants in summary process proceedings in the Boston Housing Court. Throughout much of its history, SULAB was under the clinical direction of John David Schatz.

SULAB also provided the locus for development of several other Law School clinical programs:

S.U. Clinica Legal was initiated 1985 as Su Clinica, a clinical program associated with SULAB. Renamed S.U. Clinical Legal in 1991, it continued to provide legal assistance, primarily in housing cases, to indigent Spanish-speaking clients in Chelsea and was staffed by second- and third-year students fluent in Spanish. Participants worked out of the Greater Boston Legal Services office at 274 Broadway in Chelsea. In 1993, Asian-language speakers were added to the program to address the needs of Chelsea's diversifying population; and in September 1994, an evening component (S.U. Clinica Legal Evening Clinic) was added to the S.U. Clinica Legal Landlord-Tenant Clinic in Chelsea, to provide an opportunity for a full clinical experience for Evening Division students. By 1995, the Director of the S.U. Clinical Legal program was Prof. Stephen J. Callahan; its clinical director was Martin Espada.

The Battered Women's Advocacy Project, which during the first two years of its existence had been an "outside" clinical program, was added to SULAB in 1986. It was separated and listed separately from SULAB by 1991. Directed in 1995 by Christine Butler, an attorney specializing in Family Law and an expert in Abuse Prevention, it was a one-semester, three-credit clinical course offered primarily to law students in their last two years of Law School involving the representation of victims of family abuse. The majority of clients were women seeking protection from abusive spouses or partners, but all victims of domestic violence were represented. Students appeared in court to represent their clients in ex parte and contested hearings to obtain restraining orders to prevent further abuse, and to determine future child custody, support, and related matters. Students also staffed a "crisis line" at the Law School to give legal advice to domestic violence victims in order for them to understand and to pursue their civil and criminal remedies, and to offer them representation at the court proceedings. Client referrals also came from various sources such as shelters for battered women and the courts.

A Mental Health Clinical Program (tentatively to be associated at first with SULAB) was approved by the faculty in 1990, but not immediately initiated. Under exploration and development by Prof. Linda C. Fentiman, it contemplated a three-credit, one-semester course in which students would represent mentally-disabled residents of state institutions.

The Legal Internship Program (known as the Outside Clinical Studies Program from its foundation in 1976 until 1991) provided opportunities for students to gain two credits per semester for supervised legal work performed for a government or non-profit agency. The student was required to perform 90 hours of uncompensated legal service for the agency as well as to satisfy the requirements of a classroom component that met one hour each week. Coordinated for two decades by Prof. Charles B. Garabedian from its inception until his death in February 1991, the program was directed after 1991 by Prof. Gerard J. Clark.

A Moot Court program was begun at the Law School in 1965. Its first director was Prof. Charles B. Garabedian. He served throughout the 1970s, and was succeeded, as advisor to the student-run Moot Court Board (which was established in 1973), by Prof. Richard G. Pizzano.

In 1981, the Moot Court Board organized and administered six annual programs: The Justice Tom C. Clark Annual Moot Court Competition, begun in 1971; the First Year (Moot Court) Program (in cooperation with the Legal Practice Skills program); the Client Counseling Competition (1973); the Philip C. Jessup International Moot Court Competition Team Program (1973); the McLaughlin Oral Advocacy Run-Off Competition (Best Oral Advocate of each LPS section), established in 1976; and the National Moot Court Competition Team Program (in which the Suffolk Law School team usually consisted of those who had excelled in the Clark Competition). By 1989, the Moot Court Board had more than doubled its responsibilities, organizing and administering five annual intraschool programs, seven appellate advocacy teams, and three trial teams. The intraschool programs were: the Tom C. Clark Competition, the First Year Moot Court Program, the Walter H. McLaughlin First Year Oral Advocacy Competition, the Annual Mock Trial Competition (begun in 1984-85), and the Second Year Trial Program (inaugurated in 1987-88). The appellate advocacy teams included the Constitutional Law Team (the Craven Constitutional Law Competition), the Patent Team, the International Law team, the National Team (the National Trial Competition), the Securities Team (the Irving R. Kaufman Securities Law Moot Court Competition), the Tax Team (the Stetson Tax Moot Court Competition held in St. Petersburg, FL), and the F. Lee Bailey Team (the Bailey team competed in a competition sponsored by the National University in San Diego). Two trial teams represented Suffolk University in the National Trial Competition and one team in the ATLA Trial Competition (sponsored by the American Trial Lawyers Association). All Moot Court activities focused upon developing expertise in oral advocacy, legal writing, and administrative skills. By 1995, the Moot Court Board organized and administered four annual intraschool competitions: the Justice Tom C. Clark Competition; the Walter McLaughlin Oral Advocacy Competition; the Second-Year Day/Third-Year Evening Mock Trial Competition; and the Third-Year Day/Fourth-Year Evening Mock Trial Competition. It also supported thirteen regional and national interschool appellate advocacy and trial teams. Numerous successes were enjoyed by these teams: the ABA National Trial Competition Team; the ATLA Trial Team

(Suffolk University Law School won the 1995 national competition); the Constitutional Law Team; the Environmental Law Team; the Information Technology and Privacy Law Team; the Insurance Law Team; the Intellectual Property Law Team; the Jessup International Law Team (Suffolk University Law School won the 1995 regional competition); the National Invitational Trial Tournament of Champions Team (Suffolk University Law School earned fifth place in 1994); the National Moot Court Team; the Patent Law Team; the Securities Law Team; and the Tax Law Team. In 1995-96, the Moot Court program at Suffolk University Law School was among the most diverse in American legal education.

34 By 1994-95, none of the seven SOM academic departments had honors courses/programs; 4 out of 7 had affiliations with national academic honorary societies.

35 By 1994-95, 10 out of 14 CLAS academic departments had honors programs/courses; 9 out of 14 had affiliations with national academic honorary societies.

36 The Government Department also demonstrated an impressive skill at finding ways to combine the desirable and the possible in conceiving and then successfully marketing its new master's program in Professional Politics (1993-94) and in obtaining and administering a $650,000 grant from DeWitt Wallace-Reader's Digest for Suffolk University and the Right Question Project to develop a program to help low-income families monitor and improve their children's education. In addition, the Sargent era saw the College enter into full-scale internationalization under the guidance of Associate Dean David L. Robbins, as well as the fruition of Cultural Diversity in the Curriculum Committee efforts in the adoption of a CLAS core curriculum diversity requirement and a Black Studies interdepartmental minor in 1994. Finally, several additional interdepartmental minors (Studies in Religion 1994, Latin American Studies 1995) were initiated, possibly marking the beginning of a trend toward increased interest in interdisciplinary studies.

37 When fully operational, its functions easily superseded the University's previous computer/data processing resources: a small business computer in the Business Office, a service bureau in Lexington used by the Alumni Office, and time-sharing services purchased by the University.

38 In the School of Management, where the first Dean, Donald Grunewald, had urged the Board in 1968 to empower the Deans to set up a Computer Science curriculum, response to the acquisition of the PRIME 750s in 1979 was swift: in November 1979, Nancy Clemens Croll was appointed the SOM's first Director of Academic Computing. In June 1980, the School approved a Computer Information Systems (CIS) major, and the establishment of a corresponding academic department. On February 17, 1983, the John P. Chase Computer Room, eventually to be reserved for SOM use, was dedicated. The College moved a bit more circumspectly. Dr. Paul Ezust and Dr. Eric Myrvaagnes had since 1976 (joined by Dr. Walter Johnson in 1977) been detailed to analyze the College's computer needs. In April 1979, "computer science" tracks were established within the Biology, Chemistry, Physics, and Mathematics majors, and in June 1979 a CLAS Physical and Computer Science Applications Certificate program was introduced. But it was not until 1981 that a Computer Science major was approved in the College, the Department of Mathematics renamed the Department of Mathematics and Computer Science (with Ezust as its chair), and Myrvaagnes appointed as CLAS Director of Academic Computing. In 1983, Physics Department chair Walter Johnson inaugurated a Computer Engineering Technology program which by 1988 had become Computer Engineering. It was not until 1990 that the College's dispersed computer workrooms were consolidated in a CLAS Computer Laboratory. By 1989, the Law School had provided an office computer for each faculty member, along with the capability of accessing Lexis and Westlaw directly from those office terminals, and had engaged a full-time computer technician and an assistant

(1988); by 1995, it had also established computer workrooms for Law School students both inside and outside the Law Library.

39 Holdings of Suffolk University Libraries:

1980-81: Law Library 102,500 volumes; Library for the Colleges 90,000 volumes, 24,000 microtexts, 2,500-volume Museum of Afro-American History collection.

1989-90: Law Library 182,000 volumes; Library for the Colleges 99,000 volumes, 558,000 microforms, 2,500-volume Museum of Afro-American History collection, 2,100 periodical subscriptions, and 660,000 Fenway Library Consortium volumes.

1994: Law Library 173,620 volumes, 44,923 Microtexts, 11 CD-ROM titles, 5,628 serial subscriptions; Sawyer Library 107,000 volumes, 171,000 microtexts, 1,350 periodical subscriptions, 15 CD-ROM titles, 4,000-volume Collection of Afro-American Literature, 2,008,000 Fenway Library Consortium volumes.

1995: Libraries ranked in top 20 of 111 college and university libraries in Massachusetts by American Library Association; Law School E. Albert Pallot and Stephen P. Mugar Libraries, 104,624 microforms, 173,249 serials, books, and periodicals, 80,000 standard books, 11 CD-ROM titles; Mildred F. Sawyer Library, 386,000 volumes, 135,190 microtext volumes, 5,010 periodical subscriptions, 26 CD-ROM titles.

40 Installation began during the summer of 1994, and the public catalogue portion of the system was up and running in October 1994. Funding for the Sawyer Library's share of the start-up cost was made possible by a generous grant (of $104,000) from the Davis Educational Foundation.

In January 1994, the Sawyer Library's CD-ROM local-area-network (LAN) was installed. Users could thus search ABI Inform, InfoTrac, PsychLit, ERIC, and Ethnic Newswatch at any one of the five terminals in the Library, and at any 8386-level PC connected to the University's fiber optic "backbone." Other databases would be added as funds permitted. The purchase of network hardware and software was made possible by two grants from the Sawyer Charitable Foundation (in 1992 and 1993) totalling $21,263. During academic 1994-95, Director Hamann aimed to expand the Sawyer CD-ROM LAN to its full capacity of 17 disk drives.

41 Total Suffolk University alumni 1906-1990, 39,023; living alumni 36,324; Total degrees 1906-90, 96 Associates (51AA, 20ABA, 25AS); 15,982 Bachelor's (3272BA, 4371BS, 7301BSBA, 177BSGS, 837BSJ, 24BSPA); 8,711 Master's and Advanced Certificates (308MA, 578MAE, 5114MBA, 1298MED, 9MEC, 791MPA, 444MS, 50MSB, 17MCO, 33MSC, 4MHR, 16APC, 49CAGS); 16,184 Law (15,582JD, 15JDP, 587LLM).

Total Suffolk University alumni 1906-1995: 31,803 total active alumni; 12,093 Law School only; 7,947 CLAS only; 10,784 SOM only; 979 with degrees from more than one Suffolk University school.

The 1994-95 Suffolk University Law School catalogue (p. 15) says: "Today the Law School has one of the largest law alumni in the nation, numbering approximately 13,000 and representing every aspect of the profession in the judiciary as well as the bar, the legislature and governmental service."

35-40% of alumni addresses, in general, change each year.

42 As early as February 1991, President Sargent and Vice-President Flannery were meeting with the Development staff "to work out the details of future operations and activities of that office." In September 1991, Sargent reluctantly announced to the Board that, under the circumstances, he thought it would be best "that Kelley be promoted to Senior VP and that the President undertake to find a new VP for Institutional Advancement." The latter responsibility turned out to be rather more odious than anyone expected. An initial appointment, of David L. Murphy as Vice-President for Development in January 1992,

never really "gelled": by the spring of 1993, both Kelley (who died in September 1992) and Murphy were gone.

43 Suffolk University Board of Trustees, Minutes, November 12, 1986; June 3, 1992.

44 When Suffolk University gave up its rental space in Charles River Plaza in 1981, most of the displaced offices moved to the newly completed 12-story building at 8 Ashburton Place. The Athletics office, however, was moved from Charles River Plaza to the original Ridgeway Building at 148 Cambridge Street. It remained there until that building was razed in 1989 to permit construction of the new Ridgeway Building (1989-91), during which the Athletics office was temporarily housed above the Store 24 on the southeast corner of Temple and Cambridge Streets. Upon completion of construction in 1991, the Athletics office relocated to the new Ridgeway Building, which also contained the University's first gymnasium.

In February 1983, the Office of Institutional Advancement (which had been housed in Charles River Plaza until 1981, and in the Sawyer Building at 8 Ashburton Place since that time) and the newly created Office of Institutional Research moved to rented space at 11 Beacon Street. The University had held a lease at 11 Beacon since 1979. When the decision was made in 1989 to rent the 25th floor at One Beacon Street, that new rental space absorbed all of the University offices that were, at that time, housed on the sixth, seventh, and twelfth floors of 11 Beacon Street.

Suffolk University Physical Plant, 1996: Eight buildings located on Beacon Hill in the heart of downtown Boston; 500,000 gross square feet of space; 40-acre Robert S. Friedman Field Station at Cobscook Bay, Maine; leased office and classroom space at One Beacon Street and 20 Ashburton Place, Boston; eleven-story urban dormitory at 150 Tremont Street, Boston; site for new Law School building at 110-120 Tremont Street, Boston.

On July 13, 1962, Suffolk University's Board of Trustees voted to maintain the locale of the University in Boston. On the recommendation of Trustee Joseph E. Sullivan, the Trustees established a Suburban Building Committee on April 14, 1971, to reexamine the University's suburban options. At its meeting on June 1, 1988, the Suffolk University Board of Trustees voted to reaffirm its commitment to the development of the University's Beacon Hill campus and decided not to give further consideration to the possibility of moving to "Parcel One" (a Commonwealth-owned West End tract of land including the Hurley-Lindemann Building), which had been offered to the University on April 29, 1987.

45 President Sargent in August 1995 appointed Suffolk's first University Professor, to offer lectures and courses in all three of the University's academic units (Law School, CLAS, SOM). The individual designated to fill the new position was Associate Justice Joseph R. Nolan of the Massachusetts Supreme Judicial Court. Justice Nolan had the distinction of being the only jurist to sit on all four tiers of the Massachusetts court system (District court, Superior court, Appeals court, and Supreme Judicial Court). He had also served for twenty-five years as a member of the Law School's adjunct faculty.

46 The merger agreement with the New England School of Art and Design (NESAD) was finally signed on March 1, 1996. In 1995, NESAD enrolled 320 students, employed a faculty of 60 full-time and adjunct instructors, and offered programs in graphic design, interior design, decorative arts, and fine arts. As part of the merger agreement, NESAD sold its building at 28 Newbury Street in Boston's Back Bay and leased new quarters in the edifice that formerly housed Paine Furniture at 75 Arlington Street.

Whether in merger/acquisition negotiations, land purchase transactions, bond issues to finance new building, annual budget projections/adjustments, or in mundane daily account-management, Presidents Fulham, Perlman, and Sargent all shared one constant (and one great asset): University Treasurer Francis X. Flannery. By 1995, Flannery was not only an institution at Suffolk;

he was approaching the status of legend. If legends are discernible by the company they travel in, observe this: In 1964, Flannery first came to Suffolk University as Assistant Treasurer to Judge Frank J. Donahue, the great and powerful; in doing so, he replaced, in effect, after 23 years in the office and in her 37th at Suffolk, the formidable Dorothy M. McNamara, "Miss Suffolk...the heart of the University." Six years later (following a fatal half-year sojourn in the post by former Boston Mayor John B. Hynes), Flannery succeeded Judge Donahue as University Treasurer. At the time of his retirement, the herculean Judge had served twenty years as Treasurer; in the spring of 1995, Flannery began his twenty-sixth. Appointed University Vice-President (as well as Treasurer) in July 1972, Flannery by 1995 had accumulated a tenure in that office which outdistanced his nearest rival (the venerable Judge John E. Fenton, Sr., University Vice-President for 18 years) by a half-decade. Vice-President/Treasurer Flannery had even served, on two separate occasions, as Acting President: in the Fulham/Perlman interregnum (July 30-September 4, 1980) and in the six-week interval between the Perlman and Sargent Presidencies (July 1-August 15, 1989). Whatever might have happened and did not during the period 1970-95, it was certain that whatever *did* could not have done so without Treasurer Flannery's having had a significant hand in it. By the time of his work with President Sargent to coax the new Law School Building into existence, Frank Flannery's status had attained a new plateau: while none of us is truly indispensable, his was the honor of having his colleagues regard his absence as inconceivable.

47 "The alumni, faculty and student body believe [noted Law Prof. Charles P. Kindregan in 1983] it is possible for Suffolk to continue its mission of providing opportunity for those who will serve the community while aspiring to excellence . . . Opportunity and excellence should go hand-in-hand, but the movement toward yet greater excellence sometimes creates a tension within the [University] community. . . . [T]his is a healthy tension, reflecting a viable concern with developing excellence while continuing the historic mission of [the University]." (Charles P. Kindregan, Jr., Coordinator, Faculty Self-Study Task Force, Suffolk University Law School Self-Study, 1983 [approved by the Faculty on March 10, 1983]).

48 Toward the common University goal of preparing students for responsible community service, all three academic units required by 1994 practical ethics courses as part of their "core" curricula, the Law School offered special scholarships for students entering public-interest law, and the College's Government Department introduced (1994) New England's only master's degree program focusing on "Professional Politics." An indirect, but telling, indication of successful outcomes in this regard was the fact that Suffolk University students recorded, throughout the Perlman and Sargent administrations, one of the lowest default rates on Guaranteed, Stafford, and Supplemental student loans to be found at any Commonwealth of Massachusetts institution.

Default rate on Guaranteed Student Loans: UMass (Boston) 24%, Northeastern University 11.9%, UMass (Amherst) 9%, B.U. 8.2%, B.C. 6.6%, Suffolk 4%, among the lowest in New England. (Suffolk University Board of Trustees, Minutes, November 18, 1987)

49 Suffolk University Strategic Planning Committee, Revised University Mission and Goals Statement (approved by University Strategic Planning Committee, April 1993); Suffolk University Strategic Planning Committee, Summary of Goals for Suffolk University Five-Year Strategic Plan, 1991-96 (approved by University Strategic Planning Committee, June 18, 1991).

50 Gleason L. Archer, "Status of Suffolk University, January 16, 1939," p. 26.

Bibliography

Archer, Gleason L. "Archer's Evening Law School: History and Statistics" (ca. 1907), unpublished.

Archer, Gleason L. *Building a School.* Boston: By the Author, 1919.

Archer, Gleason L. *Fifty Years of Suffolk University.* Boston: By the Author, 1956.

Archer, Gleason L. *The Impossible Task.* Boston: Suffolk Law School Press, 1926.

Archer, Gleason L. "Journal II" (1920-32) and "Journal III" (1932-34), personal journals, unpublished.

Archer, Gleason L. "Program for the Accreditation of Suffolk University (Special Report to the Board of Trustees, April 10, 1947)."

Archer, Gleason L. "Status of Suffolk University, January 16, 1939," unpublished.

Beecher, Lyman, *Autobiography,* 2 volumes. Edited by Barbara M. Cross. Cambridge: Belknap Press, 1961.

Boston Historic Conservation Committee (Walter Muir Whitehill, Chairman). *Beacon Hill: The North Slope.* Boston: By the Committee, 1963.

Boston 200. *Boston: The Official Bicentennial Guidebook.* New York: E.P. Dutton, 1975.

Castanino, Gary P. "Beacon Hill: Continuity and Change 1960-70." Paper prepared for the Beacon Hill Civic Association. Boston, 1972.

Chamberlain, Allen. *Beacon Hill.* Boston: Houghton Mifflin, 1925.

Drake, Samuel A. *Old Landmarks and Historic Personages of Boston.* Detroit: Singing Tree Press, 1970.

Handlin, Oscar. *Boston's Immigrants 1790-1880,* revised and enlarged edition. New York: Atheneum, 1977.

Knights, Peter Roger. *The Plain People of Boston 1830-60: A Demographic and Social Study.* PhD Dissertation, Wisconsin, 1969.

McIntyre, A. McVoy. *Beacon Hill: A Walking Tour.* Boston: Beacon Hill Civic Association, 1975.

Marston, Everett C. *Origins and Development of Northeastern University.* Boston: Northeastern University, 1961.

National Center for Education Statistics. *Projections of Educational Statistics to 1997-98.* Washington: U.S. Government Printing Office, 1988.

Robb, Christina. "Names." *Boston Globe Calendar,* 19 May 1977, pp. 12-13.

Seaburg, Carl. *Boston Observed.* Boston: Beacon Press, 1971.

Stark, James H. *Stark's Antique Views of Ye Towne of Boston.* Boston: James H. Stark, 1901.

Suffolk Journal, 1936-40, 1946-95.

Suffolk University Board of Trustees. Minutes, 1911-93.

Suffolk University College of Liberal Arts and Sciences catalogues, 1934-95.

Suffolk University College of Journalism catalogues, 1936-41.

Suffolk University flyers and pamphlets, 1907-95.

Suffolk University Law School catalogues, 1907-95.

Suffolk University School of Management catalogues, 1937-44, 1976-95.

Thwing, Anne Haven. *Crooked and Narrow Streets of the Town of Boston 1630-1822.* Detroit: Singing Tree Press: 1970.

Warden, G.B. *Boston 1689-1776.* Boston: Little Brown, 1968.

Western Interstate Commission for Higher Education, *High School Graduates: Projections by State, 1986-2004.* Boulder: By the Commission, 1988.

Whitehill, Walter Muir. *Boston: A Topographical History,* 2nd edition. Cambridge: Belknap Press, 1968.

Winsor, Justin, ed. *The Memorial History of Boston,* 4 volumes. Boston: James P. Osgood, 1881.

Acknowledgments

The following individuals have been incalculably helpful to me in constructing Chapters Eight and Nine in my mind, and then in getting them out: Sharon Artis-Jackson, John F. Brennan, David Caristi, John Castellano, John C. Deliso, Marguerite J. Dennis, James P. Diamond, Francis X. Flannery, Edmund G. Hamann, Deborah A. Levinson, Sam Lopez, Cindy Lucio, Christine A. Perry, Lynda J. Robbins, Melissa R. Robbins, Michael R. Ronayne, Jenny Ross, Daniel A. Sankowsky, David J. Sargent, Nancy C. Stoll, and Midge Wilcke.

Presidents of Suffolk University

Gleason L. Archer	1937–1948
Walter M. Burse	1948–1954
Robert J. Munce	1954–1960
Dennis C. Haley	1960–1965
John E. Fenton	1965–1970
Thomas A. Fulham	1970–1980
Daniel H. Perlman	1980–1989
David J. Sargent	1989–

About the Author

David L. Robbins, Professor of History at Suffolk University, received his AB from Colgate in 1968. Six years later, he was awarded a Ph.D., with concentrations in intellectual and educational history, by Yale University. Robbins has been a Fulbright Scholar (University College, London), a Danforth Fellow, and a Woodrow Wilson Fellow. He joined the faculty of Suffolk University's College of Liberal Arts and Sciences in 1974, and became Associate Dean of the College in 1988. During 1994, he taught, as a Fulbright Faculty Scholar, at Charles University in Prague.

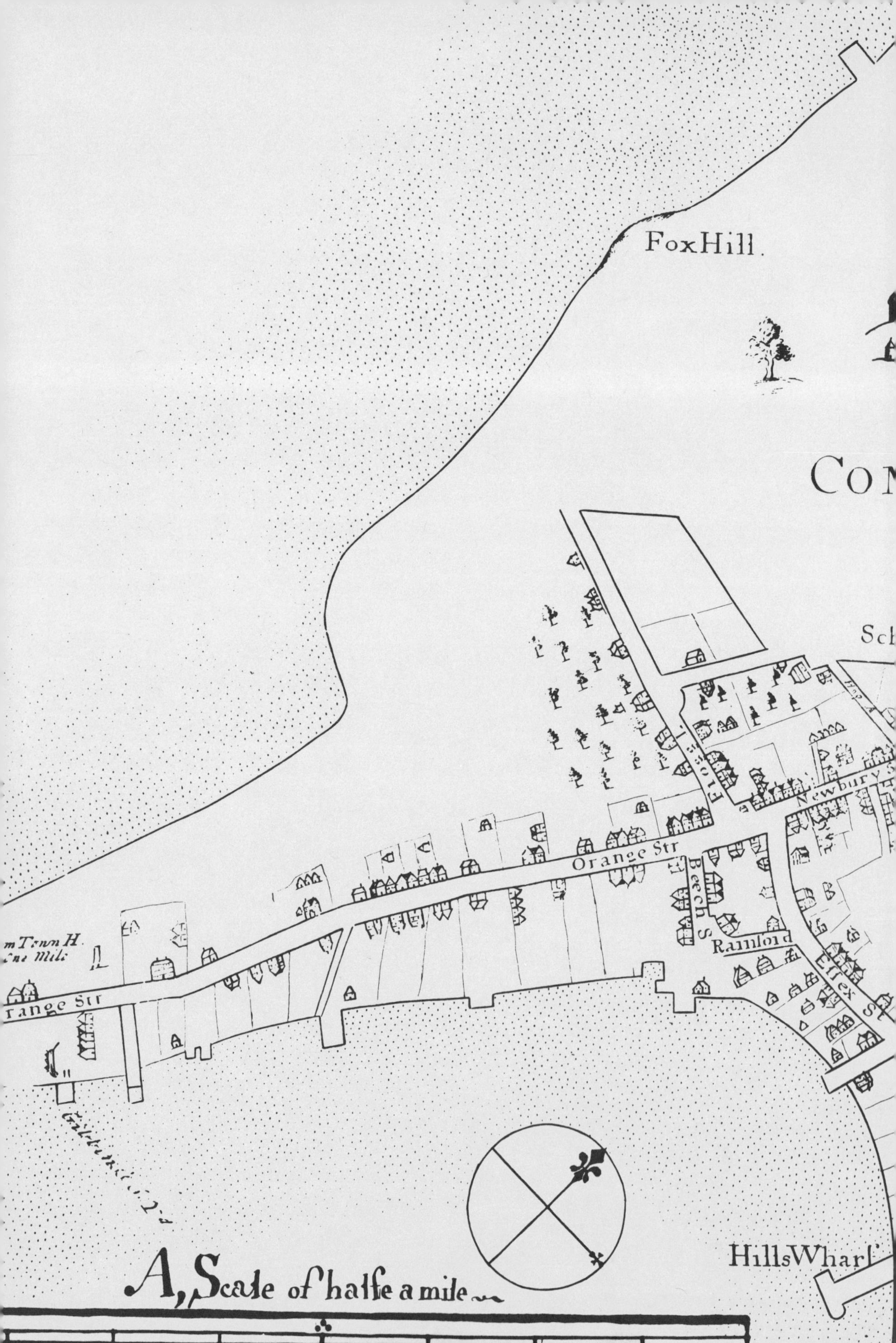

Fox Hill.
Com
Sch
Orange Str
Beech S
Frog S
Newbury S
Rainford
Essex St
range Str
Hills Wharf
A, Scale of halfe a mile